Polar Tourism

Polar Tourism

TOURISM IN THE ARCTIC AND ANTARCTIC REGIONS

Edited by

COLIN MICHAEL HALL
University of Canberra, Australia

and

MARGARET E. JOHNSTON
Lakehead University, Canada

JOHN WILEY & SONS
Chichester · New York · Brisbane · Toronto · Singapore

Other Wiley Editorial Offices

John Wiley & Sons, Inc., 605 Third Avenue,
New York, NY 10158-0012, USA

Jacaranda Wiley Ltd, 33 Park Road, Milton,
Queensland 4064, Australia

John Wiley & Sons (Canada) Ltd, 22 Worcester Road,
Rexdale, Ontario M9W 1L1, Canada

John Wiley & Sons (SEA) Pte Ltd, 37 Jalan Pemimpin #05-04,
Block B, Union Industrial Building, Singapore 2057

Library of Congress Cataloging-in-Publication Data

Polar tourism: tourism in the Arctic and Antarctic regions / edited
by Colin Michael Hall & Margaret E. Johnston.
    p. cm.
    Includes bibliographical references.
    ISBN 0-471-94921-3
    1. Tourist trade—Polar regions. I. Hall, C.M. (C. Michael)
II. Johnston, Margaret E.
G155.P713P65 1995
338.4'7919804—dc20   94-32093
                                                                    CIP

British Library Cataloguing in Publication Data

A catalogue record for this book is available from the British Library

ISBN 0-471-94921-3

Typeset in 10/12 pt Palacio from editors' disks by
Mathematical Composition Setters Ltd, Salisbury, Wiltshire.
Printed and bound in Great Britain by Bookcraft (Bath) Ltd.

This book is dedicated to John S. Marsh and Valene L. Smith who have unfailingly given us intellectual stimulation and encouragement in many ways through the years, and who continue to inspire us in the field of polar tourism research

and to

The Wandering Islands

Contents

Figures

Tables

Contributors

Rosamunde J. Codling
8 Rosary Road, Norwich NR1 1TA, United Kingdom

Kim Crosbie
Scott Polar Research Institute, University of Cambridge, Lensfield Road, Cambridge CB2 1ER, United Kingdom

Bruce Davis
Institute of Antarctic and Southern Ocean Studies, University of Tasmania, GPO Box 252C, Hobart, Tasmania, 7001, Australia

Alexandre Davydov
The Pomor University, Arkangelsk, Russia

Debra J. Enzenbacher
Scott Polar Research Institute, University of Cambridge, Lensfield Road, Cambridge CB2 1ER, United Kingdom

C. Michael Hall
Tourism Programme, University of Canberra, PO Box 1, Belconnen, Australian Capital Territory, 2616, Australia and New Zealand Natural Heritage Foundation, Palmerston North, New Zealand

Tom D. Hinch
Department of Recreation, University of Alberta, Edmonton, Alberta T6G 2H4, Canada

Janet Hughes
Institute of Antarctic and Southern Ocean Studies, University of Tasmania, GPO Box 252C, Hobart, Tasmania, 7001, Australia

Margaret E. Johnston
Centre for Northern Studies and Department of Geography, Lakehead University, Thunder Bay, Ontario P7B 5E1, Canada

Jan O. Lundgren
Department of Geography, McGill University, 805 Sherbrooke St West, Montreal, Quebec H3A 2K6, Canada

Diana Madunic
58 Walkover St, Thunder Bay, Ontario P7B 1L2, Canada

John Marsh
Frost Centre for Canadian Heritage and Development Studies, Trent University, Peterborough, Ontario K9J 7B8, Canada

Klas Sandell
Geography, Department of Social Science, University of Orebro, PO Box 923, S-701 30, Orebro, Sweden

Susan Staple
Canadian Studies Programme, Trent University, Peterborough, Ontario K9J 7B8, Canada

Bernard Stonehouse
Scott Polar Research Institute, University of Cambridge, Lensfield Road, Cambridge CB2 1ER, United Kingdom

Arvid Viken
Department of Tourism, Finnmark College, N-9500 Alta, Norway

Lev Vostryakov
Arkangelsk Region Administration, pr.P. Vinogradova 49. 163061, Arkangelsk, Russia

Mariska Wouters
15 Park Road, Palmerston North, New Zealand

Preface

The original idea for this book was generated in the back of a bus and over a number of beers during the 1992 International Geographical Union Commission on Tourism and Leisure Symposium in Telluride, Colorado. During our conversations on issues of sustainable tourism development it became readily apparent that there was a substantial gap in the available literature and knowledge on touristic activities in the northern and southern polar regions. It is hoped that this book will now fill some of that gap.

Over the past two years numerous people have assisted us with research, advice and the production of the book. Help with research and the development of ideas has come from Dick Butler, Thor Flogenfeldt, Geoff Kearsley, John Marsh, Brian and Delyse Springett, Valene Smith, Arvid Viken and Mariska Wouters. Further help with research, comment on drafts and the all-important moral support has come from Nicolette Bramley, Brenda Daugherty, Helen Gladstones, John Jenkins, Vanessa O'Sullivan, Jacqui Pinkava, Christine Petersen, Jane Saunders, Dave Twynam and Josette Wells.

Financial and administrative support has been kindly provided by the Lakehead University Centre for Northern Studies, Lakehead University Department of Geography and the Faculty of Communication, University of Canberra. Roberta Ferguson and Janice Hunt assisted with typing and organisational assistance at Lakehead University, while Ann Applebee, Stuart Christopherson, Susan McDougall, and Sue Wright assisted likewise at the University of Canberra. Maps were produced by Cathy Chapin and photographic reproduction was by Peter Puna both at Lakehead University. Robert Clarke, Pierre Germain, Sandra Haywood, Frigg Jorgensen and Laura Seddon helped with research and/or the reading of parts of the draft manuscript.

We would like to give a great deal of thanks to Iain Stevenson and everyone at John Wiley for their continued support. The editors would also like to give special thanks to the International Association of Antarctica Tour Operators (IAATO) for permission to reproduce IAATO's guidelines for tour operators and visitors to Antarctica. Finally, we would like to thank all the contributors for their support of the project and making the job of the editors that much easier.

C. Michael Hall   Margaret E. Johnston
O'Connor   *Thunder Bay*

1 Introduction: Pole to Pole: Tourism Issues, Impacts and the Search for a Management Regime in Polar Regions

C. MICHAEL HALL AND MARGARET E. JOHNSTON

PENGUINS AND POLAR BEARS: TOURISM AT THE POLES

For so long the destination of explorers, adventurers and scientists, the polar regions are now thriving tourism frontiers and rank among the world's premier tourist destinations. Recent years have seen a rapid expansion of tourist activity in the north and south polar regions. The poles have become highly attractive places to visit because of improvements in technology, the end of the cold war, changes in consumer preferences, increased accessibility, and the never-ending search for new, marketable tourist products. Increasing numbers of tourists are seeking to visit these remote regions in order to experience relatively undisturbed natural history, impressive natural beauty, and interesting cultural and historic features. However, the polar regions are fragile environments, vulnerable to invasions of tourists, like other wilderness areas. Thus the growth of touristic activity of various kinds presents substantial management and regulatory challenges for government agencies.

The north and south polar regions are also destinations for large numbers of vicarious travellers. Television documentaries such as the wildlife series *Life in the Freezer*, narrated by naturalist David Attenborough, and the travel documentary *Pole to Pole*, by former Monty Python member, Michael Palin, have brought the beauty, wonder and harshness of the polar environment into living rooms the world over. The extent to which such programmes encourage people to visit the Arctic and Antarctic is unknown. However, they do create a climate of interest and awareness in these regions, and perhaps reinforce the correct impression that these areas are more accessible than ever before.

Polar Tourism: Tourism in the Arctic and Antarctic Regions
Edited by C. Michael Hall and Margaret E. Johnston. © John Wiley & Sons Ltd, 1995

Nature-oriented polar documentaries and books are part of the development of greater environmental awareness in Western society. In recent years, this growing movement has encouraged substantial interest in nature-oriented tourism and adventure travel. Wilderness areas, national parks and reserves, and other lands which remain in a relatively undisturbed state are prime attractions for travellers who are seeking 'green', 'adventure', 'appropriate' or 'eco-tourism' experiences. Eco-tourism refers to two different dimensions of tourism which, although interrelated, pose distinct management, policy, planning and development problems. First, eco-tourism as 'green' or 'nature-based' tourism is essentially a form of *special interest* tourism which refers to the motivations of a specific market segment, and the products generated for that segment. Second, eco-tourism is any form of tourism development which is regarded as environmentally friendly (Hall, 1992b). Among the eco-tourism destinations increasing in popularity are the polar regions. The development and growth of special interest tourism, particularly the adventure, educational and environmental market segments, and advances in transport and polar technology, have led to a substantial increase in tourist visitation to the Antarctic and Arctic polar regions.

Visitor numbers in Antarctica and the sub-Antarctic Islands are still relatively small, yet there has been considerable research and management interest in the phenomenon of tourism in the southern circumpolar world which appears to be out of all proportion to these numbers. This mirrors the consuming public interest in the Antarctic which developed in the 1980s and continues to grow in the 1990s, and the tremendous scientific interest in the region (see Beck, 1989). As an extreme environment, remote from industrialisation and most peoples' direct experience, the Antarctic represents a frontier for more than tourism. More so than the Arctic, the Antarctic has become a global symbol of the state of the natural world.

Part of the Antarctic's appeal for the general public, of course, lies in its well-publicised fragility which is embodied in images of the comic, yet easily damaged penguin colonies. Penguins are personally unfamiliar to most people, yet they create a rather different empathy with the environment than polar bears, for example, which can pose physical danger for humans, and the less spectacular bird and animal life of the Arctic. Penguins are a symbol of fragility, encapsulating the warnings of scientists and conservationists about the sensitive Antarctic ecosystem, and the great impact of human activity on vulnerable species. This close, well-publicised link between the Antarctic and penguins has fostered a popular image based on this one attribute (Smith, 1993). There is no similar symbol of the Arctic that fixes an image for the general public. Instead there are many symbols, sometimes conflicting, which comprise Arctic images. Yet it is our contention that there is much to be gained by considering the two polar regions, despite their differences. The major issues are the same: regulation of tourists, protection of the environmental and cultural heritage, management of transnational space, and effects on local populations.

As this book indicates, tourism in polar regions is significant for a number of reasons. The management of tourism in the global commons of the Antarctic and in the 'last unmanaged frontier' (Bloomfield in Beck, 1989, p. 92) of the Arctic poses a number of challenges. However, many management activities are directed at controlling the numbers of tourists at particular sites, without recognition that tourism growth has broader implications. The possibility exists for commercial tourism operations to support scientific research programmes, to bring economic development to remote Arctic communities, and to subsidise government scientific operations. Furthermore, there is the possibility of tourism helping justify claims to Antarctic sectors and to the still disputed territorial waters in the Canadian Arctic Archipelago (Reich, 1979; Beck, 1990a, b; Anderson, 1991; Hall, 1992a, 1994; Hall and Johnston, 1992). However, tourists may also disrupt scientific programmes and local communities through their very presence, the requirement of emergency services, impact on wildlife, or the dismantling of archaeological and historic sites. In other words, tourism has the potential to dramatically affect the polar environments, a situation which has already occurred in several islands and on the Antarctic continent itself (Lyster, 1984), and has been noted as a concern for the Arctic (Colin, 1994; Mason, 1994). In the Arctic, an added challenge in polar tourism lies in its cultural and economic impact on indigenous populations and other residents. Tourism has tremendous potential to aid economic development in northern communities; it also has potential to disrupt communities. Additionally, the existence of tourism with other uses of the natural environment, both subsistence activities and industrial operations, carries with it potential for conflict (Marsh and Johnston, 1984; Anderson, 1991).

Although situated at opposite ends of the earth, a comparative approach to the analysis of tourism development, management and policy in the northern and southern polar regions can shed substantial light on the problems and experiences shared between the two regions. Table 1.1 highlights some of the significant characteristics of the Antarctic and Arctic regions affecting the framework within which tourism operates in these areas. A fundamental difference for management between the two regions is the degree to which national sovereignty or jurisdiction, and hence a binding legal structure, applies. In the northern polar areas, countries have clear sovereignty over all of the land, and much of the coastal and ocean areas, although some disagreement does still exist over the definition of international waters. However, in the Antarctic, legal sovereignty is disputed for all except the sub-Antarctic islands. The lack of sovereignty

Table 1.1. Comparative aspects of tourism within the Antarctic and Arctic regions

Antarctic	Arctic
● Disputed sovereignty over land and ocean areas	● Relatively clear sovereignty over land areas
● Sub-Antarctic islands relatively clear sovereignty	● Dispute exists over definition of international waters
● Scientific bases used as a means of reinforcing territorial claims	● Scientific bases used as a means of reinforcing territorial claims
● Tourism used as a means of reinforcing territorial claims	● Tourism used as a means of reinforcing territorial claims
● Conservation operates under international management regime except on sub-Antarctic islands	● Conservation primarily operates under a national management regime, including designation of national park areas
● Military presence minor	● Significant military presence
● Mineral resource exploration and mining under moratorium	● Substantial mineral resource exploration and mining
● Significant fishing and whaling	● Significant fishing, whaling, grazing and hunting
● No indigenous peoples	● Indigenous peoples seeking economic and political self-determination
● Tourism operates in a legislative vacuum, laws can only be made by countries with respect to their own citizens	● Tourism is clearly subject to national and regional legislative control except in disputed international waters
● Tourist access is extremely difficult, sea and air only	● Tourist access though difficult is available by air, land and sea. Northern regions of North America and Europe have well-established air networks and a good sub-Arctic road network
● Extremely harsh climate	● Harsh climate but a relatively mild summer (other than Canadian High Arctic and Greenland)
● Extremely sensitive physical environment	● Extremely sensitive physical environment
● Cultural tourism relates to historic sites and current scientific and government use	● Cultural tourism relates to historic sites, living aboriginal culture, archaeological sites and current industry uses
● Range of tourists from generally passive sightseers to recreational expeditions to the Pole or traversing the continent	● Range of tourists from passive sightseers to recreational expeditions to the Pole or other challenges

Source: After Hall and Johnston (1992).

represents a most fundamental and immediate problem for environmental and tourism management, given the lack of applicable national law and hence regulation of tourist and environmental activities. Nevertheless, the sheer size of both regions makes the application of regulations by an enforcement agency somewhat problematic. Therefore it is likely that codes of practice and international agreements will be significant in the Arctic and Antarctic regardless of sovereignty.

The other major difference between the two regions is the existence of indigenous peoples in the Arctic. The Antarctic has not experienced continuous human habitation until this century and even then it has been limited to the scientific bases. The Arctic, however, is occupied by groups of native peoples, many of whom are currently seeking, or have achieved, greater political and economic independence from central governments, and at the same time, are seeking to revive and retain elements of their traditional culture in light of European cultural influence.

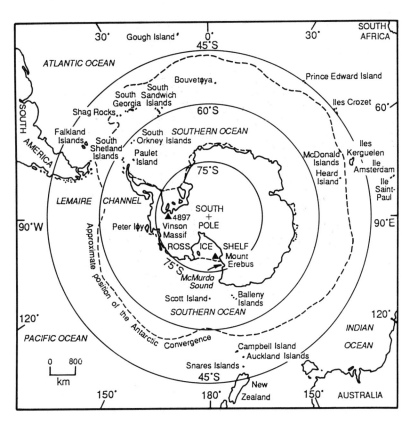

Figure 1.1. Map of Antarctica and sub-Antarctic islands

Despite these two substantial differences between the Arctic and Antarctic regions, many other characteristics are similar. The harsh climate and physical environment, the high degree of endemism among fauna and flora, an extremely sensitive environment, and the increasing attraction of these harsh landscapes for tourists have created a number of common elements in the management of these regions. Therefore, the study of polar tourism patterns, policy, issues and management within these two areas would appear to have the potential to yield a number of insights into the means by which the natural and cultural significance of the polar regions can be maintained, and the world's environmentally sensitive and remote areas managed for tourism.

The territory considered in this book includes the polar regions of the Arctic and Antarctic as well as parts of the sub-Arctic and the sub-Antarctic. The Antarctic is easy to delineate by its continental boundaries. The particular areas of the sub-Antarctic being examined in this book range from

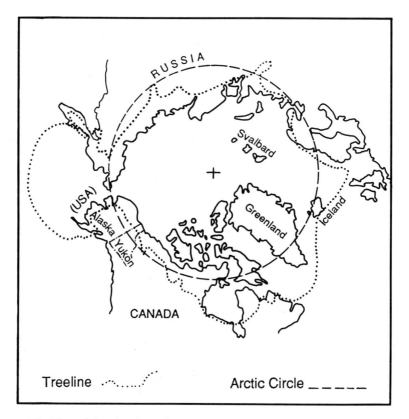

Figure 1.2. Map of the Arctic region

37° 15′ S (Tristan da Cunha) to 60° S (the boundary of the area subject to the Antarctic Treaty); despite temperate latitudinal locations, they evidence the effects of the harsh polar climate combined with the influences of the cold Antarctic waters (Figure 1.1). Various delineations of the Arctic exist; the most common are based on indicators of climate (e.g. the treeline) or solely on latitude (e.g. the Arctic Circle at 66° 33′ N) (Figure 1.2). The two, of course, are only generally comparable (see Hammar, 1989, and Directorate for Nature Management, 1993). Prevailing winds and physiography have resulted in an Arctic climate and vegetational pattern which deviates considerably from lines of latitude. This is particularly evident in Canada, Greenland and Iceland where an Arctic climate dominates substantially southward of the Arctic Circle, and in Russia and Norway, where ameliorating forces have created a sub-Arctic climate within large sections of the Arctic Circle.

DEFINING POLAR TOURISM

Polar tourism is difficult to define. For example, any discussion of Antarctic tourism by Antarctic Treaty parties is often automatically linked to the management of non-governmental activities. However, Hemmings et al. (1991, p. 3) assert that, 'it is tourism, rather than non-governmental activities per se, which has been the publicly acknowledged problem. Yet when it comes to actually drafting something, the terms of reference suddenly become wider than merely tourism'.

Several researchers have attempted to define tourism and tourists in the Antarctic context. In a definition which is clearly more encompassing than would appear necessary for the Arctic, Enzenbacher (1992a, p. 17) defined tourists as

> visitors who are not affiliated in an official capacity with an established National Antarctic Program. They include both fare-paying passengers, whose numbers are usually reported reliably by tour operators, and private expedition members and adventurers aboard sea or airborne vessels, whose numbers are more difficult to determine.

The International Union for Conservation of Nature and Natural Resources (IUCN) (1992, p. 1) also makes a distinction between commercial and private tourism activities for management purposes, because 'Operations by commercial tour companies, whether shipborne or aircraft supported, are usually larger in scale, involve more people, have greater potential for environmental impact or disruption of activities, and, therefore, demand greater management effort.' Similarly, Hemmings et al. (1991) also divide tourism in Antarctica into commercial and non-commercial ventures. They categorise the principal tourism activities into large group tourism, adventure tourism and recreation. Non-governmental activities such as journalism, science or independent assessment of human activities are not included under the heading of tourism.

As discussed in Chapters 10 and 12, the Antarctic Treaty parties are divided on how to define Antarctic tourism. Chile, France, Germany, Italy and Spain have produced a draft Annexe on Tourism (Chile, France, Germany, Italy, Spain Submission 1992, p. 3) in which they distinguish between an organised group visitor, who is a person taking part in a trip prepared by a 'tour organiser'; and an independent visitor, who is any person who organises on his/her own account a trip to Antarctica. In the case of the Antarctic, defining 'tourism' and 'tourists' is important because of the legal and administrative difficulties inherent in managing transnational territory. Clearly, however, in the management context any visitor to polar regions, regardless of who organised the trip, may have considerable impact on the environment. Certainly, there is the expectation that visitors whose trip has been organised by a tour operator are potentially subject to greater levels of control.

Hall (1992a, p. 4) argued that tourism in the Antarctic and sub-Antarctic context can be defined as 'all existing human activities other than those directly involved in scientific research and the normal operations of government bases'. This definition covers the activities of commercial tourism operations, non-government expeditions and the recreational activities of government personnel. However, the situation in the northern polar regions is clearly different because of the presence of resident populations and a range of commercial activities including mining, grazing and fishing. Definitions of tourism used in the Arctic and sub-Arctic context are typical of definitions of tourism in much of the world: 'Tourism [is] the relationships and phenomena arising out of the journeys and temporary stays of people travelling primarily for leisure or recreational purposes' (Pearce, 1989, p. 1). In some cases, this definition is operationalised merely as visitors to the particular jurisdiction. For example, much of the tourist information collected and disseminated by the Northwest Territories and Yukon Territory is about visitors to the territory, often calculated through border crossing statistics, and does not necessarily cover internal pleasure travel. Internal resident tourism is important within these territories and yet it is ignored. Therefore, for the purposes of this book, polar tourism is defined as 'all travel for pleasure or adventure within polar regions, exclusive of travel for primarily governmental, commercial, subsistence, military or scientific purposes'.

THE GROWTH OF ANTARCTIC AND SUB-ANTARCTIC TOURISM

It is difficult to establish with absolute certainty the exact numbers of tourists that have visited Antarctica. Information is often scattered, ambiguous or incomplete, and often inconsistently reported by the Antarctic Treaty parties (Enzenbacher, 1991, 1993, in print; Wouters, 1993). Nevertheless, since Antarctica emerged as a tourist destination 35 years ago, over 45 000 tourists are estimated to have visited (Enzenbacher, 1993, p. 142). The majority of tourists are ship-borne (Table 1.2). Of the total landed since 1957–58, nearly 45 per cent travelled during the seasons 1987–88 to 1991–92. During the 1990–91 season, at least 4842 tourists visited Antarctica, representing a 600 per cent increase from 1985–86 (782 visitors) (Enzenbacher 1992a). At least 6495 tourists visited the Antarctic during the 1991–92 season, presenting the largest tourist presence ever recorded in a single season (Enzenbacher, 1993). During the 1992–93 season, over 8000 tourists could have visited Antarctica if all planned tours were conducted (Madden, 1993b; NZAS, 1993). Tourists now outnumber the total number of scientists and support staff based in Antarctica (estimated at 4000) during the Austral summer. A detailed breakdown of tourist numbers to Antarctica since 1980 is provided in Table 1.3.

Visitation to sub-Antarctic islands is also rapidly increasing. Islands close to existing Antarctic tourist destinations such as the Antarctic Peninsula (e.g. South Georgia and the Falkland Islands) and the Ross Sea (e.g. Campbell Island and Macquarie Island) are receiving ship-borne visitation (see Chapters 15 and 16 by Wouters and Hall). The expansion of ship-

Table 1.2. Estimated numbers of seaborne tourists in Antarctica from 1957 to 1993

Year	No. of tourists	Year	No. of tourists
1957–58	194	1978–79	1048
1958–59	344	1979–80	855
1965–66	58	1980–81	855
1966–67	94	1981–82	1441
1967–68	147	1982–83	719
1968–69	1312	1983–84	834
1969–70	972	1984–85	544
1970–71	943	1985–86	631
1971–72	984	1986–87	1797
1972–73	1175	1987–88	2782
1973–74	1876	1988–89	3146
1974–75	3644	1989–90	2460
1975–76	1890	1990–91	4698
1976–77	1068	1991–92	6317
1977–78	845	1992–93	7037

Note the absence of tourist activity from the end of the 1958–59 season until the 1965–66 season. Numbers of seaborne tourists after the 1979–80 season include yachts when known.
Source: Enzenbacher (1993, p. 144, 1994, p. 106).

Table 1.3. Known numbers of tourists in Antarctica from 1980–81 to 1992–93 inclusive and their totals

Year	No. of seaborne tourists	No. of airborne tourists	Total no. of tourists
1980–81	855	n/a	855
1981–82	1441*	*	1441
1982–83	719	2	721
1983–84	834	265	1099
1984–85	544	92	636
1985–86	631	151	782
1986–87	1797	30	1827
1987–88	2782	244	3026
1988–89	3146	370	3516
1989–90	2460	121	2581
1990–91	4698	144	4842
1991–92	6317	178	6495
1992–93	7037	185	7222
Totals	33 261	1782	35 043

Notes: n/a—the number of airborne tourists during this season is unknown.
Figures for airborne tourists are likely to be low as data are fragmentary.
* In 1981–82 some passengers were both airborne and ship-borne.
Source: Enzenbacher (1992, p. 142, 1994, p. 105).

borne tourism in the Antarctic may well see the development of circum-polar tour routes, which potentially may include visits to other sub-Antarctic islands, including Heard Island, which have been isolated from the effects of tourist visitation.

Exact numbers of visits made by small or non-commercial expeditions to Antarctica and the sub-Antarctic islands are difficult to obtain, and many visits may never be reported. In addition, there is a lack of uniformity in reporting procedures by commercial operators, making the exact statistics of Antarctic visitors difficult to determine (Enzenbacher, 1993; Wouters, 1993). The number of private expeditions is also on the increase, and includes voyages by private and chartered yachts, overland crossings of the continent and visits to the South Pole (IUCN, 1991).

The patterns and processes of future Antarctic tourism are difficult to predict in detail (Enzenbacher, 1991). Interest and activity will almost certainly increase. However, such factors as cost, accessibility, weather and the availability of transport all play a role in determining levels of activity. Indeed, there is already growing interest in recommencement of overflights from Australia, and cruise ship operators have plans to increase the number of voyages to the Ross Sea region and the sub-Antarctic islands (Wouters, 1993).

THE GROWTH OF ARCTIC AND SUB-ARCTIC TOURISM

The number of tourists in the Arctic and sub-Arctic is far greater than in the southern polar regions. There is a much longer history of touristic activities, considerably greater accessible land area, more destinations, many more access routes from relatively close markets, and a wider variety of attractions. As in the Antarctic, tourists travel by water and air; however, by far the most common mode of transport is land-based as there is road access to many parts of the Arctic and sub-Arctic. The main draw in this region is the natural landscape. Nature-based activities predominate as they do in the southern polar region: an untouched wilderness is the chief attraction. Within this, there continues to be an important consumptive element to Arctic and sub-Arctic tourism which is absent in the south. Hunting and fishing experiences have traditionally had strong markets and have been met by both commercial and non-commercial opportunities. Despite the tremendous growth in non-consumptive uses and a growing environmental ethic which decries sport hunting and fishing, the popularity of these activities shows no signs of abating. Cultural activities based on aboriginal lifestyles and crafts, and historic events, locations or artefacts are also increasingly significant.

For numerous reasons, it is impossible to estimate worldwide numbers of visitors in the Arctic and sub-Arctic. There are eight countries with Arctic and/or sub-Arctic territory, and, with the exceptions of Greenland and Iceland, the statistical reporting boundaries within them do not match the delineation of the Arctic or sub-Arctic. This makes gathering of statistics for the defined areas difficult. For example, Kempf *et al.* (1994) suggest that 100 000 tourists visit the Arctic each summer. However, their definition of the Arctic relies on administrative boundaries. It therefore includes tourist numbers for the entire Northwest Territories of Canada, all of which is not Arctic, and does not include numbers for the Arctic portion of mainland Norway. Furthermore, different reporting systems, sporadic record-keeping, and former policies of secrecy add to the problem. But most importantly, tourists do not necessarily physically leave one continent and arrive at another. Many destinations in the Arctic and sub-Arctic are without border crossings, checkpoints or other accurate means of determining whether travel is tourism-related. Another difficulty in establishing numbers stems from the type of trip: for example, it should be relatively easy to obtain passenger numbers for all large cruise ships (as Marsh and Staple have done for the Canadian Arctic, Chapter 4); however, it might be equally difficult to track numbers of independent yachts and small commercial cruises. In some cases, we can find statistics for specific places and regions, and some of these are given in chapters in this book.

The tremendous growth in Arctic and sub-Arctic tourism has occurred in the last 25 years (see Kempf *et al.*, 1994). However, touristic activities have been in evidence for over a century, with travel often linked to exploration. As Marsh (1987, p. 303) stated, 'it is difficult to distinguish some of the later explorers from some of the earliest tourists in the [Canadian] North'. There was a similar link between exploration and tourism in the Scandinavian Arctic when polar tourism received a boost in 1827, after Himalayan explorer, Robert Everest, visited North Cape, a northerly point on the mainland of Norway (Jacobsen, 1994). For much of its history, Arctic tourism was the preserve of the wealthy and so numbers remained low. Not until the post Second World War period did the tourist market expand rapidly, for the same sorts of reasons that Antarctica emerged as a tourism destination around the same time (and tourism in general began to increase): post-war optimism, available transportation, rising incomes, increased holidays, and the growth of broader public interest in the environment and conservation.

Evidence of the size of the increase comes from the Northwest Territories in Canada, which comprises a large Arctic area, and a smaller but road-accessible sub-Arctic. It is estimated that there were about 600 tourist visits to the Northwest Territories in 1959; by 1992, the number of tourists was estimated to be 56 000, with 85 per cent of these visiting in the summer months (Department of Economic Development and Tourism, 1993). Table 1.4 illustrates the tremendous growth of Arctic and sub-Arctic tourism in recent years. Though not necessarily impressive in comparison to tourist numbers in major tourism destination regions of the world such as the Caribbean or the Mediterranean, Northwest Territories figures are none

Table 1.4. Growth of Arctic and sub-Arctic tourism, 1988–93

	North Cape	Svalbard camping/nights[*]	Northwest Territories
1988	140 000	1431	33 000
1989	169 642	1437	47 600
1990	172 500	1444	47 600
1991	183 745	1932	47 600
1992	200 467	1790	47 600
1993	224 028	2184	n/a

[*] Camping/nights includes all persons camping beyond Longyearbyen, but does not distinguish between type or tourist (e.g. hiker, skier).
Sources: Department of Economic Development and Tourism (1993); SAS North Cape Hotels; Info-Svalbard.

the less impressive when compared to the yearly Antarctic total. However, northern destination regions with greater road access have correspondingly higher tourist numbers. For example, the total summer tourism in the mainland part of Arctic Norway is estimated at 500 000 (Sletvold, 1993, p. 1).

Tourism in the Arctic and sub-Arctic will probably continue to grow in the future as the appeal of opportunities for eco-tourism, adventure tourism and cultural tourism continues to grow. While many other destinations in the world are well developed, the Arctic and Antarctic have lagged behind. There is vast potential for further development, particularly as aboriginal peoples develop tourism skills and begin to take charge of tourism in their communities, and as the opening of the Russian Arctic to foreigners enables circumpolar tourist travel in the 'Mediterranean of the North'.

THE ENVIRONMENTAL IMPACTS OF POLAR TOURISM

The polar regions are often described as eco-tourism destinations (Janiskee, 1991). However, the perceived wilderness nature of the Arctic and Antarctic, while drawing visitors interested in their outstanding natural values may, paradoxically, lead to their destruction. Three types of visitation may be identified in the polar regions, each with its own requirements in terms of infrastructure, pattern of tourism, and consequent impacts on the physical environment: airborne or overflights, ship-borne and land-borne (Table 1.5).

Overflights provide the most minimal disturbance of the polar environment and do not necessarily require permanent land-based facilities. In Antarctica, overflights use large jets which depart from outside the region; these were popular in the 1970s until operations ceased following the crash of an Air New Zealand flight in 1979 (Dingwall, 1993). The recommencement of overflights on New Year's Eve 1994 is testimony to their great popularity. In the northern hemisphere, overflights are much more likely to be low-flying, small aircraft with a dozen or fewer passengers who depart from small northern centres within the region. Hydrocarbon residues from aircraft fuel can be distributed over a wide area by winds (Swithinbank, 1993), while low overflights may cause disturbance to feeding, frighten animals and affect breeding behaviour. For example, regular low overflights of penguin colonies have been shown to cause panic stampedes or desertion of nests with considerable loss of eggs by crushing or from subsequent predation by skuas' (HRSCERA, 1989, p. 10). In the north, the main wildlife concerns relate to disturbance of ungulates such as caribou, as well as birds.

The possible impacts of ship-based tourism on the polar environment are more substantial. The most significant concern is the potential for water

Table 1.5. The environmental impacts of tourism infrastructure in polar regions

Type of activity	Infrastructure characteristics	Nature of impacts
Overflights	No requirement for permanent land-based facilities in region	Fall-out from engines; disturbance of wildlife due to noise which may affect breeding and feeding activities; disturbance due to plane crashes
Ship-based	No requirement for permanent land-based facilities as long as ship carries sufficient fuel and supplies	Generally transient environmental effects, although substantial pressure may be placed on regularly visited shore-based attractions; water pollution from oil spills and sewage; disturbance to wildlife; potential introduction of bird and plant diseases; introduction of exotic flora; disturbance due to shipwreck
Land-based	Support infrastructure including the provision of all-weather airstrips capable of handling large commercial aircraft; accommodation facilities; possible combination of tourist facilities with scientific bases and local communities. Other infrastructure may include road or train network, gift shops, interpretive/information facilities, tracks and trails, waste disposal facilities	Increased competition with flora and fauna for ice-free land and fresh water supply; water pollution; disposal of sewage and rubbish; degradation of specific sites with high visitation levels; disturbance to wildlife including both breeding and feeding patterns; potential introduction of bird and plant diseases; introduction of exotic flora and fauna. Potential damage to built heritage through souveniring, trampling and changes to microclimate. Disruption of permafrost for construction. Permanent roads and airstrips cause erosion, slumping, river siltation and drainage problems

Source: Adapted from Hall (1992a).

pollution due to inadequate sewage and waste disposal, fuel spills and the possibility of shipwreck (see Marsh and Staple, Chapter 4). For example, the grounding of the Argentine resupply/tourist vessel *Bahia Paraiso* in Antarctic waters in 1989 (Herr *et al.*, 1990), highlights the dangers of travel in polar waters. As illustrated by the grounding of the *Exxon Valdez* in Alaska, large-scale shipping accidents may require time-consuming and costly environmental clean-up operations. A further concern with ship travel is the possibility of ships encountering Arctic pack-ice as it moves, and, in extreme cases, of ships being frozen in. These situations require the assistance of ice-breaking ships, again a costly rescue activity for the affected country and/or company.

As ships are self-contained they have only a low level of interaction with the environment (HRSCERA, 1989; Enzenbacher, 1992b). Cruise-ship passengers do not generally spend many hours on land. Nevertheless, these tourists can have potentially adverse effects due to their numbers placing significant pressures on locations of tourist interest (HRSCERA, 1989). Repeated visits, even by well-regulated tours, can destroy a fragile plant cover (Wace, 1990); litter and human waste might also be of concern. Therefore, given that ship-based tourism is extremely hard to regulate because of the mobility of cruise operations and their capacity to visit remote locations, the length of time that visitors spend on land and the activities they undertake may well require further regulation (Codling, 1982; Wouters, 1993).

Permanent land facilities and infrastructure will have the greatest impact on the polar environment. The establishment of tourism facilities poses major problems of sewage and waste disposal, food and water supply, and the provision of accommodation, gift shops, information centres, and postal and medical services for example. Furthermore, the development of land-based tourism operations necessitates the construction or upgrading of tourism infrastructure such as communication and transport networks, including all-weather airstrips, landing pads, and roads (Hall, 1992a). Much infrastructure in the northern hemisphere generally has been built for commercial or government reasons. However, incremental increases in tourist use have required maintenance, improvements and even expansion of existing systems. Moreover, new facilities have been constructed specifically for tourists, notably trails, lodges and campsites.

In both polar regions, the provision of permanent tourist facilities poses the greatest threat to the environment. The simple presence and activity of tourists, even when occurring in an acceptable manner and in designated locations, also pose threats to the physical and social environment (see Valentine, 1992). Furthermore, inappropriate behaviour of visitors can be particularly deleterious to the environment: improper waste disposal, disturbing or killing wildlife, unsuitable travel through sensitive areas, and removing wood for fires are sources of potential negative impacts. Tourism can build support for conservation and may help finance it. However, as several chapters in this book illustrate, unless adequate controls are placed on tourist visitation in environmentally sensitive areas, there is a strong possibility that tourism will damage the very landscape that attracts the tourists in the first place.

THE ECONOMIC DIMENSIONS OF POLAR TOURISM

All tourism brings with it some degree of economic impact. Indeed, the generation of tourist dollars is one of the key reasons for tourist development. The development of a tourism industry might be pursued by communities which have no other source of income, communities which are seeking to strengthen their economic base, and communities whose traditional industries are declining. While the economic dimension of polar tourism appears to have the most significance for the Arctic and sub-Arctic, given the vastly larger tourist numbers and the presence of permanent settlements, it is none the less important in the Antarctic as well. In both polar regions, tourism can serve as an alternative to extractive uses of the environment, particularly if tourists mobilise to protect land and water that is currently used or potentially usable for other commercial activities. However, in much of the Arctic and sub-Arctic, tourism operates in conjunction with other uses of the environment. Other economic activities might include industrial exploitation such as hydroelectricity and mining, or traditional aboriginal hunting, fishing and grazing activities. It is important to note that such activities are not necessarily solely subsistence and often have a commercial component.

Tourism has been suggested as a means of community economic development in most parts of the world, and appears to have great relevance for remote northern communities. The creation of Katannilik Territorial Park in the Northwest Territories in Canada was a component of government initiatives 'to facilitate visitors achieving their objectives while at the same time creating an important economic benefit to local communities' (Downie, 1993, p. 51; see also Val, 1990; Hinch, Chapter 8). In Svalbard, tourism is being viewed as a potential saviour of the community of Longyearbyen should the long uneconomical coal-mines cease operation. Tourism currently employs 50 people directly, and another 50 indirectly (Viken, Chapter 5); clearly, some further development of the industry is necessary if an entire community of over 1000 people is to be supported by this one sector. The key for Longyearbyen, Svalbard and indeed many other northern communities, is to encourage tourists to spend money locally. One of the major problems in the north, particularly in places like Svalbard which experiences a dominance of cruise tourists, and the Arctic part of the Northwest Territories which is dominated by air travel, is that much of the money generated by tourist travel is spent on transportation and therefore accrues outside the region. A major element in the tourism policy of the Northwest Territories is to encourage 'community tourism' so that local people determine the path tourism shall take and local ownership of business is increased (Hinch and Swinnerton, 1992). In a 1990 database of commercial adventure-related operators in eastern

Canada, eight were based in the Northwest Territories and seven were based externally, two of these in the United States (Tourism Research Group, 1990).

Although tourism can bring money to communities, it also costs money to host visitors. Facilities are required, and investment is needed in businesses which serve tourists (e.g. local transport, restaurant, hotel). Furthermore, 'Because local businesses are often forced to "import" goods and services in order to cater to tourist demands, much of the money that reaches the communities "leaks" out before it has a chance to generate "downstream" jobs and income' (Milne et al., in press). In addition, there are often social impacts associated with the influx of visitors and tourist dollars, which might, in fact, outweigh any economic benefits (see Hinch, Chapter 8; Marsh and Staple, Chapter 4; also Smith, 1989). Social impacts might be especially problematic in the Arctic and sub-Arctic where tourists come into contact with indigenous peoples and northern lifestyles.

THE INTERRELATIONSHIP OF TOURISM WITH SCIENTIFIC WORK

Impacts of tourism in the polar regions are generally considered in view of environmental degradation. It has been suggested by Hall (1992a) in the Antarctic context, that control of tourists and their impacts might best be facilitated through the location of facilities near scientific bases. While the impacts on the environment might be minimised by situating the tourist infrastructure near existing bases, this may have negative impacts on scientific research. Scientific bases may have to provide costly search and rescue services, greatly reducing their ability to perform research, and disrupting the work of scientists. It can even cause social stress to the people who are based for a season or even a whole year in Antarctica (Sage, 1985). The sudden appearance of new faces ashore often proves unsettling for otherwise isolated research stations, and visits tend to be followed by outbreaks of minor infections among base personnel (Wace, 1990, p. 339).

Tourism can interfere directly with scientific work and indirectly through impacts on the cultural heritage of polar regions. In Antarctica and the sub-Antarctic Islands, a number of cultural and industrial (sealing and whaling) sites exist, as well as the remains of several early exploration bases. These have substantial historic significance. Similarly, in the Arctic, sealing, whaling, mining, exploration, missionary, trading, military and archaeological sites are vulnerable to tourist visitation. In both polar regions, cultural sites and artefacts can easily be destroyed by souveniring, vandalism, fire or other damage, with consequent substantial impact on archaeological and historical research.

Although commercial operators might be responsible for disrupting scientific work, they might also be involved in scientific research which could be useful in the management of the environmental impacts of humans on the polar environment. For example, in 1989 Southern Heritage Tours, a New Zealand nature tourism company, organised and funded a survey on the distribution of Rockhopper penguins on the Auckland Islands in the New Zealand sub-Antarctic islands (Russ, 1992). However, such activities may be deemed 'inappropriate' for commercial operators and thus threatening to government agencies, where nature conservation agencies do not regard commercial activities as appropriate on conservation reserves (Hall and Wouters, 1994). Linked to this is a concern noted in the Canadian Arctic regarding the activities of recreational expeditions who declare themselves scientific parties but whose primary aim is not, in fact, to obtain scientific data but to reach a predetermined goal such as traversing a particular island or skiing to the Pole (Johnston, 1993). Groups such as these do not necessarily evidence the attitudes and approaches to the environment that a government agency would expect of a truly scientific party. Yet tourism can also enable scientific research to proceed by sharing the costs of transporting personnel and cargo, or by providing all the necessary money to undertake the polar travel when government financing is not forthcoming (see Gusarova and Kempf, 1994).

SOVEREIGNTY AND POLITICAL DIMENSIONS OF POLAR TOURISM

Sovereignty is an important concept in international law and politics (Crawford, 1979). There are several ways in which territorial sovereignty may be acquired: 'occupation of terra nullius; prescription, by which title is gained by possession adverse to the abstract titleholder; cession, or transfer by treaty; accretion, where a gradual deposition of soil changes the shape of the land; and, finally, conquest' (Triggs, 1986, p. 2). Tourism can be an important expression of sovereignty, serving as an example of effective occupation. Furthermore, tourism may serve as an economic linkage between the disputed territory and the claimant state, thereby giving further weight to any argument of effective occupation (Hall, 1994).

Tourism is currently being used to support territorial claims in both the north and south polar regions. In the Arctic, continental sovereignty is not disputed. However, conflict does exist over the definition of territorial and international waters, such as through the Northwest Passage. Therefore, the creation of national parks and protected areas in the Arctic by the Canadian government, and the development of special-interest tourism activities in these parks, may be seen as a means of supporting Canada's territorial claims to the northern islands and to the surrounding waters, just as military and other commercial activities are (Hall and Johnston, 1992; see also Anderson, 1991). In contrast, no nation has legal sovereignty over any part of Antarctica. Several states (Argentina, Australia, Chile, Ecuador, Great Britain, France, New Zealand and Norway) claim territory but these claims are not generally recognised by the international community (Auburn, 1982; Triggs, 1986; Farmer, 1987) (Figure 1.3 shows the extent of Antarctic claims). The legal status of the lands and resources of the continent is subject to the conditions of the Antarctic Treaty which was signed on 1 December 1959, and came into effect on 23 June 1961 (see Enzenbacher, Chapter 12). Although the Antarctic Treaty makes no specific reference to tourism, measures and recommendations relating to tourism and non-government expeditions have been adopted at almost every biennial Antarctic Treaty Consultative Meeting (ATCM) since the 1966 meeting in Santiago, while more recently debate is occurring on whether to establish a specific protocol or convention to regulate tourism within the Antarctic Treaty framework (Nicholson, 1986; Hall, 1992a; Hall and Johnston, 1992). However, from the perspective of claimant nations,

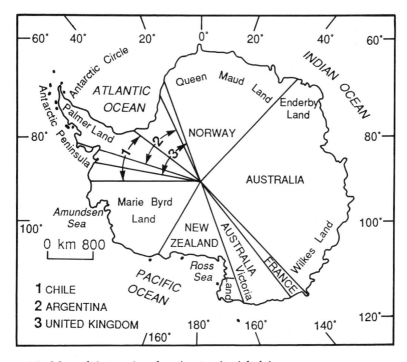

Figure 1.3. Map of Antarctica showing territorial claims

tourism in Antarctica also offers a potential mechanism to justify territorial claims and a possible source of funds to subsidise stations and scientific research (Reich, 1979).

Tourist activity on the Antarctic Peninsula is given the greatest support by Argentina and Chile. Although this is, in part, because of their geographic locations, the primary reason for their sanction of tourism in their territorial areas, including use of airbases, is that it provides support for their territorial claims to the peninsula. Similarly, Australia is also using tourism, and control of tourist activity, as a means of maintaining its claim. In the absence of organised and regular tourism to the Australian Antarctic Territory (AAT), the Australian government tended to take a generally neutral position on tourism and non-government expeditions to the Territory until the late 1980s (Bergin, 1985; Hall, 1992a). However, the pressure on the Australian government by conservation groups to act on a variety of Antarctic environmental issues, the negotiations on the renewal of the Antarctic Treaty, the rise of commercial interest in the tourism opportunities provided in the AAT, and the need to maintain a viable Australian presence in Antarctica have led to the first steps being taken towards the development of an Australian Antarctic tourism policy within the context of Australia's broader Antarctic policy objectives including, significantly, to 'preserve its sovereignty over the [Australian Antarctic Territory], including rights over the adjacent offshore areas' (HRSCERA, 1989, p. 2).

Despite the generally clear sovereign control in the northern polar region, as one of the few remaining regions in the world not covered by international agreements, it has been suggested that the Arctic is the 'last unmanaged frontier' (Bloomfield in Beck, 1989, p. 92). International cooperation in the Arctic has been increasing in recent years, particularly with progressive openness of Russia (Beck, 1989; Ilyina and Mieczkowski, 1992). Government organisations such as the Northern Forum have been created, and they join regional and circumpolar aboriginal associations in the aim of sharing knowledge and resources, and working for common goals. In 1989 the Circumpolar Universities Association was formed at Lakehead University in order 'to encourage cooperation and promote higher learning and research in northern areas of the world'. In the early 1990s considerable efforts were undertaken towards forming an Arctic environmental council to establish conservation and environmental protocols. A major step in protecting Arctic environments has been taken in the compilation of documents by the Working Group on the Conservation of Arctic Flora and Fauna (Directorate for Nature Management, 1993). This spirit of cooperation appears to have the momentum to continue, and may well result in the adoption of an international agreement similar to the Antarctic Treaty System (see Beck, 1989), and perhaps the adoption of a visitor code for the Arctic (see Mason, 1994) and a code of operator ethics for the Arctic and sub-Arctic.

CONCLUSION

> The polar regions are similar—cold, remote from civilisation, difficult for people to live in, and beautiful or dreary, exciting or boring, according to taste. But they are different too, as though a Creator had set out to design two ends for the earth, fundamentally the same but different in as many curious and interesting ways as possible (Stonehouse, 1990, p. 13).

The polar regions are among the world's last tourism frontiers. Their relative isolation has helped preserve a relatively pristine environment which increasingly has been viewed favourably in a world seeking unique tourist experiences. The growth of interest in 'green', 'eco-tourism' or 'nature-based' forms of tourism has focused attention on the management of tourist visitation in polar regions and they are often regarded as benchmarks or potential models for visitor management in other environmentally sensitive areas (Wouters, 1993; Hall and Wouters, 1994). Therefore, the study of tourism in the Antarctic, Arctic and sub-polar regions is valuable not only in terms of its potential contribution to an understanding of tourism and polar studies, but also in terms of tourism in other valued environments.

This book provides a number of chapters each looking at specific aspects of tourism in the northern and southern polar regions. As indicated in this introduction, a number of common themes runs through each chapter, identifying the need for appropriate tourist management regimes in polar regions and the sensitivity of the polar environments, but also clarifying the substantial differences which exist in the political/legal regimes which regulate tourism, in the spatial patterns of tourist visitation, in the economic impacts of tourism, and in the presence of indigenous and resident populations in the northern polar region.

Each polar region is examined in a series of chapters, the first of which introduces the key issues and patterns of tourism in each polar region. Chapters 2–9 discuss tourism in the Arctic and sub-Arctic, while Chapters 10–16 discuss tourism in the Antarctic and sub-Antarctic.

Patterns and issues in Arctic and sub-Arctic tourism are examined by Johnston (Chapter 2) who notes the major elements affecting tourism in the northern polar regions. Historical and spatial aspects of tourism in the Arctic and sub-Arctic are discussed in Chapter 3 by Lundgren who compares tourism space penetration processes in northern Canada and Scandinavia. The theme of space penetration is also a focus of Marsh and Staple (Chapter 4) in their chapter on cruise tourism in the Canadian

Arctic. Although essentially road-based and railroad-based tourism are well established, cruise tourism is just beginning in the Canadian Arctic. In contrast, cruise tourism has a relatively long history in Svalbard, and Viken (Chapter 5) describes the development of cruise and other tourism in Svalbard, and reports on the motivations and experiences of land-based visitors in this part of Arctic Norway. Chapter 6 by Johnston and Madunic focuses specifically on waste disposal issues related to the Yukon Territory, Canada, and considers some of the management issues given visitors' ideas about the present waste disposal regime. All three chapters make interesting comparisons with the Antarctic and sub-Antarctic experience, particularly in terms of trying to encourage people to be 'green' in terms of their attitudes towards the environment and in the search for appropriate management regimes.

The remaining three chapters on Arctic tourism highlight one of the elements of the region that distinguish it from the southern polar regions, the presence of indigenous and settled peoples and the important cultural and economic dimensions of the tourism industry. The chapter on tourism in northwest Russia by Viken, Vostryakov and Davydov illustrates the potential significance of tourism in post-Soviet Russia and the effect that this may have on local peoples and their control of tourism. The Russian experience can be compared in Chapter 8 by Hinch with that of the involvement of aboriginal people in Canada's northern tourism economy. The final chapter in the Arctic and sub-Arctic section (Chapter 9), by Sandell, adds another dimension to the story of the relationship of northern peoples to tourism with an analysis of the relationship between the right of access to land, tourism, conservation, and the creation of national parks.

Chapter 10 by Hall and Wouters introduces readers to issues in Antarctic and sub-Antarctic tourism. Historical aspects of tourist visitation are discussed in Chapter 11, the precursors of tourism in the Antarctic, by Codling. The significance of the political and legal regime for the regulation of Antarctic tourism is thoroughly examined by Enzenbacher in Chapter 12 which analyses the Antarctic Treaty System (ATS) and the consequent development of appropriate management strategies. The significance of the ATS is further highlighted in the following two chapters which illus-trate the complexity of managing tourism in the Antarctic environment. Stonehouse and Crosbie examine tourist impacts and management in the Antarctic Peninsula (Chapter 13), while the complexities of management of tourism at Antarctic historic sites and monuments are discussed in Chapter 14 by Hughes and Davis. The final two chapters on tourism in the southern polar regions analyse tourist visitation and management regimes in the sub-Antarctic islands. Unlike the Antarctic, the sub-Antarctic islands are subject to uncontested national sovereignty. Therefore, the development of management strategies on these islands may be as relevant for the Arctic as it is for the Antarctic region. Chapter 15 by Wouters and Hall provides a general overview of tourism in the sub-Antarctic islands, while Chapter 16, also by Wouters and Hall, specifically examines tourism in New Zealand's sub-Antarctic islands.

The concluding chapter by Johnston and Hall (Chapter 17) on visitor management and the future of tourism in polar regions reiterates many of the concerns and issues discussed in this chapter and throughout the book. Particular attention is given to the problem of managing visitors and tourism operators in the environmentally sensitive polar regions and with sensitivity to the indigenous cultures of the Arctic and sub-Arctic. However, it is emphasised that it is impossible to prevent tourism access to the tourism frontiers of the Antarctic and Arctic. Therefore, appropriate and sustainable tourism management regimes must be put in place which simultaneously provide satisfactory visitor experiences and the requisite environmental, cultural and economic returns which will sustain the conservation and attractiveness of the polar regions for future generations.

As Stonehouse (1990, p. 194) remarked with some understatement, 'Management of polar regions is a lively field of research and discussion, with many practical consequences'. The contents of this volume are no exception in terms of debate over the current and future management of tourism in polar regions. It is the hope of the editors and individual authors that this volume will make its own contribution to the management and conservation of the polar regions.

REFERENCES

Anderson, M.J., 1991, Problems with tourism in Canada's eastern Arctic, *Tourism Management*, **12**(3): 209–220

Auburn, F.M., 1982, *Antarctic law and politics*, C. Hurst, London

Beck, P.J., 1989, Entering the age of the polar regions: the Arctic and Antarctic are no longer poles apart, *Ambio*, **18**(1): 92–94

Beck, P.J. 1990a, Antarctica enters the 1990s: an overview, *Applied Geography*, **10**(4): 247–264.

Beck, P.J. 1990b, Regulating one of the last tourism frontiers: Antarctica, *Applied Geography*, **10**(4): 343–356.

Bergin, A., 1985, Recent developments in Australia's Antarctic policy, *Marine Policy*, **9**: 180–191

Chile, France, Germany, Italy, Spain, 1992, Submission: preliminary draft, Annex VI to the Protocol on Environmental Protection to the Antarctic Treaty, Antarctic Treaty Consultative Meeting

Codling, R.J., 1982, Sea-borne tourism in the Antarctic: an evaluation, *Polar Record*, **21**(130): 3–9

Colin, M., 1994, Ecotourism and conservation policies in Canada. In Kempf, C., Girard, L, eds., *Le tourisme dans les régions polaires/Tourism in polar regions*, Proceedings of the Symposium, Colmar, France, 21–23 April 1992

Crawford, J., 1979, *The creation of states in international law*, Clarendon Press, Oxford

Department of Economic Development and Tourism, 1993, *Quick facts about the Northwest Territories tourism industry*, Government of the Northwest Territories, Yellowknife

Dingwall, P.R, 1993, Is tourism a threat to polar wilderness? Paper presented at the 5th World Wilderness Congress, Tromso, Norway, 24 September–1 October 1993

Directorate for Nature Management, 1993, *The state of habitat protection in the Arctic*, Conservation of Arctic Flora and Fauna Report No. 1, Directorate for Nature Management, Trondheim

Downie, B., 1993, Katannilik Territorial Park: an Arctic tourism destination. In Johnston, M.E., Haider, W., eds., *Community, resources and tourism in the north*, Lakehead University Centre for Northern Studies, Thunder Bay, pp. 51–60

Enzenbacher, D.J., 1991, A policy for Antarctic tourism: conflict or cooperation?, Unpublished Master of Philosophy thesis in Polar Studies, Scott Polar Research Institute, University of Cambridge, Cambridge

Enzenbacher, D.J., 1992a, Tourists in Antarctica: numbers and trends, *Polar Record*, **28**(164): 17–22

Enzenbacher, D.J., 1992b, Antarctic tourism and environmental concerns, *Marine Pollution Bulletin*, **25** (9–12): 258–265.

Enzenbacher, D.J., 1993, Tourists in Antarctica: numbers and trends, *Tourism Management*, April: 142–146.

Enzenbacher, D.J., 1994, Antarctic tourism: an overview of 1992/93 season activity, recent developments, and emerging issues, *Polar Record*, **30**(173): pp. 105–116

Farmer, W.J., 1987, The Antarctic treaty system and global interests in the Antarctic, *Australian Foreign Affairs Record*, **58**(3): 135–141

Gusarova, S., Kempf, C., 1994, Tourism and science in Siberia: the 1991 experience. In Kempf, C., Girard, L., eds., *Le tourisme dans les régions polaires/Tourism in polar regions*, Proceedings of the Symposium, Colmar, France, 21–23 April 1992

Hall, C.M., 1992a, Tourism in Antarctica: activities, impacts, and management, *Journal of Travel Research*, **30**(4): 2–9

Hall, C.M., 1992b, Issues in ecotourism: from susceptible to sustainable development. In *Heritage management: parks, heritage and tourism*, Royal Australian Institute of Parks and Recreation, Hobart, pp. 152–158

Hall, C.M., 1994, *Tourism and politics: policy, power and place*, John Wiley, London

Hall, C.M., Johnston, M., 1992, Pole to pole: polar tourism policy and development in Australia, Canada and New Zealand, paper presented at the Association for Canadian Studies in Australia and New Zealand Conference, Wellington, New Zealand, 14–16 December

Hall, C.M., Wouters, M.M., 1994, Managing nature tourism in the sub-Antarctic islands, *Annals of Tourism Research*, **21**(2): 355–374

Hammar, J., 1989, Freshwater ecosystems of polar regions: vulnerable resources, *Ambio*, **18**(1): 6–22

Hemmings, A.D., Cuthbert, A., Dalziell, J., 1991, *Non-governmental activities and the protection of the Antarctic environment: a paper for the government of New Zealand*, Antarctic and Southern Ocean Coalition (New Zealand), Wellington

Herr, R.A., Hall, H.R., Haward, M.G., 1990, Antarctica's future: symbols and reality. In Herr, R., Hall, H., Haward, M., eds., *Antarctica's future: continuity or change?*, Government Printing Office, Hobart

Hinch, T., Swinnerton, G., 1992, Tourism and Canada's Northwest Territories: issues and prospects, paper presented to the IGU symposium on Recreational Resources and Leisure in Geographical Perspective, Telluride, Colorado, 14–22 August 1992

HRSCERA (House of Representatives Standing Committee on Environment, Recreation and the Arts), 1989, *Tourism in Antarctica*, Report of the House of Representatives Standing Committee on Environment, Recreation and the Arts, Australian Government Publishing Service, Canberra

Ilyina, L., Mieczkowski, Z., 1992, Developing scientific tourism in Russia, *Tourism Management*, **13**(3): 327–331

Info-Svalbard, Visitor statistics, 1988–93

International Union for Conservation of Nature and Natural Resources, 1992, *Tourism in Antarctica (IUCN submission), XVII ATCM/INFO 18, 11 November*, IUCN, Gland

International Union for Conservation of Nature and Natural Resources (IUCN), 1991, *A strategy for Antarctic conservation*, IUCN, Gland

Jacobsen, J.K.S., 1994, *Arctic tourism and global tourism trends*, Research Report No. 37, Lakehead University Centre for Northern Studies, Thunder Bay

Janiskee, R.L., 1991, Ecotourism in Antarctica: too much of a good thing? Paper presented at the Annual Meeting of the Association of American Geographers, Miami, April

Johnston, M.E., 1993, Tourism and the regulation of adventure travel in the Canadian Arctic, paper presented at the Arctic Tourism and Ecotourism Symposium, 5th World Wilderness Conference/1st Northern Forum, Tromso, Norway, 24 September–1 October 1994

Kempf, C., Girard, L., Beirer, K., 1994, Le tourisme dans l'Arctique. In Kempf, C., Girard, L., eds., *Le tourisme dans les régions polaires/Tourism in polar regions*, Proceedings of the Symposium, Colmar, France, 21–23 April 1992

Lyster, S., 1984, The Falklands Islands Foundation, *Oryx*, **18**: 22–23

Madden, R., 1993, To boldly go with the Antarctic ice floes, *Sunday Times*, 1 August

Marsh, J.S., 1987, Tourism and conservation: case studies in the Canadian north. In Nelson, J.G., Needham, R., Norton, L., eds., *Arctic heritage: proceedings of a symposium*, Association of Canadian Universities for Northern Studies, Ottawa, pp. 298–322

Marsh, J.S., Johnston, M.E., 1984, Conservation, tourism and development in the north: case studies in northern Canada. In Duerden, F., ed., *Applied research in the Canadian north*, Occasional paper, Department of Geography, Ryerson Polytechnical Institute, Toronto, pp. 77–104

Mason, P., 1994, A visitor code for the Arctic, *Tourism Management*, **15**(2): 93–97

Milne, S., Ward, S., Wenzel, G., in press, Linking tourism and art in Canada's eastern Arctic: the case of Cape Dorset, *Polar Record*

New Zealand Antarctic Society (NZAS), 1992, Antarctic, *NZAS Bulletin*, **12**(9)

Nicholson, J., 1986, Antarctic tourism: the need for a legal regime? *Maritime Studies*, **29** (May/June): 1–7

Pearce, D.G., 1989, *Tourist development*, 2nd edn, Longman Scientific and Technical, Harlow

Reich, R.J., 1979, Tourism in the Antarctic: its present impact and future development, Unpublished Master of Philosophy thesis, Scott Polar Research Institute, University of Cambridge, Cambridge

Russ, R., 1992, New Zealand ecotourism: the role of the private sector – player and referee. In Hay, J.E., ed., *Ecotourism business in the Pacific: promoting a sustainable experience, conference proceedings*, Environmental Science Occasional Publication No. 8, University of Auckland, Auckland, pp. 190–194

Sage, B., 1985, Conservation and exploitation. In Bonner, W., Walton, D., eds., *Key environments: Antarctica*, Pergamon Press, Oxford, pp. 293–317

SAS North Cape Hotels, Visitor statistics, 1988–93

Sletvold, O., 1993, Arctic coastal tourism: the Norwegian Arctic coastline as a landscape for tourism, paper presented at the Arctic Tourism and Ecotourism Symposium, 5th World Wilderness Conference/1st Northern Forum, Tromso, Norway, 24 September–1 October 1994

Smith, V.L., ed., 1989, *Hosts and guests: the anthropology of tourism*, 2nd edn, University of Pennsylvania Press, Philadelphia

Smith, V.L., 1993, What have we learned from Antarctica: a tourism case study, paper presented to the Arctic Tourism and Ecotourism Symposium, 5th World Wilderness Conference/1st Northern Forum, Tromso, Norway, 24 September–1 October 1993

Stonehouse, B., 1990, *North Pole South Pole: a guide to the ecology and resources of the Arctic and Antarctic*, Prion, London

Swithinbank, C., 1993, Airborne tourism in the Antarctica 1991/92, *Polar Record*, **28**(166): 232

Tourism Research Group, 1990, *Adventure travel in eastern Canada: an overview of product and market potential*, Volume 2, Tourism Canada, Ottawa

Triggs, G., 1986, *International law and Australian sovereignty in Antarctica*, Legal Books, Sydney

Val, E., 1990, Parks, aboriginal peoples and sustainable tourism in development regions: the international experience and Canada's Northwest Territories. In Vining, J., ed., *Social science and natural resource recreation management*, Westview Press, Boulder, pp. 219–243

Valentine, P.S., 1992, Review: nature-based tourism. In Weiler, B., Hall, C.M., eds., *Special interest tourism*, Belhaven, London, pp. 105–127

Wace, N., 1990, Antarctica: a new tourist destination, Applied Geography, **10**(4): 327–341

Wouters, M., 1993, Promotion or protection: managing the paradox—the management of tourist visitation to Antarctica and the sub-Antarctic islands, the New Zealand situation as a case study, Unpublished master's thesis, Massey University, Palmerston North

2 Patterns and Issues in Arctic and Sub-Arctic Tourism

MARGARET E. JOHNSTON

ARCTIC AND SUB-ARCTIC TOURISM AND THE TEMPERATE VIEW OF THE POLAR REGIONS

Tourism in the Arctic and sub-Arctic takes many varied forms throughout the region, reflecting the particular economic and social resources that are available for tourism, the nature of the facility base, and domestic and international demand, as well as the special characteristics of the environment. Regardless of the form tourism takes, the chief attraction is the existence of a landscape which has alluring wilderness qualities. Within the overall appeal of the wilderness, there are numerous elements of the local environment which are attractions in and of themselves. For example, hunting and fishing, wildlife viewing, landscape photography and kayaking are distinct opportunities which attract tourists. While one of these might be the primary attraction for individual tourists, the typical pattern is that several features of the physical and cultural environment play a role in attracting visitors. This is particularly important for the multi-destination, road-based tourists who dominate Arctic and sub-Arctic tourism in North America and northern Scandinavia.

The tremendous appeal of Arctic and sub-Arctic environments for tourists today relates to their ability to present to tourists, to a greater or lesser degree, the image and the potential experience of northern or polar wilderness. As a cultural construction, the image of polar wilderness reveals our perceptions about the landscape and provides a framework for our actions in this environment. Sugden (1989) outlines the two main perceptions, or, as he states, illusions, that characterise the temperate view of the polar regions: hostile, challenging places; and fragile, sensitive environments (Sugden, 1989; see also Bone, 1992, pp. 2–3). The idea that the polar regions are hostile to human habitation developed out of the experiences of early European explorers who tended to use inadequate, 'temperate' technology in their struggles with the environment while

Polar Tourism: Tourism in the Arctic and Antarctic Regions
Edited by C. Michael Hall and Margaret E. Johnston. © John Wiley & Sons Ltd, 1995

ignoring the harmonious approach of indigenous peoples and their appropriate technology (Sugden, 1989). This view equates the Arctic with a mental and physical challenge, a land to be conquered. The conception that the Arctic is fragile relates to the simplicity of its ecosystem, the long period of time for vegetation recovery, and the effects of disturbance to the permafrost, thereby encouraging a protective attitude towards the environment (Sugden, 1989). However, according to Sugden (1989), these elements of polar environments are poorly understood, and, in fact, there is evidence to suggest that the polar regions are not as fragile as the temperate view indicates.

Undoubtedly, a non-polar or temperate bias permeates many of our perceptions and images of the polar regions; this is true of scientists as well as tourists. None the less, there can be no doubt that polar ecosystems are susceptible to change and/or degradation from excessive or inappropriate tourism (e.g. see Hall and Johnston, Chapter 1; Mason, 1994). Perhaps it should not be surprising, given the rise in the environmental movement over the past 20 years, that promotional literature prepared about Arctic and sub-Arctic places tends to emphasise the fragility of these environments, and the need for humans, especially visitors, to act responsibly. Yet, the mythology of the Arctic and the northern wilderness continues to attract hundreds of thousands of tourists each year. With large numbers of visitors to the northern polar regions, and their current and potential impacts on the environment and local populations, it may well be important that tourists continue to have a temperate view of the Arctic (and by extension, the sub-Arctic) as fragile and therefore requiring appropriate tourist behaviour. Related to this is the expectation that through appreciation and understanding of the wilderness tourism environment, polar tourists will become advocates for their preservation (Val, 1990), and that tourism will become a justification for the conservation of the local environment (Nickels et al., 1991). Indeed, 'The Arctic tourist may be essential for increasing awareness and the development of a constituency for the long-term preservation of this northern land' (Snepenger and Moore, 1989, p. 569).

The pull of the Arctic for many tourists relates not only to its apparent fragility but also to other features: it is a clean, 'pristine' and vast wilderness destination which provides tremendous opportunities for recreation, education, adventure and enjoyment (e.g. Bronsted, 1994; Kaltenborn, 1994; Milne et al., in press). To most visitors, it is also unusual, culturally and physically. Another important component of the image for tourists is 'the feeling of purity, giving the thoughts a freeway to dreams and reflections which the urban and hectic daily life scarcely gives any room for' (Viken, 1993, p. 6). Especially in the European Arctic, there appears to be 'the impression of being at the end of the world. ... It is not only a geographical end, it is also a cultural end' (Viken, 1993, p. 6). The mystic symbolism of the polar environment allows contemplation about the wider universe, and also about the individual, delicate components of a fragile ecosystem. It can be an awe-inspiring reminder of the connectedness of the global environment, or simply a place for new and unique cultural and nature-based experiences.

Definitions of Arctic boundaries reflect cultural and historical ways of describing and interpreting the region. In Europe, the Arctic Circle is the most commonly used factor in delineation, regardless of any climate and vegetation characteristics. The 'land of the midnight sun' is north of the Arctic Circle, however, even some places south of this line might be included within the Arctic boundaries. The quintessential Arctic in Europe is found, perhaps surprisingly, at North Cape (Nordkapp) in Norway (see Jacobsen, 1993), and not on Svalbard, which might appear more appropriate geographically. According to noted polar tourist researcher, Valene Smith, North Cape has greater meaning for Europeans as the northern extremity of Europe than does the North Pole, or anywhere else in the Arctic, for North Americans.[1] Jacobsen (1993) ties the sacralisation of North Cape to the Mercator representation of the world which placed it at the northern end of the world.

Though the Arctic Circle represents a special marker for the general public in Canada, the more usual way of delineating the Arctic is to distinguish it from the sub-Arctic or boreal north (see Bone, 1992), a distinction which is not necessarily part of the Scandinavian delineation. The usual boundary reflects the treeline, a zone many kilometres wide which is a product of climate and soils. North of the treeline, the landscape is dominated by a treeless tundra. In Alaska, the Arctic Circle is often used for delineation, much as it is in Europe (e.g. Snepenger and Moore, 1989). The Arctic Circle is heavily marketed as an attraction in the European Arctic, more so than it is in North America. In addition to the historical importance of the 'land of the midnight sun' (see Jacobsen, 1994), and the role of North Cape as the northern edge of Europe, this prevalence likely reflects the greater access Europeans have to the experience of crossing the Arctic Circle at the surface of the earth. While there are numerous good roads in northern Europe which take travellers across the Arctic Circle, in North America there is only one, the Dempster Highway. It is possible that this lack of opportunity has limited the attraction of the Arctic Circle.

Despite the image of the northern polar regions as relatively pristine and untouched, there is a long history of resource exploitation, settlement and tourism in many parts of the Arctic and sub-Arctic. The entire northern circumpolar world is ringed with the legacy of past and continuing military and industrial activity (see Viken *et al.*, Chapter 7). In some locations, tourists are confronted with this discrepancy between the image of a

Figure 2.1. Visitors might experience a conflict between image and reality in some northern polar locations. Here, at Tuktoyaktuk, Northwest Territories, the canoe is evidence of aboriginal lifestyles, while the military station in the background illustrates the historically important role of the northern circumpolar world in global defence (Photo credit: M.E. Johnston)

pristine, untouched environment and the reality of military installations, and oil and gas exploration, for example, requiring them to adjust their expectations (Figure 2.1). Similarly, a discrepancy might be experienced by tourists in the cultural realm when tourists expect aboriginal hosts to act or live in a particular way which is not evidenced in reality (Butler, 1994; Hinch, Chapter 8; Johnston and Madunic, Chapter 6).

TOURISM PATTERNS

Hundreds of thousands of tourists visit destinations in the northern circumpolar regions every year (Table 2.1). Though significantly greater than figures in the Antarctic and sub-Antarctic, the numbers in the north are still quite small compared to other tourism destinations (Butler, 1994; Mason, 1994). However, there is great variation within the region: for example, numbers of visitors at North Cape in mainland Arctic Norway equate to mass tourism in the Arctic context. In 1993, there were 224 028 visitors at this road-accessible site (SAS North Cape Hotels). Alaska had

Table 2.1. Numbers of Arctic and sub-Arctic tourists

Country of region	Numbers
Greenland*	< 6000
Iceland†	129 000
Svalbard‡	29 000
Northern Scandinavia§	500 000
Northern Russia	Not available
Arctic Alaska¶	25 000
Alaska in total‖	1 049 800
Yukon**	177 220
Northwest Territories††	47 600

* Bronsted (1994). Includes 1000 cruise passengers and about 2000 air excursionists many of whom spend less than a day in Greenland. Also includes scientists and researchers.
† 1988 figure in Economist Intelligence Unit (1989).
‡ 1993 figure in Viken, Chapter 5.
§ Estimate of summer visitors in Sletvold (1993).
¶ Estimate in Snepenger and Moore (1989).
‖ 1992/93 figures in State of Alaska (1994).
** 1991 figures in Yukon Department of Tourism (1992).
†† 1992 figures in Department of Economic Development and Tourism (1993).

over 1 million tourists from October 1992 to September 1993; 247 000 travelled by cruise ship, 111 800 by road and 627 600 by air (State of Alaska, 1994). However, less than 3 per cent of Alaskan tourists visit the Arctic part of the state (Snepenger and Moore, 1989). This pattern is mirrored in the Northwest Territories and Yukon in Canada where there is a major distinction in tourist numbers between primarily road-accessible destinations and those that are reached primarily, or solely, by air or water. This pattern of accessibility corresponds roughly to the Arctic/sub-Arctic division. In the Northwest Territories, visitors are concentrated in the southwestern sub-Arctic region which has good road access linked to a North American highway network (see Table 2.2). Road and/or railroad access is obviously important in both Europe and North America, enabling substantial tourist visitation. The one exception to this pattern is Alaska where arrivals by air and sea are more significant than travel by land. This probably relates to both the distance of the state from the rest of the continental USA, its biggest market, and to the ability of Alaska to meet the growing demand for cruising opportunities worldwide which have a strong northern wilderness segment.

Table 2.2. Number of visitors (business and pleasure) in Northwest Territories, summer only, by destination zones

Destination zone	Number of visitors
Arctic zones	
Arctic coast	2000
Baffin	4100
Keewatin	2400
Western Arctic	7600
Arctic total	16 100
Sub-Arctic zones	
Big River	13 200
Nahanni–Ram	5000
Northern frontier	27 700
Sahtu	2000
Sub-Arctic total	47 900
Northwest Territories total	64 000

N.B. These figures include all visitors, regardless of purpose. Of the total 64 000 visitors in the summer of 1992, 47 600 were pleasure travellers, but it is not known whether the visitor numbers reflect pleasure traveller numbers in each zone. The Arctic and sub-Arctic zones as listed here are provided by the author and not the source of the data. The destination zone boundaries do not necessarily align perfectly with the climate–vegetational zones as used in this volume, however, they correspond closely enough to be useful here.
Source: Department of Economic Development and Tourism (1993).

Access plays a key role in the development of tourism in the northern circumpolar world: transportation routes enable travellers to reach northern destinations, and also encourage the establishment of tourist facilities and services in particular places. However, the features of a tourism industry (and its long-term viability) will depend on the volume of traffic that can be encouraged. These points are taken up in Chapter 3 by Jan Lundgren, who compares the development of tourism destinations in northern Sweden and those in northern Canada, concluding that more efficient access in Sweden has resulted in a strong and well-serviced tourist destination area. In contrast, tourism in the Canadian north is affected by a progressive increase in travel costs northward due to great distance, and this has resulted in fewer tourists, fewer facilities, and greater expense for those who do travel.

A considerable amount of tourism development in northern Canada is focused upon road access, and highways in the Arctic and sub-Arctic continue to act as tourist corridors, serving as attractions as well as access (Figure 2.2). Many of these roads originally were developed as access routes for natural resource exploitation and military uses; however, tourist interest in newly opened wilderness areas soon followed.

> First come the surveyors and the contractors who plan and build the highway. Then there are the hunters and fishermen who want to get in and get theirs before they and others 'spoil' the country. On the heels of the sportsmen come guides, outfitters, small enterprises which provide gasoline, tire repairs, groceries, and possibly food and lodging ... (Jackman, 1973, p. 72).

The development of the Dempster Highway in northern Yukon and western Northwest Territories follows this pattern, and provides an example of the relationship between transportation and tourism in the circumpolar world. Although the territorial governments did not promote the 740-kilometre long Dempster Highway as a tourist corridor when it first opened in 1979, the press began to popularise it as a rugged wilderness road to the Arctic. Even before the highway was completed, articles were

Figure 2.2. The Dempster Highway serves as a tourist corridor, providing both attractions and access to the Arctic (Photo credit: M.E. Johnston)

published proclaiming the natural beauty, challenge and novelty of this wilderness (Johnston, 1984). This vast wilderness region and the rugged road bisecting it held the same appeal and mystique that attracted tourists to other northern highways: the experience of challenging Arctic or northern wilderness. Yet the Dempster has an additional attraction: it crosses the Arctic Circle, an important motivation for tourists (Crombie, 1982). As the only public road in North America which crosses the Arctic Circle, this tourist corridor provides a unique attraction for tourists; yet visitor numbers are low. In the early 1980s, tourist traffic amounted to about 1600 vehicles annually (Johnston, 1984). Use has since increased substantially, and it is estimated that about 7000 people visited the Dempster in 1988 (Northern Biomes Ltd et al., 1989). This amounts to about 4 per cent of Yukon tourists (see Yukon Department of Tourism, n.d.).

The tourism industry at the northernmost, Arctic end of the Dempster, in Inuvik, Northwest Territories, has developed gradually, and now a mix of small, local firms and a few larger southern-based companies offer sight-seeing, wildlife observation and adventure tours in the region. Similar to tours in other parts of the Arctic and in the Antarctic, many of these companies use naturalists and scientists as expert interpreters. 'Most of the commercial side tours have an interpretive component, although the knowledge and skill of each operator determines the quality of the learning experience. There are presently no guidelines for wildlife viewing from the air, nor are operators likely to be fully aware of sensitive habitat sites' (Northern Biomes Ltd et al., 1989, p. 22). The situation is perhaps typical of a fledgling tourism industry, yet it indicates the need for regulations and operator codes as tourism products and destinations are being developed.

The traditional activities of hunting and fishing continue to be important in northern tourism, but visitors in some places are now more likely to be interested in non-consumptive uses (Milne et al., in press). One of the major market segments which appears to be growing in much of the northern circumpolar world is wildlife viewing. Each year up to 20 000 tourists visit Churchill, Manitoba, and most of these visitors arrive during the 37-day polar bear viewing season which extends from the first of October into early November (Haglund, 1993). They come to watch up to 20 per cent of the world's polar bear population congregate at the shore of Hudson Bay and wait for the sea ice cover to begin to form so they can once again hunt seals for food (Haglund, 1993). Given that the polar bear watching season cannot be extended and that accommodation in Churchill during the 37 days is completely booked, the best opportunities for diversification of tourism appear to rest on the further development of bird watching in May and June (Ingebrightsen, 1993). Worldwide, whale watching is estimated to have about 4 million participants, while in northern Norway, in 1993 one operator had 8845 tourists pay the equivalent of

US$90 for a whale watching experience (Hagtun, 1993). For the most part, these tourists decided to take the tour after arriving in the locality and hearing about the trip; they came to this particular area because of its general reputation for natural attractions (Vistad and Vorkinn, 1994). Yukon Territory has also attempted to capitalise on the interest in wildlife viewing. Seeing wildlife is one of the highlights of visitors' trips in Yukon, and the wish to have more opportunities to see wildlife is consistently mentioned in all Yukon tourist surveys (Northern Biomes Ltd *et al.*, 1989). This has encouraged the development of a strategic plan to promote Yukon as a destination for wildlife viewing opportunities (Tuak Environmental Services, *et al.*, 1990). Yet wildlife viewing and scenic tourism can still have major impacts on the resource. For example, in Alaska, where cruise tourism started in 1957 with 2500 tourists, there are currently about 250 000 passengers a year being taken to view the wilderness; however, significant concerns have arisen about tourist-generated garbage and the disruption to whales caused by boat traffic (Jamet, 1994).

The need for operator codes and cooperation is evident in Arctic cruising, and it is here in particular that tourist operators can benefit from the Antarctic experience (see Smith, 1993). In Chapter 4, John Marsh and Susan Staple predict that cruising in the Arctic, especially in Canadian waters, is going to increase substantially in the near future, as operators begin to respond to the demand for Arctic cruises. These authors describe the gradual development of the industry in the Canadian Arctic, and they suggest that in order to minimise negative social and environmental impacts, existing regulations must be enforced, but also that greater community control over cruise visits is desirable, and continued education and control of tourists are needed. In their survey of Arctic cruise tourists, Marsh and Staple found that just under half the respondents had previously visited the circumpolar north, and further that one-third had been to the Antarctic. One-half expected to return to the circumpolar north, and many hoped to visit Antarctica. Thus, although there is a need to educate and control visitors in these fragile environments, the pattern of repeat visitation could mean that many cruise visitors in the high Arctic are committed to the polar wilderness and are motivated to behave responsibly. Arvid Viken (Chapter 5) similarly suggests that there is a tourist career pattern among polar travellers, noting that one-third of his sample of Svalbard tourists had been to at least one polar destination, other than Svalbard, previously. Viken identifies three categories of tourists based on their motivations and desired experiences: the conquerors, the naturalists and the scientists.

Chapters 4 and 5 consider polar tourists in the High Arctic, a group which may well be distinct from northern travellers who do not venture beyond the sub-Arctic or road-accessible areas (see Snepenger and Moore,

1989). Chapter 6 describes the perceptions and behaviour of road-based tourists in Yukon Territory regarding impacts of tourism and waste disposal. Although the disposal of human waste, garbage and waste water presents management challenges in the Arctic and Antarctic generally because of cost and climatic considerations, waste disposal is also a concern in the sub-Arctic. Margaret Johnston and Diana Madunic surveyed 600 tourists and found that although the vast majority did not believe tourism impacts had affected their experience negatively, a sizeable proportion had witnessed or experienced problems with waste disposal. With the large numbers of self-catered tourists in Yukon, these results suggest that a variety of issues require management resolution.

LOCAL IMPACTS OF TOURISM

Government agencies, politicians, entrepreneurs and other local residents often see the development of tourism as an opportunity to bring jobs and money to the local economy. However, a variety of barriers exist in northern polar tourism which might act to hinder or prevent tourism development. These vary from place to place and include factors such as the limitation, for the most part, of the tourist season to a few summer months, the local understanding of and preparedness for tourism, and the nature of the political climate and institutional framework within which tourism is developing (Keller, 1987; Anderson, 1991; Hinch and Swinnerton, 1992). In Chapter 7, Arvid Viken, Lev Vostryakov and Alexandre Davydov discuss the opportunities and problems presented by tourism development in northern Russia. With the opening of Russia to tourists, there is great potential for tourism based on a vast wilderness and significant cultural features, yet numerous barriers related to the former regime are evident, summarised by these authors as the survival of 'sovietism'. Yet the opening of the Russian north provides unique opportunities for cooperation in tourism and a focus on the unifying features of Arctic destinations. In May of 1994, the first circumpolar expedition organised by the Northern Forum took place, with 88 passengers flying to 15 Arctic cities in 8 circumpolar countries. As well, cooperative programmes are being developed across the Bering Strait among the indigenous people of Chukotka, Russia and Arctic Alaska (Novik and Tottoyo, 1994).

Tourism holds promise for communities which might have no other way to bring in revenue, and indeed, for communities which might be losing other industries (e.g. Longyearbyen, Svalbard). Currently in Greenland the tourism industry is small, with between 5000 and 6000 visitors a year, including, for example, package tourists, independent travellers and cruise tourists, and employing fewer than 150 people (out of a population of

55 000) directly and indirectly (Bronsted, 1994). However, with the intention of improving the economy, the government wishes to develop tourism to the point that annual visitation reaches 35 000, a level that is expected by 2005 (Bronsted, 1994). Many forms of tourism appear to have the potential to coexist rather than conflict with the lifestyles of local residents, and most involve small numbers that are appropriate to the size of the communities. Even a few dozen or hundred tourists over the season can bring benefits to local settlements which might seem very minimal compared with other destinations.

> Although Auyuittuq National Park Reserve will aid in the tourism development of Pangnirtung, because of the small number of visitors and the limited opportunities to spend money, its absolute economic significance cannot be equated with more southerly Canadian parks. However, the injection of even small amounts of money into a small economy such as that at Pangnirtung, where economic activities are restricted by inaccessibility and the narrow resource base, is a valued contribution (Wall and Kinnaird, 1987, p. 46).

Despite the expectations of local people and governments that tourism will benefit communities and regions, there are numerous potential negative impacts associated with it, some of which are more problematic in small, remote Arctic settlements than they are in larger road-accessible locations (see Nickels et al., 1991; Milne et al., in press). The nature of the impacts also relates to the particular form of tourism and the activities engaged in by participants. One of the main concerns is the large proportion of economic leakage associated with polar tourism: little local employment is generated and most of the tourist payment for transportation and package tours accrues to the airline and tour operators, usually located outside the region (Smith, 1993; Milne et al., in press). This pattern is typical of tourism in Alaska, Arctic Canada, Greenland and Svalbard. Even in road-based tourism, a considerable amount of money that is generated leaks out of the community to pay for imported food and gasoline, for example. It is for these reasons that the sale of locally produced souvenirs and the use of local guides are viewed as important in encouraging the retention of some tourist dollars (see Wall and Kinnaird, 1987; Smith, 1993). Indeed, in one community in the Northwest Territories, efforts are being made to develop further links between tourism and the highly successful arts and crafts sector (Milne et al., in press).

The kind of tourism that is developed affects the nature of impacts, both positive and negative, that communities experience. For example, an independent, unannounced visitor might cause more problems for a community than a group of package tourists whose arrival is known in advance (Milne et al., in press). Cruise tourism does not necessarily mean a great deal of money will accrue to the local community simply because cruise ships are self-contained. However, it is for this reason that cruise tourism is seen by some as a preferred way to deal with large numbers of tourists without having to expend a great deal of money on facilities for visitors (Bill, 1981). Yet sometimes these massive influxes of visitors can be overwhelming for a small community (see Marsh and Staple, Chapter 4). Cruise visitors bring in money, but it also costs money to provide services for them (Milne *et al.*, in press). Though most communities appear to welcome cruise ships, some might prohibit visitation for a variety of reasons. Marsh and Staple (Chapter 4) report that residents of Snowdrift, a small aboriginal community of Great Slave Lake in the Northwest Territories, feel that even occasional visits of a cruise ship are too disrupting. Similarly, a cruise ship was denied access to a national park in Greenland because it was believed by some members of the park board that the visits would disturb the wildlife (Smith, 1993).

Impacts on wildlife are also potentially impacts on local people, particularly when the local abundance of wildlife is altered through disturbance of feeding and breeding, or simply by scaring animals away. Other impacts are generated through the use of wildlife resources for tourists. In northern Russia, US$30 000 was paid for the sole rights for one season to fish one of the best salmon fishing rivers on the Kola Peninsula, thereby legally expropriating the rights of the local aboriginal population. The clients pay US$1000 to stay in a completely self-sufficient camp which requires nothing from local people (*Vanishing Frontier*, 1993). Similarly, there are concerns about tourists shooting polar bears in self-defence in the Canadian eastern Arctic: each polar bear that is shot by a tourist affects the number that the community is entitled to kill for its use.

Concerns have also been raised about the commoditisation of aboriginal culture and the ways in which tourists view local people and interact with them (Smith, 1993; Bronsted, 1994; Milne *et al.*, in press; Hinch, Chapter 8; see also Wall and Woodley, 1993). There is potential for cultural conflict between visitors and northern peoples which can manifest itself in social and physical impacts for residents, and unpleasant experiences for visitors. Though many kinds of tourism appear to complement aboriginal lifestyles, there might be difficulties in combining the two. For example, with the growing interest in wildlife viewing tours, and the seemingly complementary interest in indigenous peoples' lifestyles, there are opportunities for creating specialised tours based on the two activities in combination. Yet a potential conflict exists between how visitors and local people view wildlife. There are a number of stories circulating which illustrate this. These stories might well be exaggerated, but there is a grain of truth to them: they all hinge on the sighting of some animal (e.g. a narwhal or a seal) during a wildlife viewing tour or a traditional lifestyles tour. The actions of the tourists and the Inuit guides are in sharp contrast. The visitors immediately start snapping photographs; the Inuit, after a suitable amount of time for photo-taking, shoot the animal in question.

In addition to the issue of conflicts of culture, there is a concern with the appropriation and representation of aboriginal culture by outsiders. For example, in a rare case in Finland, non-Sami guides were used to interpret Sami lifestyles, and a non-Sami dressed and acted as a 'Sami' for tourists. This reinforces the need for local and aboriginal control of tourism. Smith (1989) described cultural tourism in Alaska in which visitors attended demonstrations of traditional activities, but had little contact with aboriginal people themselves; instead they were led by a non-aboriginal guide. After several decades, a local indigenous corporation took over management of the industry in 1977, and emphasised the use of native-owned businesses (Novik and Tottoyo, 1994). Since 1989, 20 000 visitors have been hosted by this corporation in Kotzebue and Prudhoe Bay (Novik and Tottoyo, 1994). Aboriginal control is a key component in providing tourists with an appropriate cultural experience. Reidar Erke, of the Nordic Sami Institute, commented at a conference in Tromso, Norway (September 1993): 'as long as we control it we can also say that we are selling what we call the genuine Sami culture'. Similarly, Ole Henrik Magga, President of the Sami Parliament, recommended that Sami do things for tourists that are part of their current lifestyles; if they show things that were done 200 years ago, they should be dramatised, for example, so that there is a clear distinction between present and past. These are the kinds of issues that Tom Hinch (Chapter 8) discusses in his examination of the involvement of aboriginal people in tourism in the Northwest Territories. Hinch is encouraged by the management strategies that have been developed to deal with potential negative impacts of tourism in aboriginal communities, suggesting that tourism, if managed carefully, should provide local benefits and encourage local involvement.

Local control continues to be an important part of many strategies developed for northern tourism, and reflects a key theme in sustainable tourism ideology. Klas Sandell (Chapter 9) considers the potential of locally based tourism development in the Swedish Arctic. He suggests that such an approach is the optimal way to balance competing interests regarding public access in a proposed national park. While some local access might be restricted, Sandell's 'territorial' tourism would enable local circumstances and approaches to resource management to set the context for tourism development.

The seven chapters in this section examine particular aspects of tourism in the Arctic and sub-Arctic. By no means do they comprise an encyclopaedic report on the state of northern polar tourism; nor were they intended to do so. Rather they provide a glimpse of some tourism patterns, past and present, and of the issues of tourism in this part of the world. In doing so they illustrate the great variety found in tourism in these various locations as well as the many similarities across the circumpolar north, and they indicate the numerous connections with the southern polar regions. The focus in these chapters, for the most part, is on people—both residents and tourists—and in this section there is an implicit, sometimes explicit, recognition that because of impacts on local communities and environments, tourism must be controlled. The great success of operator guidelines and a visitor code in the Antarctic are examples for the Arctic as is the international cooperation evidenced in that realm. These are themes that the final chapter addresses as it examines the appropriate control of tourists in polar regions.

ENDNOTE

1. Smith gave this analysis at the Arctic Tourism and Ecotourism Symposium of the 5th World Wilderness Conference/1st Northern Forum, Tromso, Norway, 24 September–1 October 1994.

REFERENCES

Anderson, M.J., 1991, Problems with tourism development in Canada's eastern Arctic, *Tourism Management*, **13** (3): 209–220

Bill, R., 1981, Planning for tourism in small northern communities, Paper presented to the Planning for Northern Communities Conference, Happy Valley-Goose Bay, Labrador, Canada, 28 August

Bone, R., 1992, *The geography of the Canadian north: issues and challenges*, Toronto, Oxford University Press

Bronsted, H., 1994, Tourism activities in Greenland. In Kempf, C., Girard, L., eds., *Le tourisme dans les régions polaires/Tourism in polar regions*, Proceedings of the Symposium, Colmar, France, 21–23 April 1992

Butler, R.W., 1994, Tourism in the Canadian Arctic: problems of achieving sustainability. In Kempf, C., Girard, L., eds., *Le tourisme dans les régions polaires/Tourism in polar regions*, Proceedings of the Symposium, Colmar, France, 21–23 April 1992

Crombie, M., 1982, *Dempster Highway corridor: background analysis and management recommendations*, Government of Yukon, Department of Renewable Resources, Whitehorse

Department of Economic Development and Tourism, 1993, *Quick facts about the Northwest Territories tourism industry*, Government of the Northwest Territories, Yellowknife

Economist Intelligence Unit (UK), 1989, Iceland, *EIU International Tourism Reports*, **4**: 28–48

Haglund, D.K., 1993, The autumnal polar bear migration of Churchill and its associated tourism industry, Paper presented to the Arctic Tourism and Ecotourism Symposium of the 5th World Wilderness Conference and the 1st Northern Forum, Tromso, Norway, 24 October–1 September

Hagtun, A., 1993, Whale watching, Paper presented to the Arctic Tourism and Ecotourism Symposium of the 5th World Wilderness Conference and the 1st Northern Forum, Tromso, Norway, 24 October–1 September

Hinch, T., Swinnerton, G., 1992, Tourism and Canada's Northwest Territories: issues and prospects, Paper presented to the IGU symposium on Recreational Resources and Leisure in Geographical Perspective, Telluride, Colorado, 14–22 August

Ingebrightsen, M., 1993, Polar bear safaris, Paper presented to the Arctic Tourism and Ecotourism Symposium of the 5th World Wilderness Conference and the 1st Northern Forum, Tromso, Norway, 24 October–1 September

Jackman, A.H., 1973, The impact of new highways on wilderness areas, *Arctic*, **26**(1): 68–73

Jacobsen, J.K.S., 1993, North Cape: the development of a sacred site, Paper presented to the Arctic Tourism and Ecotourism Symposium of the 5th World Wilderness Conference and the 1st Northern Forum, Tromso, Norway, 24 October–1 September

Jacobsen, J.K.S., 1994, *Arctic tourism and global tourism trends*, Research Report No. 37, Lakehead University Centre for Northern Studies, Thunder Bay

Jamet, A., 1994, Les croisières polaires—Antarctique, Arctique, Alaska. In Kempf, C., Girard, L., eds., *Le tourisme dans les régions polaires/Tourism in polar regions*, Proceedings of the Symposium, Colmar, France, 21–23 April 1992

Johnston, M.E., 1984, Conservation, tourism and development: the case of the Northern Yukon and Dempster Highway area, Unpublished honours thesis, Department of Geography and Environmental Studies Programme, Trent University, Peterborough, Ontario

Kaltenborn, B., 1994, Tourism in Svalbard: who are the visitors, and how can they be managed? In Kempf, C., Girard, L., eds., *Le tourisme dans les régions polaires/Tourism in polar regions*, Proceedings of the Symposium, Colmar, France, 21–23 April 1992

Keller, C.P., 1987, Stages of peripheral tourism development—Canada's Northwest Territories, *Tourism Management*, **8**(1): 20–32

Mason, P., 1994, A visitor code for the Arctic, *Tourism Management*, **15**(2): 93–97

Milne, S., Ward, S., Wenzel, G., in press, Linking tourism and art in Canada's eastern Arctic: the case of Cape Dorset, *Polar Record*

Nickels, S., Milne, S., Wenzel, G., 1991, Inuit perceptions of tourism development: the case of Clyde River, Baffin Island, NWT, *Etudes/Inuit/Studies*, **15**(1): 157–169

Northern Biomes Ltd, J.S. Peepre and Associates, Bufo Incorporated, and Jackson and Johnson Heritage Research and Consulting Ltd, 1989, *Dempster Highway interpretive strategy, Volume 1: Background report*, Yukon Department of Tourism, Whitehorse, Yukon

Novik, N., Tottoyo, Y., 1994, Tourism in Arctic Alaska and Chukotka. In Kempf, C., Girard, L., eds., *Le tourisme dans les régions polaires/Tourism in polar regions*, Proceedings of the Symposium, Colmar, France, 21–23 April 1992

SAS North Cape Hotels, Visitor statistics, 1993

Sletvold, O., 1993, Arctic coastal tourism: the Norwegian Arctic coastline as a landscape for tourism, Paper presented to the Arctic Tourism and Ecotourism Symposium of the 5th World Wilderness Conference and the 1st Northern Forum, Tromso, Norway, 24 October–1 September

Smith, V., 1989, Eskimo tourism: micro-models and marginal men. In Smith, V. ed., *Hosts and guests: the anthropology of tourism*, 2nd edn, University of Pennsylvania Press, Philadelphia, pp. 55–82

Smith, V., 1993, What have we learned from Antarctica: a tourism case study, Paper presented to the Arctic Tourism and Ecotourism Symposium of the 5th World Wilderness Conference and the 1st Northern Forum, Tromso, Norway, 24 October–1 September

Snepenger, D.J., Moore, P.A., 1989, Profiling the Arctic tourist, *Annals of Tourism Research*, **16**: 566–570

State of Alaska, Division of Tourism, 1994, Visitor statistics

Sugden, D.E., 1989, The polar environment: illusion and reality, *Ambio*, **18**(1): 2–5

Tuak Environmental Services, J.S. Peepre and Associates, and Vision Environmental Services, 1990, *Strategic plan for wildlife viewing in the Yukon*, Department of Tourism and Department of Renewable Resources, Whitehorse, Yukon

Val, E., 1990, Parks, aboriginal peoples and sustainable tourism in developing regions: the international experience and Canada's Northwest Territories. In Vining, J., ed., *Social science and natural resource recreation management*, Westview Press, Boulder, Colorado, pp. 219–243

Vanishing Frontier, 1993, directed by Nils Gaup and Kare Tanvik

Viken, A., 1993, The Arctic tourist experience, Paper presented to the Arctic Tourism and Ecotourism Symposium of the 5th World Wilderness and 1st Northern Forum, Tromso, Norway, 24 September–1 October

Vistad, O.I., Vorkinn, M., 1994, Images of attractions: premises for succeeding with guided tours, Paper presented to the 5th International Symposium on Society and Resource Management, Fort Collins, Colorado, 7–10 June

Wall, G., Kinnaird, V., 1987, *Auyuittuq National Park Reserve visitor survey 1984–1986*, Department of Geography, University of Waterloo, Waterloo, Ontario/Visitor Activities Branch, Environment Canada, Hull, Quebec

Wall, G., Woodley, A., 1993, Souvenir sales: a case study of the north shore of Lake Superior. In Johnston, M.E., Haider, W., eds., *Communities, resources and tourism in the north*, Lakehead Centre for Northern Studies, Thunder Bay, pp. 97–108

Yukon Department of Tourism, 1992, *Yukon tourism industry 1991 highlights report*, Yukon Department of Tourism, Whitehorse, Yukon

Yukon Department of Tourism, n.d., *Visitor exit survey 1987, part I: visitors to the Yukon basic information*, Yukon Government, Whitehorse, Yukon

3 The Tourism Space Penetration Processes in Northern Canada and Scandinavia: a Comparison

JAN O. LUNDGREN

INTRODUCTION

Tourism travel into northern and Arctic areas of Canada and northern regions of Sweden has a fairly long history. However, it is a fact that modern transport infrastructure and transport services greatly aided the early tourist development in the Swedish case in the 1890s. This is perhaps best illustrated by visitor statistics from the Abisko tourist station located on the Lulea–Narvik railway line in Norrbotten County, northern Sweden, which, in the 1935–39 period, recorded annual average overnight visitor volumes in the amount of 10 000–15 000, according to the Swedish Touring Association Yearbooks. No comparable Canadian statistics for northern or Arctic overnight facilities exist. It may perhaps suffice to mention, by way of comparison, that the S/S *Nascopie*, the Hudson Bay Company supply ship, that regularly serviced the eastern sub-Arctic and Arctic Archipelago, usually carried a small contingent of tourists. On the 1937 voyage, some 15 per cent of the 150 registered passengers were 'official tourists', the majority of travellers being government officials, company personnel and northern locals, mostly Inuit (S/S *Nascopie* Passenger List, 1937). Obviously, there existed considerable differences between the two countries in terms of northbound tourist travel at that relatively modern era.

Proponents of tourism travel into the northern parts of the two countries have in many respects expressed similar beliefs in the tourist resources of the north. Thus, according to the 1985 federal study *Tourism tomorrow: toward a Canadian tourism strategy*, 'Canada's range of tourism products compares favourably with that offered by international competition . . . For example, Canada's Arctic and the Amazon jungle would both be classified as wilderness/expedition. An Arctic Safari and an Amazon Safari are obviously different but . . . could appeal to the same adventure-seeking

Polar Tourism: Tourism in the Arctic and Antarctic Regions
Edited by C. Michael Hall and Margaret E. Johnston. © John Wiley & Sons Ltd, 1995

tourist' (Department of Environment, 1985, p. 13). The Swedish Nature Conservation Association expressed similar beliefs in the future of northern Sweden as a major tourist destination, stating that 'the uninhabited region of northern Sweden represents Europe's most extensive, contiguous wilderness, that today . . . has become a resource and a tourist attraction in its own right, competing in a tough international market place. The uninhabited region has become a natural resource—and an economic one at that' (Naslund, 1964).

This chapter is an exercise in comparing tourist destination areas and their development dynamics. In analysing conceptually any tourism space, one can usually identify geographically and functionally distinct sub-spaces, some of which are urban spaces and tend to reflect intensive travel interaction between urban/metropolitan centres. The Canadian system of cities and towns comes to mind. Others, however, involve a different kind of geographic travel-related relocation: the tourist moves from an urban habitat to a rural or natural landscape destination to engage in recreational pursuits with space-demanding environmental requirements—hiking, mountaineering, fishing, canoeing, ski touring, bird watching—often in peripheral and remote locations.

The tourism space concept may to many have a fairly innocent regional-sounding ring at first glance. However, the term is more than just a destination region. It usually incorporates both a distinct travel generator area and a tourist destination linked together by the transport mechanism. Thus, the geographically extensive tourism space phenomenon constitutes the principal, conceptual framework of the 'basic tourism system' (Hills and Lundgren, 1977; Pearce, 1979; Leiper, 1981) within which, in a developmental context the 'tourism penetration process' works. This chapter has as its main focus the analysis of two destination regions, where both the touristic resources and touristic utility of the resources, at first glance, seem to have considerable similarity: the Canadian north (north of the Canadian ecumene) and the Scandinavian tourist periphery (the less inhabited areas north and northwest of the major settlement zone in Sweden). These two destination areas will be compared with emphasis upon the three interdependent key components referred to above, and their attributes—the tourist resources composition, the market access and transport function and, finally, the destination area visitor service function. The investigative framework therefore resembles the principal conceptual make-up of the Pearce model, the difference being that the principal components are studied in both an historic–evolutionary and a geographic–comparative perspective, and not just in a static situation.

The argument for this investigative exercise is that as the two study areas have many common attributes functionally as well as geographically, the functioning and consequences of the tourist penetration process should also demonstrate considerable similarity. The proposition is one of development convergence: two boreal, peripherally located, fairly uninhabited and originally inaccessible tourist destination areas should—*ceteris paribus*—feature similar development characteristics, i.e. a tourist development with only marginal differences. The analysis will discuss the key components mentioned above starting with the tourist resources function, followed by the market access and transport function. The destination area visitor services and their geographic implications constitute the third, and final, comparative elaboration.

THE TOURIST RESOURCE BASE COMPONENT

Unquestionably, the territory north of the Canadian ecumene, or the northern Canadian tourist zone (NCTZ), broadly incorporating areas north of the Quebec City–Montreal–Ottawa/Hull baseline, and the Swedish border mountain zone (SBMZ) have certain similarities. Locationally, they are both peripheral: as one moves northwards, one quickly experiences leaving the ecumene and gradually entering successive zones of increasing habitational periphicity (National Atlas of Sweden, 1991; National Atlas of Canada, 1974). In the Canadian case, the settlement gradient and its environmental corollary moves from one extreme to another in a fairly short distance, perhaps 200–300 kilometres. This is evident travelling northward from Montreal beyond the Mt Tremblant Park and resort area towards regions further north: human occupancy is rapidly replaced by a practically inexhaustible supply of physical landscape resources with considerable outdoor recreation potential.

The Swedish case features a similar but less extreme settlement gradient for a variety of reasons. First, the ecumene baseline cannot be defined as precisely in geographic terms. One could use the Stockholm region as the starting point and would then, obviously, observe a decline in settlement density as one moves north or for that matter west. The geographic orientation of the Swedish ecumene is not linear as is its Canadian counterpart, with the possible exception for the Bothnian Gulf coast, where the urban system hugs the coastline. In addition, settlers penetrated the extensive interior hinterland many centuries ago, a process that traversed an environment that was less marginal for human occupancy than the Canadian northlands (Bylund, 1956, 1968; Arell, 1979; National Atlas of Sweden, 1991).

The Storsjo region, some 150 kilometres east of Are and the Swedish equivalent to the Whistler–Blackcombe resort area in British Columbia, is a case in point: here, the earliest settlement dates back to the twelfth century and presently, the administrative county region records a population of some 135 000 inhabitants (Statistics Sweden, 1990). Still, the region has a low population density well below 3, which makes it comparable to certain northern tourist destination zones in Canada. For the bulk of SBMZ counties the density score is below 5, a figure which, if the coastal zone along the Bothnian Gulf or the Storsjo region of Jamtland County were excluded, would be below 3 (the national average is 21). However, the Canadian north in general with its much lower population density and smaller aggregate population base (National Atlas of Canada, 1974; Wallace, 1982) represents a much greater problem for any future economic development than does northern Sweden.

In terms of geographic dimensions and climatic conditions, the two areas diverge. However, the overall dimensions (Figure 3.1) encompass a more extensive territory for the NCTZ than for its Swedish counterpart. The east-to-west extent of the Canadian Shield, conservatively measured from the westerly point of the Sault to the most accessible northbound transport infrastructure provision in the east, at Sept Isles, is approximately 2000 kilometres, which is double the north-to-south front of the Swedish tourist zone in its totality! The two territories also differ in their physical depth: here, the NCTZ may be difficult to define geographically and functionally, but if the straight-line distance Sudbury to Moosonee is used, the distance depth in eastern Canada is at least 500 kilometres and could easily be doubled. Thus, the distance imperative as such is a more powerful factor in shaping and influencing the spatial organisation of tourism in the Canadian north than in northern Sweden.

Climatically, both regions are distinctly seasonal due to their respective northern latitudes and have typical continental climates with the widest monthly variations found in Canada. The winter lows in the more south-to-north oriented Swedish space also vary, with an average January temperature of approximately $-6°$ C in the Storsjo region of Jamtland, compared to $-19°$ C in Karesuando, north of the Arctic Circle (Somme, 1960). This winter temperature amplitude disappears in July, when temperatures are virtually the same along the whole north–south length of the SBMZ (Swedish National Atlas, 1971). The seasonal temperatures influence in a major way the length of the prime tourist seasons: winter and summer seasons are strongly curtailed by the temperature regime reducing them to approximately two 10-week periods, one from mid-February to mid-April and a second one starting in late June and stretching into mid-August. The same is true for certain parts of the NCTZ (National Atlas of Canada, 1974), but proximity to metropolitan recreational hinterlands often produces a practically year-round recreational touristic utility.

A good example of the operational impact of the seasons can be observed at the Abisko tourist station in Swedish Lappland, where the summer weeks from 1 July to 15 August account for almost half (46 per cent) of the

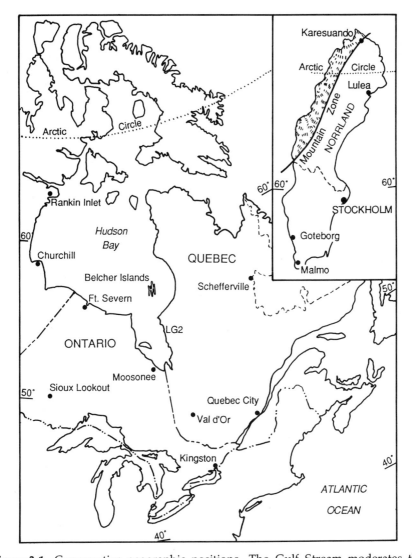

Figure 3.1. Comparative geographic positions. The Gulf Stream moderates the high latitude position of the Swedish mountain border zone, all of it north of latitude 60° N, affecting its climatic and vegetation regimes. This produces markedly milder regional climates in the Trondheim–Are–Ostersund corridor, also affected by lower topography, and in the Abisko–Narvik passage in the far north as a result of proximity to the Norwegian Sea only 50 km away. Coniferous forests dominate the Norrland region of Sweden with some latitudinal consequence on their quality and quantity. The standard 'boreal' classification of large tracts of both Swedish and Canadian Shield forest vegetation hides major differences. For example, Schefferville, Quebec at latitude 55° N is in a biogeographic environment resembling that of Karesuando at latitude 68.5° N

annual guest volume, while the winter season generates only a quarter (26 per cent). The remaining 37 weeks produce an aggregate of 12 000 guests (Svenska Turistforeningen, 1991), only 28 per cent of the yearly volume. This translates into an absurdly low daily average guest number of 46 for the bulk of the year with a bed occupancy of 11 per cent. This type of skewed occupancy is a major business dilemma in both countries and explains more than any other factor the often excessive pricing for accommodation services in remote locations. Periphicity takes its toll, indeed.

A final observation on the resource potential of the two tourist destination regions relates to the existing settlement system. Given the low population density of the two regions, the tourism phenomenon seldom 'grafts on' to local settlements and local economies. Hence, tourism impacts occur beyond, in the physical environment, affecting particular sites or locales, rather than in the settlements themselves. Further, given the principal reason for the tourist visit, the interaction with urban or village settlements is often weak. Still, both regions have settlement systems that assist the tourism penetration process. In the Canadian case the system consists of two kinds: traditional aboriginal villages, both Indian and Inuit, and more recent settlements established by southern Canadians as they have penetrated north, in the past 100 years (National Atlas of Canada, 1974; Wallace, 1982), originally as traders but later as industrial resource developers, satisfying various demands in the industrial heartland further south.

Indeed some of the earlier forms of commercial tourist services in the Canadian north were outgrowths of industrial prospecting done in the inter-war decades and greatly aided by the first generation of bush pilots (Richardson file). As mining camps became embryonic mining towns, they also developed as end-of-the-road locations from which tourists continued their journey by bush plane to fishing and hunting camps. Depending upon location, some of these towns emerged as regional transport 'hubs' for strongly seasonal tourist-based air services. Schefferville, Val d'Or, Timmins and Lynn Lake function as such remote transport service centres in addition to their original, industrial function.

The northern Swedish region functioned differently in terms of settlement/tourism interaction due to differences in history and geography. Primarily, the settlement penetration process had started earlier with a gradual push of the settlement gradient towards the mountain foothills. The southeast–northwest orientation of major valley and lake/river systems funnelled colonisation through geographic corridors, and settlement ultimately reached the treeline in the mountain zone in the early 1800s (Bylund, 1968). Thus, a system of nucleated centres existed when the modern tourism era began around 1900. Aided by historic transborder road links with Norway the subsequent tourist travel flows could centre upon strings of strategic settlements. This was for instance the case in the Sveg–Funasdalen–Roros transborder sector in the south as well as further north.

In spite of differences in settlement dynamics, northern tourism development and settlement interaction in the two countries nevertheless demonstrate some common features: the outdoor and nature-oriented visitor preferences over time have shifted the ultimate tourist destinations away from settlements and towards wilderness locations. Thus, even very substantial tourist facilities have located as often at a distance from the village settlement locations (*Hotell och Pensionat i Sverige*, 1985) as in their proximity. Still, many urban centres of the SBMZ have a high tourist function score (Pearce, 1987), such as Salen, the starting area for the world famous Vasaloppet, and Funasdalen, as well as Are–Duved, the alpine ski centre in Sweden, and further north, Tarnaby–Hemavan. Beyond these centres, along the historic transborder road links, the majority of tourist facilities—resorts, pensions and 'tourist village clusters', hiking trails with service huts, fishing camps—are dispersed throughout the landscape, with an obvious clustering around those principal landscape attractions that constitute their respective *raison d'être*. The same is true for some Canadian northern resort sites, but these locations are usually at much shorter travel distances from major urban markets.

The fundamental difference between the Canadian and Swedish situations lies in the 'ease of access' to the whole of the Swedish tourist zone: the tourist can penetrate the destination core by car, and at the end of the road find facilities offering either high service quality or simpler, more rustic overnight services (*Hotell och Pensionat i Sverige*, 1985). This range in visitor services is also reflected in the pricing, which makes the destinations more appealing to broader urban market segments. The situation contrasts markedly to that in the Canadian north where, apart from much higher travel costs (the last leg of the journey is often by air), the tourist utility of the ultimate destination (sports fishing and hunting) is more limited and also more seasonally confined. Thus, a 'northern tourist experience' as a whole tends to be more accessible, and acceptable, to people in Sweden than in Canada, both economically and in practical terms.

THE PENETRATION AS SUCH: A FUNCTION OF TRANSPORT

Transport is the 'middle function' in the basic tourism system as well as an essential factor for the development of destination areas. Examples of this are numerous on global, national and interregional scales. The growth of more efficient and extensive networks of land surface transportation started with the railway system of the 1840s, which was followed by the upgrading and subsequent development of road and motorway systems in North America and Europe (Lundgren, 1993).

The Canadian north and the northern Swedish tourist region have certain transport function characteristics that are similar. However, for the development process we must also recognise fundamental differences which exist in the two situations. Common to both regions is the historic presence of rail, which in a major way has penetrated (Wallace, 1982) both the eastern Canadian north (Sept Isles to Schefferville) and the central northern Ontario sector (Cochrane to Moosonee) as well as northern Manitoba (Winnipeg–the Pas–Churchill).

Similar railway-based penetration axes exist in northern Sweden (Figure 3.2). The most well-known line, the international iron ore line, linking together Lulea on the Bothnian Gulf coast, Kiruna in the mountain foothills and Narvik/Norway on the Norwegian Sea, was inaugurated in 1902 (Statens Jarnvagar, 1981). The route cuts through the northern part of Norrbotten County and its Lappland region, in the process providing links from sea to sea as well as southward (Hekscher, 1954). A second strategic transborder line had opened much earlier, in 1882, and linked Ostersund in Jamtland County with Trondheim in Norway. This had also produced a sea-to-sea service as well as link-ups with the national system towards the south. The third line, important to tourist travel in a more recent era, is the 'Inlandsbanan' (the interior line) which runs parallel with the foothills of the border mountain zone some 50 to 100 kilometres from the tundra terrain. This line originally started at Kristinehamn in central western Sweden, on the latitude of Stockholm, and linked together a diverse set of urban centres and villages, among them Ostersund, before finally reaching Kiruna on the iron ore line in Lappland some 1000 kilometres to the north. Thus, both the Canadian north and the northern Swedish tourist zone have featured, and still provide, railway-based passenger transport services. The principal difference between the two is a function of history: the strategic Swedish lines became operational well before 1914—the Inlandsbanan in the inter-war years—while the Canadian northbound links are of a more recent date. In Manitoba, scheduled services started in the mid 1930s while the newest line in Quebec–Labrador became operational only in 1952 (Wallace, 1982).

The implications of the different eras of railway infrastructure installations for the tourist development process are major: the opening of passenger services on the iron ore line in Swedish Lappland, coordinated with the railway passenger scheduling in the south, swayed the Swedish Touring Association to pursue a geographically remote 'mountain policy' as witnessed by the establishment of its first mountain tourist station at Abisko (Svenska Turistforeningen Yearbooks, 1904–7), a decision that compares with that of the Canadian Pacific (CP) building its first major

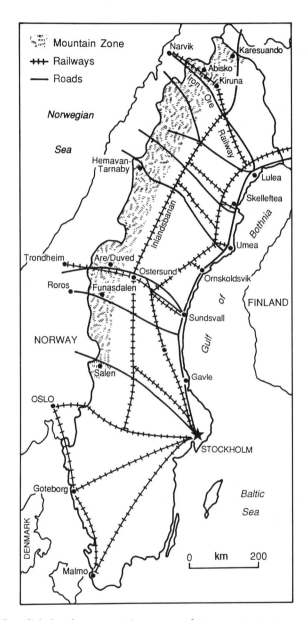

Figure 3.2. Swedish border mountain zone and transport structure

hotel, the Banff Springs Hotel, in the Rockies. However, the CP-owned rail line ran east to west, in the process literally creating the Canadian ecumene and a domestically integrated travel market. In contrast, the Swedish lines are northbound penetration axes with little two-way (or *en route*) travel potential; the lines are perpendicular to the north–south oriented national railway grid with its better geographic fit with the Swedish ecumene. No doubt, without these two east-to-west oriented links large volume tourist movements into the Swedish north would have come to naught and would, if developed at all, most likely have developed into a rather dispersed destination pattern similar to that of the Canadian north.

The railway was responsible for providing the basic, moderately priced transport service for tourists visiting the SBMZ, especially its tundra zones along the Norwegian border. In addition, a combination of other factors and interests aided in the mobilisation of important national travel market segments at an early stage. The role of the national 'tourist animator', the Swedish Touring Association, with its travel agency retailing offices and its rapidly expanding membership, was crucial to the early successes of northbound tourist travel (Svenska Turistforeningen Yearbook Statistics). As a consequence, travel flows and facility developments centred on railhead locations: Are and Storlien on the Ostersund–Trondheim line and Abisko on the iron ore line were popular before 1914.

Sometimes the early railhead-based tourist development was grafted on to existing settlements with major direct economic impact as a result. This was for instance the case for the Are–Duved complex, which in many respects can be compared with Canada's Banff–Lake Louise and Jasper locations. Looking directly north in Canada there are, however, few, if any, equivalents to these Swedish developments, except for the impressive resort developments in close proximity to the metropolitan recreation hinterlands, as the initially railway-accessible Montreal Laurentians. Stretching the comparison, the more recent Whistler–Blackcombe development north of Vancouver, also accessible by train, would perhaps also qualify. The northern Canadian end-of-the-line railheads, Churchill, Manitoba, Moosonee, Ontario, and Schefferville in Quebec–Labrador, all service tourists coming north for shorter visits and at the end of the rail line transferring to regional air transports for their ultimate destinations. However, even when train passenger flows are substantial on some Canadian lines, for example of some 60 000 travellers (1985) on the Ontario Northland Railway between Cochrane and Moosonee of which 64 per cent were excursionists, the volume is still both inadequate and too seasonal to make any substantial and matching facility development in the respective destinations economically viable.

Road accessibility into the northern Canadian and Swedish tourist spaces has even less in common than the railway systems. Here the fundamental reason seems to be that in the Canadian north road penetration hardly reached further north than the Cochrane, Ontario–Matagami, Quebec–Chibougamau–Sept Isles latitude, until the early 1980s. With the La Grande 2 hydropower development on stream a road link was built from Matagami to Radisson and further east-northeast towards Caniapiscau. Only recently can the car-travelling public use this main road to reach into the northern interior.

In areas further south an extensive bush road network has often provided adequate access to sports fishing camps and hunting lodges. This transport infrastructure provision tends, however, to become less extensive when you move some 300 kilometres north on the Canadian Shield. In western and northern Manitoba the road system has penetrated close to the Hudson Bay, at Split Lake and north of Lynn Lake. In contrast, the bulk of the northern Swedish tourism space is accessible by road (Swedish National Atlas, 1971; Discover Sweden Map, 1989). With the exception of the Abisko–Sarek National Park area in northern Lappland, even avid tourist hikers or skiers are seldom further away than 25 kilometres from a road link or a serviced trail (straight-line distance) throughout the whole northern tourism space. Thus, even most of the core areas of the region can be accessed by inexpensive family transport, which is hardly the case in northern Canada. Furthermore, the more historic railway system provided at an early stage a bulk transport economy potential that made the development of large-scale accommodation facilities at strategic locations a viable option, while the historic, and in more recent times, upgraded and expanded road system permitted a complementary car-based traffic influx, that often linked up with mountain villages in off-railway locations. As a result, the more recent travel inflow into the region diffused on a much wider scale, as did economic, cultural and environmental impacts. The early railway lines, on the other hand, were responsible for an earlier form of mass tourism in the mountain zone, which has yet to materialise in the Canadian north.

Critical to the growth of tourism in northern Canada has been the initiation of air services, which on the whole were of little consequence for Swedish tourist development. In fact, airline development in Canada in general and the establishment of air services in the north in particular are closely related. This was noticeable as early as the 1920s, when the first northbound air passenger services were launched out of Winnipeg. The system developed rapidly: in 1930 it had reached deep into the north and Arctic along both shores of Hudson Bay (Richardson file), although scheduled operations tended to be less extensive. In Manitoba, Ilford/Gillam was serviced as early as 1934, while in Ontario the most northerly scheduled destination was Big Trout Lake, halfway between Sioux Lookout and Ft Severn on the shore of Hudson Bay. Services did exist to places further north but on demand only: one could fly into Fort Chimo on Ungava Bay or alternatively fly the 'milk run' following the two shorelines of James Bay and Hudson Bay to Baker Lake, NWT and Povungnituk, Labrador, respectively.

The northern links in the system were not major, but their very existence demonstrated both the market need and the business economics of air services that catered for a variety of market segments, the northbound tourist market being one, albeit a small one. To these regular services should be added numerous, smaller bush pilot operations flying out of the nodes in major carrier networks, such as that of the Canadian Airways (Richardson file).

The tourist traffic volume was in this early era modest, because the journey could be both expensive and dangerous. Only with the introduction of larger aircraft after the Second World War, and, around 1970, jet air services on more strategic long-haul runs did travel time to remote northern destinations shrink. For instance, the Montreal–Frobisher Bay journey that took approximately seven hours in 1957 was reduced by half in 1970 (Nordair flight schedules). Likewise, air fares declined in relative terms but never enough to trigger any major market response. With the jet service, the nominal ticket price almost doubled between 1957 and 1970 (Nordair flight schedules 1957–85). In the North American tourist travel market context, with its rather short legal vacation time period allocation, the importance of good access and thereby short travel time for tourists is crucial. No doubt the 'real' tourist frontier moved northward very quickly during the 15-year period that saw the northern air services transformed from propeller technology of the 1930s, and as late as the 1950s, to jet propulsion in the early 1970s.

THE DESTINATION AREA SERVICE FUNCTION

The final step of our analysis involves destination-area based tourist services, especially the accommodation enterprise. This type of service operation acts as a final demand-derived calibrator of tourist expenditures in the destination area, which, depending upon geographic location, introduces the economic component of the tourism impacting process to the destination environment.

If certain features of the two regions' geographic and functional attributes so far accounted for have demonstrated considerable similarities it must be stated that in terms of destination area services the northern Canadian and northern Swedish tourist destination regions are distinctly different. This contrasts with tourist development processes as they have manifested themselves elsewhere; coastal resort strips, mountain tourist areas or lake front developments all tend to have, at least in a more contemporary era, regardless of geographic location, a convergent trend rather than the opposite (Pearce, 1987).

Indeed, one of the major criticisms of modern tourism has been just on that point, its homogenising power, its tendency to transform ambience, place uniqueness and the particular 'sense of place' that a destination possessed prior to discovery as potential tourist venues and indeed was the true appeal or principal attraction. Mass tourism has overwhelmed destinations and has, in the process, often set in motion a development of 'standardising' facets running counter to long-term strategies that often aim at maintaining geographic distinctiveness and original, high quality attractions (Turner and Ash, 1974).

The two northern regions have certain comparable services, that in practical terms offer visitors on one hand first-class resort experiences and on the other simpler and more rustic overnight accommodation. In northern Sweden, the early trend was towards railway-based large-scale hotel/resort services, which for instance still dominate the Are–Storlien corridor west of Ostersund and the Abisko–Riksgransen section of the iron ore railway line in Lappland, where, in the latter case, the facilities are also at considerable distance from any substantial village settlements. The majority of the larger operations are in quite isolated locations (*Hotell och Pensionat i Sverige*, 1985), which reduces the direct economic and cultural impact of tourism.

Since the Second World War with the advent of car-based tourist travel, a new locational trend has been towards highway locations near villages which is the case for places such as Salen, Funasdalen and Hemavan–Tarnaby. In such locations, the tourism function index (TFI) tends to be high with tourism quickly replacing traditional elements in the local economy. In spite of the dangers associated with tourists invading rural villages, the locals seem to be willing to accept the risk. The benefits are simply too great and the alternatives too few, in the long run, not to chance it.

A final, and different, feature of the Swedish case, is its friendly, family-oriented, promotional image (Brochure samples 1991–93). The physical environment is projected as 'congenial' and easy for any tourist to come to terms with and enjoy, through hiking, skiing, or eco-tourism—or for that matter such familiar water recreation pursuits as windsurfing—north of the Arctic Circle! Facilities in the Canadian north are on the whole simpler and aimed more at true wilderness sports, hunting and fishing, as well as mobile forms of outdoor recreation such as hiking and canoeing. Therefore, they often take on a 'camp air' or are executed out of fairly modest cabin style facilities.

The final feature of this comparative application of tourism in the north relates to the tourist's use of the land resource in the destination area. It is generally recognised that tourists tend to concentrate spatially around major attraction features or along strategic linear routes within a destination area. Thus, in relative terms, the tourist 'consumes' only a small percentage of the available resource lands of a destination (see National Atlas of Sweden, 1993). This occurs whether the destination is suburban, cultural or nature-based. In the jargon of the behavioural geographer, the tourist's distance–decay gradient is steep.

The Swedish north is an extensive territory with both gentle and rugged terrain. Therefore, the majority of tourists, be they summer or winter visitors, operating out of some principal overnight base fishing camp, a tourist village, a village-located pension or a resort, usually confine their day activities to a distance range of at the most some 10–20 kilometres. However, backpacking is popular and usually operates over longer distances, greatly aided by an extensive trail system, which originally centred upon the main resort/railway stops. The year-round hiking trail system was initially a Swedish Touring Association creation, with the first links of the King's Trail laid out as early as 1907, starting at the Swedish Touring Association Abisko mountain station and reaching deep into the first national park, the Sarek and the Kebnekajse alpine area. Today, the trail system penetrates practically the whole mountain zone (National Atlas of Sweden, 1993, pp. 106–107). The network is still serviced by the Swedish Touring Association but in collaboration with regional government authorities.

The only equivalent in North America to the overall spatially integrated character of the Swedish trail system can be found in New England, especially in the Green and White Mountain ranges. The difference between the two systems rests, however, with the fact that the New England mountain trail network operates over more clearly delimited areas for trail use and trail planning, within the respective forest reserves only. It also services a much greater market only a few hours' car drive away— the heavily populated metropolitan Boston–New York City corridor. The considerably more extensive northern trail system in Sweden is much less exposed, as travel-generating markets are much smaller and intervening opportunities more numerous, the latter a function of the right-of-way tradition (known as the right of all people to 'trespass').

In functional terms, the Canadian north operates differently from its Swedish counterpart. The range of accommodation services equals that of the Swedish situation, to a degree. However, the more capital-intensive tourist operations tend to be located closer to tourist-generating metropolitan–urban areas, as is the case with Quebec's resort system, and they are generally linked to the market through the road network and only occasionally by rail. Such facilities usually provide recreational opportunities on the premises as they are often centred on some specific recreational landscape resource, such as a fine lake and beach, a big mountain, or a nearby national or provincial park. The resorts often function as private recreational domaines or enclaves and are therefore not an integral part of the nearby village, although a cluster of resorts in a given location can initiate the development of a village; Whistler in British Columbia, Tremblant in Quebec and Jasper in Alberta come to mind. The integration with the surrounding landscape is, therefore, usually weak, a function of difficult terrain, vegetation and also land ownership in the Canadian case, which represents no major problem in Sweden.

What makes the Canadian north unique is, generally speaking, its different recreational–touristic vocation, which is a function of its practically omnipresent extensive and impressive wilderness environment found in few other parts of the circumpolar north. Thus, traditional forms of outdoor recreation—fishing, hunting and exploring—constitute the principal market base for commercial camp owners and tour operators, an experience that can be savoured both at short distances from the Canadian ecumene but also in truly remote northern locations.

The geographic depth of the destination zone where the majority of these enterprises are located varies: in Quebec, accessibility is extremely good with large concentrations of such facilities often only a two–three hour drive from major urban areas (Fédération des Pourvoyeurs du Québec, 1984). This is the case with two principal regions on both sides of the Saugenay Fjord and Lac St Jean, and the same is true also for the La Mauricie sector north of Trois Rivières and the Gatineau region north of Ottawa/Hull. Other clusters, however, are remote: the Gouin Reservoir area lies some 300 kilometres north of Montreal and the Temiscaming region at about the same distance upstream from Ottawa. North of 50° N latitude, transport by floatplane becomes the norm, while in Manitoba, for instance, one can easily reach 57° N latitude by car (Lynn Lake, Split Lake).

In terms of the type of tourist facilities there is little geographic variation throughout the various Canadian northern zones. Their touristic function is basically the same. However, they may vary from the point of view of visitor comfort and satisfaction, which is reflected in prices charged, and above all in terms of resource management. Here, the files on Quebec outfitter operations can be used as examples, because they are remarkable on this point, but there is no reason why the resource dimensions of the enterprise would differ in other provinces with a northern tourist frontier, where 'fish and game' is the principal attraction. A sample of some large enterprises typical of the region is presented in Table 3.1.

The data suggest that the Canadian outfitter operations are truly spatial enterprises in a manner akin to the areal imperative of the traditional farm unit. Clearly, access to and control over a large resource-rich space makes

Table 3.1. Quebec-based sports fishing/hunting camp operations

Enterprise	No. of lakes	Territory (km^2)	Guest capacity (persons)
Domaine des Cent Lacs	65	401	47
Pourvoiries Jesmer	125	355	115
Domaine Picard	100	212	200
Club Beachene	17	205	66
Pourvoyeur L. Lareua	112	181	85

Sources: Fédération des Pourvoyeurs du Québec (1984/1988) and Service des Pourvoiries, Gouvernement du Québec (1993).

for a competitive operation as well. Provided that the fish or game resource is maintained over the years, the enterprise is a sustainable commercial operation—indeed a version of sustainable tourism. The type of commercial tourist operations referred to above makes the Canadian north indeed unique with no real equivalents in northern Swedish tourist areas. Admittedly, sports fishing is popular and fishing camp operators exist, but they rarely have the 'Caesars of the Wilderness' quality (Newman, 1985) of many Canadian enterprises.

A number of factors have contributed to this different development: the most outstanding factor affecting the two situations differently rests with the extensive, almost endless spatial dimensions and the physical environmental homogeneity that characterise the Canadian north, admittedly with a distinct zonation as you move north. Therefore, the areal size of the outfitter business units can be much larger than those found in the Swedish north, simply a reflection of the overall abundance of supply of resource lands in the form of terrain, river and lake systems. As a consequence, when outfitters (camp developers) have in the past staked out their claims they tended to make them extensive. The northern Swedish landscape has smaller dimensions and is also more varied per distance unit and offers, consequently, a wider range of outdoor recreational utility, but always in smaller areal units.

The second factor relates to the degree of human occupancy of land: the Canadian situation is very much a function of a lack of human occupancy of the land that makes for literally uninhabited, extensive spaces with few obstacles to 'casting the net wide', thus producing land-extensive enterprises; in contrast, the northern Swedish land resources have been exploited by people through centuries and are presently owned by both a tradition-ally local sedentary population and semi-nomads, the Sami. Thus, most land has a less controversial legal ownership status than is the case in the Canadian north. Consequently, any comparable land-extensive commercial development would be politically more difficult to implement in Sweden; the Swedish tourist operations tend therefore, on the whole, to be more 'localised', and compare with the recreational domaine with its geographically more concentrated visitor-related activity set. Hence, the operational logistics are simpler, because the territorial dimensions are more modest.

SUMMARY AND CONCLUSIONS

Concluding remarks about the development process of two quite different but at the same time similar tourist spaces are always difficult to make. The variables used in this analysis are never strictly the same, neither spatially nor in their functional format. Some differ markedly, although at first glance they may strike one as similar.

The two northern tourist spaces compared have indeed many similarities: they are distinctly 'northern', and hence prone to strong seasonality. They are both large. Human occupancy is scarce, although the Swedish space is less marginal and features a long settlement history. Some forms of transport infrastructure developments are similar, especially in earlier eras of development with the advent of railways, but tend later to differentiate. Given the many similar characteristics referred to above, the results of the tourist penetration differ. The Swedish north has emerged as a fully fledged tourist space, with a wide range of destination services throughout its territory and with no real reduction in tourist services as one traverses the region. In contrast, the Canadian north suffers from a more sharply declining south-to-north service gradient, which has a negative effect on market appeal northwards; this in turn reduces the visitor inflow. The railways in northern Sweden have been, and are, strategic and economic travel devices which is hardly the case in northern Canada. The more efficient access situation in northern Sweden makes northbound tourism popular, which generates higher travel volumes and reasonable prices. The demand/supply/consumption relationships are more consumer friendly for northern tourist travel in Sweden than in Canada, where the same set of factors so far have activated high-priced, specialised, smaller travel markets, with limited potential for larger volumes in the future, weak scale economy and high prices. This characterisation becomes more pronounced the further north the tourist travels and it is on these factors that the real development divergence of the two regions rests.

REFERENCES

Arell, N., 1979, *Kolonisationen i Lappmarken, (the colonisation of Lappland)*, Esselte Studium, Stockholm

Bylund, E., 1956, Koloniseringen av Pite Lappmark t.o.m. 1867 (the Colonisation of the Pite Lappmark Region before 1867), *Geographica*, **30**, Uppsala University, Sweden

Bylund, E., 1968, *Generationsvagor och bebyggelsespridning (Generation waves and settlement diffusion)*, Ymer Arsbok/Yearbook, Esselte, Stockholm

Department of Environment, 1985, *Tourism tomorrow: toward a Canadian tourism strategy*, Department of Environment, Ottawa

Discover Sweden Map 1989

Fédération des Pourvoyeurs du Québec, 1984–88, *Répertoire*

Hekscher, E., 1954, *An economic history of Sweden*, Bonniers, Stockholm

Hills, T., Lundgren, J., 1977, The impact of tourism in the Caribbean—a methodological study, *Annals of Tourism Research*, **4**(5): 248–266

Hotell och Pensionat i Sverige (Hotels and Pensions in Sweden), 1985, Svenska Turistforeningen, Stockholm, Sweden

Leiper, N., 1981, Toward a cohesive curriculum in tourism—the case for a distinct discipline, *Annals of Tourism Research*, **8**(1): 69–84

Lundgren, J., 1993, *European tourist space and tourist travel networks—past, present and future*, European University Institute Colloquium Papers, Doc. IUE 121/93 Col.18, Florence

Naslund, M., 1964, Odemarkernas varde och anvandning for fritidsandamal (The utility and use of wilderness for outdoor recreation), *Sveriges Natur*, **4**: 106–113

National Atlas of Canada, 1974, *Canada surveys and mapping*, Published by Macmillan Co. of Canada in association with the Department of Energy, Mines and Resources and Information Canada, Ottawa

National Atlas of Sweden, 1991, *Population distribution map series*, Swedish National Atlas Publishing, Stockholm

National Atlas of Sweden, 1993, *Cultural life, recreation and tourism*, Swedish National Atlas Publishing, Stockholm, Sweden, pp. 106–107

Newman, P., 1985, *Company of adventurers*, vol. I, Viking, Penguin Books, Markham

Nordair flight schedules, Montreal

Pearce, D., 1979, Toward a geography of tourism, *Annals of Tourism Research*, **6**(3): 245–272

Pearce, D., 1987, *Tourism today—a geographical analysis*, Longman Scientific and Technical, Harlow

Richardson file, Hudson Bay Company Archives/Provincial Archives of Manitoba, Winnipeg

Service des Pourvoiries, 1993, Gouvernement du Québec

Somme, A., 1960, *A geography of Norden, Oslo, Norway*, J.W. Cappelens Forlag, Oslo

S/S *Nascopie*, 1937 Passenger List, Hudson Bay Company Archives, Winnipeg

Statens Jarnvagar, 1981, *125 Anniversary/S.J.* Statens Jarnvagar, Stockholm

Statistics Sweden, 1990, *Statistical Abstract of Sweden 1990*, Statistics Sweden, Stockholm, Sweden, pp. 28–30

Svenska Turistforeningen, 1991, *Operational Statistics for STF Abisko Tourist Station 1982–91*, Svenska Turistforeningen/STF (Swedish Touring Association), Stockholm, Sweden

Svenska Turistforeningen Yearbooks 1904–7, Stockholm, Sweden

Svenska Turistforeningen Yearbook Statistics, Stockholm, Sweden

Swedish National Atlas, 1971, Generalstabens Litografiska Anstalts Forlag, Stockholm, Sweden

Turner, L., Ash, J., 1974, *The golden hordes*, Constable and Company Ltd, London

Wallace, I., 1982, The Canadian Shield: the development of resource frontier. In L.D. McCann, ed., *Heartland and hinterland: a geography of Canada*, Prentice-Hall, Scarborough, Ontario, pp. 373-409

4 Cruise Tourism in the Canadian Arctic and its Implications

JOHN MARSH AND SUSAN STAPLE

INTRODUCTION

Once considered a dying industry, likely to be replaced by fast air travel, cruising is now one of the fastest growing segments of the travel industry. The recent period of growth in the cruise industry began in the 1970s when cruise ship operators began to offer a mass market product to a broader and younger clientele, and not just the rich and elderly. As a result, the cruise industry has continued to grow and prosper into the 1990s.

Such growth has many implications. While much of it has occurred in traditional destinations, there has been a geographical spread of cruising, so few areas of the world will remain 'off the beaten path' (Edwards, 1988). There will be increasing economic, environmental and social impacts, both positive and negative, in a wider range of destinations. Accordingly, we are now witnessing the expansion of cruising and its impacts in the Canadian Arctic.

The aim of this chapter is first to outline briefly the growth of the cruise industry and its economic, environmental and social impacts. Then, the evolution of the industry in the Canadian Arctic will be traced. Thereafter, information is provided on the characteristics of a sample of passengers on a cruise in this area. Finally, some conclusions and suggestions are offered regarding the cruise industry in this region.

GROWTH OF THE CRUISE INDUSTRY

The cruise industry is quickly pursuing market segmentation, product diversification and new destinations (Richardson, 1988). Accordingly, more cruise ships, with more tourists, are visiting more places. The number of cruise ships has been increasing in recent years. Between 1990 and 1992, there was a 35 per cent increase in international cruise ship berths (Tourism Canada, 1992). Some of the increase results from the construction of new

Polar Tourism: Tourism in the Arctic and Antarctic Regions
Edited by C. Michael Hall and Margaret E. Johnston. © John Wiley & Sons Ltd, 1995

ships, and some from the remodelling of other types of ship. For example, in 1993, the British Columbia Ferry Corporation added two 'superferries', with a capacity of 2100 passengers and 470 cars, to its fleet. Several ice-breakers from the former Soviet Union and a Chilean naval personnel carrier have been used for cruises (Marsh, 1992).

It has been noted that 'in the past twenty years, the growth in the cruise industry has been nothing short of astonishing. In 1971, half a million North Americans took a cruise vacation, and by 1991 that figure had dramatically increased to four million' (Loverseed, 1992, p. D4). The number of cruise passengers embarking from North American ports increased from 1.43 million in 1980 to 2.88 million in 1987, an annual average growth rate of 10 per cent (Duke and Ference, 1988).

In order to attract passengers in this competitive market, cruise companies have had to become more creative with the type of vacation packages they offer to the public. This creativity has produced theme cruises, specialty cruises, adventure cruises and even 'cruises to nowhere'.

Due to the high level of competition, many discount rates are being offered. Furthermore, as cruise vacations are all inclusive, they are often relatively inexpensive compared with other types of vacation. It has been pointed out, for example, that 'a 13 day Baltic cruise beginning in London and ending in Amsterdam with Holland America Line is offered for US$5542 per person for a luxury outside cabin, including air fare (from Canada). A comparable tour of seven cities with land transportation and deluxe hotel rooms would cost $10 072 per person, or 45 per cent more' (Immen, 1992a, p. F3).

Even cruises to destinations such as Antarctica are now being offered at lower rates than previously. For example, in December 1992, Blyth and Company Travel offered a cruise to Antarctica aboard the Canadian vessel MV *Northern Ranger*, and it was noted that 'while fares on other cruise ships offering Antarctic voyages start at U.S.$5,900 per passenger and can easily soar to more than U.S.$10,000, Blyth offered basic accommodation on the Northern Ranger at U.S.$2,995' (Immen, 1993, p. F5). Thus, cruises are becoming more affordable to more people. The attractive rates for many cruises result in some ships being sold out a year or more in advance (Fodor's Travel, 1991).

It has been projected that the number of cruise passengers embarking from North American ports will increase from 5.1 million in 1994 to 6.1 million in 1997 (Duke and Ference, 1988). Thereafter, the cruise market is 'expected to grow to ten million passengers by the year 2000' (Macleod, 1990, p. 37).

The cruise industry is expected to continue to expand because many people have yet to take a cruise and many who have will take another. In 1988, only 3 per cent of the US market had yet taken a cruise. According to Duke and Ference (1988) 'experience has shown that a large and increasing proportion of passengers (30 per cent in 1988) are repeat cruise patrons. Thus the challenge for the cruise industry is to continue to diversify cruise itineraries in order to maximise the potential for repeat passenger sales'.

The prime cruising regions include the Caribbean and the Bahamas, the Mexican Riviera and Panama Canal, the Mediterranean and Alaska (Richardson, 1988). The Caribbean is by far the most popular cruise destination, accounting for 42 per cent of cruise-bed-days in 1988 (CLIA, 1988). Other regions, which historically have not been important destinations, but which are gaining in popularity include South America, the northeastern United States and Canada, as well as the polar regions of Antarctica and the Canadian Arctic (Enzenbacher, 1992). Between 1983 and 1988, Alaska and Canada accounted for under 10 per cent of cruise-bed-days but both gained an increased share of the market. The growth of the cruise industry, its potential for more growth, and its geographic diversification, mean its impacts will be greater and more widespread.

ECONOMIC, ENVIRONMENTAL AND SOCIAL IMPACTS

All tourism has a wide variety of economic, environmental and social impacts that may be positive or negative (Mathieson and Wall, 1982). The substantial and sustained involvement of companies and coastal communities in cruise tourism reflects the many positive economic impacts of the industry. According to Williamson (1992), for example, 'British Columbia has managed to build an estimated $125 million-a-year industry (perhaps $300 million with the indirect spin-offs) out of foreign owned cruise ships based in Vancouver'. On the other hand, cruise tourism requires a substantial capital investment in infrastructure from ships to ports, and involves substantial and sustained operating costs. Thus, Clarke (1992, p. J1) noted that 'in Miami, the world's greatest cruise port, officials are making plans to add new terminals to the present twelve, and, in the Caribbean, several islands are scrambling to construct new port facilities'.

The industry also has an environmental impact resulting from the shipping activity, the behaviour of passengers and the need for coastal infrastructure. Cruise tourism may encourage an appreciation of the environment, and generate support and funds for environmental protection, but can also degrade the marine and adjacent terrestrial environment.

Cruise ships use energy, may cause pollution, and affect marine species. Pollution may include oil, sewage, grey water (that used for washing), and garbage. Especially serious impacts may result if ships are wrecked. For example, an Argentine ship carrying tourists was wrecked off Anvers

Island in Antarctica. 'This gave substance to fears regarding oil spills because there is already evidence of adverse impacts caused by the ship on krill and birdlife' (Beck, 1990, p. 343). Another cruise ship ran aground in Antarctica in 1991, and a passenger vessel in the Baltic Sea in 1994. The lack of good navigation charts and aids, as well as challenging weather conditions, in some areas now visited by cruise ships contribute to the potential for such impacts.

With some 250 cruise ships plying through the world's waters, the marine waste problem is substantial. This can be appreciated from the fact that Carnival Cruise Lines 1452-passenger *Holiday* churns out 9 tonnes of waste per day (Wilson, 1992). Current regulations only partly address this problem. 'By international treaty, ships are banned from dumping plastic anywhere, and they are prohibited from dumping anything else within three miles of shore. Food and paper can be dumped at sea when it is chopped to one inch' (Wilson, 1992, p. D1). However, it is difficult to enforce such regulations.

Some cruise lines have responded to the problems of waste disposal by implementing recycling programmes, using compactors to cut the volume of waste, increasing space for storing waste until it can be disposed of properly on land, and installing incinerators to burn the waste on board ship (Wilson, 1992). For example, 'the $50 million, 164 passenger *Frontier Spirit* has state-of-the-art garbage facilities that set a new standard for an industry dependent on clean waters. The ship will freeze its food and plastic waste, grind its glass to sand, and burn the rest through specially filtered incinerators' (Warren, 1990, p. C8).

Unfortunately relatively little is known about the impacts of ships on marine species. However, concern is being expressed about potential or actual detrimental impacts in various locations. For example, in the Caribbean coral reefs have been damaged by cruise ship anchors and chains. In Antarctica, cruise ships repeatedly bring tourists to certain penguin colonies that may be vulnerable to such visitation. Concern has been expressed that cruise ships in Glacier Bay, Alaska may be affecting both the humpback whales and Stellar sea lions, which are key components of the park ecosystem, and major tourist attractions. According to Akre (1993, p. F7):

> For more than a decade, the ships have loomed large in a debate over the park's health and its role in preserving a rare marine ecosystem. As the park has become more popular, the cruise industry has pressured the U.S. National Park Service and Congress to sharply increase the number of ships allowed inside the park. Environmentalists oppose an increase for fear more ships will drive away the rare humpback whales. The park can only be reached by water or air, but last year a record 215,897 people made the trip, the vast majority by cruise ships. Of most concern to conservationists is the

ship's possible effects on the humpbacks, an endangered species under U.S. Federal Law, and Stellar sea lions, which are classified as threatened. Between 1982 and 1991, the population of humpbacks fluctuated between 10–28 per year. During those years, the Park Service increased the limit on ship visits twice, to the current 107. The U.S. Park Service is currently hurrying to complete a management plan that will set the ship visits for the future.

Cruise tourism also has social impacts on industry personnel, passengers and the communities visited. It provides employment and income, and enhances the lives of passengers, but may disrupt communities, particularly small communities in developing regions. For example, the MS *Norweta* offers excursions on Great Slave Lake in the Northwest Territories, that stop at Snowdrift, a 150-year-old Chipewyan village with a population of 270, only accessible by air or water. The elders of the village have argued that even occasional visits by the ship constitute too great an invasion for this close-knit village (Allerston, 1992).

Some cruise lines are realising the problematic impacts they may have on ports of call. For example, Princess Cruises took the initiative in Alaska to remove the *Royal Princess* from the region. The cruise line acknowledged that the region's tiny port towns could not cope with the 1200 passengers the ship was putting ashore at one time (Peisley, 1988).

Evaluating impacts is generally complicated by a lack of information and because, as Anderson (1991, p. 209) notes, '"tourism impact" is a relative concept, for what may be too much in one area may be quite manageable in another. The precise delineation of impact is always a culturally based concept'. So, until more is known, and agreements are reached about such impacts, a cautious approach to developing cruise tourism is warranted.

THE EVOLUTION OF THE CRUISE INDUSTRY IN THE CANADIAN ARCTIC

The first real cruise to the Canadian Arctic was organised by Salen Lindblad in 1984 (Snyder and Shackleton, 1986). The MS *Lindblad Explorer*, with 98 passengers, traversed the Northwest Passage from east to west. The next cruise through the Passage was made by the *World Discoverer*, with 140 passengers, in 1985. Another cruise using this ship in 1986 was unable to pass west through the Passage due to ice conditions west of Bellot Strait.

There were no further cruises until 1988, when two were offered. Society Expeditions offered a cruise using the *Society Explorer*, with 100 passengers, through the Passage. Special Expeditions offered a cruise using the *Polaris*, with 80 passengers, along the coasts of Greenland and Baffin Island. The next cruise in the region, though outside Canadian territory, was in 1991, when Quark Expeditions ran one to the North Pole using the nuclear powered *Yamal*, with 100 passengers.

In 1992, five cruises were proposed. Blyth and Company Travel ran a cruise through the Passage using the *Kapitan Khlebnikov* (Green and Green, 1992). This vessel is an ice-breaker, chartered from the Far Eastern Shipping Company of the former Soviet Union. The complete cruise actually involved sailing between 3 continents and across 10 international boundaries in an exploration of some of the world's most northerly areas and settlements. It ventured further north in the Canadian Arctic than any other passenger ship in history. Thus, one journalist noted: 'it was the only ship this year to move along the coast of Ellesmere Island, a part of the world that is so far north, you would not be able to find it on most maps' (Immen, 1992b, p. F1). The ship came equipped with a helicopter and a fleet of zodiacs to carry passengers close to ice floes and inland for numerous shore excursions. The helicopter took small groups of passengers to the Geodetic Hills on Axel Heiberg Island, the site of a fossilised forest. The passengers were also able to hike in a glaciated mountain valley on the island, probably only ever seen by a handful of people. A total of 52 passengers participated in this cruise; 30 of them were Canadian, 12 were German and 10 were from the United States.

Seaquest Cruises also ran a cruise through the Passage using the *Frontier Spirit*, with a capacity of 184 passengers. Quark Expeditions again offered a cruise to the North Pole. Addison Travel Marketing offered two cruises on the Mackenzie River, using the MS *Norweta*, with a capacity of 40 passengers.

In 1993, Blyth and Company Travel proposed an ambitious programme of cruises. The *Akademik Ioffe*, another ice-breaker, that carries 150 passengers, was expected to make two cruises to the eastern Arctic and Davis Strait, two cruises to Greenland and the eastern Arctic, and one cruise to Davis Strait, Baffin Island and Hudson Bay. However, none of these cruises occurred because the Canadian Coastguard would not certify the ship as it did not meet Canadian safety standards. This company did, however, use the *Kapitan Khlebnikov* again to visit the Passage and the High Arctic. Transocean Cruises used the MV *Columbus Caravelle*, with 250 passengers, for a cruise to Newfoundland and Greenland.

Various other cruises were organised through the Northeast Passage and to the North Pole and Greenland. For example, Quark Expeditions used the *Kapitan Khlebnikov* in an attempt to circumnavigate Greenland, but this was not possible and the ship did not enter Canadian waters.

Over the 10 years since cruises to the Canadian Arctic began, there has been an increase in the number of companies involved, the cruises offered, the passenger capacity of ships and the range of destinations. However, it is noteworthy that some proposed cruises have been cancelled, and several have been unable to follow their proposed routes due to ice conditions.

CHARACTERISTICS OF CRUISE PASSENGERS

To date, very little information has been obtained on the characteristics of passengers on cruises to the Canadian Arctic. Accordingly, a study was undertaken of passengers on a cruise aboard the *Kapitan Khlebnikov* to the Northwest Passage and High Arctic offered by Blyth and Company Travel in 1993. As several researchers were interested in undertaking such a study, the survey prepared by the authors was combined with those prepared by researchers from McGill University, the Scott Polar Institute and Blyth and Company Travel to produce a single survey. A total of 89 passengers completed the survey, which was self-administered on board the ship, the results then being forwarded to the authors.

Fifty-two of the respondents were female and 37 male. Their ages ranged from under 20 to over 70, a majority (55) being over 60 years. Fifty-one were travelling with family, 30 alone and 8 with friends. A slight majority (46) were on their first trip to the Arctic. Those returning had been to a wide array of places, notably the Canadian Arctic, Alaska, Scandinavia and northern Russia.

Among the reasons given for taking this trip, 69 mentioned wildlife, equal numbers (47) mentioned recreation and education, 37 mentioned photography, 33 history and 27 conservation. Other reasons given by individuals for taking the trip included: geographic exploration, the Russian ice-breaker and ice-breaking, geology, mycology, plant life, as well as adventure, excitement and patriotism, interest in all aspects of Canada, and to see a part of Canada not seen before.

Forty-two were Canadian and 29 American, the rest having other, mainly European, nationalities. Similarly, 39 of the passengers resided in Canada, 30 in the United States, and the rest in Europe, Bermuda and Australia. A majority (49) were members of conservation or wildlife societies, especially the World Wildlife Fund, Nature Conservancy and Canadian Wildlife Federation. The passengers were generally highly educated, 27 having completed postgraduate study, and 39 college or university. Nearly half (41) were retired, the rest having a range of occupations, particularly in professional and technical fields.

Passengers cited a variety of things they were mainly interested in seeing on the trip. Forty-nine cited wildlife, 16 Inuit people, 11 scenery, 9 ice, 9 plants, while another 28 features were cited by between one and seven people. The cruise provided various opportunities to go ashore to visit natural areas or communities. The most popular landing was Lake Hazen on Ellesmere Island, cited by 20, followed by Illulissat (16) and the Geodetic Hills (12). Many reasons were given for identifying a landing as their favourite, notably: glaciers, beauty, scenery, remoteness, Inuit people and uniqueness. A majority (62) purchased goods while ashore, especially local crafts (45), but also clothing, non-local souvenirs and food or drink.

The passengers heard about the cruise in diverse ways. Thirty-one noted it in magazines or newspapers, 21 were informed by friends or acquaintances, and 25 learned about it from a travel guide.

Most of the passengers talked with the staff naturalists accompanying the cruise, especially while on the ship. Forty-two talked with such naturalists over 10 times while on the ship, and 28 over 10 times while on shore.

Passengers brought numerous pieces of equipment to enhance or record their trip. Seventy-eight reported bringing a camera, 72 binoculars, 17 camcorders, while 33 had nature guidebooks.

Fifty-eight passengers felt there should be more nature protection areas in the Arctic, but 22 said they did not know, and 8 said no. Sixty-eight passengers said tourism was impacting the natural environment, 9 said it was not, and 10 said they did not know. Of 68 respondents, equal numbers (19) said the impacts were positive, negative or both. Various positive impacts were cited, such as increase in jobs, provide income, awareness of fragile environment and increased knowledge. Various negative impacts were cited, such as stress on fragile environment, and negative for flora, as well as local community impact, impact on traditional life, and Inuit life affected by the money.

Forty-seven of the passengers expected to return to the Arctic, 10 not to return, while 31 said they did not know if they would return. While a majority (56) had not visited Antarctica, a substantial number (32) had been there, most to the Antarctic Peninsula. Of those who had not visited Antarctica, 18 planned to do so.

The respondents also provide numerous comments concerning tourism and conservation in the Arctic. Many advocated control of tourism to protect the region's environment and communities. For example, one passenger suggested: 'cruising companies should be vigorously controlled to ensure that they do not allow passengers to cause disturbance to birds or other animals, damage to plants and leave behind any litter'. Another commented: 'Although it is very interesting to visit native villages, I can't help feel that we are really invading the people's privacy by swarming en masse over their territory (homes and property), photographing their homes, possessions, and themselves as if they were oddities or in a zoo. Maybe videos and cameras should be banned, and I must admit that I have been as guilty, if not more guilty, of this invasion of privacy, which I am beginning to regret'.

It was also suggested that more benefits of tourism should accrue to the communities visited. Thus, passengers noted: 'Try to think of some way to make the tourist visit a more positive contribution to the areas visited.

I can't tell that they derive any real benefit from being stared at and patronised by the boat load of tourists who tramp around taking pictures and intruding into private lives;' 'Tour operations should be small scale and operated by local residents thus injecting money and investing directly into the local economy'.

CONCLUSION

The cruise industry has expanded rapidly in recent years. Increasingly, vessels are travelling to the most remote areas of the world, such as Antarctica and the Arctic. Cruises to the Canadian Arctic began with one in 1984 and many more have travelled to this region since. The use of ice-breakers has enabled new areas, even the North Pole, to be reached, but ice conditions still prevent some cruises from following their intended routes.

Cruises may have various positive and negative economic, environmental and social impacts. Given the fragility of some of the Canadian Arctic environment and the vulnerability of small, remote, largely aboriginal communities to impact, great care must be exercised in using the area for cruise tourism. Existing regulations regarding shipping safety and pollution (Canada, 1989), and access to parks, historic and archaeological sites will help protect the region. However, their effectiveness will depend on enforcement and cruise operator cooperation. Cruise passengers must always be educated and guided to ensure appropriate non-destructive behaviour on the land and in communities (Stonehouse, 1990). Furthermore, community control over, and benefits from, cruise visits should be increased. Lessons have been learned elsewhere, for example in Antarctica (Hall, 1992), that should aid in ensuring cruise tourism will be a beneficial activity in the Canadian Arctic.

ACKNOWLEDGEMENTS

The assistance of the Royal Canadian Geographical Society, Blyth and Company Travel and George Hobson is gratefully acknowledged, but the opinions expressed are strictly those of the authors.

REFERENCES

Akre, B.S., 1993, Glacier Bay: cruise lines, conservationists at centre ice, *The Globe and Mail*, 20 March, F7
Allerston, R., 1992, Classy cruising on Great Slave Lake, *Up Here: Life in Canada's North*, **8**(3): 42–45

Anderson, M.J., 1991, Problems with tourism in Canada's eastern Arctic, *Tourism Management*, **12**(3): 209–220

Beck, P.J., 1990, Regulating one of the last tourism frontiers: Antarctica, *Applied Geography*, **10**: 343–356

Canada, Government of, 1989, *Arctic Waters Pollution Prevention Act*, Supply and Services Canada, Ottawa

Clarke, J., 1992, The crowded seas, *The Toronto Star*, 14 November, J1

CLIA (Cruise Lines International Association), 1988, *The cruise industry: an overview*, CLIA, New York

Duke, G., Ference, D., 1988, *Profile of the eastern Canadian cruise industry*, Tourism Canada, Ottawa

Edwards, F., 1988, *Environmentally sound tourism in the Caribbean*, University of Calgary Press, Calgary

Enzenbacher, D.J., 1992, Tourists in Antarctica: numbers and trends, *Polar Record*, **28**(126): 17–22

Fodor's Travel, 1991, *Fodor's 91: cruises and ports of call, choosing the perfect ship and enjoying your time ashore*, Fodor's Travel Publications, New York

Green, G., Green, J., 1992, In the wake of ghost ships, *Up Here, Life in Canada's North*, **8**(1): 48–56

Hall, C.M., 1992, Tourism in Antarctica: activities, impacts, and management, *Journal of Travel Research*, **30**(4): 2–9

Immen, W., 1992a, Baltic tour proves cheaper by sea, *The Globe and Mail*, 28 November, F3

Immen, W., 1992b, Breaking the ice: Northwest Passage with the Russians, *The Globe and Mail*, 5 September, F1–2

Immen, W., 1993, All at sea in the Antarctic, *The Globe and Mail*, 6 February, F5

Loverseed, H., 1992a, Cruise line steams along historic rivers, *The Globe and Mail*, 16 September, D4

Macleod, K., 1990, Cruise conventions growing: more companies set sail for meetings, *Financial Post*, **84**(19): 37

Marsh, J., 1992, Tourism in Antarctica and its implications for conservation, paper presented at 4th World Congress on National Parks and Protected Areas, Caracas, Venezuela, 10–21 February

Mathieson, A., Wall, G., 1982, *Tourism: economic, physical and social impacts*, Longman, London

Peisley, T., 1988, New developments in world cruising, *Travel and Tourism Analyst*, May–June: 5–19

Richardson, W., 1988, *Position paper: Canadian cruise industry*, Tourism Canada, Ottawa

Snyder, J., Shackleton, K., 1986, *Ship in the wilderness: voyages of the MS Lindblad Explorer through the last wild places on earth*, Dent and Sons, London

Stonehouse, B., 1990, A traveller's code for Antarctic visitors, *Polar Record*, **26**(156): 56–58

Tourism Canada, 1992, *The tourism intelligence bulletin*, Industry, Science and Technology Canada, Ottawa

Warren, M., 1990, Cruise ships seek to bury garbage-dumping image, *The Globe and Mail*, 21 November, C8

Williamson, R., 1992, Cruises spark a new gold rush, *The Globe and Mail*, 30 October, A7

Wilson, C., 1992, Cruise lines respond: making a dent on sea-dumping, *The Globe and Mail*, 25 March, D1

5 Tourism Experiences in the Arctic—the Svalbard Case

ARVID VIKEN

FROM EXPEDITIONS TO TOURISM

Tourism to the Svalbard Archipelago in the European upper Arctic is not new: tourists have been enjoying this part of the northern polar regions for over 100 years. During the nineteenth century, travel to Svalbard was a prestigious preserve of the wealthy. The trip was always something of an expedition, and travellers undertook it for adventure. Some wrote about their journeys on their return; some even brought along painters to have visual documentation of their travel. The first organised and commercial tour to Svalbard took place in 1871 (Norderhaug, 1982). The activities in the 1890s included a regular tourist route from Norway; a cruise from Germany, a hotel establishment, and even a tourist newspaper, the *Spitzbergen Gazette* (Norderhaug, 1982). However, tourist business activities on the archipelago were not very successful and after two years the hotel was abandoned. Nevertheless Svalbard has held its position as a cruise destination ever since.

Tourism was not the first use of the archipelago. For commercial and scientific travel, the northern polar areas have been significant for centuries. People visited Svalbard for fishing, whale hunting, trapping and exploration. Polar expeditions brought new knowledge about the world, and were a catalyst for Norwegians' fascination with the Arctic. The Norwegian polar explorers are national heroes, and many Norwegians have followed in the footsteps of Nansen and Amundsen. But most of the 'explorers' of today are not really exploring. Today's practitioners do not normally finance their trip by themselves, rather they have commercial sponsors. They are modern adventure tourists. One of the national heroes in the 1990s is a young Norwegian who has gone cross country skiing to both the North and the South Pole, the latter as a solo traveller. One still may meet people obviously from the upper classes, doing an adventurous tour to Svalbard

Polar Tourism: Tourism in the Arctic and Antarctic Regions
Edited by C. Michael Hall and Margaret E. Johnston. © John Wiley & Sons Ltd, 1995

with their own yacht. They are the modern version of the aristocratic adventurers from the turn of the century. The early polar bear and polar fox trappers are another type of adventurer seen as a model for today's tourists. The early trappers spent the extremely cold winter months in the wilderness alone in small and primitive cabins. The stories and myths about their life are numerous and widely known on the Norwegian mainland. Up until the 1960s there was also trophy hunting departing from Tromsø. Today some young men verify their manhood by going on 'expeditions' along the Svalbard coast. Some of them are inspired by the explorers, others by the trapper life, and still others practise a traditional form of outdoor recreation in a new area.

This touristification of polar expeditions is connected to a very important cultural trait in Norway. There are strong national feelings based on nature and wilderness. Until recently, farming, fishing, hunting and harvesting in the wilderness were central in Norwegian daily life. But in the epoch of modernity, time is divided between work and leisure, and for most people the old functional outdoor life is now a leisure activity. Since the last century this *wilderness life*, as it may be called, has been a major leisure activity in Norwegian society (Pedersen, 1993). These non-commercial activities in the outdoors are, for many, a lifestyle in which people walk in the forests and mountains, fish, pick berries or ski. During the previous century an aesthetic dimension was gradually added to the functional. As the national romantic wave reached the country, the perception of Norwegian nature changed from useless and ugly to beautiful. With improvements in transport technology, people were able to travel further afield for their wilderness life, even to Svalbard as the archipelago became accessible by regular flights in the 1970s (Figure 5.1). In the 1970s and 1980s the Norwegian wilderness life has been commercialised. In fact, much of it is tourism, though this is not admitted by the most extreme practitioners. As Ryan (1991) observes, many tourists do not like to be tourists; they aim to become, or at least to be looked upon as, non-tourists. Similarly others have described them as anti-tourists (Aubert, 1969; Jacobsen, 1989). Yet, the split between tourism and wilderness life is deeply rooted in the Norwegian culture and language. If something concerns both activities, it must be emphasised, as it is in a 'plan for tourism, *and* wilderness life on Svalbard' (Kaltenborn, 1991).

The purpose of this chapter is to describe the nature and extent of tourism on Svalbard, with an emphasis on the touristic experience itself. General statistics will be complemented by the results of a preliminary investigation carried out among visitors in 1992. For a period of one month, a questionnaire was placed in the tourist information office in Longyearbyen, Svalbard. The sample consists of 227 respondents.

Figure 5.1. About 8000 tourists arrive in Svalbard by air each year, many of whom travel beyond Longyearbyen (Photo credit: M.E. Johnston)

TOURISM IN THE SVALBARD ARCHIPELAGO

Svalbard is an archipelago situated around 1000 kilometres north of the Norwegian mainland (Figure 5.2). Almost 70 per cent of the islands are permanently covered with ice. There are three main settlements, two Russian and one Norwegian. The existence of these settlements is partly political, but it is also based on a mining industry. Svalbard has no original inhabitants: there are no first or indigenous peoples. This is a significant difference compared with other Arctic areas. It also implies that most residents are not permanent citizens, and the tourists not real outsiders, compared with a 'normal' local settlement. Svalbard is under Norwegian sovereignty, but at the same time the islands are an international area for industrial and commercial activities, regulated by an international treaty from 1920. For centuries many nations have had activities in the area. The English and Dutch hunted whales in the sixteenth and seventeenth centuries (Norderhaug, 1982), and the Swedes, Americans, Italians, Russians, Americans and others have all used Svalbard as a base for polar expeditions. The English started the coal-mining industry in the 1880s; later the Norwegians and Russians opened mines. Today many nations use the archipelago for scientific fieldwork. In the tourism industry there

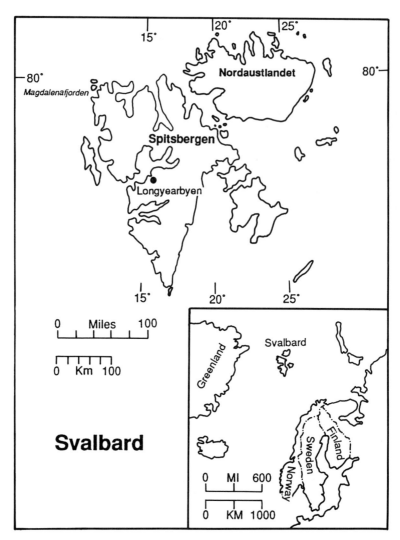

Figure 5.2. The Svalbard Archipelago is located 1000 km north of Norway

have been English, French, Dutch and German firms operating on the islands during the 1980s. Only the Norwegian industry is significant today. The tourism industry employed around 50 persons on a year base in 1993, more than 100 if all indirect effects are included (Høyfødt, 1994).

There are several types of travellers to Svalbard and its surrounding ocean. The largest category includes tourists cruising on an ocean liner, with one or two stops on the archipelago. This is mass tourism. Almost

21 000 visitors were registered in the cruising category in 1993 (Info-Svalbard, 1993). Most of these visitors go ashore in Magdalenafjorden, a place known for its cultural heritage as well as its natural beauty. However, it is primarily the heritage which brings the tourists ashore, and this is related to both whaling and explorer activities. Due to climate, remnants from earlier days are better preserved on Svalbard than in most other places.

Around 16 000 persons travel to Svalbard by air yearly. Around half of the air travellers are leisure tourists (Info-Svalbard, 1993), many of them visiting family and friends. The other half includes local residents, ordinary business travellers, and what we may call *delegation tourists*, people with an official mission, but who also undertake a lot of tourist activities. Many of these people are government employees, others are in business or are doing field research. For many of these people there is a mixture of personal motives and job duties that brings them to Svalbard. Probably, it was the same mixture which brought many of the trappers and even some explorers to the Svalbard area. However, this chapter will not examine delegation tourists, but will instead focus on leisure tourism.

Airborne visitors fall into some major categories. The first group are tourists staying a few days in Longyearbyen, the Svalbard 'capital', at the most doing day trips in the surrounding areas. Our data indicate that 34 per cent of the leisure tourists are in this category. The second main group, 24 per cent of the sample, arrives by air, then tours by coastal cruise liner. Some of them combine this with a stay in Longyearbyen or in a base camp somewhere on the coast. The third category are the trekkers, most of them doing their trekking near Longyearbyen. The fourth category contains different kinds of self-catering 'explorers', going by kayaks or zodiacs along the coast, using Svalbard as an arena for true adventure travel (Hall, 1992). The fifth category are visitors on courses or excursions, e.g. courses in glacier climbing, survival training or wildlife safaris, or undertaking special interest activities (Weiler and Hall, 1992). The trekkers, adventurers and excursionists together represent 42 per cent of the sample. In winter and spring there are some other categories, snowmobile safaris and skiing being the most popular ones. The activity of flightseeing, not unusual in the Antarctic (Hall and McArthur, 1993), is extremely rare on Svalbard. In general, tourism in Svalbard may be characterised as nature tourism or nature-based tourism, which is 'primarily concerned with the direct enjoyment of some relatively undisturbed phenomenon of nature' (Valentine, 1992, p. 108).

THE SVALBARD TOURISTS: EXPERIENCED AND LEARNED

Tourism on Svalbard is an international business. The guest books in the museum and in the tourist information office show that visitors come from countries all over the world. The Norwegians dominate and account for 33 per cent of the sample. Almost 60 per cent are from other European countries, and 8 per cent are from non-European countries. Most of the tourists give Svalbard as the main destination for their voyage. Twenty per cent give Svalbard as one of many stops in their round trip, and most of these go only to Longyearbyen. In the northern part of the Norwegian mainland, a round trip is the main summer tourist pattern, and only a few visit one specific destination (Viken, 1991).

Eighty per cent of travellers are on their first trip to Svalbard, 13 per cent had been there once before. Of those going beyond Longyearbyen, the proportion of first time visitors is 72 per cent, compared to 90 per cent among those going only to Longyearbyen. This suggests that people who have visited Svalbard before are more inclined to travel around the archipelago than are first time visitors. This phenomenon on Svalbard, for some, seems to require two trips. There is not enough evidence to suggest that Svalbard appeals to a market segment called polar tourists. However, 3.5 per cent of the sample have been in the Antarctic, 4.9 per cent to northern Canada, 9.8 per cent to Greenland and 27.8 per cent to Iceland. One-third of the sample had visited at least one of these destinations, perhaps indicating that there is a tourist career pattern among a small group of European tourists, going step by step towards the pole. Polar tourism thereby fits the general pattern of travel behaviour: people expand their territories as they get more experienced (Lundgren, 1974; Ryan, 1991).

For most people, a tourist trip to Svalbard is something of an expedition. Preparations can take months, on average six, and even eight for those going out in the archipelago. This is about the same planning period as observed for the American Arctic (Snepenger and Moore, 1989). The tourists look upon themselves as well informed, with only 20 per cent characterising their knowledge as poor. One striking point is that the information sources are manifold, not dominated either by catalogues and brochures (37 per cent), or travel books (30 per cent), but by other types of books (52 per cent). Another investigation shows that among tourists to the Norwegian mainland only 17 per cent had used such information resources (Viken, 1991). There are, however, significant differences between those ending in Longyearbyen, with 34 per cent reading books, against 64 per cent among those going out in the archipelago. The explorer traditions with thorough preparations are obviously kept up.

THE TOURISM EXPERIENCE ON SVALBARD

The visitors surveyed were posed some questions about their various experiences. A factor analysis of the survey results indicates that there are three different tourist types: the conqueror, the naturalist and the scientist. The following section examines the character of these groups and uses conversations with tourists on Svalbard to illustrate the nature of their experiences.

The *conquerors* are those for whom it is of major importance to have been to Svalbard, one of the world's most peripheral areas. They experience Svalbard as a unique destination. The conquest may involve different motives and forms. It is an intrinsic affair for some, and extrinsic for others providing for external rewards (Pearce, 1993). For some people it is primarily a symbolic act. To come to Svalbard is to consolidate and manifest the fact of being one of the masters of the world. The most adventurous activities performed are connected with some risks. As others have showed, risks may have a positive impact on the experience (Johnston, 1992). The Svalbard tourists do not deny this aspect, but none mentioned risk taking as a challenge, only as a factual aspect of travelling in these remote areas. One-fourth of our sample had been out in the archipelago without guides, trekking, kayaking or on a coastal ride by zodiac. For these people, the intention is to master the extreme conditions, knowing and showing how to survive in polar areas. They are not exploring unknown land, but perhaps unknown sides of themselves. For others it is the status which is most important. A trip to Svalbard is a sign of being a great traveller. It is said that it is not the place one is born, but the places one has visited which tells who one is. The value of a voyage is convertible, paying off in business or private life (Baudrillard, 1989). There are probably other reasons why conquest may be important. Most of the tourists come from countries which have competed for the conquest of polar areas for centuries. For some people this national heritage may well be a reason to visit the area, representing a clear link with earlier periods of polar exploration.

The *naturalists* could also be described as nature aesthetes. The group is constituted of people for whom closeness to nature, silence and beauty and, to some degree, the Arctic wildlife is most important. Their behaviour is less adventurous; they are more what have been called outdoor recreationists (Ewert, 1991): they are nature lovers without a scientific approach, they are primarily gazing (Urry, 1990). The category also contains people who find Svalbard suitable for contemplation and who find recreation in 'going back to nature'. Fiske (1989) talks about the beach as an arena where human beings tend to be more natural, or living more like an animal than anywhere else. Arctic nature apparently has a similar naturalising effect. Nature is forceful, reminding the human being of its natural origin. For most people this closeness to nature contrasts with their urban and extremely structured daily life. In fact, it is said that urban people are alienated from landscapes, and are trying to overcome it by going to places like the Grand Canyon (Neumann, 1992). Probably Svalbard is in the same category. The category also represents the modern version of the bourgeois visitors who came to admire Norwegian nature a century ago, though only a few went to Svalbard. People who visit Svalbard are not 'average' tourists, but relatively wealthy people who are able to afford the expensive trip.

The *scientists* are people for whom what is learned is the most important benefit of the visit, especially in regard to wilderness, glaciers and wildlife. This group also consists of people following the explorer traditions. The early explorers had scientific missions when they went north, and some of these tourists are similar in that they have an investigative attitude towards their tourism experience. This group of Svalbard tourists can be considered within Ryan's (1991) perspective of tourism as an investigative process. Almost everybody in the Svalbard sample believed the acquisition of knowledge was an important aspect of being there, which perhaps is a reflection of the high education levels of most of the tourists to Svalbard (Kaltenborn, 1991). The thorough preparations of Svalbard tourists indicate that knowledge seeking is more a lifestyle than a need-driven motive for travel. However, it also reflects a general trend: knowledge-seeking tourists are expected to be common in most destinations in the future (Jacobsen, 1994).

Unfortunately, questionnaire data can only provide a rather superficial presentation of the Svalbard tourist experience. Talking to people brings some additional perspectives. The nature environment of Svalbard is perceived as extraordinarily beautiful under good weather conditions. The experience brings a special mood to people. It is a kind of total pleasure or joy, which has been described by the concept of *jouissance* (Barthes, 1975; Kristeva, 1980). This total feeling is 'sexual, spiritual, physical, conceptual at one and the same time' (Kristeva, 1980, p. 16). The *jouissance* of beach experiences is discussed by Fiske (1989). He argues that the beach may bring a person to an exalted mood, a state which he also describes with terms like orgasmic and ecstatic. Central to this theory is that a multitude of senses are stimulated, and the feelings are accumulated and are thereby very strong. This is probably a good description of the mood a tourist experience in the High Arctic may bring about, and fits in with the views of many who write about the north. For example, Barry Lopez regards Arctic nature as spiritual, sacred, mythic and mystic (1986).

LANDSCAPE AS TEXT

Landscapes such as the Arctic can be read as texts. A text may be interpreted distinctly by different people, and there also is a diversity of interpretations of a tourist attraction or event. From a semiotic point of view, a text or an image can be seen as different types of signs which are interpreted by the people who happen to be confronted with them. The first type of sign a place or a tourist attraction may be is a visual expression, a kind of picture or icon (Heradstveit and Bjørgo, 1986). The attraction might be seen as nice or unpleasant, but this is a question of culture and taste which does not give any particular meaning. The Svalbard glaciers look magnificent, even for people seeing a glacier for the first time. The second category of signs are those giving meaning: this is the sign's indexical side. A person with knowledge about glaciers can understand the indexical side and is able to assess, for example, whether it is dangerous, whether it is inclined to calf, and perhaps how thick and old the ice is. The weather prophets and meteorologists are specialists in reading signs in nature. The third type of interpretation of a sign is not closely connected to the sign itself. The sign is merely a symbol, something representing something else, often something essential to humans. Seeing a calving glacier one may start thinking of the enormity of the forces of nature, and the inferiority of the human being. In front of the ice edge in the north, one may start thinking about the end of the world and eternity.

The three interpretations of a sign may all take place at the same time, reinforcing each other. The glacier is visually impressive, but the impression is stronger if one has knowledge about its age and dangers, and if one feels it as a symbol of eternity and nature's superiority. The three interpretations may also be phases in a process. First tourists see something which evokes their curiosity, without knowing what it is. The next step is to investigate it, or to listen to a narrator. The understanding may bring the tourist to the third phase, to thoughts far away from the sight or event. All three interpretations may give the tourist a feeling of *jouissance*. To experience something extraordinarily beautiful is pleasurable, and most people get a good feeling understanding or mastering something. The almost ecstatic or 'religious' feeling standing in front of a huge waterfall, or being on a mountain summit, is known by most outdoor recreationists. The interpretation is always influenced by the interpreter. This may be the tourist, but he or she can also be assisted by local people, or professional mediators. Who does this is of great significance. On Svalbard the experience of nature is normally much richer when one is accompanied by an ornithologist or another natural scientist. The life of the early trappers is much more interesting when told by one of them. Most things are enriched if presented by a narrator, the textual transfer having social and psychological dimensions (Ricoeur, 1988). Even on Svalbard, where nature is so pure and untouched, human interpretation turns the tourist experience into a cultural phenomenon.

The questionnaire given to Svalbard tourists did not include questions about which aspects of Svalbard nature are fascinating. However, discussions with individual tourists provide some ideas. First, there is the pureness. There are few places in the world where nature is as untouched as in the Svalbard Archipelago. Second is the very fact that nature is dangerous; this is something almost everybody knows, and finds a bit frightening. Third, Svalbard is not like anything else in the world: the glaciers, the fauna, the shape of the mountains are unique. Fourth, there are, in fact, many variations and contrasts: black mountains, white snow, desert and vegetation, good weather which can suddenly worsen and, of course, illustrations of how close life is to death. Finally, the natural environment of Svalbard is extremely photogenic, an important feature, in a world where people see things increasingly through camera lenses and video screens (Urry, 1990; Neumann, 1992).

TOURISM THREATS

The existence of untouched nature is central to tourism on Svalbard, but this exposes it to many threats from outside. In the questionnaire, tourists were asked if they had some concerns about tourism in Svalbard. Thirty per cent saw pollution and traces of human activity in the environment as problems. The observations giving rise to this concern probably do not reflect tourist activities, but rather come from other industries, and from leisure activities performed by the locals. As in the Antarctic, tourism is not the major pollution threat (Hall and McArthur, 1993). Nevertheless, to secure the long-term experiences, there may be a need for tourism regulation. Tourists were asked for their opinion about regulation. A factor analysis of these questions gives one category who are against restrictions, and three categories who are in favour of restrictions. Of those who favour restrictions, one group would regulate tourism through a strategy of not organising anything for tourists, thinking that without trails, bridges, snowmobile safaris, coastal cruises and so on, the tourist will not come and nor will problems be created. Another group believed that avoiding hotel development may be a way of regulating tourism. The last group preferred a kind of access control with an upper limit for the number of tourists per year. This is a policy which is applied in different places around the world, and which may be possible on an archipelago like Svalbard.

Tourism on Svalbard probably deserves descriptors such as 'green' or 'sustainable' tourism. So far the damage caused by tourism is small. The environment is extremely vulnerable, and it takes years to restore vegetation, and hundreds of years for vehicle tracks to disappear from the tundra. The cultural heritage is unique, but sites may be easily ruined if people are not aware of the heritage status. There is a widespread consensus that sustainability, both ecological and cultural, must be a major principle for the tourism development strategies on the islands (Kaltenborn, 1991).

But the traces of modern society are already there, and so the traces of earlier times are threatened.

CONCLUSION

This chapter has given an overview of tourism to Svalbard on a general level, and more specifically how people are experiencing it as tourists. People come to Svalbard for the sake of having been to the edge of the world, or to experience nature in one way or another. The interest in Svalbard is greater than ever. Its history is adventurous, its accessibility has increased considerably, and the images of the island have changed. How people look upon a place is very much a question of who is informing them. For most people Svalbard has always been totally unknown. A few have read books and seen paintings. In Norway some time ago most people had heard stories about brave people, explorers, trappers and miners, travelling and living under extreme conditions. Today, there are a variety of informants: the tourism industry, the media, even friends and neighbours who have been there, and not least, Svalbard is also presented by artists. A very popular action film was made with Svalbard as the major location some years ago. Kåre Tveter, one of Norway's most honoured painters today, has used Svalbard nature as a major theme for some years. This has given the archipelago much publicity and a changed image which suits the trend towards a growing body of gazing tourists (Urry, 1990). The tourism business sees the value of this publicity as it did 100 years ago. Painters were then one of the target groups mentioned in the advertisements showing Svalbard as offering picturesque mountains for artists. The art of painting is still the most noble one. The aura of the painting reinforces the aura of nature (Benjamin, 1975). This is good publicity. This mirrors the nineteenth century, and is also known from the Canadian Arctic where visual arts help form people's images of nature (Löfgren, 1990; Johnston, 1991) and their taste. Even though this emphasises the cultural aspects of the Svalbard experience, compared to most modern tourist destinations, Svalbard is still a unique alternative to the dominating tourism world of hyperreality (Eco, 1986).

REFERENCES

Aubert, W.,1969, *Det skjulte samfunn*, Pax forlag, Oslo
Barthes, R., 1975, *The pleasure of the text*, Hill and Wang, New York
Baudrillard, J., 1989, Ekstasen og inertien, *Sosiologi i dag*, 4: 34–54
Benjamin, W., 1975, *Kunstverket i repreoduksjonsalderen*, Gyldendal, Oslo
Eco, U., 1986, *Travels in hyperreality*, Picador Pan Books, London

Ewert, A., 1991, Adventure travel and tourism, description and overview, paper presented at the Heritage Interpretation International Third Global Congress, Honolulu, November

Fiske, J., 1989, *Reading the popular*, Unwin Hyman, Boston

Hall C.M., 1992, Review. Adventure, sport and health tourism. In Weiler, B., Hall, C.M., eds., *Special interest tourism*, Belhaven Press, London, pp. 141–158

Hall, C.M., McArthur, S., 1993, Ecotourism in Antarctica and adjacent Sub-Antarctic islands: development, impact, management and prospects for the future, *Tourism Management*, April: 117–122

Heradstveit, D., Bjørgo, T, 1986, *Politisk kommunikasjon*, Tano, Oslo

Høyfødt, S., 1994, *Reiselivsnæringens økonomiske og sysselsettingsmessige betydning på Svalbard*, Acta Consult, Tromsø

Info-Svalbard, 1993, *Smånytt fra Info-Svalbard*, 1/93, Longyearbyen

Jacobsen, J.K., 1989, Før reisen fantes oppdagelsen, etter reisen finnes turismen, *Ottar*, 175: 35–48

Jacobsen, J.K., 1994, *Arctic tourism and global tourism trends*, Lakehead University Centre for Northern Studies Research Report No. 37, Lakehead University, Thunder Bay

Johnston, M.E., 1991, The Canadian wilderness landscape as culture and commodity, *International Journal of Canadian Studies*, 4: 127–144

Johnston, M.E., 1992, Case study. Facing the challenges: adventure in the mountains of New Zealand. In Weiler, B., Hall, C.M., eds., *Special interest tourism*, Belhaven Press, London, pp. 159–169

Kaltenborn, B., 1991, *Forvaltningsplan for turisme of friluftsliv på Svalbard*, Norsk Institutt for Naturforskning, Lillehammer

Kristeva, J., 1980, *Desire in language*, Basil Blackwell, Oxford

Löfgren, O., 1990, Längtan til landet annorlunda. In Sahlberg, B., ed., *Längtan til landet onnorlunda*, Gidlunds/Sveriges Turistråd, Stockholm, pp. 9–49

Lopez, B., 1986, *Arctic dreams*, Picador, London

Lundgren, J.O.J., 1974, On access to recreational lands in dynamic metropolitan hinterlands, *Tourist Review*, 29(4): 124–131

Neumann, M., 1992, The travelling eye. Photography, tourism and ethnography, *Visual Sociology*, 7: 22–38

Norderhaug, M., 1982, *Svalbard. Mennesket i den siste villmark*, Universitetsforlaget, Oslo

Pearce, P., 1993, Fundamentals of tourist motivation. In Pearce, D.G., Butler, R., eds., *Tourism research*, Routledge, London and New York, pp. 113–134

Pedersen, K., 1993, Gender, nature and technology: Changing trends in 'wilderness life' in Northern Norway. In Riewe, R., Oakes, J., eds., *Human ecology: issues in the north*, Canadian Circumpolar Institute, Edmonton

Ricoeur, P., 1988, *Från text till handling*, Symposion Bibliotek, Stockholm

Ryan, C., 1991, *Recreational tourism: a social science perspective*, Routledge, London and New York

Snepenger, D.J., Moore, P., 1989, Profiling the Arctic tourist, *Annals of Tourism Research*, 16: 566–570

Urry, J., 1990, *The tourist gaze*, Sage, London

Valentine, P.S., 1992, Review. Nature-based tourism. In Weiler, B., Hall, C.M., eds., *Special interest tourism*, Belhaven Press, London, pp. 105–127

Viken, A., 1991, *Destinasjon nordkalotten*, FDH-rapport No. 3, Alta

Weiler B., Hall, C.M., eds., 1992, *Special interest tourism*, Belhaven Press, London

6 Waste Disposal and the Wilderness in the Yukon Territory, Canada

MARGARET E. JOHNSTON AND DIANA MADUNIC

One of the most enduring themes in Arctic and sub-Arctic tourism is the attraction of 'untouched' wilderness. The image of a pristine environment draws many thousands of visitors to circumpolar destinations in search of unique, rewarding experiences that are based largely on the appreciation of nature. As with most tourist destinations, a primary challenge in polar tourism is in achieving a balance between protecting natural and cultural environments and enabling visitors to experience those environments (Bloomfield, 1986; Manning, 1989; Tourism Advisory Group, 1991). Certainly it is easier for managers to achieve this balance when visitor movements can be controlled through site and route management, and when visitors themselves display appropriate awareness and motivation. This balancing becomes more difficult when visitor behaviour is spatially and temporally diffused, and when visitor awareness and motivation vary.

The emergence of green tourism and eco-tourism has been hailed as an important step towards achieving this balance and thereby maintaining the environmental health of wilderness destinations. Green tourism and eco-tourism respond to the needs of tourists who are aware of the detrimental impacts of mass tourism and are motivated to act with sensitivity towards the environment (see Silverstein, 1991; Smithers and Geisenger, 1991; Tourism Advisory Group, 1991). However, not all circumpolar visitors share these concerns. Many are unaware of, or unconcerned about, their impacts upon the environment, local people and the cultural landscape. Furthermore, even when tourists are motivated by green ideals, opportunities to practise those ideals might be inadequate in some destinations.

Regardless of tourists' motivations, negative environmental impacts are clearly evident at many polar sites and are currently being addressed in a variety of ways (Johnston, 1993; Mason, 1994). Nature-based tourism can

Polar Tourism: Tourism in the Arctic and Antarctic Regions
Edited by C. Michael Hall and Margaret E. Johnston. © John Wiley & Sons Ltd, 1995

have major impacts on wildlife and environmental integrity (e.g. Valentine, 1992). In combination, or separately, these effects have the potential to change irreversibly the attraction itself, an outcome that can have a striking impact on the image of the destination, visitor experiences and the health of the tourism industry. Given the level of damage already evident and the existence of conflict between tourists and local residents, it seems desirable to develop a code of behaviour which informs visitors of environmentally and culturally appropriate practices (Mason, 1994).

Formal codes of behaviour for Arctic tourists are rare (Mason, 1994), although broader legislation can limit tourist behaviour in a variety of ways (e.g. fishing, hunting, collecting and camp-fire regulations). Svalbard, the archipelago under Norwegian jurisdiction, is one Arctic destination which has a formal set of rules for tourist behaviour (Mason, 1994; see Johnston and Hall, Chapter 17). More common are the specialised codes designed for parks and other protected areas, manifested in the signs and literature which outline expectations of visitor behaviour (e.g. Environment Canada Parks Service, 1992). Usually legislation supports these rules, which generally are based on the 'take nothing but photographs; leave nothing but footprints' theme that solicits visitor acceptance of the minimum impact philosophy. It is interesting in this context to note, however, there might be particularly 'fragile' polar sites in which even footprints are not acceptable (Stonehouse, 1990). Mason (1994) argues that there is a need for a visitor code for the Arctic as a whole, which extends beyond local, regional and national efforts at management of impacts; this could be part of an international conservation strategy for the region. In several circum-polar locations, the tourist industry has undertaken self-regulation through the adoption of operator codes of ethics. For example, in the Yukon Territory, Canada, the regional tourism industry association has adopted the Canadian Code of Ethics for Sustainable Tourism Development. Operator codes, visitor behaviour codes and government regulations should be developed 'in partnership with all entities affected by visitors [to] eliminate overlap and help make guidelines more comprehensive' (Blangy and Wood, 1994).

YUKON TOURISM AND WASTE DISPOSAL

Yukon Territory (Figure 6.1) covers 484 000 square kilometres and contains just under 5 per cent of the land mass of Canada (Bone, 1992). Except for a small portion in the extreme north, Yukon is part of the sub-Arctic climate-vegetational zone. Tourism is based on the attraction of a vast forest, mountain and tundra wilderness, and interesting cultural features related to the gold rush period and native lifestyles. Visitor impacts on the Yukon environment have been identified, and a particular concern of

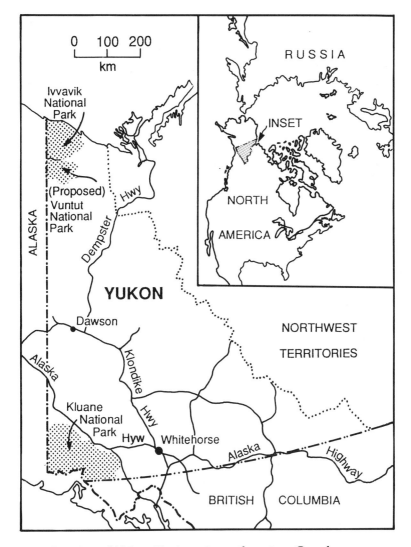

Figure 6.1. Location of Yukon Territory in northwestern Canada

residents and land managers is the proper disposal of garbage and human waste. This chapter examines this element of tourism impacts by discussing the perceptions and behaviour of tourists themselves, and then considering their implications for government management and the promotion of Yukon as a northern wilderness.

The proper disposal of garbage, sewage and waste water is important at all tourist destinations. Improper disposal can generate behaviour changes in animals, present health hazards for both wildlife and visitors, lead to the spread of exotic flora, and cause aesthetic losses in the tourist experience (Valentine, 1992; see also Environment Canada, 1987). Litter is garbage which is disposed of in an inappropriate manner, usually at an unacceptable location (e.g. thrown on a roadside, buried at an illegal dump, jettisoned into a river). Litter comprises discarded material such as glass and plastic, as well as larger items such as camping equipment and car parts. Although we tend to think of litter as scenically unappealing but relatively harmless, it includes any kind of foreign material which may or may not have a negative impact on the environment. Also of concern in a wilderness environment is the disposal of sewage and grey water (that used for washing), particularly when discharged from holding tanks of recreational vehicles, a common mode of tourist transport in Yukon. Although mass tourism is not yet in evidence in the Arctic, 'Litter and other human waste is becoming a significant problem, mainly because no one is taking responsibility for clearing it up' (Mason, 1994, p. 94). In the sub-Arctic, particularly in road-accessible areas, this problem has the potential to be much larger.

Improper disposal of unwanted items is quite evident in Yukon:

> Every spring when the snow melts this fact is again brought to light. And the problem is not limited to our communities and roadways. The banks of the Yukon River itself are strewn, in many places, with refuse left behind by local and visiting river travellers. Other popular rivers and wilderness areas have also been affected (Yukon Department of Renewable Resources, 1990b, p. 26).

However, until the enactment of the Yukon Environment Act (1991), littering was only prohibited in communities and along highways: no general law prohibited littering in wilderness or off-road areas (Yukon Department of Renewable Resources, 1992a). Under the new Act, littering is illegal on all public lands, and any material which is considered litter according to the definition used in this law must be disposed of in roadside litter barrels, at designated disposal grounds, or through regular community garbage disposal. This legislation defines litter as 'any rubbish, refuse, garbage, paper, packaging, containers, bottles, cans, manure, human or animal excrement, sewage, the whole or part of an animal carcass, the whole or part of a vehicle or piece of machinery, construction material or demolition waste that is abandoned or discarded' (Yukon Department of Renewable Resources, 1992b, pp. 56–57).

Presently, the Yukon Department of Renewable Resources is developing anti-litter campaigns to assist visitors and residents in complying with this aspect of the new Act. In addition, efforts are being taken to inform visitors about minimal impact camping and the commitment of Yukon to environmentally appropriate behaviour. The new legislation also addresses the disposal of waste from the holding tanks of recreational vehicles. Under this law, the discharge of sewage and waste water from the holding tanks of vehicles and boats is restricted to designated areas; violators can be penalised (Yukon Department of Renewable Resources, 1992a). The Act itself is not a visitor code. It is general legislation directed at all individuals in the Yukon; however, this component of the Act clearly has greater potential to affect visitors than do other sections. In this respect then, it serves as a general framework for visitor waste disposal behaviour much as a visitor code would.

This chapter describes litter and waste perceptions and behaviour of a sample group of tourists who were travelling in Yukon in the summer of 1992. The study, undertaken in conjunction with the Yukon Department of Tourism, used a questionnaire administered to 603 tourists at visitor reception centres, tourist attractions, recreational vehicle parks, campsites and museums in the southern, road-accessible part of the Yukon. Two subgroups of visitors—private automobile travellers and recreational vehicle travellers—receive special attention in this report.

Particular attention is paid to the interpretations held by these tourists regarding their own impact on the environment. While many of those surveyed did not indicate concern with, or experience of, the negative effects of tourism on the environment, there are indications that management efforts to improve disposal of waste are required. These efforts should take the form of education, promotion of a 'green' awareness, and some facility construction related specifically to the needs of recreational vehicle travellers.

WILDERNESS AND TOURISM IN YUKON TERRITORY

The importance of the tourism industry as a vital sector of the Yukon economy is indisputable. As a generator of income, tourism ranks second to mining (Yukon Department of Tourism, 1992). Nearly half of all Yukon businesses are related to tourism, and it is the largest private sector employer in the territory (Yukon Department of Tourism, 1992). Fifteen per cent of the Yukon labour force is either directly or indirectly employed in tourism (Tourism Canada, 1991). Border crossing statistics for the peak tourist season, June to September, show that in recent years visitor numbers have been in the order of 175 000 to 195 000 (Yukon Department of Tourism, 1992).

In the 1980s, Yukoners and their government continually emphasised the importance of tourism in the economy and the importance of the wilderness for tourism. Wilderness and tourism were discussed as parts of broader planning programmes undertaken to help the territory elaborate its goals, priorities and desired actions on the economy in general and the management of natural resources (e.g. Yukon government, 1988; Yukon Department of Renewable Resources, 1990a). Within the broad frameworks, the role of tourism development was elaborated, reinforcing the importance of the wilderness environment for tourism: 'Wilderness provides the essential character of this region. . . . [Among other functions,] it forms a central theme for our tourist industry' (Yukon Department of Renewable Resources, 1990a, p. 23).

The Yukon Conservation Strategy was designed to assist the government in managing Yukon's natural resources for continued economic, social and environmental well-being, expressed in the catch-phrase 'sustainable development'. This document describes the place of wilderness in the Yukon economy and culture, and examines the role of tourism in Yukon's use of resources. The wilderness theme is particularly strong in the proposed areas of tourism development for the 1990s. Of the six proposed government actions, four are directly applicable to encouraging wilderness and wildlife tourism opportunities and are currently being acted upon by Tourism Yukon. They are:

- develop a range of opportunities to view and interpret wildlife, both in the backcountry and along territorial highways;
- provide interpretive programmes to inform our tourists about the Yukon's wilderness and wildlife;
- develop opportunities that will encourage our visitors to participate in wilderness experiences . . .;
- develop trails and other recreational opportunities to allow our visitors to experience the wilderness (Yukon Department of Renewable Resources, 1990a, p. 26).

Given the continuing emphasis on wilderness and wildlife for tourism, the protection of that environment and its image is necessary. In addition to providing new wilderness-type attractions for visitors, the Yukon Conservation Strategy outlines the plans to promote tourists' understanding of conservation efforts and their importance in Yukon. Furthermore, one of the themes to be used in tourism marketing is to 'promote the Yukon as an "environmentally aware" territory, so our visitors understand that Yukoners care about the environment and its resources' (Yukon Department of Renewable Resources, 1990a, p. 26). The ideas developed in this strategy have become the basis for environmental education efforts now in place.

VISITORS AND THE WILDERNESS ATTRACTION

In this study of Yukon visitors, the specific focus on litter and waste disposal was set within the context of the role of wilderness and wilderness-type activities as attractions for tourists. Visitors were asked to select from a list of attractions including both cultural and natural features those which had attracted them to visit Yukon (Table 6.1). Scenery and the wilderness was selected most frequently (66 per cent) with the Alaska Highway Anniversary next (51 per cent). This special event was both a historical and a wilderness attraction, for it commemorated the fiftieth anniversary of the building of the Alaska Highway through the southern Yukon wilderness in 1942. For some visitors, this was a primary attraction; for others it was an added incentive that encouraged them to visit in 1992 rather than in any other year. For others, the anniversary events were an additional attraction but they would have visited Yukon regardless, and 'it just happened to be the year of the anniversary'.

Other listed attractions were also selected by substantial proportions of the sample: Klondike Gold Rush history (36.2 per cent), national parks (33.8 per cent), native culture and history (30.7 per cent) and outdoor activities (27.5 per cent). Though both sub-groups were generally similar in their responses, substantially more of the recreational vehicle travellers were attracted by the Alaska Highway Anniversary, and substantially more private automobile travellers were attracted by the national parks. Additional attractions for respondents, which were not listed on the questionnaire, included visiting family and friends, and work-related activities. Nine per cent stated that travelling through Yukon was the only way to arrive at their ultimate destination, the state of Alaska.

Table 6.1. Features which attracted Yukon visitors

Feature	Respondents (%)
Scenery and the wilderness	66.0
Alaska Highway anniversary	51.0
Klondike Gold Rush history	36.2
National parks	33.8
Native culture and history	30.7
Outdoor activities	27.5
Only way to reach Alaska	9.0
Other	19.0

Source: Survey data.

Wilderness and wildlife also featured strongly in the actual activities of tourists, primarily in a passive way, though about one-third of the sample went fishing or day hiking. Only about 7 per cent undertook overnight hiking and canoeing. Wildlife viewing and scenery are clearly, and not surprisingly, important elements in the tourism experience in Yukon. A great deal of enjoyment can be gained simply by driving the roads of the Yukon and watching scenery from a vehicle or from scenic viewpoints (see Yukon Department of Tourism, n.d.2). The link between driving highways and viewing wilderness is a strong one in Yukon, and has encouraged the popularity of remote roads such as the Dempster Highway, although, as in all Yukon attractions, there is an important cultural component experienced when visiting communities and historic sites along highways.

TOURISM AND NEGATIVE IMPACTS

One of the main goals of the study was to determine visitors' awareness of and concern with possible negative impacts of tourism on the environment. Twenty-eight per cent (171) of the respondents indicated that they had noticed what they considered to be negative impacts of tourism on the Yukon environment (Table 6.2). The most frequently mentioned impact was litter, garbage and other pollution such as graffiti and illegally dumped holding tank waste water, observed by 90 of these 171 respondents. Also mentioned were impacts on wildlife (41 respondents), described by individuals as 'less wildlife than expected' or 'no wildlife to be seen' and the occurrence of roadkills. Dissatisfaction with the amount of wildlife seen appears to be a consistent complaint of tourists in Yukon (Johnston, 1984; see Yukon Department of Tourism, n.d.2). Seven people noted that they had seen more wildlife in a previous visit to the Yukon, and numerous others believed that tourism caused wildlife to leave the area. Six stated

Table 6.2. Perceived negative impacts of tourism noted by visitors

Impact	Number of respondents
Litter, garbage and pollution	90
Unspecified impacts of tourism and human activity	55
Wildlife impacts	41
Trees, flowers affected	15
Impacts of highways, paths	15
Other impacts	27

Source: Survey data.

that they believed the diets of wild animals had been affected by the tourist presence, chiefly through litter consumption. Effects on flora were also noted, with impacts on trees and flowers, and trampled vegetation described. The existence of highways and forest paths was related as detrimental to the environment as was overused campsites.

Fifty-five respondents stated that all human activities, or specifically tourism and tourists, have an impact on the environment, although 13 said they had not yet seen the negative impact of tourism during their trip in Yukon. One tourist stated: 'You can't have a tourism industry in a pristine, wilderness environment because they contradict each other.' Four respondents predicted that with more tourists visiting the Yukon or with more roads being built and therefore more tourists, inevitably there would be an increase in negative environmental impacts. Three stated that tourism was becoming 'too commercialised' and that this was having a negative effect on the environment, while one tourist explained that 'tourists don't appreciate the wilderness'.

There evidently was awareness of existing or potential negative impacts of tourism on the environment; however, there were also some respondents who considered tourism to be beneficial to the environment in ways which reflect a philosophical link with the tenets of eco-tourism (see also Marsh and Staple, Chapter 4). Eight individuals stated that tourism had a positive impact on the environment, notably through encouraging education and awareness, and allowing individuals the opportunity to take care of the environment. One person stated that it was through tourism that parks and protected areas were established.

In an interesting side-note, people who are members of wilderness conservation or environmental groups appear to be more aware of detrimental impacts than non-members. Of the respondents, 97 (16.1 per cent) were members of at least one of these kinds of group, with no noticeable differences in membership rates between the two sub-groups of recreational vehicle and private automobile travellers. Nearly half (47) of those who were members of these kinds of groups stated that they had noticed negative impacts of tourism on the wilderness environment. This contrasts markedly with the proportion of respondents who were not members who had noticed an impact: only 24 per cent of non-members reported noticing impacts. This difference is statistically significant, indicating that members of conservation-oriented groups appear to be more likely to notice negative impacts of tourism, though no suggestion is being made here as to why.

LITTER AND ILLEGAL DUMPING

Although 14 per cent of all respondents indicated that one of the negative impacts of tourism on the environment was the presence of litter, only

6 per cent of the sample (37 individuals) had seen litter during their trip in Yukon. However, most of these respondents stated that litter did, in fact, detract from the experience. For the remaining few individuals, a common sentiment expressed was: 'I have noticed litter, but I wouldn't say it has detracted from my vacation experience because the word 'detract' is much too strong a word'.

Of those who felt litter detracted from their experience, many believed it was 'out of place' or 'inappropriate' in Yukon. One person remarked 'You notice the litter here more, because it breaks the perfectness of the scenery'. However, others explained that they expected to see litter: 'With so many people coming through Yukon, there is bound to be some litter around'. Still others compared Yukon to their place of origin, replying that: 'Yukon has nowhere near the amount of litter that is in my home town, so it really is not that bad a problem here'.

Although segments of the local population may believe that littering by tourists is a problem, only a small proportion of visitors noticed litter and found it to be a problem. This supports the results of an 1987 comprehensive tourist survey in Yukon in which visitor comments were overwhelmingly positive. Negative comments primarily focused on the poor state of the roads and the high cost of gasoline; less frequently mentioned was the presence of litter (see Yukon Department of Tourism, n.d.2). However, litter appears to be a more frequently recognised problem in the Northwest Territories. Frequent comments about excessive litter in town sites and along roads were given by tourists surveyed in 1982 in the Northwest Territories (Department of Economic Development and Tourism, 1982). Furthermore, tourists suggest that one of the five most necessary improvements in Northwest Territories tourism is litter clean-up (Acres International Limited, 1990).

With different ideas about environmental integrity, Yukon residents might be more concerned about their relatively cleaner environment than are the tourists. There was an indication that some tourists might expect Yukon to display a strong concern for the environment. One tourist 'expected Yukon to be one of the leaders in protecting the environment, and advocating for its preservation since they have one of the last pristine wilderness environments. I'm surprised that they don't at least have recycling'. Given that Yukon has a recycling programme, it would appear that the improvement needed is in educating the tourist public and showing visitors, as the Yukon Conservation Strategy recommends (Yukon Department of Renewable Resources, 1990a), that Yukoners care about their environment. Six per cent of the respondents suggested that recycling facilities be made available for tourists, indicating that visitor education about recycling sites or, perhaps, expansion of the programme is appropriate.

As in most jurisdictions, Yukon has provided designated sites for disposal of litter and other material for tourists and residents alike. There was some indication in this study that tourists would like to see more sites available for the disposal of garbage. Although under 4 per cent of the visitors had difficulty finding a designated place to dispose of garbage, 18 per cent of the respondents suggested that the creation of more disposal sites would reduce the amount of litter in tourist areas.

A particular concern in Yukon Territory is the dumping of recreational vehicle holding tanks in non-designated areas. This issue was a particular focus for the sub-group of recreational vehicle travellers ($n = 357$), 6 per cent of whom stated that they had witnessed illegal dumping, confirming that this a problem. Thirty per cent of the respondents stated that they had experienced difficulty in finding or using a designated dumping site. This proportion is extremely important in view of the large numbers of such tourists travelling through Yukon each year. In 1987, the last year in which a comprehensive tourist survey was done, 11 per cent of all tourists between June and September, just over 21 000 people, were travelling by recreational vehicle, and 19 per cent (37 526) were travelling in a camperised vehicle or pulling a trailer (Yukon Department of Tourism, n.d.1). Although there is annual fluctuation in visitor numbers and there may be some changes in mode of travel, extrapolation from the 1987 survey and the results of the 1992 survey indicate that a sizeable number of Yukon tourists may well be experiencing difficulty in complying with the regulations on the discharge of holding tanks.

Part of the difficulty stems from the nature of the facility base. At some point during their trip in Yukon, 14 per cent of the respondents had difficulty in actually finding a designated dumping site, 8.4 per cent could not find a site at all (and apparently disposed of waste illegally), and 6.7 per cent found there to be an insufficient number of sites available. The remainder indicated that they had difficulty in finding an affordable site. The two major issues here are a lack of adequate signage to direct visitors, and a lack of facilities in convenient locations (e.g. campsites).

These results suggest that improvements are needed to make dumping of holding tanks more convenient to users and more easily located. Respondents were asked to select from a list all those improvements they thought were needed to remedy the situation. One-third of the group suggested more disposal sites were necessary generally, while a further 10 per cent specified that additional sites were needed at locations such as rest stops, roadsides or centrally within towns. Improvements to signage and written information on disposal site locations was suggested by 42 per cent of respondents. Twenty-seven per cent of the recreational vehicle travellers were completely satisfied with the availability, location and signage of dumping sites.

CONCLUSION

Many tourists are, in fact, aware that they are having an impact on the very environment that has attracted them. Nearly 30 per cent of this sample stated that they had seen negative impacts of tourism on the environment they are visiting. However, it is somewhat surprising that relatively few of the respondents believed that the most frequently mentioned impact, litter, affected their experience in a negative manner. Despite the presence of litter, and the concerns of local residents and land managers that litter is detracting, this particular tourism impact did not diminish the experience for the vast majority of tourists. One possible reason for this is that the tourists surveyed originated in locations with relatively greater amounts of litter; the lesser amount in Yukon did not particularly offend people. There is some evidence in the responses of this kind of reasoning. There is also evidence that the presence of some litter was insufficient to mar an otherwise extremely enjoyable trip. Despite the perceptual gap regarding litter in a 'pristine' environment, the Yukon government has determined that this particular tourism impact is unacceptable. However, if the vast majority of tourists do not notice litter, or mind it, then it may prove difficult to encourage complete compliance with current garbage regulations.

This lack of concern with litter likely reflects fundamental features of the survey group. This was a large, heterogeneous sample of road-based visitors. Back-country users and self-defined eco-tourists might well respond differently. This is suggested in several studies of the environmental attitudes and perceptions of back-country users and eco-tourists. For example, in a study of Auyuittuq National Park Reserve, most visitors were pleased with the facilities, yet some were dissatisfied with overflowing toilets and garbage bins, and many visitors 'expressed concern regarding the impact of over use on the sensitive Arctic environment' (Wall and Kinnaird, 1987, pp. 37–38). A study of trekkers in Thailand found that 70 per cent of respondents believed that trekkers have an impact on the environment (Dearden and Harron, 1994). The primary environmental concern of the Thailand study population, both before and after the trek, was garbage disposal; after the trek, the lack of toilet facilities also became prominent (Dearden and Harron, 1994). Among cruise tourists to Antarctica surveyed by Marsh (1991) there was no general agreement on whether tourism was degrading the environment: 52 per cent of the sample ($n = 91$) believed tourism was responsible for impacts such as pollution and disruption of nature. A group of 1015 Nahanni National Park Reserve (Northwest Territories) recreational river users was surveyed between 1984 and 1986 (Graham and Grimm, 1987). Nearly 80 per cent stated that they believed river users were not damaging the river environment; however, of those who believed negative tourism impacts were occurring, the most frequently noted impact was erosion and litter stemming from campsite use or overuse (Graham and Grimm, 1987).

Highway users who are primarily passively experiencing the local environment are the most common group of visitors in Yukon. However, this fact should not discount the needs and attitudes of specialised tourists who visit the more remote areas of Yukon and for whom the active experience of wilderness and a 'pristine' environment is likely more important. Additionally, eco-tourists might be more aware and concerned about litter in communities. In the Thailand study, tourists believed that cultural differences in attitudes towards garbage were evident in the endemic garbage 'problem' in Thailand (Dearden and Harron, 1994). A similar concern may well be experienced in some communities in Yukon, the Northwest Territories and other northern destinations (see Hinch, Chapter 8). Visitors and residents may well have differing culturally based ideas about what is undesirable in the environment and what is an acceptable element of the landscape (Figure 6.2).

A unifying theme for promotion of tourism in Yukon could link the conservation and environment ideals of the Yukon Conservation Strategy

Figure 6.2. Potential for conflict exists where visitors and residents have differing ideas about what constitutes litter and garbage (Tuktoyaktuk, Northwest Territories) (Photo credit: M.E. Johnston)

with the development of an extensive visitor code for Yukon which invites tourists to join Yukoners in celebrating and caring for the wilderness. The Department of Renewable Resources is committed to promoting Yukon as an 'environmentally aware' destination and encouraging visitors to participate in environmentally friendly and conservation efforts during their visits (Yukon Department of Renewable Resources, 1990b). In addition to outlining the guidelines for behaviour, the promotional material for a visitor code could answer the needs of visitors to know where waste disposal facilities are.

Given that 5.6 per cent of tourists expressed a need for recycling services for visitors, 5.3 per cent stated that litter detracted from their vacation experience, and 30 per cent of the recreational vehicle travellers had difficulty using holding tank disposal facilities, there appears to be a need to improve services. Particularly important is the need for an improvement in the number and location of dumping sites and their signage. The 'reduce, reuse, recycle' theme has become a part of daily life, and it is important that Yukon extend such services to its visitors. This desire for further information and an improvement in facilities appears to offer a golden opportunity for providing visitors with the cues they need to follow acceptable paths in helping sustain both the image and the reality of wilderness in Yukon.

ACKNOWLEDGEMENTS

This study was completed as a result of cooperation between the Lakehead University Centre for Northern Studies and the Yukon Department of Tourism Development Branch. We thank the department and the following individuals for assistance in the survey and for comments on this chapter: John Spicer, Robert Clarke, Pierre Germain, Cathryn Paish, Jeff Hunston, Bengt Pettersson and Pat Paslawski. Funding was provided by the Northern Scientific Training Programme and the Lakehead University Senate Research Grants Committee.

REFERENCES

Acres International Limited, 1990, *Northwest Territories visitors survey summer 1989*, Prepared for the Department of Economic Development and Tourism, Government of the Northwest Territories, Yellowknife

Blangy, S., Wood, M.E., 1994, Developing and implementing ecotourism guidelines for wild lands and neighbouring communities. In Kempf, C., Girard, L., eds., *Le tourisme dans les régions polaires/tourism in polar regions*, Proceedings of the Symposium, Colmar, France, 21–23 April 1992

Bloomfield, J., 1986, Tourism initiative in Alberta. In *Tourism and the environment: conflict or harmony*, Society of Environmental Biologists, Edmonton, pp. 9–16

Bone, R., 1992, *The geography of the Canadian north: issues and challenges*, Oxford University Press, Toronto

Dearden, P., Harron, S., 1994, Alternative tourism and adaptive change, *Annals of Tourism Research*, **21**(1): 81–102

Department of Economic Development and Tourism, 1992, *Visitors to the Northwest Territories 1992*, Department of Economic Development and Tourism, Yellowknife, Northwest Territories

Environment Canada, 1987, *Wilderness management plan Kluane National Park Reserve*, Environment Canada, Ottawa

Environment Canada Parks Service, 1992, *Auyuittuq National Park Reserve*, Minister of Supply and Services Canada, Ottawa

Graham, R., Grimm, S., 1987, *Synopsis of visitor survey: Nahanni National Park Reserve*, University of Waterloo, Waterloo, Ontario

Johnston, M.E., 1984, Conservation, development and tourism: the case of the Northern Yukon and Dempster Highway Area, Unpublished honours thesis, Department of Geography and Environmental Studies Programme, Trent University, Peterborough, Ontario

Johnston, M.E., 1993, Tourism and the regulation of adventure travel in the Canadian Arctic, paper presented at the Arctic Tourism and Ecotourism Symposium, 5th World Wilderness Conference/1st Northern Forum, Tromso, Norway, 24 September–1 October

Manning, R.E., 1989, Opportunities for linking wilderness and tourism. In *Managing America's enduring wilderness resource*, Tourism Centre, Minnesota Extension Service and Minnesota Agricultural Experiment Station, St Paul, pp. 629–633

Marsh, J., 1991, The characteristics of a sample of tourists visiting Antarctic, Paper presented at the Annual Meeting of the Ontario Division of the Canadian Association of Geographers, Ottawa, Canada, 26 October 1991

Mason, P., 1994, A visitor code for the Arctic, *Tourism Management*, **15**(2): 93–97

Silverstein, J., 1991, The emergence of the 'green tourist', *The Globe and Mail*, 27 April

Smithers, J., Geisenger, H., 1991, Polar tourism: an opportunity for environmentally sensitive economic development. In *The role of circumpolar universities in northern development*, Proceedings of the 1st Annual Conference of the Association of Circumpolar Universities, Lakehead University Centre for Northern Studies, Occasional Paper No. 4, Lakehead University, Thunder Bay, pp. 102–114

Stonehouse, B., 1990, A traveller's code for Antarctic visitors, *Polar Record*, **26**(156): 56–58

Tourism Advisory Group, 1991, *Tourism advisory group report to the Conservation Strategy Committee of the Saskatchewan Round Table on Environment and Economy*, Government of Saskatchewan, Regina

Tourism Canada, 1991, *Federal tourism strategy Yukon Territory*, Ministry of Industry, Science and Technology, Ottawa

Valentine, P.S., 1992, Nature-based tourism. In Weiler, B., Hall, C.M. eds., *Special interest tourism*, Belhaven Press, London, pp. 105–127

Wall, G., Kinnaird, V., 1987, *Auyuittuq National Park Reserve visitor survey 1984–1986*, Department of Geography, University of Waterloo/Visitor Activities Branch, Environment Canada, Hull, Quebec

Yukon Department of Renewable Resources, 1990a, *Yukon conservation strategy for our common future*, Yukon government, Whitehorse, Yukon

Yukon Department of Renewable Resources, 1990b, *Protecting our Yukon environment: Discussion towards development of a YUKON ENVIRONMENT ACT*, Yukon government, Whitehorse, Yukon

Yukon Department of Renewable Resources, 1992a, *A guide to the Yukon Environment Act*, Yukon government, Whitehorse, Yukon

Yukon Department of Renewable Resources, 1992b, *Statutes of the Yukon Environment Act*, Yukon government, Whitehorse, Yukon

Yukon Department of Tourism, n.d.1, *Yukon visitor exit survey 1987, part I: visitors to the Yukon, basic information*, Yukon government, Whitehorse, Yukon

Yukon Department of Tourism, n.d.2, *Yukon visitor exit survey 1987, part III: visitors to the Yukon, comments*, Yukon government, Whitehorse, Yukon

Yukon Department of Tourism, 1992, *Yukon tourism industry 1991 highlights report*, Yukon government, Whitehorse, Yukon

Yukon Government, 1988, *Yukon economic strategy Yukon 2000 building the future*, Yukon government, Whitehorse, Yukon

7 Tourism in Northwest Russia

ARVID VIKEN, LEV VOSTRYAKOV AND
ALEXANDRE DAVYDOV

EXPERIENCING RUSSIA

Tourism in northwest Russia is filled with paradoxes. In many ways, Russia is a modern, dynamic society; in other ways it is more or less like a museum. This mixture of modernity with tradition and heritage makes it an interesting tourist destination. Tourists with cross-cultural competence suitably mixed with a bit of ethnocentricity may find interest and enjoyment in unexpected and surrealistic events during their stay. Northern Russian society today provides something very essential to tourism experiences: the unfamiliar, unexpected and occasional. For some people it may be too different, the encounter being somewhat of a cultural shock. A tourist trip to northwest Russia is like doing scientific fieldwork: to have a satisfying outcome, one needs knowledge about the places or phenomena which will be investigated (Figure 7.1). However, tourism is very time specific and there are reasons to believe that it will be changed.

This chapter discusses the opportunities and problems of tourism development in northwest Russia, or the Russian north as it also is called. This includes the areas around the White Sea—the Kola Peninsula and the Archangel region (Figure 7.2). The chapter commences with a discussion of the history of the region (see also Hosking, 1991, 1992; Richmond, 1992). It is followed by a brief description of the area's tourism resource base. Some general problems in Russian society and how they influence the tourism industry will also be discussed. Finally, several issues related to strategies for tourism development will be analysed.

THE RUSSIAN NORTH: CLOSE TO THE WORLD, FAR FROM MOSCOW

The area described as northwest Russia is a huge territory, the size of France and Great Britain combined. There are only around 4 million

Polar Tourism: Tourism in the Arctic and Antarctic Regions
Edited by C. Michael Hall and Margaret E. Johnston. © John Wiley & Sons Ltd, 1995

Figure 7.1. Tourists require cross-cultural competence and some knowledge of their destination to have a successful trip in northwest Russia (Murmansk, Russia) (Photo Credit: M.E. Johnston)

inhabitants in the area, 70 per cent of them living in urban areas. Most of the territory is wilderness with an Arctic climate.

People living in the north are called 'northerners' and are traditionally said to have a special type of mentality. They have a peaceful past. This is where different nationalities and ethnic groups have lived in peace and cooperation for centuries. For various reasons this part of Russia avoided involvement in Russian wars until the Second World War. The northwest is where the Russian 'peasant people' met the Finno-Ugric 'people of the forest' and the Viking 'people of the sea' more than a thousand years ago. These encounters gave rise to commercial and cultural activities which distinguished the northwest from the rest of Russia. The northerners became a frontier people, merchants and sailors, an extroverted and open people, differing considerably from the conservative Russian peasants. For hundreds of years most of Russia had a dominating nobility 'owning' the peasants, but not in the north. Here they were the 'property' of the state. This influenced the societal atmosphere, making it more liberal than in southern Russia. Foreigners may notice that people of the north are relaxed—they take their time—and they are open minded and interested in talking to everybody about everything.

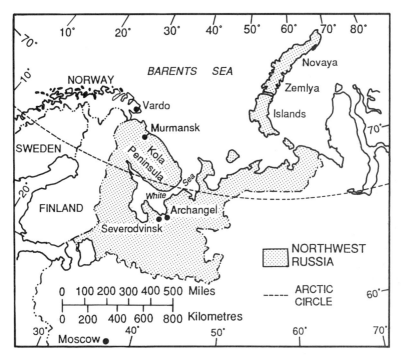

Figure 7.2. Map of northwest Russia showing its regional setting in northern Europe

Archangel (founded in 1584), the biggest city on the White Sea, was the first Russian seaport, and a model for the founding of St Petersburg. The city grew into a central position in the maritime culture of northern Europe, and northwest Russia became a meeting place for Russian and Western cultures. As such, it has had a central position in Russian society since the late Middle Ages. At the same time it was a long distance to the capital (Moscow or St Petersburg), the climate was cold, and the forests and wilderness made travel to the north a dangerous affair. The area was looked upon as a European Siberia, and since the seventeenth century was used for deportation of prisoners and exiles from the south.

From the sixteenth century, due to military threats from Sweden and England, the northwestern Russians built big fortress-style monasteries. The remnants of these serve today as an important base for tourism. During the cold war northwest Russia again had a strategic military position. However, the remnants of the cold war are a threat both for the inhabitants and for tourists: the old-fashioned nuclear installations on the Kola Peninsula; the nuclear bomb testing island Novaya Zemlya; the 'nuclear city' of Severodvinsk just outside Archangel where the enormous nuclear submarines were built; the military marine base in Severomorsk on the Kola Peninsula; and the Russian space centre, the Plesetsk cosmodrome, south of Archangel. Though threatening, these installations are monuments from an important historical period, and are not without interest to tourists.

The increasing strategic importance of northwest Russia during the Soviet period also increased the area's economic importance. Cities such as Murmansk (500 000), Severodvinsk (270 000) and others have been built since the Second World War. An enormous industry supplies the military forces. The submarine shipyard of Severodvinsk has around 70 000 employees, although some of the military production is currently being replaced with civil production. The timber industry has been of great importance for centuries; northern Russia now produces half of the total amount of Russian timber exports. The fishing industry is also export oriented, and the fishing fleet considerable. Two of the world's largest shipping companies are also situated in the area, indicating a significant trading position. The area is clearly integrated in the modern world of technology and international affairs, but also suffers from enormous pollution and ecological problems, which threaten both local people and the tourism industry. For example, the Chernobyl event in 1986 showed the industry's exposed position: the disaster was reflected in the tourism arrivals all over Europe that year and the following year (Hall, 1991), especially in arrivals from overseas (Zallocco, 1989).

Although there were a variety of industries in the area, the military-oriented industries were the ones with priority during the Soviet period. The economic conditions and technological level of these industries make a clear contrast to the low technological level of other branches of industry and business, and to the standards of living for ordinary people. Very many live without a water supply to their houses and with a bathroom in the backyard. In the business sphere computers are scarce, and the technologies in hospitals and universities are far behind Western standards. This makes the area full of contrasts, difficult for many of the locals, often interesting for tourists.

THE TRAVEL AND TOURIST TRADITIONS OF NORTHWEST RUSSIA

For many decades the main experience in going to the Soviet Union as a tourist from the West was the very fact of going there. The Kola Peninsula, except the city of Murmansk, and the Archangel region were closed to foreigners until 1990. Today the borders have been opened, as have the political, societal and cultural spheres. The Russian openness has given the world a new concept, *glasnost*. Efforts have been made to re-establish old trading relationships between the northern countries in Europe. During the period before the Bolshevik revolution there was an established trade between Norway and Russia, known as the *pomor* (coastal) trade (Niemi, 1992). The Russians brought timber and grains to Norway, fish and other goods back to Russia. There was a scheduled steam liner between Archangel and the Norwegian neighbouring town, Vardø. Russian merchants brought their children to Norway so that they could learn the language and mode of behaviour of their neighbours. Some 100 Norwegians settled along the northwest Russian coast. They lost contact with their old country after the revolution, and some of them were executed in the Stalin period (Niemi, 1992). Today relatives across the border are re-establishing the relationships.

Another historic root of tourism in the Russian north is the pilgrimage, seen in the Russians' voyages to northern monasteries and sacred places. Today we may look upon this as a form of special interest tourism (Hall and Weiler, 1992). The most famous destination for the pilgrims, or pilgrim tourists as they were called in the Soviet period, was the monastery on the Solovki Archipelago. Most of the pilgrims (around 90 per cent) came from or passed through Archangel. Here the transfer operations were handled by two tourist operation centres, or *podvorye*. Each centre included a hotel, and the guest rooms were even equipped with *icons*. The Solovki monastery had three vessels. In the archipelago of Solovki there were also hotels, one of them, which was inside the monastery walls, still exists. For pilgrims, the Solovki monastery was the 'Northern Paradise'. Besides religious contemplation, the stay might have included outdoor activities. There were many sacred places, chapels and crosses which could be reached by foot or by rowing through canals and lakes. Each sacred spot had plates with inscriptions and information about the place or monument. One may clearly see the contours of a well-organised tourism attraction system, with an attraction core or set of cores, an information system, and tourists (Leiper, 1990a). At its peak there were just over 200 000 pilgrims a year. The tourist trails have now been re-established by the monastery museum, and the monastery itself was reconsecrated in 1992. Eighteen monks were living in the monastery in 1993. To the visitors they sell icons, now made of light metal, and 'work' as tourist guides, making the monastery tour as authentic as possible for tourists.

During the Soviet period the tourism industry expanded everywhere in the Union. Accommodation capacity measured in beds, expanded from fewer than 0.5 million in 1940 to 2.5 million in 1988 (Shaw, 1991). Tourism in the Soviet period was first seen as important for health and recreation reasons; later tourism policies were primarily propagandistic. For the last 40 years the policy has been to expand capacities and to bring tourism to new districts. But still the central part of the country is the most developed. In the northwest mostly traditional tourist facilities were built, with less emphasis on health-oriented institutions (Shaw, 1991), probably reflecting the accommodation needs of the military forces and the industry.

For a long period international tourism was not desired by the Soviet regime, and there were many constraints for foreign visitors. After the Stalin period foreign tourism has gradually been accepted and expanded, from around 700 000 foreign visitors in 1960 to 2 million in 1970, 5 million in 1980, and around 8 million in 1989 (Shaw, 1991; Witt, 1991). For a long time most of the foreign tourists were from other socialist countries (Shaw, 1991). Due to the territorial restrictions, no foreign visitors, except for official guests and those going to Murmansk from Finland, Sweden and Norway, visited the northwest before 1990.

During the Soviet period tourism was organised by the state, the trade unions and the party. Tourism was, as everything else, strongly regulated (Hall, 1991). The commercial organisation for international tourism in the Soviet period was Intourist. Since the onset of *glasnost* many commercial operations catering for international tourists have been established. In the northwest, new firms are popping up all the time, many of them established by former employees of Intourist or Sputnik, the tourist organisation for young people.

There are still many constraints facing businesses (Hall, 1991), and it will take a considerable period of time before international quality services are offered to foreign tourists. Nevertheless, there is a long history of international travel in northwest Russia, providing a foundation for building a tourist industry which is more international in focus than that which existed during the Soviet period.

THE NORTHWEST RUSSIAN TOURISM RESOURCE BASE

From a resource point of view, Russia is a rich country. The explanation of the poverty that to some degree exists in the country today may mainly be traced back to resource allocation patterns which have existed for hundreds of years. For example, in the communist period up to one-third of the GNP is said to have gone to the military forces. What was left for general infrastructure and welfare was far less than the average in the West.

The resource base for tourism development in northwest Russia is the wealth of potential attractions, fundamental to a tourist industry. Northwest Russia is primarily a huge wilderness, mainly consisting of a forest, taiga and tundra. The landscape is not as spectacular as in Scandinavia, but it has many romantic places, impressive rivers, interesting geological features, and many natural curiosities, such as caves and sinking lakes. There are rich salmon rivers, and a good inland and coastal fishery. In the Archangel region there are about 244 000 lakes, 138 000 rivers and 15 nature reserves. The territories for hunting and trapping are enormous. The species hunted cover birds such as ptarmigans and black cocks, and game animals such as moose and bear. Local outfitters and professional hunting and fishing guides cater for hunters and anglers. The quality demands in the accommodation sector are lower for this group than for mass tourists. With high quality on the core products, the Russians can charge international prices in special interest activities. Due to import and export restrictions, hunting by tourists is primarily aimed at shooting trophies. However, the importance of hunting and fishing to the local population may well lead to conflict between tourists and the host community as they seek to utilise the same resource.

Northwest Russia's history is well documented and much of its heritage has been preserved. The rank of historical monuments is almost endless. There are about 800 archaeological sites, 200 of which have been excavated, 8 monasteries, hundreds of churches, prehistoric sites such as labyrinths and rock carvings, many interesting pre-revolutionary cultural sites, and monuments from the Soviet period. The vast territory covered with forest has given rise to a considerable timber industry and the development of traditional wooden architectural and artistic practice. Archangel is, in the eyes of many people, the 'European timber capital'. There is a huge production of wooden handicrafts and souvenirs, including icons and balalaikas. Recently, Russians have gone abroad with their handicraft, selling it all over Europe, as they have realised that their handicraft and souvenirs are in demand (Cohen, 1993). However, this also might make it less interesting for tourists to visit the source of such handicraft. Traditions in performing arts have been maintained throughout the Soviet period, although often with a changed content, reflecting the 'right' ideology. The closed borders of the Soviet period encouraged a huge domestic cultural production, not the least television. As a tourist one feels the rich cultural traditions and that there are many possibilities which might entertain one. Folk dancers perform for tourists, and local festivals are quite common. Even more interesting for many tourists is to meet local people and to talk to people who have been living in one of the biggest social and political experiments ever seen. Moreover, the people of the north are curious and interested in talking to tourists as the area was closed for decades. The stories they tell are filled with irony or bitterness for the lost generations. As Hosking states (1991), every elderly person has something tragic to tell from the Soviet period.

SOVIETISM: A BARRIER FOR TOURISM DEVELOPMENT

Russian society will be marked by communism for years. The former regime apparently produced as many problems as it solved, and set society back politically, economically, infrastructurally and scientifically. The

Russians lie far behind the West in many respects. The most fundamental gap is mental. The Soviet way of thinking and acting can only work within a Soviet regime. Though the regime is dead, its mentality has survived. The phenomenon may be called *sovietism*. Probably the concept should include three aspects. First are the massive manifestations of the old regime, which have to be dealt with and solved today: the military force, the armament industries, the collective farms, the party, the lack of maintenance and respect for public values, and the neglect of environmental questions, and something that might be called volumism. For the tourism industry this means low technical quality (Grönroos, 1984). The hotels are old and badly maintained. The sanitary conditions in particular are often far below a minimum Western standard. Another result is that almost everything is very big: the hotels, spas and other types of tourist resorts. These facilities are not necessarily what is needed to be developed in the tourism industry. The volumism is also reflected in the way many people are thinking about the future: they are expecting or hoping for large-scale international tourism, probably not very realistic in the north.

This has something to do with a second aspect of sovietism: the mindset of Russians. There is a noticeable difference between actual and mental time. People want to be modern, but they think and behave like they did 10 or 30 years ago. It is usual to hear Russians talking negatively about the Soviet regime, but behaving as if it still was a reality. Very often the old system can be recognised: authoritarian leaders, bureaucracies and corruption. Decision making is often unclear: nobody seems to know the rules, or whose responsibility a case is. People do not rely on each other—for years there was a well-organised system for reporting suspicious behaviour to the Party (Hosking, 1991), and still there seems to be a sharp distinction between the private and public spheres, with people not caring about the latter (Richmond, 1992). In the tourism industry one of the consequences is low functional quality (Grönroos, 1984). It is, for example, often uncertain about who is the owner and who is the one to decide. It often seems to be impossible to get decisions taken about maintenance and renovations, and the costs of it. The cost sides of running a business are often overlooked. People want to build new hotels with Western quality, although most places lack infrastructure, knowledge and people to develop and run such businesses. Many of the projects launched are unrealistic, and suffer from the lack of all kinds of analyses. On the interpersonal level, the sovietism is seen in a total lack of service attitude. If you need a taxi the problem is yours, the hotel receptionist does not see that this is something he or she should worry about.

The third aspect of sovietism is the negative feelings people have about their own country as it is today. This can be expected as a natural reaction to the previous lack of freedom, but some people obviously are overreacting, and the conception of Western society is often twisted. In the tourism industry this may primarily be noticed in all the efforts done to westernise hotels, restaurants and souvenir production. One consequence of this may be authenticity problems, if this trend is not changed. Fortunately there is much to be proud of in the pre-revolutionary history and the rich Russian culture.

Some of these problems might be more important in the north than in the south, especially in the future. Northwest Russia has been relying heavily on military forces and state subsidies. This will likely be changed, through disarmament and the process of privatisation. The enormous natural resources in the north may give room for new industries which compensate for part of this support, but probably not all. There is no reason to believe that tourism will contribute noticeably in the near future. Due to the Arctic climate, tourism is highly seasonal. Wilderness tourism throughout the year will be on a small scale, and of limited importance in economic development and employment generation. Nevertheless, tourism will be utilised in some communities as a means to bring some economic benefits to the region, while some small-scale operators may be successful in catering for the special interest travel market.

THE FUTURE: CHALLENGES AND PITFALLS

Despite its long history of trading and contact with the West, and with pilgrimage, northwest Russia has hardly any experience with contemporary *international tourism*. This means that there is only a minimum of tourist infrastructure and very little experience with foreign visitors. The potential attractions are many and often of excellent quality, but having a resource base is not the same as having products. Most of the resources must be looked upon as raw material. Pre-announced groups are usually well treated and given interesting and specially tailored programmes, but very little is organised for the independent tourist. The Russians are used to doing things together with others and there exists a group mentality (Richmond, 1992). They seem to believe that this is the case with international tourists. However, the international trends are the opposite, with people travelling more and more without groups. Very little is prepared for those tourists in the north; there are only a few scheduled tours and site excursions, and information systems are poorly developed.

The tourism industry in northwest Russia is in the early stages of its development. For decades hotels have been looked upon as public goods, and the staff were employed by the state. There are some smaller private hotels and some individual tour operators, all looking upon each other not only as competitors but, more or less, as enemies. There is no collaboration, no common tourism organisations, no common regional marketing bodies, no apparatus for professional training, no signs of a real industry, not even a fragmented one (see Leiper, 1990b).

As during the Soviet period, tourism is now serving an ideological function. In the Soviet period tourism was an arena for communist indoctrination (Shaw, 1991). Today efforts are being made to break down the same ideology. There are many exchange programmes and collaboration projects where Russians are brought to the West to learn, and Western experts and businesses are going into Russia. Western companies are involved in oil exploration, shipbuilding, and in the fertiliser industry. There is a risk that such industries will adopt the pattern well known in the Third World with international companies exploiting the raw materials, and manufacturing and selling the products in an international market with only a small proportion of the value accumulated going back to the Third World country. This may be regarded as a form of economic imperialism (Crick, 1989). The tourism industry in northwest Russia might well fall into this pattern. Many have suggested the joint venture project as the road to international tourism in Russia (Buckley and Witt, 1990; Witt, 1991). This may be appropriate from the point of view of the international tourism industry, but might also mean that Russians will lose control over the industry, with profit leaving the country. It is, however, looked upon as a risky business to go into northern Russia and few joint ventures have been established in the tourism industry. Should there be a political regression, the northern regions for military reasons would probably be the first to be closed to foreigners.

Tourist trips to northern Russia, as to all Russia except Moscow and St Petersburg, should be marketed as alternative tourism (Smith and Eadington, 1992) or special interest tourism (Weiler and Hall, 1992). There are increasing markets for these types of tourism, which suit the trend towards serious leisure. Learning and self-realisation are now important incentives for travelling. People who are serious about their interests are probably less concerned about accommodation and transport standards. They may be characterised as experience oriented or allocentric tourists, in contrast to the safety and comfort oriented, the psychocentric tourists. There are two main types of special interest tourism, one corresponding to the uniqueness of the activities, the other to the uniqueness of the place or destination (Weiler and Hall, 1992). 'Cruising' with an ice-breaker to the North Pole can be done only in the Arctic; going on a cruise may be done almost everywhere. Northwest Russia may be a new arena for people's special interests, not least for people attracted by wilderness. The area may also offer activities and experiences which are place specific; the whole country is a very special destination today.

Ilyina and Mieczkowski (1992) propose scientific tourism as a priority in Russia in the coming years. The idea is to bring in Western specialists to what they describe as the 'Russian laboratory'. They point out different ways this may be done, from scientific expeditions on the one hand, to using scientists as guides for special interest tourists on the other. The north is one of the areas they identified as suitable for such activities. The idea is well-regarded and supported by many Russians. Several more or less scientific expeditions were arranged during the summer of 1993. Russian academics are as good as any in many fields, but generally there is a lack of modern equipment. However, as in the business sphere, there is a risk of an unbalanced cooperation and a danger of developing a sort of academic imperialism.

The current extreme openness must be seen as a reaction to the fact that the Russians have been like prisoners in their own country for 70 years. One common reaction to the openness and the newly achieved freedom is to reject everything in the society which can be connected to the Soviet regime. This implies a belief that everything is better in the tourists' origin countries, a typical attitude in developing countries, in their encounters with the modern tourist (Schwaller, 1992). Russians serve hamburgers and Coca Cola, cheap Italian champagne instead of good Russian, and they take the tourists to striptease clubs. There are Western (or believed Western) style cafés and restaurants; the one outside the Solovki monastery looks like a Western saloon. This is probably not the most appropriate strategy. Tourists want to see and experience unique Russian culture, not copies of the West. In the future, the restoration of Russian pride is a major challenge. There is, of course, no contradiction between Russian traditions and culture, and modernity. Probably tourism could be a positive force in this process. The images people have of themselves reflect the images held by others. Being popular among tourists may strengthen self-esteem; there are several examples of tourism used in the process of revitalisation of local identity (Friedman, 1990).

The excitement of going to Russia today is that the trip differs from most others and is based on a limited cultural knowledge. In cultural theory one speaks of low or high contextual cultures (Hall, 1976; Dahl and Habert, 1990). Russia is probably tending towards the last category. To understand what is said or happens, one has to have insight into the Russian culture. The interpretation must be based on signals from the context in addition to the words which are said or the event observed. This may be a bigger problem in the northwest than in central Russia. With the exception of Murmansk, people are not used to foreigners and the tourism industry is poorly developed. This implies a widespread need for 'cultural brokers' (Nunez, 1989; Nash, 1989) who mediate between the host population and the tourists. To be good hosts, tourist guides and tour leaders need cross-cultural competence. In the hands of a tourist company one is always surrounded by guides, interpreters and 'body guards'. This is a tradition from the Soviet period when the tourists had to be controlled. However, such situations are unlikely to appeal to special interest travellers who are seeking to experience first-hand the cultural and physical environment in which they are travelling.

As an arena for cultural and wilderness-based special interest tourism, the image of the area should correspond to the nature of the resource base. 'The Cultural Russian Arctic' might be an appropriate image slogan for this area. The word 'Arctic' is well known, as is the word 'Russian'. There is much evidence that it is good business to use the name of the country in promoting destinations (Salzer, 1990). 'The Russian Arctic' will have some associations for everybody. However, there is another side to the image of the area, in which the region is perceived as a cold war monument, and one in which the pollution and the nuclear threat are probably the greatest in the world. This image may be another reason not to proceed quickly with tourism development. Therefore small-scale tourism, in combination with travelling due to activities in other sectors, using the existing facilities, might be a primary strategy for northwest Russia. This is not only the most realistic strategy, it is also a way to avoid the negative effects associated with fast development and mass tourism.

CONCLUSION

This chapter has outlined some of the background, opportunities and problems of tourism development in northwest Russia. Going there is a unique and memorable experience. The main reasons for this are the wilderness, culture and heritage, and the Soviet monuments. Another motivation is probably the lack of industrialisation in the tourism industry. One is guaranteed to be confronted with all aspects of Russian society and culture.

Russia is currently undergoing a process of westernisation. The challenge for the Russians, as for every other national culture, is to become a member of international society and global culture without losing uniqueness and identity. This should be possible as there is not necessarily a conflict between local identity and internationalisation (Urry, 1992). However, the signs which can be seen today give reasons to be alert: the belief in capitalism is without boundaries, and the wilderness is for sale, as is everything else. There are reasons to believe that the internationalisation process may proceed quickly in the northwest, due to the new openness and its historical trade traditions. But the tourists are not numerous and there is no base for large-scale tourism. The market demands are not of a type which necessitates huge demands for international investments. This gives hopes for the future, a tourism development under Russian control. In 1993 the Scandinavian countries and Russia established an international region called the Barents Region, constituting the northernmost regions in Scandinavia, and northwest Russia. It was established primarily for the purpose of including northwest Russia in the international family of the north. The region is a political and administrative unit with funding from the participating states. There are a number of matters to be resolved in cultural, environmental and industrial fields. One of these is tourism. There is optimism in the region. The Scandinavian countries see many business opportunities and have undertaken investment in Russian firms and joint ventures. Hopefully there will be a balanced development. In the beginning, the cooperation has very much had the character of Norwegians, Finns or Swedes making fast money in Russia. At the same time the Russians are learning how to think and behave in business. This may be good for both parties, but there is a risk of exploitation. The way to success in tourism lies not primarily in joint ventures and internationalism, but in Russian control with a flavour of Russianness throughout.

REFERENCES

Buckley, P.J., Witt, S.F., 1990, Tourism in centrally-planned economies of Europe, *Annals of Tourism Research*, **17**(1): 91–104

Cohen, E., 1993, Introduction. Investigating tourist arts, *Annals of Tourism Research*, **20**(1): 1–8

Crick, M., 1989, Representations of international tourism in the social sciences: Sun, sex, sights, savings and servility, *Annual Review of Anthropology*, **18**: 307–344

Dahl, Ø., Habert, K., 1986, *Møte mellom kulturer. Tverrkulturell kommunikasjon*, Universitetsforaget, Oslo

Friedman, J., 1990, Being in the world: globalization and localization, in *Theory, Culture and Society*, 7(2–3)

Grönroos, C., 1984, *Strategic management and marketing in the service sector*, Studentlitteratur/Chartwell-Bratt Ltd, Lund/Kent

Hall, C.M., Weiler, B., 1992, Introduction. What's special about special interest tourism. In Weiler, B., Hall, C.M., eds., *Special interest tourism*, Belhaven Press, London, pp. 1–14.

Hall, D.R., ed., 1991, *Tourism and economic development in Eastern Europe and Soviet Union*, Belhaven Press, London

Hall, E.T., 1976, *Beyond culture*, Doubleday, New York

Hosking, G., 1991, *The awakening of the Soviet Union*, Harvard University Press, Cambridge, Massachusetts

Hosking, G., 1992, *A history of the Soviet Union*, Fontana Press, London

Ilyina, L., Mieczkowski, Z., 1992, Developing scientific tourism in Russia, *Tourism Management*, **13**(3): 327–331

Leiper, N., 1990a, The tourism attraction system, *Annals of Tourism Research*, **17**(3): 367–384

Leiper, N., 1990b, Partial industrialization of tourism systems, *Annals of Tourism Research*, **17**(4): 600–605

Nash, D., 1989, Tourism as a form of imperialism. In Smith, V., ed., *Hosts and guests: the anthropology of tourism*, 2nd edn, University of Pennsylvania Press, Philadelphia, pp. 37–52

Niemi, E., ed., 1992, *Pomor. Nord-Norge og Nord-Russland gjennom 100 år*, Gyldendal

Nunez, T., 1989, Tourist studies in anthropological perspective. In Smith, V., ed., *Hosts and guests: the anthropology of tourism*, 2nd edn, University of Pennsylvania Press, Philadelphia, pp. 265–274

Richmond, Y., 1992, *From nyet to da, understanding the Russians*, Intercultural Press, Yarmouth, Maine

Salzer, M., 1989, *Länders image*, LIU EKI/WP8907, Lund University, Lund, Sweden

Schwaller, C., 1992, 'As others see us': The role of cultural awareness in European tourism, paper presented at Tourism in Europe Conference, Durham

Shaw D.J.B., 1991, The Soviet Union. In Hall, D.R., ed., *Tourism and economic development in Eastern Europe and Soviet Union*, Belhaven Press, London, pp. 119–141

Smith, V., Eadington, W.R., eds., 1992, *Tourism alternatives*, University of Pennsylvania Press, Philadelphia

Urry, J., 1992, Europe, tourism and the nation state, Tourism in Europe, mimeo.

Weiler B., Hall, C.M., 1992, *Special interest tourism*, Belhaven Press, London

Witt, S.F., 1991, The development of international tourism in Eastern Europe, paper presented at New Horizons in Tourism Education and Research Conference, World Tourism Education and Research Centre, University of Calgary

Zallocco, R.L., 1989, Market analysis. In Witt, S.F., Moutinho, L., eds., *Tourism marketing and management handbook*, Prentice-Hall, London, pp. 239–244

8 Aboriginal People in the Tourism Economy of Canada's Northwest Territories

TOM D. HINCH

INTRODUCTION

The Northwest Territories (NWT) is in transition, and its people, governed by an aboriginal majority in their legislative assembly, are dealing with this change on many fronts. From an economic perspective, the NWT is still undergoing the transformation from a predominantly subsistence economy to a predominantly wage-based economy. The government of the NWT is striving for greater economic independence as the ability and willingness of Canada's federal government to provide financial support declines and as residents of the NWT seek more control over their own destiny. New socio-cultural concerns are emerging with the decline of traditional activities of hunting, trapping and fishing, an increasing exposure to southern media, new educational curricula, and a myriad of other factors. Maintaining a sense of cultural identity has been an ongoing challenge in the face of this rapid change. Furthermore, new technologies have amplified the impact of human activity on the natural environment. As a result, aboriginal residents of the NWT are having to reassess their relationship with their environment and develop approaches to resource management that remain consistent with their values.

A changing political framework, in which northern people have gained greater decision-making power, represents one level of the response to the challenges facing the NWT. This devolution of power includes the scheduled creation of the new territory of Nunavut in the eastern regions of the present NWT as well as the ongoing settlement and negotiation of numerous aboriginal land claims. While this trend towards local and regional control has facilitated a more democratic response to the issues facing northerners, approaches are still being developed to deal with the challenges found in this polar region.

Polar Tourism: Tourism in the Arctic and Antarctic Regions
Edited by C. Michael Hall and Margaret E. Johnston. © John Wiley & Sons Ltd, 1995

The development of tourism appears to represent one of the more promising strategies which northern people can use to achieve their economic, socio-cultural and environmental goals in a sustainable context. The intent of this chapter is to examine and assess the potential of tourism as an effective agent for change particularly as it relates to the aboriginal majority in the NWT. To this end, the chapter will be divided into three main sections, the first of which will examine the current status of tourism in the NWT including the involvement of aboriginal people in this sector of the economy. Next, the issues associated with tourism in the context of the NWT's aboriginal people will be considered. Finally, existing approaches for the management of tourism will be reviewed in the context of their implications for the aboriginal population.

TOURISM AND NORTHERN HOSTS

The northern tourism economy

Just as the NWT as a whole has undergone dramatic change over the past 30 years, so has tourism activity within the territories. While only 600 non-resident pleasure travellers were estimated in 1959 (Department of Industry and Development, 1972) over 47 600 were estimated during the summer of 1989 (Department of Economic Development and Tourism (DEDT), 1990a). These 1989 figures are small relative to many southern destinations but they are substantial in this context, representing a 78-fold increase over this 30-year time period.

As the number of visitors has increased so have their reasons for visiting. While pleasure visitors in the 1960s came primarily for fishing and hunting, today's visitors have a much more diverse range of interests including general touring and sightseeing, adventure travel and eco-tourism (Hinch and Swinnerton, 1993). Notwithstanding this diversification, the two most prevalent forms of pleasure travel in the NWT are visiting friends and relatives along with general touring (Acres International Limited, 1990).

The contribution that these visitors make to the NWT economy is substantial. Tourism Canada (1990) estimated that in 1989 the tourism industry in the NWT generated approximately $54 million in revenue and accounted for 2.7 per cent of the gross territorial product. Over 2500 or one in 20 NWT residents were either directly or indirectly employed in tourism. Tourism presently ranks as the third leading export of the Territories behind minerals, and oil and gas and it is seen as a growing industry (DEDT, 1990b). Tourism is also viewed as an activity in which these economic benefits can be targeted to areas not necessarily favoured by other types of economic activity and to areas that are populated by indigenous people.

The attraction of aboriginal cultures

Images of aboriginal people and their cultures have long been used to promote travel to Canada and its northern regions. The implicit rationale for this type of promotion is that tourists will be drawn to these destinations because aboriginal cultures are attractive. This idea has been explicitly stated and examined in a number of studies conducted in the late 1980s by a variety of aboriginal associations and government agencies (Csargo, 1988; Native Council of Canada, 1987; Tourism Canada, 1988). The demand for aboriginal-based tourism attractions with an outdoor adventure or a cultural orientation was seen to be particularly strong in the long-haul markets of Germany, France, Britain and Japan.

There are a variety of aboriginal tourism experiences currently available. Visiting attractions like heritage villages or interpretive centres is one of the most popular types of aboriginal tourism experience. Shopping opportunities represent a second category and involve purchases of goods such as native crafts, clothing, art or jewellery. A third variation occurs when visitors seek and obtain specific native experiences such as traditional wilderness outings, visiting native communities, and attending dance performances or powwows. Finally, guided native hunting or fishing experiences can be considered a fourth category of aboriginal tourism products.

On the basis of perceptions of demand and supply, the government of the Northwest Territories (GNWT) has endorsed aboriginal cultures as key elements of its attractiveness as a tourist destination. This strategy is, in part, based on research which shows that visitors to the NWT feel that people and culture are the two most interesting features of the NWT after the natural environment (Acres International Limited, 1990). Even within aboriginal communities themselves, there is a general feeling that aboriginal cultures are one of the primary attractions for visitors (RT and Associates Ltd, 1992).

Local hosts figure prominently in the promotional descriptions contained in the NWT visitors guide (DEDT, n.d.1). Numerous images of aboriginal people appear throughout the publication with the majority illustrating traditional activities but also interspersed with more contemporary images. The text emphasises the 'exotic' nature of the Dene, Métis, Inuit and non-aboriginal cultures, the sense of community, and the genuine hospitality of all northerners. The following excerpt highlights this message:

> Some people think the North is a cold place. But we think it's warmer than most, in terms of the human heart.

Your northern journey is a collage of open, friendly faces: shyly grinning children at a village playground, young mothers in Inuit amautis (parkas for mother and child), Dene elders gather at church. . . .

You'll meet native northerners in many roles: as guides, interpreters, entrepreneurs and professionals, they're happy to share their knowledge on the land, cultures and its wildlife. They'll show you living tradition. And they'll introduce you to 'the new North' where they're living in harmony with people who have come to the Northwest Territories from all over Canada and the world. . . .

Come North, and share our vibrant cultural tradition (DEDT, n.d.1, pp. 11–13).

ABORIGINAL PEOPLE AND THE BUSINESS OF TOURISM

Despite a government strategy 'to promote a community based and regionally disbursed tourism industry . . .' (DEDT, 1990c, p. 13), tourism activity is not evenly distributed throughout the NWT nor are its benefits evenly distributed across cultural groups. The NWT contains a population of approximately 57 000 residents who live in just over 60 widely dispersed communities with many of these having less than 600 residents. The mosaic of ethnic groups includes Dene (17 per cent), Inuit (including Inuvialuit) (37 per cent), and Métis (7 per cent) and non-aboriginals (39 per cent). Inuit peoples form the majority in the eastern portions of the NWT while the Dene and Métis are concentrated in the western portion of the NWT around Great Slave Lake, the MacKenzie River Valley and in part of the Mackenzie Delta. Non-aboriginals dominate the major urban centres which also contain considerable Métis populations (Bureau of Statistics, 1991; Outcrop Ltd, 1990).

Tourism activity in the NWT increased dramatically from 1979 to 1988 but these increases were not spatially uniform and therefore they did not affect all residents to the same extent (Table 8.1). In 1979, 92 per cent of all summer pleasure visitors had a primary destination in one of the three western tourism zones of Big River, Northern Frontier or Western Arctic. By 1988, this figure had fallen to 84 per cent of all pleasure visitors (DEDT, 1990c). Notwithstanding this shift, the ongoing imbalance indicates that the Inuit do not experience the same level of tourism activity and, as a consequence, impacts in their communities as do other groups in the NWT.

In contrast to the slow spatial adjustment in visitation, there has been a much more substantial adjustment in terms of the distribution of the ownership of tourism businesses (Table 8.2). Aboriginal residents increased their share of tourism businesses from 18 per cent in 1979 to 35 per cent in 1988. This is a substantial increase in both relative and absolute

Table 8.1. Distribution of summer pleasure visitors in Northwest Territories, 1979 and 1988

	1979		1988	
	%	No.	%	No.
Zone				
Big River (South Slave–Deh Cho)	28	6320	25	8250
Northern Frontier (North Slave)	37	8300	34	11 350
Western Arctic (Sahtu and Mackenzie)	27	6080	25	8250
Arctic coast (Kitikmeot)	0	200	2	690
Keewatin	0	320	5	1720
Baffin	6	1280	8	2740
Total	100*	22 500	100*	33 000

* % columns do not equal 100% due to rounding.
Source: After DEDT (1990c).

Table 8.2. Distribution of travel businesses by ownership

	1979		1988	
	%	No.	%	No.
Ownership				
Aboriginal resident	18	34	35	130
Non-aboriginal resident	42	81	40	148
Non-resident	40	78	25	94
Total	100	194	100	372

Source: After DEDT (1990c).

terms but it still demonstrates that aboriginal tourism ownership (35 per cent) is less than the proportion of aboriginal people in the NWT population (61 per cent).

Small and medium-sized communities are plagued with some of the highest unemployment rates in the NWT (e.g. Rae Lakes, 56 per cent and Gjoa Haven, 52 per cent) and they also have the highest concentration of aboriginal settlement (DEDT, 1990b). If the culture of aboriginal communities represents a tourism resource, then tourism development within these communities may help combat the high unemployment rates. Recent surveys of the residents in several communities in the eastern half of the NWT demonstrate a high level of support for tourism development and a widespread belief that it would lead to substantial economic benefits within the community (Nickels *et al.*, 1991; RT and Associates Ltd, 1992). In an argument in support of tourism training, Haywood (1991) suggested that some northerners remain suspicious of tourism and how it will affect their traditional lifestyles. Notwithstanding these concerns, at least one of the tourist associations located in a predominantly Inuit region has made a concerted effort to encourage local employment associated with tourism activity (Arctic Coast Tourist Association, n.d.). In a poster distributed throughout the region, a broad range of tourism employment opportunities are described including those associated with hotels and lodges, outfitters, arts and crafts, tour operators/guides, taxi operators, travel agents/airline agents and tourism groups like the association itself.

SELECTED ISSUES

Aboriginal cultures have traditionally viewed life holistically while non-aboriginal societies in North America have tended to focus on isolated parts of the whole. Fundamental philosophical differences such as this one can create tension between aboriginal hosts and the largely non-aboriginal guests. The global tourism industry in which the NWT is increasingly operating is also dominated by non-aboriginal values and philosophies. This section of the chapter examines the issues associated with this involvement from the perspective of a non-aboriginal observer. Issues will be categorised in terms of their economic, socio-cultural and environmental dimensions in order to facilitate this discussion. It should, however, be recognised that these dimensions are interrelated.

The economic dimension

Tourism development in the NWT is driven by anticipation of economic benefits. Services and attractions are made available to visitors in exchange for monetary payments, a portion of which will accrue to the local destination with the balance accruing to the various intermediaries who make it possible for the tourist to visit the destination. The north faces a variety of challenges in terms of participating in this business in a way that will optimise its share of these tourist dollars. Like other Arctic and sub-Arctic destinations, the NWT faces the paradoxical situation of its geography being both one of its major assets and one of its major liabilities. Visitors from primary market areas face relatively long and expensive travel arrangements not only to get to the NWT but also to travel to different destinations within them. As with any other industry based in a remote region, the high cost of transportation represents a barrier (DEDT, 1990b). It has been estimated that the cost of doing business in the NWT is 60 per cent higher than in southern Canada. Similarly, its Arctic and sub-Arctic climate restricts the vast majority of tourism activity to a very short summer season. Visitation at other times of the year must take into account the harsh climate and limited daylight. From a business perspective, the compression of this season presents a challenge in terms of cash flow but from a cultural perspective, seasonal activity in and of itself is not an unusual hardship. Nevertheless, specific conflicts with other seasonal activities such as hunting and fishing might pose a problem in some communities.

Related barriers to tourism development include the difficulties of obtaining financing through standard financial institutions and the lack of communication between the broader tourism industry and aboriginal communities. Regarding the first barrier, many northern communities do not even have a local financial outlet let alone one that is knowledgeable and supportive of tourism. In respect of the second barrier, regional tourism associations along with the GNWT are beginning to facilitate the necessary contact with the largely non-aboriginal tourism trade operations located in distant market areas.

Increased aboriginal participation in Arctic and sub-Arctic tourism is supported by the interest of tourists in aboriginal cultures, the apparent compatibility of traditional activities of hunting and fishing with consumptive tourist activities, and the attractiveness of aboriginal traditional knowledge of the environment. However, it must be recognised that tourists are becoming more sophisticated and demanding all the time. Haywood (1991, p. 402) has suggested that not all of the skills and interests that characterise traditional northern lifestyles complement the more communicative and service-oriented aspects of managing visitors. The culturally sensitive development of these skills and attitudes has been recommended by a number of individuals and agencies (Haywood, 1991; DEDT, 1990c) and is currently being addressed through community-based outreach programmes offered by the Arctic College and the Tourism Training Institute.

At a more fundamental level is the question of whether aboriginal cultures hold values that are compatible with participation in the 'business of tourism'. Traditional views suggest that aboriginal cultures 'tend to be communal, not individualistic' and that 'individual ownership of chattels and property is not highly esteemed' (Hollinshead, 1992, p. 49). These values would seem to run counter to the underlying *laissez-faire* materialistic philosophy normally associated with the tourism industry. Rather than being diametrically opposed, it appears that the positions of aboriginal people in the north and of the non-aboriginal tourism industry are beginning to converge or at least be more accepting of alternative business models. While community values still remain paramount in northern aboriginal cultures, greater concern for the individual is also emerging. Similarly, although the tourism industry still seems firmly entrenched in the economic rhetoric of Adam Smith, there is a growing recognition that the long-term success of tourism depends on the support of the destination community and that a community approach to tourism development is needed (Murphy, 1985). The difficulty that these separate value orientations present was summarised in a brief to the Royal Commission on Aboriginal Peoples by the Canadian National Aboriginal Tourism Association which made the statement that: 'The main challenge for aboriginal people who enter the industry is to be culturally oriented "BUSINESS" people' (Parker, 1993, p. 259).

Socio-cultural dimension

While the anticipated economic benefits of tourism may be the driving force for the increasing involvement of aboriginal people in the tourism industry of the NWT, the argument that tourism may actually strengthen traditional cultures is also very important. Purported socio-cultural benefits include: the revival or at least compatibility of tourism with traditional social and material cultures; the promotion of a greater under-standing and appreciation between the interacting cultures; and the development of infrastructure such as airports which will benefit the local community even in the absence of tourists (Mathieson and Wall, 1982; Nickels *et al.*, 1991). Counter-arguments focus on the marginalisation of aboriginal participants in the tourism industry, the negative impacts of the commoditisation of culture, and the problem of a 'demonstration effect' associated with tourism activity.

The emergence of aboriginal entrepreneurs and participants in the tourism industry has not been without its costs. Parallels exist in the NWT to the marginalisation of aboriginal tourism operators described in Smith's (1989) study of aboriginal participation in tourism in Alaska. Although the transition from traditional subsistence to wage-based economies has progressed beyond that which existed in Alaska in the early 1970s, a comfortable balance has not yet been reached. Aboriginal people who have established financially successful tourism businesses run the risk of being viewed as deserting their culture and even demeaning it by treating it as a resource for personal benefit. While this reaction varies from community to community and individual to individual, it can cause isolation and stress for aboriginal entrepreneurs.

Commoditisation is said to occur when the culture of a community becomes part of a system of exchange (e.g. a product which has a monetary value). Expressions or manifestations of culture such as colourful local costumes and customs '. . . come to be performed or produced for touristic consumption' (Cohen, 1988, p. 372). Critics have, therefore, argued that contrary to claims that tourism can revive traditions, it actually attacks the very core of a culture by turning the authentic into the inauthentic, destroying those things that give meaning to a culture (Greenwood, 1977). While there can be little doubt that the commoditisation of culture for tourism does occur in the NWT, its impacts must be considered in the broader context of present-day life in the north. Traditional markets for the products associated with hunting and trapping are declining. If economic independence is viewed as desirable, then northerners must consider other sustainable options. Welfare dependence or relying solely on large-scale non-renewable resource extraction may present far greater challenges to the cultural integrity of northern people than the challenges associated with mitigating the undesirable impacts of cultural tourism.

Concern also exists about the negative influence associated with the 'demonstration effect' in which local residents aspire to the material standards and consumer patterns displayed by wealthy tourists. The inability of locals to attain these objectives is said to create frustration and dissatisfaction within destination communities (Nickels et al., 1991).

Environmental dimension

The natural environment, in concert with northern people and their cultures, represents the essence of the NWT's attraction as a tourism destination (Acres International Limited, 1990). Rather than being separate, these entities are intimately intertwined. Aboriginal people have traditionally seen themselves as being inseparable from nature, an integral part but not paramount (Hollinshead, 1992). Advocates of aboriginal tourism see it as an opportunity for indigenous people to stay close to the land and teach others about these values (Parker, 1993). The industry parallel to the idea of 'coexisting with Mother Nature' is the concept of sustainable tourism (Tourism Stream Action Strategy Committee, 1990). While the terminology may be different, there appears to be agreement that tourism activity presents the opportunity for economic development while maintaining the integrity of the physical and cultural resource. Economic development based on non-renewable resource industries is not as easily justified within this value system.

Notwithstanding the close association between the natural environment and aboriginal people in the NWT, there are challenges in this area of tourism development. In addition to the lower standard of living found in many northern communities relative to their southern counterparts, one of the most striking characteristics of northern communities from a tourist's perspective is the prevalence of refuse and litter. Visitors have identified the clean-up of this litter as one of the five most needed improvements for tourism in the NWT (Acres International Limited, 1990). Difficulties arise though when the cultural context of this refuse is considered. Do the skeletal remains of butchered game constitute litter even though aboriginal cultures may have treated these remains in a similar fashion for hundreds of years? Would a sanitised community still reflect the cultural integrity of the resident community? A similar issue may emerge in terms of the selected tourist segments who come north for non-consumptive activities. Conflicts may occur when these groups interact with other tourists who are visiting for consumptive activities or with local residents as they conduct their traditional hunting, trapping and fishing practices. Does a bird watcher want to stay at the same lodge as a trophy angler? What are the likely reactions of eco-tourists to a whale hunt that may coincide with their visit to a coastal village? Some type of management intervention potentially will be required to minimise conflicts.

DELIVERY APPROACHES

Clearly there are no easy solutions to the challenges facing the aboriginal people of the NWT in their efforts to maximise benefits while minimising negative impacts of tourism. Nevertheless, general development strategies along with specific mechanisms of implementation are beginning to emerge.

Economic strategies and mechanisms

Current economic development policy in the NWT is intended to: reduce employment and income disparities between and within communities and regions; promote growth and diversification; and ensure that the NWT residents receive a larger share of economic benefits than they have in the past (DEDT, 1990b). Within this policy, tourism is identified as a sector that offers considerable promise in meeting these objectives and in achieving the involvement of local communities (DEDT, 1990c). The primary supporting mechanisms for these objectives include a series of business development programmes offered by the GNWT. These programmes are designed to overcome barriers to economic development by providing business loans, investment contributions, joint venture opportunities with the GNWT, business advice and venture capital contributions (DEDT, n.d.2). Aboriginal people are favoured under many of these programmes by the simple fact that applications from smaller communities, where higher concentrations of aboriginal people tend to reside, are eligible for a greater percentage of project funding than are applications from major centres.

Parallel policy and strategy exist at the federal level in Canada as exemplified by the *Canadian aboriginal economic development strategy* which is intended to promote more effective participation by aboriginal people in Canada's economy (Government of Canada, 1989). The most relevant programme elements for tourism emerging from this policy include: assistance for business development in the form of funding and consultation; financial incentives that encourage aboriginal people to enter joint ventures with other firms in the mainstream economy such as the long-standing partnership behind the Bathurst Inlet Lodge; and the establishment of community economic development organisations that are designed to enable aboriginal communities and their people to define their own economic future (Department of Indian Affairs and Northern Development, 1991).

While the barriers such as the difficulties of obtaining capital funding seem to be addressed in both GNWT and federal programmes, the successful attainment of policy goals is dependent upon at least three underlying requirements. The first is that the devolution of political control must be matched by a similar process in terms of control of economic development (RT and Associates Ltd, 1993). This control is especially important from a tourism perspective to ensure that local communities can determine the nature and scale of development with which they are comfortable (Keller, 1987). The second requirement is that local residents must become skilled and knowledgeable about tourism if they are to appreciate the consequences of their decisions regarding economic development and are to participate effectively in the 'business of tourism'. While outside resources may be required, training and education programmes should be culturally sensitive and initiated from within local communities (Haywood, 1991). Finally, while the present programme initiatives related to joint ventures may provide an important mechanism for the training and education of local aboriginal people, to do so, aboriginal people should be active partners, not silent partners whose primary contribution is limited to the financial assistance that they have levered.

Socio-cultural strategies and mechanisms

Socio-cultural tourism issues in the NWT were identified as marginalisation, commoditisation, and the demonstration effect. Official tourism policy is strongly in support of the principle of culturally compatible development (DEDT, 1990c), yet it is difficult to operationalise programmes that ensure that this principle is implemented. One of the most direct responses to the danger of creating marginalised tourism entrepreneurs has been the shift towards regional and community-based tourism planning. Examples of this include support for the eight regional tourism associations made up of local representatives but funded largely through the GNWT (DEDT, 1990c). Similarly, community tourism action planning initiatives conducted at a local level help the community to influence the nature of the development and their share of the benefits and costs associated with the development. Under this approach, tourism development is not something that happens to communities but rather it is something that happens within them.

The issue of commoditisation of culture is a complex one but its negative impacts are likely to be minimised if informed aboriginal people are in control of the development process. One of the dangers of external tourism control is that culture may be seen as static and locked into traditional patterns even though local people are in a much better position to determine the appropriate balance between traditional and contemporary elements. Notwithstanding the trend towards self-determination, the packaging of culture is still a difficult exercise. One of the mechanisms that is currently being used in the NWT can be categorised as staged authenticity in which a cultural demonstration, such as drum dancing, is recognised as a form of theatre by both its presenters and its audience (MacCannell, 1973). This approach facilitates a cultural exchange in conjunction with the control of unwanted impacts. The operation of a summer cultural camp at N'dilo just outside Yellowknife represents a good example of this form of programme. Visitors, as well as residents, are invited to the N'dilo camp where they may observe and interact with Dene elders involved in traditional summer activities. A fee is charged upon admission and souvenirs may be purchased at the camp. A variation of this approach is offered at Pangnirtung in the Baffin region where the Angmarlik Interpretive Centre combines traditional exhibits with an area where local Inuit elders informally meet with visitors over coffee or tea.

Finally, the problem of the demonstration effect must be put into the broader context of contemporary life in the NWT. Tourists represent just one of many sources of exposure that aboriginal people have to outside cultures and likely, a much less significant one than television broadcasts originating from large urban areas outside the territory. The advantage that tourism offers is that the physical presence of the tourists allows for interventions designed to make both the tourist and the resident more sensitive to concerns such as the demonstration effect. Promotional publications, like the 1993 Explorers' guide (DEDT, n.d.1), are beginning to educate potential visitors about aboriginal cultures before they arrive while upon arrival, cultural demonstrations and exhibits are developing additional understanding of contemporary as well as traditional aspects of life in the north. In those cases where problems continue to exist, the direct regulation of visitors by local communities should be considered as it is in aboriginal communities in the southwestern USA (Sweet, 1991).

Environmental strategies and mechanisms

Some of the most powerful mechanisms available for the control of the environmental challenges posed by tourism exist in the form of the management frameworks associated with parks and reserves. Although the establishment of these protected areas may have occurred for a variety of reasons, the fact is that parks tend to attract and concentrate tourists in selected areas. The management frameworks associated with these parks, therefore, enable the behaviour and subsequent impacts of tourists to be influenced. While these areas were often imposed on local aboriginal people in the past, the creation of new parks and similar jurisdictions now requires detailed negotiations between the national and territorial governments with aboriginal groups. The experience in the NWT has been that the establishment of new protected areas will be accepted much more readily by aboriginal societies if 'the legal status of the land in question is first settled to their satisfaction' (Seale, 1992, p. 8). This native land claims process has been going on for more than 15 years in the NWT and has helped to define aboriginal rights on matters related to renewable resource management and economic development as well as landownership. As a result of their strong negotiating position, aboriginal groups have acquired greater control over wildlife management, as well as the planning, management and operation of territorial and federal parks (Val, 1990). These negotiated settlements have resulted in a convergence of environmental values as expressed through the management and regulation of these new parks.

The agreement for the establishment of a national park on Banks Island in the western NWT is a case in point (GNWT, 1992). Signatories to the agreement included representatives from the government of Canada, the GNWT and the Inuvialuit. Rights for the Inuvialuit that are incorporated into the agreement include: guarantees of animal harvesting, continued use of cultural resources within the park, consultation related to visitor management, preferential hiring for park personnel, and preferential treatment in relation to business opportunities associated with the park. The Banks Island agreement is indicative of the increased level of control and self-determination that aboriginal people are exhibiting in relation to the environment of the north.

The mixed message that tourists get when they see refuse in northern communities remains a seemingly minor but perplexing problem. Efforts to rectify this issue through clean-ups have only met with limited success. Education is likely the best mechanism for dealing with litter. As aboriginal people learn more about the needs and concerns of tourists, they will be in a better position to reduce this dissonance. Solutions will likely involve more clean-ups and the education of visitors in terms of aboriginal views on the environment as it relates to community appearance.

CONCLUSION

The aboriginal people of the NWT are becoming more active and are participating more fully in the business of tourism throughout the NWT. Growing involvement has presented both challenge and opportunity. As opportunities are seized and progress is made in respect to any given challenge, further opportunities and challenges arise. It is therefore unlikely that there will be a point in this process at which all of the pluralistic goals of aboriginal people are achieved. The needs and aspirations of aboriginal people in the NWT are diverse, complex and dynamic as are those of the other participants in the global tourism industry. No ideal stable state of equilibrium exists in which all of these needs and aspirations can be met. While tourism development does not represent a panacea for the aboriginal people of the NWT, if carefully managed, it can offer progress towards their goals.

Notwithstanding the dynamic nature of the process of tourism development and the role of aboriginal people in this process, a number of principles can be drawn from the preceding discussion. First, just as the NWT is undergoing a devolution of power in terms of its political structure, greater local control of tourism development is required. This should not be interpreted to mean that the federal and territorial governments should withdraw from tourism development, for to do so would contribute to the further fragmentation and the effective loss of power at all levels. It does mean, however, that real decision-making must be shared with local communities. A second principle is that tourism education is essential if progress is to be made in terms of the complex issues that arise from tourism development. Both the hosts and the guests should be the target of these education programmes. Third, because these issues are so complex and because there are so many external factors that influence them, tourism should not be treated as the sole strategy for economic development in any community. It should be viewed as one component of a diversified strategy. Finally, tourism development should be kept to a scale that allows for effective local control. Rapid growth and large-scale development generally do not match the local resources needed to maintain control. As these principles continue to be introduced and ingrained in policy and programmes, the role of aboriginal people in the business of tourism throughout the NWT is likely to grow in a meaningful way.

REFERENCES

Acres International Limited, 1990, *Northwest Territories visitors survey summer 1989*, Prepared for the Department of Economic Development and Tourism, GNWT, Yellowknife

Arctic Coast Tourist Association, n.d., *Careers in tourism*, brochure, Cambridge Bay, NWT

Bureau of Statistics, 1991, *Statistics Quarterly*, **15** (3), GNWT, Yellowknife

Cohen, E., 1988, Authenticity and commoditization in tourism, *Annals of Tourism Research*, **15**: 371–385

Csargo, L., 1988, *Indian tourism overview*, Policy Development Branch, Economic Development Section, Indian and Northern Affairs Canada, Ottawa

DEDT (Department of Economic Development and Tourism), 1990a, *Quick facts, Marketing Section, Tourism and Parks*, GNWT, Yellowknife

DEDT, 1990b, *Building on strengths: a community based approach*, GNWT, Yellowknife

DEDT, 1990c, *Tourism: the northern lure*, GNWT, Yellowknife

DEDT, n.d.1, *Canada's Northwest Territories, 1993 explorers' guide*, GNWT, Yellowknife

DEDT, n.d.2, *Strategy for business development, Programs that mean business*, GNWT, Yellowknife

Department of Industry and Development, 1972, *Northwest Territories tourism investors' handbook*, GNWT, Yellowknife

Department of Indian Affairs and Northern Development, 1991, *Building a future*, Indian and Northern Affairs Canada, Ottawa

GNWT (Government of the Northwest Territories), 1992, *An agreement for the establishment of a National Park on Banks Island*, GNWT, Yellowknife

Government of Canada, 1989, *The Canadian aboriginal economic development strategy*, Government of Canada, Ottawa

Greenwood, D.J., 1977, Culture by the pound: an anthropological perspective of tourism as cultural commoditization. In Smith, V.L., ed., *Hosts and guests: the anthropology of tourism*, University of Pennsylvania Press, Philadelphia, pp. 129–138

Haywood, K.M., 1991, A strategic approach to developing hospitality and tourism education and training in remote, economically emerging and culturally sensitive regions: the case of Canada's Northwest Territories. In *New Horizons*, Conference Proceedings, The University of Calgary, Calgary

Hinch, T.D., Swinnerton, G.S., 1993, Tourism and Canada's Northwest Territories: issues and prospects, *Tourism Recreation Research*, **18**(2): 23–31

Hollinshead, K., 1992, 'White' gaze, 'red' people—shadow visions: the disidentification of 'Indians' in cultural tourism, *Leisure Studies*, **11**(1): 43–64

Keller, P., 1987, Stages of peripheral tourism development—Canada's Northwest Territories, *Tourism Management*, **8**(1): 20–32

MacCannell, D. 1973, Staged authenticity: arrangements of social space in tourist settings, *American Journal of Sociology*, **79**(3): 589–603

Mathieson, A., Wall, G., 1982, *Tourism: economic, physical and social impacts*, Longman Scientific and Technical, Harlow

Murphy, P.E., 1985, *Tourism: a community approach*, Methuen, New York

Native Council of Canada, 1987, *An inventory of Métis and non-status Indian tourism opportunities*, Ottawa, Canada

Nickels, S., Milne, S., Wenzel, G., 1991, Inuit perceptions of tourism development: the case of Clyde River, Baffin Island, NWT, *Etudes/Inuit/Studies*, **15**(1): 157–169

Outcrop Ltd, 1990, *Northwest Territories data book*, Outcrop Ltd, Yellowknife

Parker, B., 1993, Aboriginal tourism: from perception to reality. In Reid, L.J., ed., *Community and cultural tourism*, Conference Proceedings of the Travel and Tourism Research Association—Canada 1992, Regina, Saskatchewan, pp. 14–20

RT and Associates Ltd, 1992, *Kitikmeot CEDO survey of community economic development needs and aspirations*, RT and Associates Ltd, NWT

RT and Associates Ltd, 1993, *Kitikmeot economic development delivery models*, RT and Associates Ltd, NWT

Seale, R.G., 1992, Aboriginal societies, tourism, and conservation: the case of Canada's Northwest Territories, Paper presented at the 4th World Congress on National Parks and Protected Areas, Caracas, Venezuela

Smith, V.L., ed., 1989, *Hosts and guests: the anthropology of tourism*, 2nd edn, University of Pennsylvania Press, Philadelphia

Sweet, D.S., 1991, 'Let 'em loose': Pueblo Indian management of tourism, *American Indian Culture and Research Journal*, 15(4): 59–74

Tourism Canada, 1988, *The native tourism product: a position paper*, Government of Canada, Ottawa

Tourism Canada, 1990, *Federal tourism strategy Northwest Territories*, Industry, Science and Technology Canada, Government of Canada, Ottawa

Tourism Stream Action Strategy Committee, 1990, *An action strategy for sustainable tourism development*, Globe '90, Vancouver, Canada

Val, E., 1990, Parks, aboriginal peoples and sustainable tourism in development regions: the international experience and Canada's Northwest Territories. In Vining, J., ed., *Social science and natural resource recreation management*, Westview Press, Boulder, pp. 219–243

9 Access to the 'North'—But to What and for Whom? Public Access in the Swedish Countryside and the Case of a Proposed National Park in the Kiruna Mountains

KLAS SANDELL

INTRODUCTION

The right of public access to the countryside is a basic element of outdoor life and tourism in Sweden. This *allemansrätt* (every person's right) is not a statute, but rather it exists in the 'free space' left between various restrictions, these being principally economic interests (e.g. agriculture and forestry), local people's privacy (e.g. restricted areas around houses), and preservation (e.g. areas closed in order to protect rare species). For example, one is permitted to camp for a night, to bathe, to traverse any land (at least on foot), to traverse any lake or river, to pick flowers, berries and mushrooms and to light a fire *provided* that none of the said restrictions is infringed. This means that the right of public access is interpreted from case to case. There is an obscure field at the interface of what is permitted for the public (e.g. tourists) and what is ruled out by the claims of landowners, local inhabitants and nature conservancy authorities (Figure 9.1).

This chapter will first outline the right of public access in Sweden, particularly with regard to increased international integration and the recent interest in nature-oriented tourism as a form of environmental education. The case of a proposed national park in the Kiruna Mountains north of the Arctic Circle in Sweden will then be used as an illustration of how the right of public access can be regarded as a crossroads where various interests intersect. If Sweden in general is more interesting for nature-oriented tourism (due to, for example, its sparse population and right of public access) compared with the rest of Europe, its northern part, with its high

Polar Tourism: Tourism in the Arctic and Antarctic Regions
Edited by C. Michael Hall and Margaret E. Johnston. © John Wiley & Sons Ltd, 1995

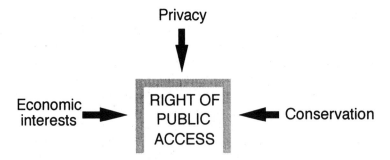

Figure 9.1. Traditional restrictions and 'free space' in the countryside. The right of everyone to move freely, pick flowers, etc. in the countryside is here identified as the 'free space' left between the traditional restrictions of (i) economic interests, (ii) privacy and (iii) conservation

mountains, is the most manifest example of this opportunity. 'The interior north includes extensive areas of a truly wilderness character, sometimes described as the last remaining wilderness areas in Western Europe' (Aldskogius, 1987, p. 15). Therefore, if we want to study polar tourism and the right of public access, tourism-oriented national parks in the north of Sweden will be of special interest.

FROM RURAL INTEGRATION TO URBAN CONSUMPTION

With roots in peasant society

Traceable at least back to the county laws of the Middle Ages, the right of public access can be regarded as a 'tradition' deriving from pre-industrial society—the tradition, that is, of being able to move about the countryside undisturbed, provided that one did not disturb or damage the property of the local inhabitants. Generally one was not entitled to take away or damage anything of economic value, for example trees, crops, birch-bark and acorns (which were used to feed the animals). In principle this rule still applies. What was 'left over'—picking flowers, berries and mushrooms, or making a camp-fire and staying overnight—became a part of what we now refer to as the right of public access. It can also be noted that when, for example, berries were of special economic interest there was discussion of the need to limit the right of public access (Ahlström, 1992b). As in other cultural spheres, the right of public access was also to some extent a question of supporting the interests of those without property. The survival of this right to the present day is largely attributable to the fact that Sweden has vast areas of extensively used land and a sparse population.

From the beginning of the present century, demands emerged for the protection of certain areas and certain species through national parks, protective legislation and bird sanctuaries, for example. There arose a need for open-air and wilderness areas as arenas for recreation and as a part of various educational endeavours, not the least of which was the attempt to create a sense of national fellowship and identity. There was also an abundance of myth-making about the special Swedish 'feeling for nature' (Sandell and Sörlin, forthcoming). All this was quite different from the production focus of the rural people (Löfgren, 1987). Parallel with shorter working hours, holiday legislation and a higher general economic standard, outdoor recreation became an important aspect of physical resource planning and policy.

Looking for hard facts about current outdoor life in Sweden we can note that: 'The dominant outdoor activities are walks for pleasure and exercise, cross-country strolling and visits to open-air bathing-places. Each of these activities is practised by some 80 per cent of the population in the 16–74 age-range' (Statistics Sweden, 1987, p. 115; my translation here and in all other cases). Some 60 per cent of those in this age-range say that they walk in the forest at least once a month or almost every week (Statistics Sweden, 1987, p. 42).

In modern times the tradition of the right of public access has been bolstered by legislation. Instances of this include the protection of shores against new building and other obstacles to mobile outdoor life; the obligation of the landowner in specific circumstances to make arrangements to let people pass through his/her fences; the identification and recognition of areas of specific interest for outdoor recreation as part of national physical resource planning; the inclusion of matters of conservancy and responsible use in legislation concerning agriculture and forestry; and the existence of a special law forbidding the driving of motor vehicles off-road for recreational purposes if there is no snow on the ground (which is important from the point of view of non-mechanised outdoor recreation).

INTERNATIONAL INTEGRATION AND THE RIGHT OF PUBLIC ACCESS

Today Sweden is becoming more and more internationally integrated, and tourism is an important part of this process. 'What is it, then, that attracts foreign tourists to Sweden? ... Putting it briefly, one might say that it is the countryside that attracts people, and the fact that Sweden does not really have a mass tourist industry' (Sahlberg et al., 1993, p. 91). This means that Sweden's attraction for foreign tourists is closely related to the right of public access. In general, traditions of right of public access to the countryside seem to be associated with the sparsely populated circumpolar

countries. There are similar but, from the point of view of tourism, sometimes more restricted situations in Norway and Finland. (In Norway there
is a special law regarding the right of public access.) But it is hardly
possible to speak of any right of public access in Denmark, or further south
in Europe. In a comparison of the Nordic countries, Vogel (1990, p. 125)
states that:

> The types of leisure activities in the Nordic countries are quite similar owing
> to common cultural traditions, similarities in settlements and climate, etc.
> About 15 activities have been studied. The results indicate that outdoor life
> and exercise have a strong position in the Nordic countries.

It has been argued that the Nordic tradition of *friluftsliv* (open-air life) is
characterised by simplicity and popularity, emphasising its difference from
the more commercialised and specialised outdoor activities of North America
and Continental Europe, which are asserted to be more motorised, 'high-
tech' and action-oriented—far from the tradition of the right of public
access (see Sandell, 1991a for further references and Reed and Rothenberg,
1993 for a discussion of *friluftsliv* and the Norwegian roots of deep
ecology).

In short, today we have a combination of three themes with regard to the
right of public access in the Swedish countryside. First, the fact that 'There
is probably not such an extensive right of public access as the Swedish in
many—if indeed any—other parts of the world' (Ahlström, 1982, p. 76).
Simultaneously, 'It cannot be sufficiently emphasised that the utilisation of
the right of public access is first and foremost a question of judgment'
(Rosén, 1979, p. 13). In addition to this the increased integration in Europe
involves the perspective that 'Sweden can become Europe's open-air
recreation area' (*För en rikare fritid*, 1990, p. 16).

Currently, there are frequent examples of problems related to tourists
and their (mis)use of the right of public access. Such problems are, thus
far, largely related to the most intensely used tourism areas, mainly in the
southern parts of Sweden. There is also a widespread concern about the
right of public access if Sweden were integrated further with the rest of
Europe, for example as a member of the EC/EU (European Community/
European Union). For example, this is reflected in two recent surveys
carried out among municipalities and among organisations dealing with
outdoor recreation and in which Swedish membership in the EC was
seen as a major threat to the right of public access (Ahlström, 1992a;
Naturvårdsverket, 1993).

This has brought to the fore the question of legislating the right of public
access. It has also been proposed that this right be limited to Swedish
citizens and permanent residents (Westerlund, 1991, p. 143). So far,

however, no major group has claimed that the right of public access should be defined by law. On the contrary, many reasons for the maintenance of the present situation have been put forward by, for instance, organisations dealing with outdoor recreation and the Swedish Environmental Protection Agency. The main reason has been that as this is a question of a tradition bound with judgement, consideration and regional variations, any law would probably limit the right of public access, instead of preserving or widening it.

How governmental reports have dealt with the further integration of Sweden into the rest of Europe (mainly EC/EU) and the right of public access is important with regard to tourism and recreation policy. In May 1991 it was stated: 'It can further be noted that the Swedish right of public access is not affected either by the EEA (European Economic Area) agreement or a future membership of the EC . . .' (*Konsekvenser* . . ., 1991, p. 88). Two years later, however, some problems were noted, for example, perhaps 'a land-owner might invoke the EC legislation protecting personal liberty and rights in order to claim that his ownership right is infringed by the right of public access' (SOU, 1993a, p. 363). But it was still claimed that no major problems would occur. Shortly after this, though, it was suggested that the right of public access should be included in the Constitution (but without any definition of its contents) parallel with greater emphasis on the right of private ownership (SOU, 1993b, p. 28, 86). Even though the latter discussion is also a part of a wider ideological context, it suggests (together with the surveys and arguments referred to above) that the right of public access might be threatened by European integration, perhaps mainly through conflicting views of ownership. We will perhaps have to take into consideration that public resistance may turn out to be so strong that the European integration (at least in the form of EC/EU membership) will itself be threatened by the question of the right of public access.

ENVIRONMENTAL PERCEPTIONS AND ENVIRONMENTALISM

It is frequently claimed that close contact with nature encourages a sense of respect, care and active environmental involvement. Many factors are, of course, involved in using outdoor recreation as a means of attaining greater environmental awareness, for example, the type of activity, the depth of the environmental involvement and other (perhaps conflicting) sources of inspiration and information. In any case, it could be argued that the qualities of the landscape and the adaptation of activities to the landscape probably are crucial elements in respect of public environmental awareness and of the attainment of attitudes and lifestyles in line with a more sustainable development (see e.g. Sandell, 1991a and forthcoming).

Thus, while the right of public access is a means to an end for conservation and environmental awareness, the defence of this right is at the same time an important aspect of conservation.

Considering the current large-scale monocultures of modern agriculture and forestry it seems necessary to add 'industrialisation' and 'specialisation' of the landscape as a fourth limitation of the 'space left' for the public right of access, in addition to the three limitations discussed in the introduction to this chapter. It must be remembered that not only is the 'free space' left for the right of public access restricted by what is not allowed, but also the value or content of this free space could be restricted by, for example, noise and landscape exploitation. The increasing 'industrialisation' of agriculture and forestry makes it physically more complicated to traverse a landscape on foot. There are no ditches, no intermediate zones between field and forest, no pastures, but instead dense 'spruce fields' of the same age. Hägerstrand (1988, p. 46) states: 'These shifts [from pastures to forest, etc.] taken together mean that the landscape which once upon a time had gradual transitions between settlements and deep forest has been replaced with a new landscape, constituted by monotonous blocks with sharp edges'. Even though counter-strategies are now being carried out in order to give greater weight to conservation and aesthetic perspectives, the trend remains conspicuous (cf. Bernes, 1993).

There is, however, also another (and perhaps more important) aspect of the limitation of the right of public access caused by the 'industrialisation' of the landscape, namely the reduced access to 'free nature'. It is a question of reduced access to a landscape which to a large extent follows natural rhythms in time and space (i.e. where the location, behaviour and features of many landscape elements such as animals, trees, water and land-forms are in accordance with ecological processes, not human rationale). As an illustration one may quote Laquist (1990, pp. 18–19), who, in a depiction of the Swedish forest of the future, writes: 'It is no longer a pleasure to be in the forest. Not now that its variety and multiplicity have disappeared. The joy of discovery and flights of imagination have been hewn away by forestry. ... The Swedish forest of the future is a plantation'. This further specialisation of the landscape (including special areas set aside for recreation purposes) will probably be an important aspect of everyone's perception of nature (and therefore of environmental policy) in the future.

THE CASE OF A NATIONAL PARK IN THE KIRUNA MOUNTAINS

The 'northern wilderness'

Looking for good opportunities for nature-oriented tourism in Sweden we could note the tradition of 'going north'. Already the founding of the Swedish Touring Club in 1885 was closely linked with the increasing interest in the Swedish high mountains as a recreation area. In addition, the 'exotic' Laplanders and a poor understanding of the high mountains as a cultural landscape made it a 'wilderness' for the urban people from the south. As the Laplanders' ownership of the land was not fully recognised it was also easy to establish relatively large parts of the high mountains as national parks. Today, 22.5 per cent of the total land area in the northernmost county of Sweden is protected in different ways for the purposes of preservation, conservation and recreation (Grundsten, 1992, p. 156). This could be compared with about 1–2 per cent in the south of Sweden. The Swedish population is also distributed very unevenly with only 10 per cent living in the northern half of the country. Therefore, polar tourism and its interrelationship with the right of public access and national parks are of utmost importance with regard to nature-oriented tourism in Sweden.

Background for the proposed park

During the latter part of the 1980s there was a debate concerning the possibilities of establishing a large national park in the area around Lake Torneträsk, involving two smaller existing national parks, a number of marked trails, mountain huts and the Abisko tourist centre. If established, it will be one of the largest national parks in Europe (4360 square kilometres; Figure 9.2).

Looking into the historical background for the current interest in tourism in this area it could be noted that in 1903 the railway between Narvik, Norway and Kiruna, Sweden (a mining community which is now a town of about 21 000 inhabitants, with its own airport) was opened. Even though the railway was intended primarily for the transportation of iron ore, it nevertheless came to play an important role for tourism as it made the 'wilderness' in the area around Lake Torneträsk easily accessible. In 1909 Abisko National Park (one of the first such parks in Sweden) was established in the area. Marked trails and mountain huts were established, used for hiking in the summer and for cross-country skiing in the winter. In 1976 the area was included in one of 25 primary recreation areas in Sweden, and at the beginning of the 1980s a road was built parallel to the railway between Kiruna and Narvik. This is reflected in an increase in the number of people staying in or passing through the area: from 200 000 in 1980 to 650 000 in 1989 (Bäck, 1993, p. 107). A part of the area is also included in the Unesco list of special biospheres for research and environmental studies (Naturvårdsverket, 1989, p. 41).

The intention behind the plan for a large national park in the area is that 'it is good for nature conservancy if much larger groups of people than at

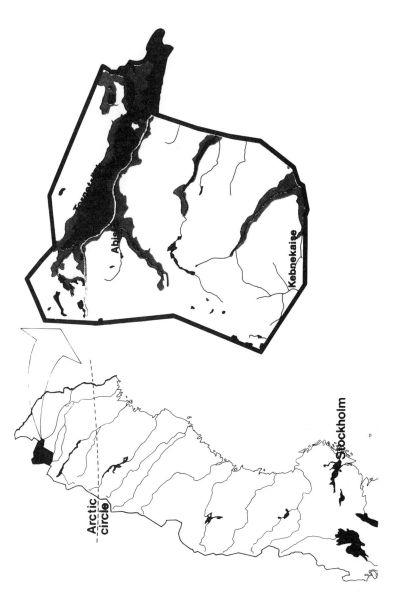

Figure 9.2. The location of the proposed national park in the north of Sweden (drawn by Marie-Louise Modéer)

present can be given the possibility of genuine and first-rate experiences of nature' (Naturvårdsverket, 1989, p. 6).

In a manner that from an international point of view is unique, the landscape offers a combination of on the one hand mountain steeps and alpine topography, and on the other hand the vast and roadless brush moors of the Swedish fells. No other area in Europe outside Sweden offers within an area of comparable size both stupendous massifs and unexploited roadless wilderness-type landscape. Here are to be found Kebnekaise, Sweden's highest mountain, Abisko with its extraordinarily rich vegetation, the lovely lake Torneträsk, etc., etc. The proposal for a national park in the Kiruna mountains involves a widening of the traditional Swedish view of the national park concept. . . . The national park is to be established . . . in order to strengthen the area's legal protection against exploitation, to raise its status and attraction value, and to bring into being in a practical sense a co-ordinated administration that protects nature, is outward-looking, is locally based and generates jobs. Thus the goal is that there should be a high degree of interplay between nature conservancy and regional development (Naturvårdsverket, 1989, pp. 8–9).

An important element of the plan for the proposed national park is the designation of six zones in order to separate different types of recreation and protection requirements. In the largest zone, the 'wilderness', the guiding principle is that the right of public access shall be unrestricted. The marked trails will constitute another zone, and along the trails there will be bridges and cabins. Protection zones involve a ban on visiting or other restrictions of the right of public access owing to the needs of conservation, research and reindeer keeping. These protection zones are to be utilised, however, but with restraint. There will be zones where snowmobiling is prohibited, except for use in connection with work. The road across the area, and a strip 3 kilometres wide along each side of it, will be a special zone where buildings and other such exploitation will be permitted. Lake Torneträsk will constitute the sixth zone, with special regulations. Another interesting aspect of the proposed national park is the plan for using professional rangers for information, education and guiding besides service and supervision. It is also planned that the tourist centre in Abisko shall include attractive exhibitions, a big cinema and shops (Naturvårdsverket, 1989).

Meeting-place or field of conflict?

Even though various interested parties were represented in the working group for the national park, there appeared such a clash of interests that the plans have now been put on the shelf for an indefinite period. The main obstacle would appear to be the resistance from local groups, principally in Kiruna, who are afraid that their use of the area would be curtailed, partly because of possible restrictions on such current outdoor activities as, for instance, the use of snowscooters. There seems also to be a fear that in the future there could be more severe restrictions than those now proposed, for instance, with regard to hunting and fishing. Also, a general scepticism regarding the intentions of central authorities appears to be an important component of the local opposition.

Various interests clash when it comes to defining who is the public with the right of access, and defining the nature of that access. Keeping in mind the four above-mentioned restricting factors for the right of public access (economic interest, privacy, preservation and changes in the landscape), it is possible to regard the park proposal as constituting in certain of its elements a meeting-place, or perhaps more accurately a field of conflict, for various interests.

With regard to economic interests, local people's concern in fishing and hunting for their own consumption is probably a major obstacle for the proposed park. Ore prospecting for employment opportunities in the future and the localisation of employment with regard to research and conservation are other examples of clashes of economic interests in this case (Kirunafjällens nationalpark, 1987; Svar till . . ., 1988). It is clearly stated in the plan, though, that reindeer keeping will not be subject to restrictions (Naturvårdsverket, 1989, p. 12).

Privacy is probably one of the major sources of opposition to the park proposal, even though very few people, in fact, live in the proposed park area itself, and is mainly due to the differences in outdoor recreation habits between local people (e.g. from Kiruna) and tourists (e.g. from Stockholm or abroad). The local people are often very much in favour of snow-mobiling, accessibility through the use of roads, and activities like hunting and fishing. The tourists from far off, however, often accord high priority to silence, hiking, scenic views and cross-country skiing. In an appeal (with about 12 000 signatures) from Kiruna it was asserted that: 'The establishment of a "Kiruna national park" is a clear intrusion upon the "right of public access"' (Nej till . . ., 1988).

Preservation, or conservation, was a major reason for the park proposal. A general problem is of course to what extent the goal of conservancy is threatened by the large number of visitors planned. It is claimed in the proposal, however, that the area 'can tolerate a substantially increased number of visitors provided that suitable measures are taken' (Naturvårdsverket, 1989, p. 6). The use of different zones (cf. Bäck et al., 1989) and of professional rangers must be seen as a vital element of this strategy. It is also interesting to note that one of the main goals behind the proposal (e.g. with regard to the park centre) is 'to create an understanding of the need for nature conservancy' (Naturvårdsverket, 1989, p. 25). In other words, one purpose of the park is to increase the interest in the type of functions that the park and the instigating authority themselves represent. Though of course there need be no conflict of interests in this, it may at the same time be one of several underlying reasons for the local scepticism.

The question of *industrialisation* and *specialisation* of the landscape is also relevant with regard to the proposed park. Obviously, because of the railway and later the road, the accessibility of the region has already increased dramatically. If, on the other hand, the protection zones for reindeer keeping (the only occupation in the area that really involves large-scale use of land) should be very extensive in space and/or time, it would mean a somewhat reduced physical accessibility. But since there are no other plans for agriculture or forestry in the area, this is probably a minor problem in this case (cf. Bernes, 1993; Bostedt and Mattsson, 1993). On the other hand there is reason to draw attention to the risk of standardised experiences of nature in line with the discussion above with regard to a

Figure 9.3. Contemporary and traditional restrictions on 'free space' in the countryside. The right of everyone to move freely, pick flowers, etc. in the countryside is here identified as the 'free space' left between the traditional restrictions of (i) economic interests, (ii) privacy and (iii) conservation, but currently also (iv) the increasing industrialisation and specialisation of the landscape. In addition to these general restrictions various examples with regard to the proposed national park discussed in the text are given

landscape with 'less free nature'. Studies have shown that the majority of tourists do not venture far from the central points of departure (Bäck, 1993, p. 107); and if the road-zone (6 kilometres across) becomes heavily exploited and the number of visitors is very large, then there is the risk that the landscape will be an arena for prefabricated experiences. Here the inventiveness, attitude to nature, energy and resourcefulness of the rangers will have a crucial role to play, especially if the goal of environmental education is taken into account. In addition it is necessary to remember the risk of adverse external environmental influence on the landscape, in line with the discussion above concerning environmental perception and environmentalism. Even today the hikers in certain southern parts of the Swedish mountain chain (in Härjedalen) have been advised to avoid the natural water in the area because of the acidification (Sörlin, 1992, p. 272), and large liming projects are carried out to counteract this.

In summary, there are many interested parties involved in the various restrictions on the right of public access which is the point of departure for the proposed national park (and also, with variations, for nature-oriented tourism in general in Sweden). Furthermore, these interested parties have up to now had such incompatible perspectives that it has not been possible to carry out the project (Figure 9.3).

'TERRITORIAL' TOURISM—AN OPENING?

It could be argued that a basic question with regard to tourism development (and other development as well) is to what extent it takes its point of departure from a territorial perspective, i.e. an endeavour to adapt to the local natural and cultural context (cf., e.g. Friedmann and Weaver, 1979; Sandell, 1988, 1991b). Today, the potential of a locally based, small-scale, ecological, nature-oriented, eco-tourism is increasingly being discussed (Moulin, 1980; Müller, 1990; Andersen et al., 1990; För en rikare fritid, 1990, pp. 16–17; Bergfors, 1990, pp. 41–42; Faarlund, 1990; Grahn, 1991; Aronsson, 1993; and also the introduction to this book). Here, a territorial approach is often emphasised and elements of such a perspective can also, to some extent, be traced in the national park proposal studied here.

A tourism that really finds its point of departure in the local context would probably lead to less distrust of the long-term intentions of central authorities and other external interested parties than appears to exist today. A major factor in this respect is quite simply that it is impossible for external interests to exploit a true territorial tourism. With regard to the conflicts around the right of public access, a territorially based tourism seems to be the most sustainable approach as the tourism (and the tourists' interests in having access) will be well grounded among the local population.

other words, one purpose of the park is to increase the interest in the type of functions that the park and the instigating authority themselves represent. Though of course there need be no conflict of interests in this, it may at the same time be one of several underlying reasons for the local scepticism.

The question of *industrialisation* and *specialisation* of the landscape is also relevant with regard to the proposed park. Obviously, because of the railway and later the road, the accessibility of the region has already increased dramatically. If, on the other hand, the protection zones for reindeer keeping (the only occupation in the area that really involves large-scale use of land) should be very extensive in space and/or time, it would mean a somewhat reduced physical accessibility. But since there are no other plans for agriculture or forestry in the area, this is probably a minor problem in this case (cf. Bernes, 1993; Bostedt and Mattsson, 1993). On the other hand there is reason to draw attention to the risk of standardised experiences of nature in line with the discussion above with regard to a

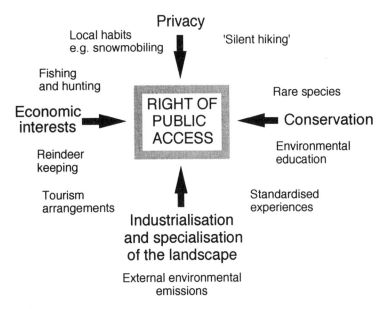

Figure 9.3. Contemporary and traditional restrictions on 'free space' in the countryside. The right of everyone to move freely, pick flowers, etc. in the countryside is here identified as the 'free space' left between the traditional restrictions of (i) economic interests, (ii) privacy and (iii) conservation, but currently also (iv) the increasing industrialisation and specialisation of the landscape. In addition to these general restrictions various examples with regard to the proposed national park discussed in the text are given

landscape with 'less free nature'. Studies have shown that the majority of tourists do not venture far from the central points of departure (Bäck, 1993, p. 107); and if the road-zone (6 kilometres across) becomes heavily exploited and the number of visitors is very large, then there is the risk that the landscape will be an arena for prefabricated experiences. Here the inventiveness, attitude to nature, energy and resourcefulness of the rangers will have a crucial role to play, especially if the goal of environmental education is taken into account. In addition it is necessary to remember the risk of adverse external environmental influence on the landscape, in line with the discussion above concerning environmental perception and environmentalism. Even today the hikers in certain southern parts of the Swedish mountain chain (in Härjedalen) have been advised to avoid the natural water in the area because of the acidification (Sörlin, 1992, p. 272), and large liming projects are carried out to counteract this.

In summary, there are many interested parties involved in the various restrictions on the right of public access which is the point of departure for the proposed national park (and also, with variations, for nature-oriented tourism in general in Sweden). Furthermore, these interested parties have up to now had such incompatible perspectives that it has not been possible to carry out the project (Figure 9.3).

'TERRITORIAL' TOURISM—AN OPENING?

It could be argued that a basic question with regard to tourism development (and other development as well) is to what extent it takes its point of departure from a territorial perspective, i.e. an endeavour to adapt to the local natural and cultural context (cf., e.g. Friedmann and Weaver, 1979; Sandell, 1988, 1991b). Today, the potential of a locally based, small-scale, ecological, nature-oriented, eco-tourism is increasingly being discussed (Moulin, 1980; Müller, 1990; Andersen et al., 1990; För en rikare fritid, 1990, pp. 16–17; Bergfors, 1990, pp. 41–42; Faarlund, 1990; Grahn, 1991; Aronsson, 1993; and also the introduction to this book). Here, a territorial approach is often emphasised and elements of such a perspective can also, to some extent, be traced in the national park proposal studied here.

A tourism that really finds its point of departure in the local context would probably lead to less distrust of the long-term intentions of central authorities and other external interested parties than appears to exist today. A major factor in this respect is quite simply that it is impossible for external interests to exploit a true territorial tourism. With regard to the conflicts around the right of public access, a territorially based tourism seems to be the most sustainable approach as the tourism (and the tourists' interests in having access) will be well grounded among the local population.

The industrialisation of the landscape, discussed above, will also be hampered by a more territorial approach as a multidimensional utilisation of the landscape will be of great value for tourism.

Some of the 'pure' naturalists who want to avoid civilisation completely (even if local and small-scale) and external tourist entrepreneurs might lose by an increase of interest in territorial tourism. Another group that might lose in such a situation is the local population who are not sufficiently involved in environmental matters as to be prepared to alter their leisure habits (e.g. in the studied case, to change from snowscooters to skis due to the demand from the tourists), and who at the same time have no occupational link with the landscape (e.g. through fishing or reindeer keeping—and in other areas through agriculture or forestry) or with commercial tourist activities.

By way of conclusion, however, I should like to move in the other direction and draw attention to another group that would gain by a more territorial tourism, the group of all of us. We should gain through the reduction both in effluents and in the consumption of non-renewable resources (if, for example, transportation is limited and carried out with renewable sources of energy), besides the leisure qualities involved and the potential for rural development.

ACKNOWLEDGEMENTS

Financial support from the Swedish Council for Planning and Coordination of Research, the help of Malcolm Forbes with the English translation and the map drawn by Marie-Louise Modéer are gratefully acknowledged. I should also like to express my appreciation for valuable comments from colleagues, principally I. Ahlström, H. Aldskogius, I. Elander, S-G. Hultman, S. Jäggi, S. Sörlin and T. Strömberg, and for informative discussions with different persons involved in the Kiruna case.

REFERENCES

Ahlström, I., 1982, *Allemansrätt och friluftsvett: en bok för friluftsfolk om konsten att umgås med natur, markägare och annat friluftsfolk*, Liber, Stockholm
Ahlström, I., 1992a, *Hoten mot allemansrätten*, Firma Friluftsplanering and FRISAM, Stockholm
Ahlström, I., 1992b, Allemansrätten: en sedvana att vårda. In *Naturia, Europa och allemansrätten*, Brevskolan, Stockholm, pp. 7–15
Aldskogius, H., 1987, Geographic research on tourism and recreation in Sweden, Paper presented at the 83rd Annual Meeting for the Association of American Geographers, Portland, Oregon
Andersen, A.B., Moen, B.F., Thoroddsson, T., Väisänen, P.K., Zettersten, G., 1990, *Naturvägledning i Norden*, NORD 1990:52, Nordiska Ministerrådet, Copenhagen

Aronsson, L., 1993, Sustainable tourism systems, Paper for the Second International School of Rural Development, 28 June–9 July, 1993, Centre for Development Studies, University College Galway, Ireland

Bäck, L., 1993, The Torneträsk region. In Aldskogius, H., ed., *Cultural life, recreation and tourism*, The National Atlas of Sweden, Almqvist & Wiksell International, Stockholm, pp. 106–107

Bäck, L., Josefsson, M., Strömquist, L., 1989, Land capability, recreational land-use and conservation strategies in a sensitive mountain environment: a method study from the Kiruna mountains, Sweden, UNGI Report No. 73, Dept of Physical Geography, Uppsala University, Uppsala

Bergfors, U., 1990, *Allemansrätten ur rättsekonomisk synpunkt: historia, regelverk och dagsläge*, Report No. 115, Inst. f. skogsekonomi, Sveriges Lantbruksuniversitet, Umeå, Sweden

Bernes, C., 1993, *The Nordic environment: present state, trends and threats*, Nordic Council of Ministers' Nordic Environment Report Group, NORD 1993:12, Copenhagen

Bostedt, G., Mattsson, L., 1993, *The value of forest nature for tourism and the effects of forestry modifications: results from two Swedish case studies*, Report No. 163, Inst. f. Skogsekonomi, Sveriges Lantbruksuniversitet, Umeå, Sweden

Faarlund, N., 1990, Om møtet med fri natur som metode i miljøundervisningen, *Mestrefjellet*, **37**: 21–23

För en rikare fritid, 1990, Ett diskussionsunderlag, Sveriges Turistråd, Landstingsförbundet, Svenska Kommunförbundet, Stockholm

Friedmann, J., Weaver, C., 1979, *Territory and function*, Edward Arnold, London

Grahn, P., 1991, Using tourism to protect existing culture: a project in Swedish Lapland, *Leisure Studies*, **10**(1): 33–47

Grundsten, C., 1992, Protected countryside. In Bernes, C., Grundsten, C., eds., *The environment*, The National Atlas of Sweden, Almqvist & Wiksell International, Stockholm, pp. 152–163

Hägerstrand, T., 1988, Krafter som format det svenska kulturlandskapet. In Heurling, B., ed., *Mark och vatten år 2010*, Bostadsdepartementet, Stockholm, pp. 16–55

Kirunafjällens nationalpark, 1987, Från kommunkansliet, Kiruna kommun, 1987-12-29, undertecknat av Gunnar Pettersson, kommunstyrelsens ordförande, (Pronouncement with regard to the proposed national park in the Kiruna mountains from the local authority in Kiruna)

Konsekvenser av ett svenskt EG-medlemsskap maj 1991, 1991, Utrikesdepartementets handelsavdelning, Allmänna förlaget, Stockholm

Laquist, A., 1990, Det är nu vi väljer vilken skog vi vill ha, *Sveriges Natur*, Stockholm, **1**: 18–23

Löfgren, O., 1987, Känslans förvandling: tiden, naturen och hemmet i den borgerliga kulturen. In Frykman, J., Löfgren, O., *Den kultiverade människan*, Liber, Stockholm, pp. 21–127

Moulin, C.L., 1980, Plan for ecological and cultural tourism involving participation of local population and associations. In Hawkins, D.E., Shafer, E.L., Rovelstad, J.M., eds., *Tourism planning and development issues*, George Washington University, Washington DC, pp. 199–211

Müller, H., 1990, *For en reiselivsutvikling i harmoni med menneske og natur* (oversatt av Jäggi, S.), Hovedforedrag ved konferanse om reiseliv arrangert på Oppdal, Norge, 12–14 februar av FOR-UT forskningsinstitutt for Friluftsliv

Naturvårdsverket, 1989, *Kirunafjällens nationalpark: rapport från en projektgrupp*, Report No. 3595, Naturvårdsverket, Stockholm

Naturvårdsverket, 1993, *Allemansrätten: En enkätundersökning*, Naturvårdsverket, 10 March, mimeo

Nej till Kiruna nationalpark! Namninsamling från den 12 augusti 1988, Från kommittén för 'Nej till Kiruna nationalpark' till Kiruna kommunstyrelse och kommunfullmäktige, 1988-09, undertecknat av Sten Erik Innalla, Erik Klint, Helge Lampinen och Atle Talo, (An appeal with regard to the proposed national park in the Kiruna mountains to the local authority in Kiruna)

Reed, P., Rothenberg, D., eds., 1993, *Wisdom in the open air: the Norwegian roots of deep ecology*, University of Minnesota Press, Minneapolis and London

Rosén, B., 1979, *Allemansrätt—allemansskyldighet*, Rabén & Sjögren, Stockholm

Sahlberg, B., Sehlin, H., Vidén, L., Wärmark, A., 1993, Tourism in Sweden. In Aldskogius, H., ed., *Cultural life, recreation and tourism*, The National Atlas of Sweden, Almqvist & Wiksell International, Stockholm, pp. 80–91

Sandell, K., 1988, *Ecostrategies in theory and practice: farmers' perspectives on water, nutrients and sustainability in low-resource agriculture in the dry zone of Sri Lanka*, (diss.), Linköping Studies in Arts and Science, No. 19, Linköping

Sandell, K., 1991a, Outdoor recreation—re-creation or creation?, *Nordisk Samhällsgeografisk Tidskrift*, **14**: 35–46

Sandell, K., 1991b, 'Ecostrategies' and environmentalism—the case of outdoor life and *friluftsliv*, *Geogr. Ann.*, **73B** (2): 133–141

Sandell, K., forthcoming, *Perceptions of landscapes—perspectives on nature*, Swedish Council for Planning and Coordination of Research, Stockholm

Sandell, K., Sörlin, S., forthcoming, Naturen som fostrare: friluftsliv och ideologi i svenskt 1900-tal, *Historisk Tidskrift*

Sörlin, S., ed., 1992, *Humanekologi: naturens resurser—människans försörjning*, Carlssons, Stockholm

SOU (Statens Offentliga Utredningar), 1993a, *EG och våra grundlagar*, Justitiedepartementet, Stockholm (Government Official Reports) 1993:**14**

SOU, 1993b, *Fri- och rättighetsfrågor, del A, regeringsformen, delbetänkande av fri- och rättighetskommittén*, Justitiedepartementet, Stockholm (Government Official Reports) 1993:**40**

Statistics Sweden, 1987, *Levnadsförhållanden*, Rapport No. 56, Fritid (Official Statistics of Sweden, Living Conditions, Report No. 56, Leisure), Statistics Sweden, Stockholm

Svar till Kiruna kommun angående Kirunafjällens nationalpark, 1988, Från Länsstyrelsen i Norrbottens län och Statens Naturvårdsverk, 1988-05-31, undertecknat av Jan-Olof Hedström, länsråd samt Lars Erik Esping, avd. chef. (Answer to the local authority in Kiruna with regard to the proposed national park in the Kiruna Mountains from the County Government Board of Norrbotten and the Swedish Environmental Protection Agency)

Vogel, J., 1990, *Leva i Norden, levnadsnivå och ojämlikhet vid slutet av 80-talet*, Nordisk statistisk skriftserie, No. 54, Nordiska statistiska sekretariatet, Copenhagen

Westerlund, S., 1991, *EG:s miljöregler ur svenskt perspektiv*, Naturskyddsföreningen, Stockholm

10 Issues in Antarctic Tourism

C. MICHAEL HALL AND MARISKA WOUTERS

> Antarctic tourism is not controversial, everyone agrees it's inevitable. What's controversial is how it's done (Parfitt, 1988, in Enzenbacher, 1991, p. 102).

Tourism is now recognised as a legitimate Antarctic activity. However, there is substantial debate over the appropriate means by which tourism should be controlled and managed at both the macro and micro planning and policy levels. This chapter introduces the reader to some of the issues surrounding the development of Antarctic tourism and the search for an appropriate management regime which are discussed in this and the following chapters.

ANTARCTIC TOURISM

Tourism in Antarctica is highly seasonal (Janiskee, 1991). Due to the harshness of the climate, access to the continent is restricted to the Austral summer between late October and early March. This is also the time of year when there are 24 hours of sunlight a day. Such a limited tourist season will clearly have implications for the management of Antarctic tourism.

The majority of Antarctic tourists originate from northern hemisphere countries and then assemble in Australasia or South America for transit to Antarctica (Wace, 1990). According to Enzenbacher (1992a), Americans currently comprise the largest percentage of Antarctic tourists. These passengers are usually older and affluent, as the cost of an Antarctic cruise is substantial (Madden, 1993). However, Wouters (1993) noted that individual carriers may have substantial variations in tourist origin. In 1993 the *Kapitan Khlebnikov* carried approximately 36 per cent Australian visitors, 34 per cent from the United States, 10 per cent German and the remainder came from Great Britain and South Africa (Sanson, 1993). Passengers on the *Frontier Spirit* cruise in January–February 1993 consisted of about 50 per cent Japanese, about 25 per cent German, Austrian and Swiss, about 20 per cent American and about 5 per cent Australian. Many had travelled on the

Polar Tourism: Tourism in the Arctic and Antarctic Regions
Edited by C. Michael Hall and Margaret E. Johnston. © John Wiley & Sons Ltd, 1995

ship and/or visited Antarctica before. The average age was early to mid-fifties. As many of the passengers were non-English-speaking nationals, staff experienced difficulty instructing visitors ashore (Cooper, 1993). The variation in tourist profiles may be due to departure points, as the *Kapitan Khlebnikov* travelled from Fremantle to Bluff (New Zealand), and the *Frontier Spirit* used Bluff as both departure and arrival point.

FORMS OF ANTARCTIC TOURIST ACTIVITIES

Antarctic tourists have a wide-ranging choice of land- or sea-based services to travel to Antarctica. Travel within the continent can consist of travel by foot, skis, snow machines, wheeled and over-snow vehicles, zodiacs, helicopters or aircraft. Zodiacs are a particularly popular form of travel, as they provide safe and reliable transport to normally inaccessible coastal areas, while limiting the number of tourists landing at a particular site at any given time (Enzenbacher, 1991).

Seaborne tourism

Tourism by ship and air began slowly in the late 1950s, when the Chilean and Argentinian governments organised the first tourist expeditions to the Antarctic Peninsula (Brewster, 1982). Ships have the easiest access to Antarctica as aeroplanes are easily affected by changing weather patterns and the difficulty of finding safe landing sites (see Table 1.2). Seaborne passengers normally make up more than 90 per cent of Antarctic tourists (Stonehouse, 1992; Enzenbacher, 1993). During the 1991/92 and 1992/93 seasons, this proportion increased to over 97 per cent (Enzenbacher, 1992a, 1994a) (see Table 1.3). However, Antarctic shipboard tourism has grown irregularly. In 1974–75, the numbers of passengers rose to a height of more than 3500, but declined to fewer than 1000 in 1980. During the southern summer 1990–91, more than 4600 tourists are estimated to have visited Antarctica, and during 1991–92, over 6000 (Stonehouse, 1992).

The first tourist cruise was made by an Argentine vessel, *les Eclaireus*, to the Antarctic Peninsula in 1958. (For historical aspects of Antarctic tourism see Reich, 1980; Headland, 1994; Codling, Chapter 11.) Since then, cruise ships have visited the northern tip of the Peninsula annually. The number of available cruises is increasing rapidly. In 1989–90, 5 ships offered 21 cruises in the Antarctic. During the 1991–92 season 10 cruise ships, one military vessel and one chartered vessel, made a total of 53 Antarctic cruises (IAATO, 1992; Enzenbacher, 1993). Visitation was focused on the Antarctic Peninsula with only two working out of New Zealand to the Ross Sea (Wouters, 1993).

Expedition/educational cruising is the most popular form of Antarctic tourism (Hart, 1988; Smith, 1994). The concept of 'expedition cruising' coupled with education as a major theme, began with Lars-Eric Lindblad in 1966, and has been followed by most cruise operators (IAATO, 1992; Stonehouse, 1992). During the 1980s, Lindblad Travel and Society Expeditions, both American tour operators, offered the majority of cruises to Antarctica (Enzenbacher, 1991). A number of new operators entered the market during the 1991–92 season, but Society Expeditions carried the most passengers with a total of 1803 aboard 16 Antarctic cruises, more than 29 per cent of the market share (Enzenbacher, 1993).

The Antarctic Peninsula is the most frequently visited area of Antarctica due to its proximity to South American ports. It also has a relatively milder climate than anywhere else in Antarctica, and relative freedom from pack-ice compared with other parts of the Antarctic coast. Furthermore, it has diverse and abundant wildlife offering photo opportunities, and the largest concentration of Antarctic research stations, to which visits are included in most tours (Enzenbacher, 1992a, 1994c).

Nearly all Antarctic cruises begin from Punta Arenas (Chile), Puerto Williams (Chile) or Ushuaia (Argentina). This is because the crossing of the Drake Passage to the Antarctic can be made in 48 hours as compared to up to 10 days from Hobart (Australia) and Christchurch (New Zealand), which are also traditional departure points for Antarctic expeditions (Hall, 1992). Other cruises, often involving the same ships, leave southern ports in New Zealand and Tasmania to visit the McMurdo Sound, Cape Adare, and Commonwealth Bay sectors, usually including Macquarie Island and some of the southern islands of New Zealand. Other areas on the continent are less frequently visited (IUCN, 1991; Stonehouse, 1992). Circumnavigation of the Antarctic continent is very rare.

Cruises vary in length, but may last 12–15 days, with 4 or 5 days actually spent landing at different sites (Enzenbacher, 1992b). In one typical documented cruise involving 48 passengers and lasting 28 days, only about 18 hours were spent on land (HRSCERA, 1989). Enzenbacher (1992b) noted that advertised prices for 10–30 day cruises during 1992–93 ranged from US$2850 to US$16 475. A typical 12-day cruise costs between US$5000 and US$7000, generally not including transportation to the cruise departure point. Guest lecturers are present on the ships, and passengers are usually put ashore in zodiacs to inspect penguin rookeries, scientific bases, locations of former whaling stations and historic sites.

Private yachts have been manned solo or may carry up to 20 fare-paying passengers (Enzenbacher, 1992a). These yachts tend to concentrate their activities in the Antarctic Peninsula region. In most Austral summers about half a dozen yacht cruises are available around the Peninsula (Dingwall, 1990). Activities range from sightseeing to chartering services for film crews, as well as supporting research studies by Antarctic Treaty party scientists (IAATO, 1992).

Accommodation for tourists at the Chilean station Teniente Marsh on King George Island off the Antarctic Peninsula and a seasonal base camp consisting of tents at Palmer station run by Adventure Network International, are presently the only land-based tourism facilities (HRSCERA, 1989; DSIR, 1990; ANI, 1992–93). However, from time to time there have been proposals to create further tourist infrastructures, which will be discussed later in this chapter.

Airborne tourism

Airborne tourism includes sightseeing overflights of Antarctica without landing, independent adventurers making brief visits in specially equipped light aircraft, and land-based tourists flown in on package deals (Wace, 1990; Swithinbank, 1993). Tourist overflights began in 1956 with a flight carrying 66 passengers from Chile to Antarctica (Swithinbank, 1993). Overflights became regular only from 1977 when Qantas and Air New Zealand began flights to the Ross Sea and adjacent coasts, carrying up to 4000 passengers per season (IUCN, 1991; Swithinbank, 1993). These operations were suspended when an Air New Zealand DC-10 crashed on Mount Erebus in 1979 with the loss of all aboard (Beck, 1986). Prior to the crash some 11 000 passengers had travelled on the 11-hour journey from New Zealand, during which some 90 minutes were spent over Antarctica (Reich, 1980). The Erebus disaster underlined the hazards of polar navigation and the danger of inadequate briefings and safety precautions (Brewster, 1982). Stonehouse (1992) argued that this disaster ended a form of tourism that was growing in popularity and which appeared to offer considerable potential for expansion with minimal environmental effects.

In 1982, the first sizeable party of tourists was flown from Punta Arenas to Teniente Rodolfo Marsh Station on King George Island where they joined a cruise ship. The aircraft returned to Punta Arenas with another group returning home after finishing their cruise. However, these soon ended due to the unreliability in timing due to weather conditions (Swithinbank, 1993). Flights landing tourists at Marsh Station for a few hours or a few days began in 1983 (Wace, 1990). Visitors are accommodated at the first Antarctic 'hotel', Guest House (also called the Hotel Estrella Polar). Visitors are taken on field trips to penguin rookeries, whaling station remains, an elephant seal colony and glaciers. At the end of their visit, the guests fly back to Punta Arenas. Prices for this type of expedition range up from US$3990 (Wace, 1990). This allows the traveller with limited time the possibility to visit Antarctica, as such an expedition may only take six days.

Adventure Network International (ANI), based in Vancouver, Canada, has organised expeditions using ski-equipped aircraft, ships and skis to many inland destinations in the Antarctic since 1984 (Enzenbacher, 1991). ANI operates as Antarctic Air and is the only operator of private flights to the interior of Antarctica (Swithinbank, 1993). Scientists also use ANI expertise to fly them from South America to Patriot Hills, then to their own national station or field study site. ANI has been assisted by the Chilean government, which, for a price, has allowed the use of its permanent King George Island gravel runway as a staging post for ANI planes. Chile uses the tourist dollars to support its own science programme as well as a sign of sovereignty. Initially, ANI was opposed by some governments due to the risk associated with Antarctic flying. However, ANI believes that it has brought risks to an acceptable level by maintaining sufficient aircraft in the Antarctic to evacuate all personnel in the event of an accident to any aircraft (Swithinbank, 1993). The Chilean government also provides back-up guaranteeing search and rescue coverage throughout its area (Wouters, 1993).

In the 1991/92 season the major activities of Antarctic Air were in support of the Shirakawa Antarctic photographic expedition 1991–93, the Kazama motorcycle expedition to the South Pole, and a *Pole to Pole* film crew with actor Michael Palin. Some support was provided for the Norwegian Aurora Projekt on the Filchner Ice Shelf. In addition, 26 climbers in six groups were taken to Mt Vinson, the highest mountain in Antarctica (4897 metres). The season began on 11 November, and the last flight was carried out on 16 January 1992. Each flight had to cover a round-trip distance of 6200 kilometres. A total of 88 passengers were flown into Antarctica in the course of the season. The base camp at Patriot Hills was closed for the winter on 18 February, and all personnel were back in Punta Arenas by 29 February 1992 (NZAS, 1992; Swithinbank, 1992).

Land-based tourism

While the majority of Antarctic visitors travel on a cruise ship a certain amount of time is spent on shore. Similarly, tourists who arrive by plane, will also pass time on the continent itself. Land-based tourism includes all activities by tourists on the Antarctic continent and covers a wide range of visitor experiences. For example, ANI offers adventure tours as well as educational and environmental tours. Their principal form of travel to the continent is by plane from Punta Arenas to the Adventure Network's camp at Patriot Hills, which is the only private base camp and runway on the continent. Tourists can choose from a number of activities, which generally all occur from the base camp. Visitors can attempt to climb Antarctica's highest peak, Mt Vinson, travel to the South Pole by plane or overland, join a sky safari to the Ellsworth Mountains, undertake a photo safari, or ski to the South Pole (ANI, 1992–93). Land-based tourism tends to be a large component of private expeditions such as that of Fiennes and Stroud who attempted to cross the Antarctic continent unaided during the 1992/93 season (Birnbaum, 1993). The motivation for land-based tourism varies. Some visitors have an educational or scientific interest, whereas others are involved in adventure tourism or, as in the case of Fiennes and Stroud, aim to raise finance for a cause (Birnbaum, 1993).

In the future, demands for the development of tourist facilities and infrastructure such as wharfs, airstrips and hotels may occur, the construction of which would incur environmental disturbance on a greater scale than has been caused by tourism to date (IUCN, 1991). As mentioned above, Chile has already opened a hotel on King George Island, with banking and shopping facilities (ECO, 1985; May, 1988). The construction of facilities would compete with wildlife for the less than 2 per cent ice-free land in Antarctica, which tends to use these areas for breeding. Wildlife sites may also be affected by constant visitation with the likelihood of behavioural change and denudation of habitat. The establishment of tourist facilities would also pose problems in terms of sewage and waste disposal, and food and water supply (HRSCERA, 1989).

Proposals to increase tourism by constructing new hotels, airstrips, and other land-based support facilities have been circulated. In the late 1980s an Australian company, Helmut Rhode and Partners, proposed the development of 'Project Oasis' which included the construction, operation and environmental monitoring of a year-round accessible 2800 metre airport, visitor education and research centres, accommodation, hospital, search and rescue and Antarctic Treaty related organisation facilities near Davis Base, in the Australian Antarctic Territory (HRSCERA, 1989). The proposed facilities would provide for 344 visitors, 70 researchers and 174 staff, and up to 16 000 visitors per year could use the facilities. It was proposed that two Boeing flights per week would operate between Davis and Australia. However, the proposal did not go ahead following opposition by the Australian government and conservation groups (HRSCERA, 1989; Hall, 1992).

The impact of concentrated development can be clearly seen on King George Island where there are 17 major constructions including a Chilean air facility and the stations of eight nations. The impacts of station construction and siting of the stations have led to the revocation of Specially Protected Areas status on two occasions (Hall, 1992). So far tourist operations have been conducted in a responsible manner and undesirable impacts have not been severe, especially compared to environmental impacts of scientific and associated logistical activity (Dingwall, 1990; IUCN, 1991). Nevertheless, the continued growth of Antarctic tourism over the next decade will undoubtedly create pressures for the establishment of more permanent tourist facilities in Antarctica and in the more visited Antarctic Peninsula in particular.

TOURISM IMPACTS

Tourism offers both benefits and threats to Antarctica. According to the IUCN (1991, p. 55), 'all who experience its magnificent scenery and wildlife gain a greatly enhanced appreciation of Antarctica's global importance and of the requirements for its conservation'. Such visits also bring fulfilment to those seeking personal challenge and wilderness adventure. Scientific activities may also benefit since tourist visits can provide a useful link with the outside world and strengthen political support for Antarctic science, and small, independent expeditions to remote areas often make valuable scientific observations (Wace, 1990; IUCN, 1991, 1992). Johnson (1985, p. 45) experienced the reaction to tourism at scientific bases: 'there are occasional visits by tourist vessels such as the Lindblad Explorer which pass by. Such visits are viewed rather ambivalently. Any break in the monotony is to be welcomed'. However, since that time Antarctic tourism has increased dramatically and such visitation may now not be welcomed so warmly.

In contrast, there is also the potential for a number of undesirable impacts on the Antarctic environment. Although tourism may increase the number of people dedicated to the preservation of Antarctica, pressures on the environment will increase at the same time (Johnson, 1985). These include physical impacts, such as disturbance at wildlife breeding sites, trampling of vegetation or damage to sites of cultural significance (Acero and Aguirre, 1994; Hughes, 1994; Splettstoesser and Folks, 1994). Tourism can cause scientific and social impacts as well through disruption of routines at stations and of scientific programmes.

Once on the ground, tourists brought in by air do not disturb wildlife any more than tourists brought in by ship. Inland operations seldom encounter wildlife, but visitors can leave rubbish behind. Swithinbank (1993) noted that ANI was aware of these problems at the planning stage, and Patriot Hills is the only inland station in Antarctica from which all waste products are taken off the continent. However, visitors who stay over on Antarctica do require considerable land-based infrastructural support (Graham, 1989). For example, tourists who fly to Marsh Base for a three-day stay at the Chilean 'hotel' require accommodation, meals, water and basic services, all of which impact on the local environment (Enzenbacher, 1991).

The type of cruise ship visiting Antarctica can also have an indirect impact on the environment. One of the major operators in Antarctica, Society Expeditions, has a traditional capacity of less than 140 passengers.

However, some of the ships operating in Antarctica carry far more than this. Argentine ships have been known to land 1000 people at a time (Johnson, 1985). These larger operations have less emphasis on the educational aspects of Antarctic tourism and more sightseeing. These ships have no ice-hardened hull and probably have no intention to go into the ice. Antarctic tourist companies are not required to use vessels specifically built for use in ice (Enzenbacher, 1991). Peter Cox, Director of Planning and Operations for Society Expeditions (in Wouters, 1993, p. 40) argued that 'if indeed they would stay in open water and merely sightsee from the vessel, the impact on the environment would be extremely minimal. If, however, they would put passengers ashore in larger numbers and not brief and control them properly then damage could easily be done'. Enzenbacher (1991, p. 18) argued that 'cruise vessels which carry fewer than 180 passengers are considered optimal since they allow small groups to off load at landing sites that are capable of reboarding expeditiously if need be'.

Tourist visitation in the Antarctic summer coincides with the peak breeding periods for many species and may disturb wildlife breeding sites that are a key feature of the tourist attractiveness of Antarctica (Mussack, 1988; Hall, 1992). Seaborne landing sites also tend to be the principal locations of plant and animal life (Hart, 1988). Tourists could unwittingly spread bird or plant diseases and introduce new kinds of organisms (Nicholson, 1986; May, 1988). The seasonality of Antarctic tourism greatly affects the impact of visitation on Antarctic sites. Therefore, it is not only accessibility which places pressure on the Antarctic environment, but also the short season in which tourism is possible. For example, Whalers Bay, Deception Island, received 1496 passengers in the 1990–91 season, averaged over 13 visits. Maximum days between visits varied from 2 to 14 days (United States, 1991).

Visitor impact is greatly influenced by tour operator policies and the management regime for Antarctic tourism (Splettstoesser and Folks, 1994). Enzenbacher (1991) believes that when operators strictly follow the current guidelines created within the industry the potential for environmental impacts is greatly reduced. Tourists aboard self-contained vessels following responsible management practices may have minimal impact on Antarctica's environment. Lecture series aboard tourist ships and guides at landing sites are some efforts used by conscientious operators. Less dedicated tour operators do not provide guides at landing sites, informative lectures, or behavioural guidelines for tourists, which was the case of Marinsular operating *Pomaire* during the 1990–91 Austral summer (Enzenbacher, 1991). It is, however, not only important that passengers are aware, but government, operators, staff and crew members must also be educated about the effects Antarctic tourism can have on the environment (Donachie, 1994).

THE ANTARCTIC TOURISM MANAGEMENT REGIME

As long as tourists continue to desire to visit Antarctica, certain constraints will be necessary. The regulatory framework for Antarctic tourism consists of the Antarctic Treaty System (ATS), several visitor guidelines established by different organisations including the tour operators, and Antarctic Treaty parties' national legislation. The majority of the Antarctic tour operators make their passengers aware of the uniqueness of the continent, giving the visitor a special sense of achievement and consideration of this 'last wilderness'. However, tourist visitation requires a coherent and controllable management regime, which encompasses all the factors involved in Antarctica, that is, the current political system, the environment, international politics, the tour operators and the visitors. The following section will provide a brief outline of the ATS and its effect on tourism, which is examined in greater detail in Chapter 12 by Enzenbacher, as well as a brief discussion of other management proposals that have been put forward.

Antarctic Treaty System

The Antarctic Treaty is the principal international agreement that has established a legal framework for regulating relationships among states in the Antarctic. The notion for an international Antarctic Treaty arose from the highly successful international cooperation associated with research in the Antarctic during the International Geophysical Year in 1957–58. Following a conference on Antarctica in Washington in 1959, the 12 participating nations (Argentina, Australia, Belgium, Chile, France, Japan, New Zealand, Norway, South Africa, the United Kingdom, the United States of America and the USSR) agreed to the Antarctic Treaty. This Treaty was subsequently ratified and came into force in 1961. The Treaty covers the entire area south of $60°$ South, including all ice shelves, but excluding all of the rights under international law in the high seas (Article VI) (Kriwoken and Keage, 1989). This encompasses one-tenth of the world's land surface and one-tenth of its oceans (Beck, 1990a; DSIR, 1990).

The primary purpose of the Treaty is to ensure that Antarctica shall continue for ever to be used exclusively for peaceful use and shall not become the scene of international conflict. The Treaty has 14 articles which, in summary, froze contentious sovereignty claims, demilitarised the area, guaranteed free access and established science as the foundation of national Antarctic interest (Beck, 1990a; Hemmings, 1991a). Subsequent agreements under what became known as the Antarctic Treaty System (ATS), comprise the Antarctic Treaty and the recommendations of the Consultative Meeting and several Special Meetings; the Convention for the

Conservation of Antarctic Seals (CCAS), 1972; the Convention for the Conservation of Antarctic Marine Living Resources (CCAMLR), 1980; the Agreed Measures for the Conservation of Antarctic Fauna and Flora 1964; and liaison with outside bodies, especially the Scientific Committee for Antarctic Research (SCAR), thereby seeking to protect terrestrial fauna and flora, seals and marine living resources (Kriwoken and Keage, 1989; Hemmings, 1991a). In 1991, a new form of protection for the Antarctic environment was formulated, the *Protocol on Environmental Protection*, which significantly affects the deliberation of Antarctic tourism management. The implications of the Protocol are discussed in greater detail by Enzenbacher in Chapter 12. Table 10.1 summarises the Antarctic Treaty System.

The ATS has been hailed as successful to date as it is claimed that the Treaty has encouraged international cooperation while guaranteeing peace and stability in the region (Blay *et al.*, 1989; Hearder, 1989). However, despite its apparent success, the Treaty has showed signs of strain which is in the large part due to the prospect of future resource exploitation (Hearder, 1989), as the existence of commercial resources were not covered expressly by the Treaty (Barnes, 1982). The increasing numbers of acceding states also places greater pressure on the existing rather informal arrangements (Woolcott, 1990). However, Beck (1990a, p. 256) believes that the ATS has

> evolved in a flexible, pragmatic and cooperative manner, designed to accommodate new circumstances and demands as well as to fill perceived gaps in the Treaty regime through the adoption by consensus of recommendations at ATCMs and of the conclusion of additional conventions on specific issues.

Currently, self-restraint and diplomatic persuasion are practised rather than compulsive action (Kriwoken and Keage, 1989; Beck, 1990b). In addition, it is unclear whether recommendations under the Treaty are legally binding, even when approved by governments (Scully, 1990; IUCN, 1991). Various self-policing aspects of the Antarctic Treaty have not been working well, and there is no single body to investigate problems and enforce policies (Janiskee, 1991). Decision-making within the ATS is based on consensus rather than majority vote. However, once consensus has been reached, there are no direct means of enforcing ATS decisions (Harris, 1991). If legal controls are to be effective, they must be enforceable by a competent authority (Kriwoken and Keage, 1989).

The Antarctic Treaty can only be enforced against its members. The Treaty does not create obligations or rights for any third party without that party's consent (Mussack, 1988). Article VI recorded the parties' assurance that they had no intention of curtailing other states' rights on the high

Table 10.1. The elements of the Antarctic Treaty System

Elements	Characteristics	Geographical parameters
Antarctic Treaty 1961	Provides for the management of Antarctic resources. Establishes Agreed Measures, Sites of Special Scientific Interest (SSSI), and other measures for the management of Antarctic resources	North to 60° S latitude
Agreed Measures for the Conservation of Antarctic Fauna and Flora 1964	Plants, land-breeding seals, and invertebrates are protected. Established the Agreed Measures, Sites of Special Scientific Interest and other measures. Revoked Protocol	North to 60° S latitude
Scientific Committee on Antarctic Research (SCAR) Antarctica	Coordinates, initiates and promotes scientific activity	North to the Antarctic Convergence and the sub-Antarctic islands
Convention for the Conservation of Seals 1972	Protects Ross and fur seals. Established seal reserves and sealing zones	Covers area from the sea-ice zone north to 60° S latitude
Convention for the Conservation of Antarctic Marine Living Resources 1980	Applies to all marine organisms except whales, which are covered by the International Convention for the Regulation of Whaling. Provides for the establishment of marine sanctuaries	Covers area from the sea-ice zone north to the Antarctic Convergence
Protocol on Environmental Protection to the Antarctic Treaty 1991	Builds on Antarctic Treaty to extend and improve Treaty's effectiveness as mechanism for ensuring the protection of Antarctic environment. Designates Antarctica as a natural reserve devoted to peace and science and sets forth environmental protection principles for all human activities. Priority to scientific research. Mineral activity prohibited. Revoked Agreed Measures	North to 60° S latitude
Annexes to Protocol	Environmental Impact Assessment. Conservation of Antarctic Fauna and Flora. Waste Disposal and Waste Management. Prevention of Marine Pollution. Area Protection Management	North to 60° S latitude

Sources: Hall (1992); United States (1992); Wouters (1993).

seas. The traditional rule that ships sailing on, or aircraft flying over, the high seas are under the jurisdiction of their flag state continues to apply in the Southern Ocean because of Article VI (Peterson, 1986). This poses problems for the management of cruise ships which are often registered outside Antarctic Treaty countries, but may carry nationals from Treaty nations. As Nicholson (1986, p. 6) so eloquently argued,

> but what is the responsible flag state in the case of an incident involving a Panamanian registered vessel with a Greek captain, a Philippine crew, carrying a party of tourists on a charter tour organised by a travel agent in the United States under a joint arrangement with travel agents in Britain, France and Germany, and departing from New Zealand for the Ross Sea and Antarctic Peninsula?

Under the Treaty, tourism is an accepted activity in the Antarctic region, and is partially regulated. Antarctic tourism is treated as a legitimate, peaceful use of the area as long as it is properly organised and controlled (Beck, 1990b, 1994). The Antarctic Treaty consultative parties (ATCPs) have acknowledged that the growth of tourism is a 'natural development' (ATCM Recommendation VIII-9/1975) arising out of the legitimate use of Antarctica 'for peaceful purposes only' (Article 1 of the Antarctic Treaty), and that this activity requires regulation (Recommendation VIII-9/1975) because of the region's 'many unique features of historical, scenic and general scientific interest' (Recommendation VII-4/1972) (Beck, 1990b, p. 344). The ATCPs are required to ensure that its nationals, who may be part of a tourist expedition, obey the Agreed Measures (Recommendation III-VIII) and respect measures relating to protected areas and historic monuments (Mussack, 1988).

Under the ATS, Antarctic Treaty parties contribute to discussions on Antarctic tourism, but external groups also exert influence on the policy process (Enzenbacher, 1991). For example, several other Antarctic visitor guidelines have been created. One of the most influential bodies, the Scientific Committee on Antarctic Research (SCAR), has published a helpful introduction to the Antarctic and its environment, with the hope that by giving visitors some simple advice, damage to the fragile region can be avoided (British Antarctic Survey (BAS), 1984). SCAR's *A visitor's introduction to the Antarctic and its environment* (1980) was designed to inform all Antarctic visitors, scientists and tourists alike, about Antarctica's environment and life forms on land and at sea (Enzenbacher, 1991). Stone-house (1990, p. 56) provided a private suggestion for an appropriate code of conduct in the Antarctic for all who visit there (Table 10.2). This code applies to ships' crews, as well as to tourists, guides, scientists and all other visitors, and aims to be accessible and easily understood. The

Table 10.2. Antarctic traveller's code

Antarctic visitors
- Must not leave footprints in fragile mosses, lichens or grasses
- Must not dump plastic or other, non-biodegradable garbage overboard or onto the Continent
- Must not violate the seals', penguins', or sea-birds' *personal space*—start with a 'baseline' distance of 5 metres from penguins, sea-birds, and true seals and 18 metres from fur seals
  —give animals the right of way
  —stay on the edge of, and don't walk through, animal groups
  —back off if necessary
  —never touch the animals
- Must not interfere with protected areas or scientific research
- Must not take souvenirs

Antarctic Tour companies
- SHOULD apply the Antarctic traveller's code to all officers, crew, staff and passengers
- SHOULD utilise one (1) guide or leader for every twenty (20) passengers
- SHOULD employ experienced and sensitive on-board leadership
- SHOULD use vessels that are safe for Antarctic ice conditions
- SHOULD adopt a ship-wide anti-dumping pledge

Source: Stonehouse (1990, p. 57).

Council of Managers of National Antarctic Programs (COMNAP) (1992) has also produced a *Visitor's guide to the Antarctic*, which has been translated into several languages. Australia, Brazil, Japan and the United Kingdom have each published their own version of the publication. Nevertheless, most governments 'experience difficulty in ensuring that any tour or expedition provides adequate information, seeks expert advice, adheres to prior commitments and respects the provisions of the ATS' (Beck, 1990b, p. 348).

Despite several claims, Antarctica is an area under no state's sovereignty, and thereby is outside the jurisdiction of any single state. The Antarctic Treaty countries have no formally agreed approach to the exertion of jurisdiction over tourist expeditions. The parties have until now been operating their official expeditions under an unwritten understanding that flag jurisdiction will apply (Mussack, 1988; Beck, 1990b). The enforcement of rules, in domestic and international terms, and in tourist regulation, is a major problem. In theory, each nation is responsible for the actions of its nationals in Antarctica, but the practical position is rather different. Heavy-handed enforcement by a claimant state of territorial jurisdiction or application of national laws might prompt complications with non-claimants (Beck, 1990b). Nevertheless, the success of the ATS, relative to other international arrangements, 'has rested on its avoidance of confrontation on the complicated sovereignty issue', thereby enabling a spirit of cooperation (Brewster, 1982, p. 110).

HERITAGE OF MANKIND AND WORLD PARK PROPOSALS

Related to the discussion about the type of management which should be in place in Antarctica is the debate whether Antarctica in international law is *terra nullius*, that is, territory open to claim by interested parties, or *res communis*, which means that like the high seas and outer space, Antarctica belongs to the international community (Murray-Smith, 1988). This has led to a number of alternative administrative suggestions for the continent of which two, the notions of 'common heritage of mankind' and 'world park', have been advocated most frequently.

In recent times there have been demands from developing countries for a new international order on Antarctica, preferably under the auspices of the United Nations (UN) (Blay *et al.*, 1989). A number of developing countries have criticised the Antarctic Treaty as being 'anachronistic, exclusive maintenance of territorial claims (claiming that they were a potential source of international instability), and argued that Antarctica should be declared the "Common Heritage of Mankind"' (*Australian Foreign Affairs Record (AFAR)*, 1986, p. 96). The thrust of this perspective is that any benefits derived from both living and non-living resource extraction should be utilised for the benefits of all states on an equitable basis (Murray-Smith, 1988; Blay *et al.*, 1989). From the conception of the ATS, the UN attempted to gain a more active role in the management of Antarctica, and has promoted the merits of an alternative UN-based mechanism as compared to the existing ATS. To date, however, the UN has failed to make any impression on the Antarctic Treaty parties (Beck, 1992).

The 'common heritage of mankind' concept appears laudable in that all nations would be able to benefit from the possible resources the continent may contain. As the proposition for the 'common heritage of mankind' method seems to advocate utilisation of the continent's resources, tourism would be an acceptable activity. However, it would be difficult to control the potential increase in all types of activity that may occur, and tourism would thus also not be controlled effectively. This concept appears to put exploitation ahead of preservation, and this notion would not be to the benefit of the protection of the Antarctic environment (Wouters, 1993).

Antarctica is not an area which could fall within the 'common heritage for mankind' concept due to the existence of sovereignty and sovereign rights over parts of the continent and its adjacent offshore areas. Eighty-five per cent of Antarctica is subject to long-standing territorial claims (Walton, 1986). Furthermore, the Antarctic Treaty does exist, and it runs

Antarctica reasonably efficiently. It also does not exclude any nation from joining, and the consultative members alone represent 80 per cent of the world's population (Murray-Smith, 1988).

Alternatively, a number of conservationist groups have called for Antarctica to be declared a 'world park'. In 1981, the International Union for Conservation of Nature and Natural Resources (IUCN) passed a resolution at its General Assembly recommending the establishment of a world park. Herbert (1992, p. 293) defined a world park as a 'regime that preserves the natural resources, wildlife, and environment of Antarctica in a generally undeveloped state'. Advocates of the world park option wish to declare it 'off-limits to mankind' except for certain very restrictive non-consumptive purposes (Janiskee, 1991), including science and tourism; however, both of these activities would be subject to censure. Johnson (1985, p. 191) argued that,

> wildlife tourism, landscape and seascape tourism, within the context of a 'hands off Antarctica' policy, seems to be an effective riposte to those who argue that in a world where 'millions are starving', it is wrong to let any resources which are available remain unused. Tourism should not be encouraged, but as a gesture towards 'internationalisation', this is probably the least harmful to take.

Greenpeace supports the belief that Antarctica should be nominated a world park with the designation also of world heritage site. According to May (1988), Antarctica fulfils all the world heritage site requirements, strengthening the argument for its designation as a world park. This designation does not impinge on issues of sovereignty (Brewster, 1982). Although greater cooperation and information sharing would be necessary, Greenpeace believes that a world park structure can be maintained under the ATS (Doyle, 1989). However, it is doubtful that Antarctica will ever be declared a world park given the opposition of the United States and Great Britain to the concept (Janiskee, 1991).

CONCLUSION

The substantial investment of time and money involved in travelling to Antarctica as a tourist will continue to limit the growth of tourism. Nevertheless, tourist activity presents special challenges to Antarctic Treaty parties, especially as tourists are beginning to outnumber scientists and support staff in Antarctica. Continued growth will pose a threat to the Antarctic environment and the science conducted there, while at the same time, tourism has become an integral activity in Antarctica and the sub-Antarctic.

The regulatory framework for Antarctic tourism consists of Treaty recommendations backed by national legislation and guidelines, such as those for tourists and tour operators endorsed by the International Association of Antarctic Tour Operators (IAATO) (see Enzenbacher, Chapter 12; Enzenbacher, 1994b). The ATS provides a framework for the development of strategies to protect Antarctica from the effects of tourist activity. The recent Protocol is an important advancement in the regulation of human activity in Antarctica. The comprehensive review of Antarctic tourism proposed by Treaty members provides a starting point for discussion of existing tourism policy in view of current levels and forms of tourist activity. This requires extensive research into the impact of tourism, such as that discussed by Stonehouse and Crosbie in Chapter 13.

As discussed in Chapter 12 by Enzenbacher, the enforcement of legislation accepted by the ATCPs concerning any type of activity, including tourism, is difficult. Claimant and signatory national legislation may cover a broad range of tourism-related areas, including conservation, communication and transportation. However, under the Antarctic Treaty, the application of domestic legislation to other nationalities is somewhat problematic. As the regulation of tourism under domestic law would be regarded as an exercise of sovereignty by that nation, it is highly likely that this would be challenged by other signatories to the Antarctic Treaty. In turn, any moves towards an international tourism regime would require claimants to accept some derogation of their sovereignty rights (Beck, 1990b). Tourist ventures such as those encouraged by the Chilean government to strengthen its territorial claims also complicate the issue (*ECO*, 1985).

Beck (1990b, p. 346) suggests that the national dimension might prove more significant in the future, 'given the greater political interest shown in the matter at both the ATS and national levels, as well as the emerging tendency of certain ATCPs to formulate national policies towards Antarctic tourism'. However, this process often involves little more than the acceptance of Antarctic tourism conducted within the parameters of the ATS. Nations active in Antarctica generally share the management philosophy of the ATS, but Harris (1991, p. 314) believes that different groups (claimants and non-claimants) differ in approach. National priorities influence perceptions of management needs, and differences can result in uncoordinated planning. The Protocol emphasises environmental management, but has some weaknesses. It leaves individual states as the final judges of their own activities (Hemmings, 1991b, 1992). Nevertheless, as indicated in the chapters by Wouters and Hall on tourism in the sub-Antarctic (Chapters 15 and 16) national approaches towards the management of tourism in areas where jurisdiction is clear may serve as models which can then be applied to the Antarctic environment.

The IUCN (1992) asserts that agreement on consistent management policies and practices is likely to be easier than achieving unanimity in law. Many national Antarctic authorities already implement procedures and operational codes of practice to encourage environmentally sensitive tourist operations, although these vary considerably in scope and detail. Unfortunately, ATS procedure and national legislation to manage Antarctic tourism are inconsistent, emphasising the necessity to establish a more coherent and universal tourism management regime. An agreed series of guidelines should thus be developed for setting performance standards that can be uniformly applied to all tourist operations throughout the region. Development of these guidelines should take advantage of experience gained both in Antarctica and elsewhere, such as from the current approaches to tourism management in the sub-Antarctic island reserves (IUCN, 1992) and discussed by Wouters and Hall in Chapters 15 and 16.

As the following chapters on Antarctica emphasise, cooperation between tour operators and the Antarctic Treaty parties will remain integral to the development of appropriate measures to develop and manage the Antarctic tourism industry. Tourist activities should be covered under a set of regulations agreed to by all stakeholders. Therefore, regulating Antarctic tourism may well require the establishment of an international convention or a similar international regulatory setting. However, as the following chapters illustrate, such a situation will not be easily obtained given the range of commercial, economic, national and political interests involved in the management of the southern polar region and in tourism activities in particular.

REFERENCES

Acero, J.M., Aguirre, C.A., 1994, A monitoring research plan for tourism in Antarctica, *Annals of Tourism Research*, **21**(2): 295–302

ANI (Adventure Network International), 1992/93, Antarctic tours brochure, Darien

Australian Foreign Affairs Record, 1986, Australia and the Antarctic treaty system, *Australian Foreign Affairs Record*, **55**(2): 90–98

Barnes, J.N., 1982, *Let's save Antarctica!*, Greenhouse Publications, Richmond

Beck, P.J., 1986, *The international politics of Antarctica*, St Martin's Press, New York

Beck, P.J., 1990a, Antarctica enters the 1990s: an overview, *Applied Geography*, **10**(4): 247–264

Beck, P.J., 1990b, Regulating one of the last tourism frontiers: Antarctica, *Applied Geography*, **10**(4): 343–356

Beck, P.J., 1992, The 1991 UN session: the environmental protocol fails to satisfy the Antarctic treaty system's critics, *Polar Record*, **28**(167): 307–314

Beck, P.J., 1994, Managing Antarctic tourism: a front-burner issue, *Annals of Tourism Research*, **21**(2): 375–386

Birnbaum, J., 1993, Great explorations, *Time*, **141**(9): 40–45

Blay, S.N.L., Piotrowicz, R.W., Tsamenyi, B.M., 1989, *Antarctica after 1991: the legal and policy options*, Antarctica and Southern Ocean Law and Policy Occasional Paper 2, Faculty of Law, University of Tasmania, Hobart

Brewster, B., 1982, *Antarctica—wilderness at risk*, Friends of the Earth/A.H. & A.W. Reed, Wellington

Cooper, W., 1993, *Report on MS frontier spirit cruise #58 Jan–Feb 1993*, New Zealand representative, Department of Conservation Field Centre Manager, Wellington

Dingwall, P., 1990, Antarctic tourism, *IUCN Bulletin*, 21(2): 9–10

Donachie, S.P., 1994, Henryk Arctowski Station: mixing science and tourism, *Annals of Tourism Research*, 21(2): 333–341

Doyle, T.J., 1989, The Antarctic treaty: within or without? In Handmer, J. ed., *Antarctica: policies and policy development*, Centre for Resource and Environmental Studies, Australian National University, Canberra, pp. 49–60

DSIR (Department of Scientific and Industrial Research), 1990, Antarctica information brochures, DSIR, Christchurch

ECO, 1985, Tourism and colonisation in Antarctica, Preparatory meeting for 13th ATCM, *ECO*, 30(3): 1–2

Enzenbacher, D.J., 1991, A policy for Antarctic tourism: conflict or cooperation? Unpublished Master of Philosophy thesis in Polar Studies, Scott Polar Research Institute, University of Cambridge, Cambridge

Enzenbacher, D.J., 1992a, Tourists in Antarctica: numbers and trends, *Polar Record*, 28(164): 17–22

Enzenbacher, D.J., 1992b, Antarctic tourism and environmental concerns, *Marine Pollution Bulletin*, 25(9–12): 258–265

Enzenbacher, D.J., 1993, Tourists in Antarctica: numbers and trends, *Tourism Management*, April: 142–146

Enzenbacher, D.J., 1994a, Antarctic tourism: an overview of 1992/93 season activity, recent developments, and emerging issues, *Polar Record*, 30(173): 105–116

Enzenbacher, D.J., 1994b, NSF and Antarctic tour operators meetings, *Annals of Tourism Research*, 21(2): 424–427

Enzenbacher, D.J., 1994c, Tourism at Faraday Station: an Antarctic case study, *Annals of Tourism Research*, 21(2): 303–317

Graham, A., 1989, An environmentalist's perspective on the future of Antarctica. In Handmer, J., ed., *Antarctica policies and policy development*, Centre for Resource and Environmental Studies, Australian National University, Canberra, pp. 25–30

Hall, C.M., 1992, Tourism in Antarctica: activities, impacts, and management, *Journal of Travel Research*, 30(4): 2–9

Harris, C.M., 1991, Environmental management in King George island, South Shetland Islands, Antarctica, *Polar Record*, 27(163): 313–324

Hart, P.D., 1988, Bound for 60° south—taxes, tips, and transfers included: the growth of Antarctic tourism, *Oceanus*, 31(2): 93–100

Headland, R.K., 1994, Historical development of Antarctic tourism, *Annals of Tourism Research*, 21(2): 269–280

Hearder, J., 1989, The Australian government perspective. In Handmer, J., ed., *Antarctica: policies and policy development*, Centre for Resource and Environmental Studies, Australian National University, Canberra, pp. 7–12

Hemmings, A.D., 1991a, Managing Antarctica's resources, *Terra Nova*, October: 8

Hemmings, A.D., 1991b, Antarctica—a premature celebration, *Greenstone*, 2(Nov.–Dec.): 4–7

Hemmings, A.D., 1992, Antarctica not secure yet, *Forest and Bird*, **23**(2): 12–18

Herbert, B.P., 1992, The economic case for an Antarctic world park in light of recent policy developments, *Polar Record*, **28**(167): 293–300

HRSCERA (House of Representatives Standing Committee on Environment, Recreation and the Arts), 1989, *Tourism in Antarctica*, Report of the HRSCERA, Parliament of the Commonwealth of Australia, Australian Government Publishing Service, Canberra

Hughes, J., 1994, Antarctic historic sites: the tourism implications, *Annals of Tourism Research*, **21**(2): 281–294

IAATO (International Association of Antarctica Tour Operators), 1992, *Tourism in Antarctica—guidelines for a low-impact presence (IAATO submission)*, *XVII ATCM/INFO 65, 16 November*, IAATO, Kent

IUCN (International Union for Conservation of Nature and Natural Resources), 1991, *A strategy for Antarctic conservation*, IUCN, Gland

IUCN, 1992, *Tourism in Antarctica (IUCN submission)*, *XVII ATCM/INFO 18, 11 November*, IUCN, Gland

Janiskee, R.L., 1991, Ecotourism in Antarctica: too much of a good thing? Paper presented at the Annual Meeting of the Association of American Geographers, Miami, April

Johnson, S., 1985, *Antarctica the last wilderness*, Weidenfeld & Nicolson, London

Kriwoken, L., Keage, P., 1989, Introduction. In Handmer, J., ed., *Antarctica: policies and policy development*, Centre for Resource and Environmental Studies, Australian National University, Canberra, pp. 31–48

Madden, R., 1993, To boldly go with the Antarctic ice floes, *Sunday Times*, 1 August

May, J., 1988, *The Greenpeace book of Antarctica—a new view of the seventh continent*, Dorling Kindersley, London

Murray-Smith, S., 1988, *Sitting on penguins: people and politics in Australian Antarctica*, Century Hutchinson Australia, Sydney

Mussack, I.E.L., 1988, An approach to the management of tourism in the Antarctic, Unpublished MSc. Thesis, Centre for Resource Management, University of Canterbury and Lincoln College, Christchurch

Nicholson, I.E., 1986, Antarctic tourism: the need for a legal regime? *Maritime Studies*, **29**: 1–7

NZAS (New Zealand Antarctic Society), 1992, Antarctic, *NZAS Bulletin*, **12**(9)

Peterson, M.J., 1986, Antarctic implications of the new law of the sea, *Journal of Marine Affairs*, **16**(2): 137–181

Reich, R.J., 1980, The development of Antarctic tourism, *Polar Record*, **20**(126): 303–214

Sanson, L., 1993, *Report on Kapitan Khlebnikov Ross Sea/Subantarctic islands tourist cruise 12–24 Feb 1993*, Government Representative, Operations Manager, Department of Conservation, Southland Conservancy, Invercargill

Scientific Committee on Antarctic Research (SCAR), 1980, *A visitor's introduction to the Antarctic and its environment*, SCAR, Cambridge

Scully, R.T., 1990, The Antarctic treaty as a system. In Herr, R., Hall, H., Haward, M., eds., *Antarctica's future: continuity or change?* Tasmanian Government Printing Office, Hobart

Smith, V.L., 1994, A sustainable Antarctic: science and tourism, *Annals of Tourism Research*, **21**(2): 221–230

Splettstoesser, J., Folks, M.C., 1994, Environmental guidelines for tourism in Antarctica, *Annals of Tourism Research*, **21**(2): 231–244

Stonehouse, B., 1990, A traveller's code for Antarctic visitors, *Polar Record*, **26**(156): 56–58

Stonehouse, B., 1992, Monitoring shipborne visitors in Antarctica: a preliminary field study, *Polar Record*, **28**(166): 213–218

Swithinbank, C., 1992, Non-government aircraft in the Antarctica 1991/92, *Polar Record*, **28**(167): 322–324

Swithinbank, C., 1993, Airborne tourism in the Antarctica 1991/92, *Polar Record*, **28**(166): 232

United States, 1991, Compilation of data on tourist visits to the Antarctic peninsula (submission), XVI ATCM/INFO 68, 10 October

United States, 1992, *Antarctic tourism and the environmental protocol (working paper), Agenda Item 13, XVII ATCM/WP 6, 9 November*, United States government, Washington DC

Wace, N., 1990, Antarctica: a new tourist destination, *Applied Geography*, **10**(4): 327–341

Walton, D.W.H., 1986, *The biological basis for conservation of subantarctic islands*, Report of the Joint SCAR/IUCN workshop, Paimpont, France, 12–14 September 1986

Woolcott, R., 1990, Challenges and changes. In Herr, R., Hall, H., Haward, M., eds., *Antarctica's future: continuity or change*, Tasmanian Government Printing Office, Hobart, pp. 21–28

Wouters, M., 1993, Promotion or protection: managing the paradox—The management of tourist visitation to Antarctica and the Sub-Antarctic islands, the New Zealand situation as a case study, Unpublished master's thesis, Massey University, Palmerston North

11 The Precursors of Tourism in the Antarctic

ROSAMUNDE J. CODLING

In its grandeur, its vastness and, in a way, its purity the Antarctic is the most beautiful thing in the world (Cherry-Garrard, 1937).

The idea of tourist interest in the Antarctic appears incredible to many. For example, when the Antarctic Treaty Bill was receiving its Third Reading in the Parliament of Great Britain and Northern Ireland in 1967, some members of the House of Commons found difficulty in accepting that tourist visits were already taking place. The Member who concluded the debate finally commented that 'no place, however cold or wet, or hot or high or deep is beyond the quest of man's ingenuity' (Gibson-Watt, 1967). Few probably realise that tourists visited a sub-Antarctic island in 1891 and that a suggestion was made for an Antarctic cruise as early as 1910. Nevertheless, over half a century elapsed before a commercially organised voyage took place and it was not until 1966 that regular tourist cruises were established (Reich, 1980).

The precursors of developed tourism in the Antarctic fall into two categories. There are those who planned visits which, for reasons now unknown, never took place. There were also others who successfully took tourists to destinations in the sub-Antarctic, and possibly the Antarctic, but whose primary purposes were trade or mail delivery. It is known that some intrepid travellers took the opportunities available to them, but in other cases it has not been possible to ascertain how many, if any, capitalised on the availability of berths on Antarctic-bound vessels.

This chapter outlines the main events that have contributed to the development of Antarctic tourism. Individually, their influence may not have been great, but they combined to demonstrate the growing interest in visits to the southern continent. Following a brief consideration of motives for travel, the first confirmed tourist visit to a sub-Antarctic island is examined. Thomas Cook planned a cruise but it was not until the 1920s

Polar Tourism: Tourism in the Arctic and Antarctic Regions
Edited by C. Michael Hall and Margaret E. Johnston. © John Wiley & Sons Ltd, 1995

that visits probably took place using the mail delivery services to South Georgia. In the 1930s two efforts were made by Lt.-Com. J.R. Stenhouse to organise an Antarctic cruise, but both were abortive, although interest continued in both Argentina and Australia.

MOTIVES FOR ANTARCTIC TRAVEL

It is often asked why people wish to visit the Antarctic. To identify motives is complex, but a passenger on one of the first regular cruises in the mid-1960s gave this descriptive summary of her fellow travellers:

> ranging in age from 23 to 86; jaded travellers, interested amateurs, four travel agents, one or two knowledgeable housewives, one neurotic, one psycho-path, a few bona-fide and three quasi-scientists, an avid continent collector, an astronomer, a clutch of bird people ... there were as many reasons for being there as there were passengers on board (Goodwin, 1966).

The term 'avid continent collector' seems to be applicable to the botanist Joseph Banks, who accompanied Captain James Cook on his first voyage from 1768 to 1770. Initially, it was planned that he should again accompany Cook, but during preparations for his second voyage, considerable diffi-culties developed between Cook and Banks, who appears to have had an 'absurdly swollen head' (Beaglehole, 1961, p. xxvii). The botanist with-drew from the expedition, so he never had the opportunity he desired to stand on the South Pole and turn a full circle on his heel through 360° of longitude (Beaglehole, 1961, p. xxvii). Cook circumnavigated the continent, but did not see land.

For many, the beauty of the continent has been especially impressive, whatever other motives there might have been for their visit. The journals of some of the early explorers—Cook, Bellingshausen, Weddell and Wilkes for example, understandably concentrate on the hazards they faced in travelling through unknown regions. Accounts of uncharted seas, navigated by small sailing vessels with the ever-present difficulties caused by atrocious weather conditions, ice and adverse living and working conditions, form the core of their writings. But even amid these dangers, some recorded the magnificence of their surroundings. On 30 January 1841, James Clark Ross sailed on the sea now named after him and was confronted by the edge of the great ice shelf. He wrote: 'But this extraordinary barrier of ice, of probably more than a thousand feet in thickness, crushes the undulations of the waves, and disregards their violence: it is a mighty and wonderful object, far beyond any thing we could have thought or conceived' (quoted by Neider, 1973, p. 181).

Appreciation beyond basic geographical description is more readily found in the writings of those in the 'heroic age' of Antarctic exploration, about the beginning of the twentieth century. Edward Wilson was with Scott on both of his expeditions, serving firstly as second surgeon and then as head of the scientific staff. He was also an exceptionally talented artist and wrote freely about his surroundings. On the *Discovery* expedition he realised the pleasure that the landscapes of the Antarctic could give others. In his diary for 23 August 1902 he wrote:

> We had the whole of Erebus island spread out in front of us, and it was a very beautiful sight indeed. One of the thoughts that strikes one oftenest I think is what people at home would give to have a glimpse of such a sight. There was a true spring feeling in the air today which makes every thing infinitely more beautiful (Wilson, 1966, p. 175).

Wilson and many of his companions on Scott's first expedition wrote lengthy letters home, but at that time, none of their families had the opportunity to see the continent.

SUB-ANTARCTIC VISITS

Headland (1989) lists several New Zealand government expeditions to peri-Antarctic islands, starting in 1882, which are believed to have carried tourists, though details are difficult to confirm. Definite information is available about the visit by the *Gratitude* to Macquarie Island, one of the sub-Antarctic islands, in 1891. Cumpston (1968, Plate 21) includes an illustration of a card distributed by the ketch's owner, Joseph Hatch, following a visit to the island in February 1891. Four people whose photographs appear on the card were described as 'tourists'. It is intriguing to see that one of the male travellers is given the title of 'Mr' while the other three men are simply listed with their initials. This possibly reflects on their relative class status, but no other clues are given to the designations. Part of the text on the back of the card reads:

> A large number of sensational articles, telegrams and letters have appeared in the public Press all over the Australian colonies in many of which Mr Hatch, an old representative for Invercargill in the New Zealand Legislature, was very roughly handled, but subsequent events have proved his knowledge of the position to be correct.

The contentious issue appears to be the killing of seals and penguins for their oil. On the return of the *Gratitude* to the port of Bluff, Hatch gave an address at the town's Theatre Royal including a spirited defence of trade in seal and penguin oil. He is reported as commenting on the 'ridiculous nonsense of protecting the penguins' (Cumpston, 1968, p. 163). It is known that Hatch continued his trading business, but no further references have been found to tourists accompanying his voyages.

THOMAS COOK AND ANTARCTIC TRAVEL

The last years of the nineteenth century saw both Norwegian and Belgian expeditions to the Antarctic and by 1905 Great Britain, Germany, Sweden and France had also become involved in exploration and scientific work in the south. Captain Scott's first expedition took the *Discovery* to McMurdo Sound in 1901–4. Shackleton followed in 1907–9 with the *Nimrod* and travelled to within 97 nautical miles of the South Pole. Scott returned in 1910–12, finally reaching the Pole in January 1912, but dying with his companions on their return journey.

All of these expeditions were given extensive coverage in the newspapers of the day, in Great Britain as well as in Australia and New Zealand. In November 1910, *The Press*, published in Christchurch, New Zealand, carried a detailed report of preparations for Scott's second expedition, and it is in the middle of that lengthy article that reference is made to the proposals by the travel agents Thomas Cook and Sons to 'despatch a vessel to McMurdo Sound'.

The proposal must be seen against the background of social patterns of both the Victorian and Edwardian age as well as the development of the travel industry, first begun over half a century earlier by the young Thomas Cook (Brendon, 1991). During the early 1840s he had begun organising excursions but it was not until the Great Exhibition of 1851 that he also arranged accommodation for his travellers. Overseas tours followed a few years later and because of Cook's Baptist and Temperance Association background, it was considered quite respectable for ladies to travel under his guidance, giving them remarkable freedom in an age beset with strict conventions. This therefore was the background to the report in *The Press* on 4 November 1910.

Scott's second Antarctic expedition was clearly of considerable interest and had already received regular coverage. The article on that particular day concentrated on food supplies and stores. A lengthy list included '$12\frac{1}{4}$ dozen quarts anchovy paste ... 700 lbs marmalade ... 500 lbs beef marrow ... 29 cases brandy, whisky, and wines' (*The Press*, 4 November 1910, p. 9). After this inventory and a discussion of the problems relating to storage and transportation there is a series of miscellaneous notes about the *Terra Nova* and the social arrangements for the ship's officers and the scientific staff. Then follows one paragraph:

> There is a possibility of the Antarctic regions being visited by a party of tourists next year, Messrs. Thos. Cook and Sons having put forward

proposals for the despatch of a vessel to McMurdo Sound. The trip, it is estimated, will take fifty days, and it is intended that the vessel should leave some New Zealand port about the end of 1911, so as to arrive at the Antarctic in mid-summer. Already some members of the New Zealand Parliament, a number of ladies and several gentlemen interested in scientific matters, have made enquiries about the trip, which, it is likely, will include a visit to the sub-Antarctic islands of the Dominion. It is anticipated that many from different parts of the world interested in the Antarctic and desirous of an opportunity of witnessing the Aurora Australis, will probably go on the trip, in addition to many who have friends and relatives with the British Antarctic Expedition (*The Press*, 4 November 1910, p. 9).

Unfortunately, the archives of Thomas Cook in London are missing certain editions of their Cook's *Australasian Travellers Gazette*, which might have contained further information on this planned voyage and they have no other record of the proposals (Jill Lomer, Archives Development Officer, personal communication).

Twenty years later, Thomas Cook's Travel Service advertised in *The polar book*, the handbook of the 1930 British Polar Exhibition organised by Louis Bernacchi, who had been a physicist on Scott's first expedition (Anon, 1930). The single paragraph opened 'Cook's Tours to the Poles are still a thing of the future, but the Cook's and Wagon-Lits travel organisation can arrange every detail of a pleasure cruise to Spitzbergen, or Iceland, or the North Cape. They seemed happier with the Arctic, rather than the Antarctic, but were willing to organise transport of 'goods of every description ... by land, sea or air'. Both the report of *The Press* and this modest half-page advertisement must stand as reliable evidence of the intentions of a well-established and internationally known travel agency.

THE MAIL DELIVERY SERVICES

The First World War interrupted Antarctic exploration and, not surprisingly, interest in Antarctic tourism waned. Opportunities to travel south were extremely limited and it was not until the mid-1920s that a possible route became available. Even though about 1000 whalers worked on South Georgia during the whaling season (October–May), as well as a small permanent population of government officials, there was a lack of regular, direct communication with the Falkland Islands. In order to meet this deficiency the SS *Fleurus* was fitted out for service as a mail ship. She arrived in Port Stanley late in 1924 and during the next nine years carried out a regular delivery service, including visits to the South Shetlands and South Orkneys (Griffiths, 1980). Passenger fares for journeys on the *Fleurus* were established. A 'saloon' to South Georgia or Port Foster, Deception Island, would cost £10 return or £6 single, while a 'cabin' to the same destination commanded half the price. No records have been found of the number of passengers carried on any of the voyages. There was clearly the opportunity to be a 'tourist'—one who travels for pleasure—so despite the lack of data, these trips by 'an uninspiring and far from glamorous steamer' (Griffiths, 1980, p. 1358) are part of the pattern of developing interest in the Antarctic as a tourist venue.

THE PROPOSALS OF LT.-COM. J.R. STENHOUSE

Lt.-Com. J. R. Stenhouse had considerable Antarctic experience. He joined Sir Ernest Shackleton's Antarctic expedition in 1914 before serving as a naval officer in the later years of the First World War. He went to the Antarctic for a second time in 1925–27, as Commander of the *Discovery*, then used as a whaling research vessel. It must have been shortly after his return from this work that he developed and publicised his cruise proposals.

The brochure for the Antarctic cruise planned by Stenhouse bore no travel company's name. The traveller was offered 'a unique opportunity of visiting the Antarctic continent' (Stenhouse, 1929–30). It was proposed to leave Southampton about 10 December 1930 and return in late April 1931, on what was proposed to be 'the first passenger ship to cross the Antarctic circle' (Stenhouse, 1929–30). From later correspondence it appears that Stenhouse was working with British American Tours, an international travel service, with offices in London and New York.

It was proposed to travel first to New York and Havana, before using the Panama Canal to reach the Pacific Ocean, the Galapagos Islands, Tahiti and Auckland, New Zealand. In addition to this simple listing of places, greater detail is given for the itinerary for the Ross Sea:

> The ship will penetrate to the Great Ice Barrier, the limit of Southern navigation, within seven hundred miles of the South Pole, and will be the first passenger ship to cross the Antarctic circle. The destination of the cruise will be the Bay of Whales in the great Ross Barrier at which Amundsen and Byrd made their bases and from which they started on their journeys to the South Pole. During the seven days' cruise in the Ross Sea, the ship will proceed, ice conditions permitting, to McMurdo Sound, from where Scott and Shackleton started their epic journeys. Visits will also be made to the huts in which they wintered at Hut Point, Cape Evans, and Cape Royds (Stenhouse, 1929–30).

The homeward route was via Australia, Bali, Ceylon (now Sri Lanka), India, the Suez Canal, Malta, Gibraltar and Southampton. It is interesting to note that many of the places listed rank highly as areas of present tourist interest, but it is not possible from this one brochure to judge whether they were simply convenient ports of call, or whether they were chosen as added attractions to the prospective passengers. In the few lines given to the world itinerary, places are simply listed, with no further detail. It is only 'The Southern Land of the Midnight Sun' that is described:

> The Antarctic Continent, which is the only Polar Continent, has an area of over five million square miles. It is isolated from the civilised world by the seas of the Southern Ocean. Known hitherto only to explorers and whalers, this vast continent is covered in eternal ice and snow. It is a land of beauty and majesty, and presents a world of colour, brilliant and intensely pure. The scenery of its ice-clad mountain ranges, towering fifteen thousand feet, is unequalled in any other part of the world. On this great silent continent there are no trees, no flowers, no land animals and no inhabitants. It has been referred to as the greatest untapped reservoir of health left for the human race. During the Antarctic summer the sun shines throughout the twenty-four hours. A cold, dry and exhilarating climate (Stenhouse, 1929–30).

The fare was tactfully stated as being 'from £500', a sum equivalent to about £7000 in 1990 terms. Three excellent photographs by Ponting, Scott's 'camera artist' from the *Terra Nova* expedition, show the magnificent scenery and wildlife. The brochure is completed by a world map showing the cruise route and a commendable bird's-eye perspective of the Ross Sea, the ice shelf and the flanking mountains stretching towards the Pole (Figure 11.1).

The brochure has been quoted in some detail not only because of the interest that the material holds, but also because it is revealing to consider what it does not say. No details are given of the ship to be used, its size or suitability for ice work. The 'roaring forties, filthy fifties and screaming sixties' receive no attention and the severity of the weather on the continent itself is also ignored. The overall prospect seems to be a trip with the character of a pleasant Sunday afternoon boating jolly.

On 24 October 1930, the *Daily Mail* reported the planned voyage in enthusiastic terms, with emphasis on the opportunity it gave to women to set foot on the Antarctic continent. Commander Frank Worsley, who had been captain of the *Endurance* on Shackleton's Trans-Antarctic expedition was also to accompany the cruise which was to use the *Stella Polaris*. The latter part of the article also said that Lt.-Com. Stenhouse

> hopes to organise an expedition of the travellers to walk 12 miles over the ice to the hut which was occupied by Commander Byrd, the American explorer, when he flew to the South Pole and back. He hopes also to take them to the hut occupied by Scott and his party. They will travel in tents just as the explorers did and pitch camp on the ice for one night (Stenhouse, 1929–30).

The whole article stressed again the magnificence of the continent and the beauty of the wildlife that could be seen. There was no indication of

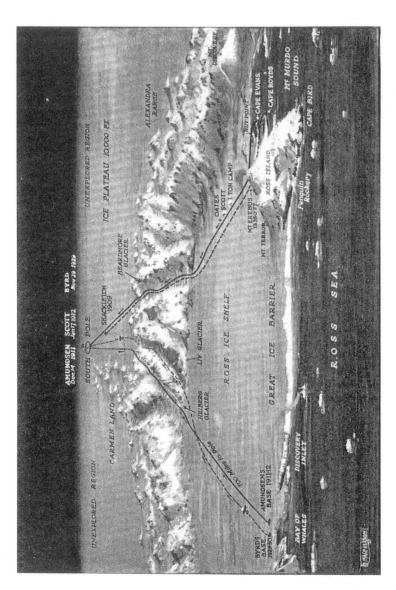

Figure 11.1. Panorama from the brochure of the proposed Antarctic cruise to be led by Lt.-Com. J.R. Stenhouse, 1930–31. The scale of the ship shown steaming away from Discovery Inlet has been greatly exaggerated. The distance between the Bay of Whales and Cape Bird is more than 750 km, so the ship is shown as being about 25 km long!

possible difficulties or dangers due to natural factors such as weather or ice conditions.

This Antarctic and world cruise never took place. No explanation has been found, but there must have been some interest to encourage Stenhouse, for he attempted to organise a similar tour in the 1931–32 season. Together with British American Tours Ltd, an itinerary was arranged, using the SS *Veendam* of 17 000 tons. Departing from New York on 15 December 1931, the same route was to be followed via the Panama Canal. It was scheduled to arrive in the Ross Sea on 27 January 1932 and depart six days later. The return route was again to be the north of Australia, and then via the Suez Canal to Gibraltar, where British passengers were to be landed. Mr Hankey, the Director of British American Tours Ltd, wrote in May 1931 that 'passengers will have a unique opportunity of visiting many places off the beaten track, which, in the ordinary course, they would never have a chance of doing' (manuscript in Scott Polar Research Institute). However, the stops were to be very short; arrival and departure at the Galapagos was scheduled for the same day and there was only a two-day stay scheduled in Bali. The plans for the cruise were still active in mid-June 1931, but it too never took place. It would be interesting to know how many had shown genuine interest, beyond merely writing for the brochure, but the records at the Scott Polar Research Institute give no further details. International unrest, leading to the Second World War and the subsequent austerity, again subdued European and American unrest and no further plans for Antarctic tourism emerged until the mid-1950s.

CONTINUING INTEREST

Two years later, in 1933, the Argentine transport ship the *Pampa* left Buenos Aires with relief personnel and provisions for the meteorological observatory on Laurie Island in the South Orkneys. According to Capdevila (1984), a group of tourists were on board, including the naval attaché from the United States embassy with his wife and family. However, the American guests decided to disembark at Ushuaia as they had doubts concerning the expertise of the crew in dangerous seas. The other travellers remained on board, and reached their goal.

Sir Douglas Mawson, the veteran Australian explorer, identified the future potential of tourism. In 1936 he concluded his presidential address to the Australian and New Zealand Association for the Advancement of Science by considering the 'prospects for economic development' (Mawson, 1936). In a quaintly worded way he suggested that 'as a winter-sports ground for diversion in summer, Antarctica would be a thrill to Australians' (Mawson, 1936). He recognised there could be transport problems. Nevertheless, he saw 'no reason to delay the despatch from our ports of modern liners on summer pleasure cruises amongst the pack ice' (Mawson, 1936).

Mawson's enthusiasm for Antarctic tourism has not always been shared, especially by scientific workers, but it has to be recognised that 'this is the most remote and unknown area of the world. Its heroic explorers belong to recent history . . . it has great scenic beauty, particularly in the relatively accessible peninsula area' (Potter, 1973, pp. 301–302). Any of these attributes can generate interest and climbers, yachtspersons and other adventurers have joined the visitors who use the cruise ships. As already suggested by Codling (1982), there is a need for both quantitative and qualitative measurement of tourist activity, with systematic monitoring, to provide a basis for balanced and workable decisions concerning its impact and it is encouraging that work has begun in these directions. Tourism in the Antarctic is now firmly established. The wanderings of a few intrepid travellers on trading or mail boats, or the proposals for a single cruise— whether in 1911 or 1930—have now developed into a far wider pattern of regular visits, fulfilling the desire of many people to see the southern continent.

REFERENCES

Anon (but possibly Bernacchi, L.C. ed.), 1930, *The polar book*, E. Allom, London
Beaglehole, J.C., ed., 1961, *The journals of Captain James Cook, Vol. II, The voyage of the Resolution and Adventure, 1772–1775*, Cambridge University Press, Cambridge
Brendon, P., 1991, *Thomas Cook*, Secker & Warburg
Capdevila, R., 1984, Las primeras mujeres que estuvieron en las Orcadas fueron Argentinas, *Artartida*, **13**: 34
Cherry-Garrard, C., 1937, *The worst journey in the world*, 2 vols., Penguin Books, Harmondsworth
Codling, R.J., 1982, Sea-borne tourism in the Antarctic: an evaluation, *Polar Record*, **21**(130): 3–9
Cumpston, J.S., 1968, *Macquarie Island*, Antarctic Division, Department of External Affairs, Canberra
Daily Mail (London), 1930, Women's Antarctic tour, *Daily Mail*, 24 October
Gibson-Watt, D., 1967, Antarctic Treaty Bill, Third Reading, House of Commons. *Hansard* columns 1593 and 1594, HMSO, London
Goodwin, M.P., 1966, Letter from the Antarctic, SPRI file ref. no. (*7): 796.51.7, Scott Polar Research Institute, Cambridge
Griffiths, R., 1980, The S.S. Fleurus and the mails to South Georgia, *Stamp Collecting*, **136**(13): 1385–1391
Headland, R.K., 1989, *Chronological list of Antarctic expeditions and related historical events*, Cambridge University Press, Cambridge
Mawson, D., 1936, Presidential Address, Australian and New Zealand Association for the Advancement of Science, Sydney
Neider, C., ed., 1973, *Antarctica*, George Allen & Unwin, London

Potter, N., 1973, The Antarctic: any economic future? In Lewis, R.S., Smith, P.M., eds., *Frozen future*, Quadrangle Books, New York

Reich, R.J., 1980, The development of Antarctic tourism, *Polar Record*, **20**(126): 203–214

Stenhouse, J.R., 1929–30, Stenhouse brochure and letters, SPRI archives folder 92 [Stenhouse, J.], Scott Polar Research Institute, Cambridge

The Press (Christchurch, New Zealand), 1910, The Antarctic expedition, *The Press*, 4 November

Wilson, E.A., 1966, *Diary of the Discovery expedition to the Antarctic 1901–1904*, Blandford Press, London

12 The Regulation of Antarctic Tourism

DEBRA J. ENZENBACHER

THE ANTARCTIC TREATY SYSTEM AND TOURISM POLICY

There is no disagreement amongst Treaty Parties that tourism and non-governmental activities must be regulated. Unregulated activities in Antarctica would lead to unacceptable impacts on the fragile Antarctic environment and criticism of the ATCPs' ability to provide for the effective governance of Antarctica.

It is therefore not a question of whether tourism and non-governmental activities should be regulated but how (ATCM, 1992b, p. 2).

Record numbers of tourists are visiting the Antarctic; more than 35 per cent of all arrivals as of 1993 (not including those overflying the continent) travelled during the three summer seasons 1990/91 to 1992/93 (Enzenbacher, 1994a). Given the increased attention to Antarctic environmental issues (Burgess, 1990; National Research Council, 1993), particularly the environmental impacts of tourism activities (Manheim, 1990; Enzenbacher, 1992; Hall, 1992), Antarctic tourism policy is becoming increasingly significant within the Antarctic Treaty System (ATS). Although environmental protection issues were not high on the international agenda when the Antarctic Treaty was signed in 1959 (Blay, 1992), Treaty meetings are increasingly focused on environmental issues (Holdgate, 1983; Barnes, 1991). An important element in the successful operation of the ATS is the flexibility of the Treaty (Scully, 1986b) that allows previous decisions to be modified or amended at any time by unanimous agreement of the contracting parties. New recommendations, employing either hortatory or mandatory language, allow Treaty parties to respond to tourism issues on an ongoing basis (Boczek, 1988). Examples of hortatory language include: 'They should exert appropriate efforts to ensure that all tourists and other visitors do not engage in any activity in the Treaty Area which is contrary to the principles and purposes of the Antarctic Treaty' (Recommendation

Polar Tourism: Tourism in the Arctic and Antarctic Regions
Edited by C. Michael Hall and Margaret E. Johnston. © John Wiley & Sons Ltd, 1995

VI-7) (Heap, 1990, p. 2602), 'They urge non-governmental expeditions to carry adequate insurance' and 'To the extent practicable, they encourage commercial tour operators to carry tour guides with experience of Antarctic conditions' (Recommendation X-8) (Heap, 1990, p. 2606). Since most are hortatory, approved recommendations are seldom enacted into national legislation (ATCM, 1992d), as a party is bound only to the extent that the wording of the recommendation requires. Once mandatory recommendations are agreed the strength of implementing legislation determines their effectiveness for each country. Indeed, some nations may enact more stringent legislation than others (Orrego Vicuña, 1988) resulting in a lack of uniformity in regulatory standards.

THE RESPONSE OF THE ANTARCTIC TREATY SYSTEM TO TOURISM ISSUES

As self-appointed stewards of the Antarctic, Treaty parties have claimed for themselves the responsibility for ensuring that human activities, including tourism, are conducted in a manner consistent with the principles of the Treaty and its instruments and to provide appropriate, comprehensive and effective regulation. Appendix A lists the signatories to the Antarctic Treaty and members of the Scientific Committee on Antarctic Research (SCAR). Such an achievement will not be easy given different governmental positions taken with respect to tourism. It is important to regulate for the Antarctic ecosystem as a whole since its parts are highly interdependent; if one part of it is harmed, all other areas will likely suffer (Couratier, 1983; Redgwell, 1990; Foreman, 1992).

Treaty parties have expressed the 'need to maintain an awareness of the activities of tourists in the Antarctic Treaty Area' [Recommendation XIII-3] (Antarctic Treaty, 1985, p. 36) and the effect tourism has had on the environment since their first meeting in 1961. Although tourism has more recently been a regular agenda topic at Antarctic Treaty consultative meetings (ATCMs), no tourism recommendations were made from 1982 to 1992 (Vidas, 1992). However, in April 1994, at the XVIIIth ATCM, the sole recommendation adopted at the meeting pertained to tourism; sets of guidance for visitors and those organising and conducting tourism in the Treaty area were drafted taking into account existing guidelines (Appendix B). What effect these sets of guidance will have is not yet known, but in some respects they are greater in scope and detail than previous guidelines. A Transitional Environmental Working Group (TEWG) was also established at the XVIIIth ATCM as a forerunner to a fully fledged Committee on Environmental Protection (CEP) following the full entry into force of the Protocol. This is significant since there is now a forum, designated to consider environmental issues, that did not exist before. It is in this working group that tourism issues are likely to be debated further. The TEWG will meet during the first week of the XIXth ATCM in Seoul so that its technical advice and recommendations may be considered, at a political level, during the second week of the meeting (ATCM, 1994a).

How well Treaty parties have responded to tourism issues has been called into question (e.g. Auburn, 1982; Nicholson, 1986; Cook, 1990; Manheim, 1990, 1992a, b; Barnes, 1991; IUCN, 1991; Suter, 1991; ATCM, 1992a; Enzenbacher, 1992; Vidas, 1992; Angelini and Mansfield, 1993). For example, the first informal Treaty meeting devoted solely to tourism issues was held in Venice from 9 to 10 November 1992 to address environmental and operational issues (Antarctic Treaty, 1991), but resulted in a standstill. An important opportunity was thereby lost, but progress may be made provided this outcome does not deter future tourism negotiations. Nevertheless, one positive development at the XVIIth ATCM was the amount of information papers (15 of 83) and working papers (6 of 30) dealing with tourism (ATCM, 1992c). Notably, a comprehensive code of guidance was tabled by the United Kingdom (ATCM, 1992e) that consolidated various guidelines into one code. Other papers assessed the nature and scale of tourism's potential problems and impacts, examined whether existing Treaty provisions adequately address them and made recommendations accordingly (ATCM, 1992b,f). The most controversial tourism document was the proposed Protocol annex on tourism (ATCM, 1992d) (see below). Tabled by five countries (Chile, France, Germany, Italy and Spain), the document met with considerable opposition.

The implementing Protocol legislation of some Treaty parties is expected to play a crucial role in regulating some aspects of Antarctic tourist activity, but Treaty recommendations and other instruments backed by national legislation and guidelines, notably those for tourists and tour operators endorsed by members of IAATO, provide the current regulatory framework for Antarctic tourism. These instruments may be described as official or unofficial. Official instruments include: (1) the Antarctic Treaty, recommendations made subsequent to its entry into force, especially those that specifically mention tourism and/or tourists (Table 12.1) and all other applicable supplementary instruments agreed within the ATS, including the Protocol; and (2) national legislation enacted by Treaty parties to implement these instruments and other applicable national laws. Notable supplementary instruments include the Agreed Measures for the Conservation of Antarctic Fauna and Flora, the Convention for the Conservation of Antarctic Seals (CCAS) and the Convention on the Conservation of Antarctic Marine Living Resources (CCAMLR). Unofficial instruments include various sets of guidelines (e.g. SCAR, 1980; the Council of Managers of National Antarctic Programs (COMNAP), 1990; Oceanites, 1990/91; IAATO, 1993a, b; National Research Council, 1993).

Table 12.1. Antarctic Treaty recommendations pertaining to tourism

Recommendation	Summary
IV-27 (1)	Information about tourist and non-tourist governmental expeditions should be provided in advance
IV-27 (2), VI-7 (2), VIII-9 (2) (a)	Conditions for visits to stations should be made known
VI-11	Tourists are discouraged from landing on newly formed islands
VII-4 (2), VIII-9,	Visitors to Antarctica not sponsored by a consultative party
X-8 Part I	Should be aware of the relevant provisions of the Treaty, recommendations and accepted practices
VII-4 (3), VIII-9 (3)	The environmental effects of tourism can be monitored
VII-4 (3), VIII-9 (2) (b)	Provision exists to concentrate on the impact of tourism should this be considered environmentally prudent
VIII-9 (2(b)) and Annex B	Areas of Special Tourist Interest (ASTIs) are created, although to date, no such areas have been designated
X-8 Part III	Tour operators are encouraged to carry experienced guides
X-8 Part II	Consultative parties should consult each other about non-governmental expeditions organised in one country and requesting assistance from another
X-8 Part II	Non-governmental expeditions should be self-sufficient and carry adequate insurance
X-8 Part IV	Commercial overflights in Antarctica are addressed
XVI-13	An informal meeting devoted to tourism issues will be convened to precede the XVIIth ATCM in Venice

Sources: Heap, (1990); Antarctic Treaty, (1991).

The Areas of Special Tourist Interest (ASTI) category was designed to direct tours to certain sites so their effects could be contained and monitored. This could be achieved if operators were encouraged to visit these sites and a reporting system were in place (Stephenson, 1993). These specially defined tourism areas have been advocated (Cousteau and

Charrier, 1992), but to date, none have been designated. The cumulative effects of Antarctic tour visits have not been established, nor is it known whether visits are best concentrated at a limited number of sites or spread out over many sites. Other recommendations may apply to tourism even if not explicitly mentioned, especially those covering 'Air safety in Antarctica' (XV-20), 'Cooperation in the hydrographic charting of Antarctic waters' (XV-19), and 'Human impact on the Antarctic environment: prevention, control, and response to marine pollution' (XV-4).

The role of the Protocol on environmental protection to the Antarctic Treaty in regulating tourism

The adoption of the Madrid Protocol revolutionised conservation measures for the Antarctic by providing the most comprehensive multilateral document on the international protection of the environment ever adopted (Blay, 1992); it will likely serve as the basis for the area's environmental management in the near future (Harris and Meadows, 1992). The annexes cover environmental impact assessment, conservation of Antarctic fauna and flora, waste disposal and waste management, the prevention of marine pollution and area protection and management, respectively. The comprehensive nature of the Protocol is significant since it ensures a more systematic and effective strategy of protection for the Antarctic; negotiations were marked by an unprecedented level of non-governmental organisation (NGO) participation (Blay, 1992).

The Protocol with annexes applies to all forms of human activity in the Antarctic, including tourism, but has yet to enter into force. To do so, it must be ratified by all parties having consultative status at the time it was negotiated. Although this is expected in the near future its entry into force is not guaranteed. The increased level of global environmental consciousness, NGO influence and the recent tendency of Treaty parties to portray themselves as environmentally responsible should result in an all-round greater willingness to ratify the Protocol (Blay, 1992). As of April 1994 nine consultative parties had ratified the Protocol: Spain, France, Peru, Ecuador, Norway, Argentina, Australia, Sweden and the Netherlands (ATCM, 1994a; *ECO*, 1994b); of these, two (Australia and Sweden) had passed domestic implementing legislation (*ECO*, 1994a). A lack of domestic implementing legislation would prevent the Protocol from having full effect.

Protocol provisions

Several sections of the Protocol are of immediate relevance to tourism in the Antarctic. Article 3 (Environmental Principles) notes that activities in the Treaty area shall be planned and conducted so as to limit adverse effects on the environment and ecosystems; plans and conduct should avoid significant adverse effects on air or water quality, detrimental changes occurring to fauna and flora and degradation of areas having biological, scientific, historic, aesthetic or wilderness significance. Under this article prior assessment of possible environmental impacts shall consider the scope of the activity, its area, duration and intensity, and cumulative impacts (by itself and in combination with other activity in the Treaty area). Also, regular and effective monitoring of human activities should occur. Priority shall be accorded to scientific research and preserving the Antarctic as an area for such research. Tourism shall take place in a manner consistent with these principles and be modified, suspended or cancelled if it results in, or threatens to result in, impacts on the environment.

Article 6 provides for parties to cooperate in the planning and conduct of activities in the Treaty area to assist in the promotion of educational programmes, preparation environmental impact assessments, and planning with a view to protecting the Antarctic environment. Article 8 states that proposed activities shall be subject to the procedures for environmental impact assessment (Annex 1). Article 11 establishes a Committee for Environmental Protection (CEP). Article 12 describes its function: to provide advice upon the collection, archiving, exchange and evaluation of information related to environmental protection, the state of the Antarctic environment and the need for scientific research. Article 13 provides for each party to take appropriate measures to adopt laws, regulations and enforcement measures to ensure compliance with the Protocol, while Article 14 arranges for inspections by observers to ensure compliance with the Protocol. Under Article 15 parties agree to respond promptly and effectively to emergencies arising from tourism, among other activities, and establish contingency plans for incidents with potential adverse environmental effects. Where such incidents occur, liability for damages is provided for in Article 16.

Environmental impact assessment procedures for human activities are provided for in Annex I of the Protocol. Initial (IEE) and comprehensive (CEE) environmental evaluations are outlined. IEEs shall be prepared unless it is determined that activities will have less than a minor or transitory impact or a CEE is in preparation. IEEs shall include a description of the proposed activity, its purpose, location, duration and intensity along with consideration of (a) alternatives to the activity and any impacts they may have; and (b) cumulative impacts in the light of existing and known planned activities. CEEs may be indicated where activities are likely to have more than a minor or transitory impact. CEEs are to be made publicly available and circulated for comment to all parties and the CEP at least 120 days prior to the next ATCM. Monitoring procedures shall be put in place to assess and verify impacts of activities that proceed following the completion of a CEE.

Annex II prohibits the taking of, or harmful interference with, native fauna and flora. A permit system for authorised activity is to be established. No species of non-native animal or plant is to be introduced on to land, ice shelves or water in the Treaty area except with a permit. Annex III provides for the amount of waste produced or disposed of in the Treaty area to be reduced as far as practicable, all wastes are to be stored. Sewage and domestic liquid wastes may be discharged directly into the sea provided that, wherever practicable, conditions exist for treatment. Similarly, under Annex IV, the discharge of oil or oily mixtures into the sea is prohibited except in cases permitted under Annex I of MARPOL 73/78. Sea disposal of all plastics, including garbage bags, and all other garbage, including glass, metal, paper, bottles and incineration ash is prohibited. Food waste may be disposed of at sea after certain treatment, but not less than 12 nautical miles from the nearest land or ice shelf.

Annex V provides for specific designation of Antarctic Specially Protected Areas (ASPAs) and Antarctic Specially Managed Areas (ASMAs) in which activities shall be prohibited, restricted or managed in accordance with management plans. ASPAs are designed to protect outstanding environmental, scientific, historic, aesthetic or wilderness values or ongoing or planned scientific research. Areas to be identified as ASPAs include those with important or unusual assemblages of species, including wildlife colonies or with the only known habitat of any species, among other things. Entry into ASPAs shall be by permit only. ASMAs may include areas where activities, such as tourism, pose risks of cumulative environmental impacts on sites and monuments of recognised historic value. Entry permits will not be required in ASMAs.

The proposed Protocol annex on tourism

As Treaty parties consider the form tourism regulations should take, a current debate centres on the proposed Protocol annex on tourism. The three main legal arguments cited by its proposers were, first, a comprehensive framework for regulating tourism which would allow states at national levels to enact homogeneous laws and regulations thereby avoiding serious inconsistencies. Second, tourism regulations would have indisputable legally binding force much stronger than current recommendations and an annex offers the most appropriate form in which to regulate tourism. Third, it would allow all Treaty parties to be involved in regulating tourism activities (ATCM, 1992d).

Those opposing maintain that the Protocol already covers all human activities in the Treaty area rendering a tourism annex redundant and/or claim a convincing case to further regulate tourism has yet to be made. Another view holds that the status quo should be maintained at least until the Protocol enters into force. However, while it is generally recognised that specific issues unique to tourist activity have arisen that are not covered by existing Treaty provisions and may need to be regulated, how the issue of the proposed annex on tourism will be resolved remains to be seen (Hay, 1993b).

Applicable national legislation

National Antarctic legislation enacted by all Treaty parties needs to be considered to assess accurately the effectiveness of Antarctic environmental and tourism regulations; the current low number of deposited Protocol ratification instruments delays this task. United States legislation applicable to its citizens in Antarctica is used as an example since they comprise the largest percentage of visiting tourists (Beck, 1990).

No single instrument legislates solely for US Antarctic tourist activity. The two legal instruments that cover US citizens in the Treaty area are the Antarctic Treaty and the Antarctic Conservation Act (ACA) of 1978 (Public Law 95-541) (NSF, 1989). The ACA implements the Agreed Measures of 1964, which have long been considered one of the most comprehensive and successful international instruments for wildlife conservation ever negotiated (Auburn, 1982). When/if the Protocol enters into force it will also apply to tourist activity.

Although the ACA does not cover all aspects of tourist activity, its provisions are relevant to the nature in which Antarctic tours are conducted given repeated localised visits to popular landing sites that often have wildlife present. For example, under the ACA it is unlawful to take, without permit, native animals or birds, to introduce species, to enter special areas or to discharge pollutants. The Act provides for penalties of up to US$10 000 and one year in prison for each violation (NSF, 1989). Treaty recommendations adopted by the United States government also have the effect of law for citizens. For example, the Comprehensive Crime Control Act of 1984 extends United States maritime and territorial jurisdiction to cover offences committed by or against its civilians in the Antarctic, therefore US tourists or operator personnel could be prosecuted for serious offences committed in Antarctica.

United States tourists will continue to be bound by ACA provisions at least until Protocol legislation is implemented. Earlier versions of introduced bills (US Congress, 1993a, 1993b) met with Administration opposition when they were seen as more stringent than the Protocol (Foreman, 1992). Domestic politics can wield enormous influence over the final version of (Protocol) implementing legislation and therefore need to be considered when developing appropriate Antarctic tourism regulations. Likewise, enforcement is a crucial issue since over-regulation of operators would likely yield unwanted results and self-regulation of the industry is neither adequate or appropriate; the challenge lies in getting the balance right.

National Antarctic programme responses to tourism

Each national Antarctic programme can develop its own policy covering tour visits to its research stations in an effort to reduce impacts on science programmes; some employ strict sets of rules limiting the number of tour visits per season (e.g. NSF, 1988; NZARP, 1990; Enzenbacher, 1991; Stephenson, 1993). For example, New Zealand undertakes the care and custody of certain historic monuments in the Ross Dependency and employs guides to accompany cruise ships having arranged to visit them (NZARP, 1990).

Practical steps have been taken by some Treaty nations to meet with Antarctic tour operators and monitor ship-borne tourism. For example, the United States provides for an annual meeting between the NSF and Antarctic tour operators (Enzenbacher, 1994b), a tourism observer programme (NSF, 1993; Enzenbacher, 1994c) and a research project on the environmental effects of Antarctic tourism as part of the long-term ecological research (LTER) project in place at Palmer Station, Antarctic Peninsula (Kiernan, 1993).

Although the annual NSF meeting has long sustained the most contact with Antarctic tour operators, recent initiatives have improved the overall scope of contact. For example, in October 1993, the first meeting of Antarctic tour operators based in Germany and government officials was held in Bremerhaven, a development which signals growing interest in, and awareness of, the need to regulate Antarctic tourism and manage its effects.

The role of the International Association of Antarctica Tour Operators (IAATO)

The International Association of Antarctica Tour Operators (IAATO) was founded in August 1991 by seven charter members (Enzenbacher, 1993a). Membership has since grown considerably and continues to change given the nature of market forces. As of 1993 it included most of the main cruise lines planning to operate in the Antarctic during the upcoming season. IAATO members meet annually in conjunction with the NSF/Antarctic tour operators meeting; attendance is compulsory as memberships, by-laws and other important issues are discussed. Since IAATO members carried 70 per cent of all Antarctic tourists during the 1992/93 season and

81 per cent the previous season their influence is considerable (Enzenbacher, 1994a). As Claus (1990) noted, 'Over the past few years we have been involved in Antarctic policy meetings, US Congressional hearings and scientific conferences, not only in the US but in Australia and New Zealand as well, where we have taken a leading role in the environmental protection of Antarctica' (Claus, 1990).

IAATO has two sets of guidelines; the first is addressed to Antarctica tour operators (Appendix C), the second is directed at Antarctica visitors (Appendix D). IAATO tour operator guidelines are intended for crew and staff members of Antarctic tour companies. The agreed principles contained within aim at increasing awareness and establishing a code of behaviour that minimises tourism impacts on the environment. The willingness of industry members to cooperate with Treaty parties in regulating tourism is crucial to the protection of the Antarctic environment (Keage and Dingwall, 1993). Tour operators maintain that current IAATO guidelines are adequate, noting tourists often serve as effective guardians of the wildlife and environment. Yet, it is not clear that self-regulation sufficiently addresses all issues arising from tourist activity as no neutral regulatory authority currently exists to oversee all Antarctic operators. Infractions of IAATO guidelines by members have been documented, but it is not known to what extent the environment is seriously affected by them (Enzenbacher, 1992).

The Scientific Committee on Antarctic Research (SCAR) and tourism

Although SCAR is not technically a part of the ATS and its linkage with ATCPs is indirect (Scully, 1986a) it is perhaps the most influential body and has a role to play with respect to tourism issues. Designated to initiate, promote and coordinate scientific activity in Antarctica, SCAR provides Treaty parties with informed advice on pertinent scientific and environmental matters including 'Antarctic ecosystems and their likely response to impact' (Heap and Holdgate, 1986, p. 209), but parties are not required to join (Appendix A). SCAR organises important international symposia and workshops; its provision of informed advice allows the ATS to benefit from input offered by a neutral body largely unbound by the politics influencing ATCM delegations.

The Council of Managers of National Antarctic Programs and tourism

The Council of Managers of National Antarctic Programs (COMNAP) is federated to SCAR and serves to exchange information and review operational matters on a regular basis; its interest in tourism issues continues to increase. All national Antarctic programmes are affected by tourism since the topic is regularly discussed within the ATS; some programmes may not receive tourists, but no programme is immune from a future request to provide emergency assistance.

In June 1992 a new COMNAP subgroup formed and reported on the impact of tourism on science and the environment, potential liability, interference with routine operations, contingency response and the prospects for formulation and enforcement of regulations. COMNAP has charged this sub-group to develop a plan for a workshop on tourism and nongovernmental activities (Antarctic Treaty, 1993). At the 1993 NSF/Antarctic tour operators meeting, Jan Stel of COMNAP requested an annual meeting with IAATO members beginning in 1994. If the offer is taken up an important channel of communication will remain open. In 1993, COMNAP tasked ICAIR (the International Centre for Antarctic Information and Research) to develop a prototype, standardised, centralised, international and accessible database on Antarctic tourism. This development addresses a gap in current knowledge of Antarctic tourist activity and will prove useful to science, tourism and environmental policy planners if parties provide the necessary information (Enzenbacher, 1994a).

LIMITATIONS OF CURRENT REGULATORY MEASURES FOR ANTARCTIC TOURISM AND THE CHALLENGE TO POLICY MAKERS

Antarctica's unique international status and unresolved issues in the ATS present special challenges when regulating tourist activity. The general success of the ATS has been well attested (Orrego Vicuña, 1986; Scully, 1986a; Watts, 1986a; Negroponte, 1987; Trolle-Anderson, 1987). No state directly involved in matters Antarctic works outside of the ATS (Watts, 1992). However, the ATS has met criticism. Troublesome issues such as jurisdiction and sovereignty, applicability and enforcement issues, liability, and implementation were side-stepped when the Treaty was negotiated in order to reach agreement; some continue to plague the ATS and may ultimately affect its ability to regulate tourism effectively.

Jurisdiction and third parties

Jurisdiction remains one of the major unsolved problems of the ATS (Quigg, 1983; Watts, 1992); issues that arise are dealt with on an *ad hoc* basis. According to Article 34 of the Convention on the Law of Treaties, treaties do not generally bind third party states to their terms without their consent. There is therefore no legal basis for steps taken to ensure compliance by third parties (Auburn, 1982; Boczek, 1988). It is not clear that tourism regulations agreed within the ATS would be binding on citizens of non-party states and it 'is unlikely that third parties will be bound by the Protocol' (Foreman, 1992, p. 877). For example, Annex IV does not apply to ships flying flags of non-state parties, a category under which many tour ships fall.

Sovereignty and territorial disputes

Another difficulty faced by the ATS is the inability to resolve sovereignty issues (Triggs, 1987; Foreman, 1992; Kaye and Rothwell, 1993). Some Treaty parties felt their authority would be undercut if they surrendered their territorial claims when (or after) the Treaty was negotiated. For example, South American claimant countries have distinct views regarding territory in their Antarctic sectors; often the area is seen as a direct extension of national boundaries. Although these views are not endorsed by other parties, they strongly influence negotiators who hold them. As a result, consensus on tourism issues may be hindered by deep-rooted territorial notions.

Area of applicability and enforcement issues

Neither the Treaty (Article VI) nor the Protocol (Article 3(1)) applies to the high seas, thereby limiting the area of regulatory applicability. The lack of enforcement procedures has led to disregard of environmental guidelines (Orrego Vicuña, 1988; Foreman, 1992) and may lessen the likelihood of compliance with Treaty provisions (Barnes, 1991). Enforcement issues for tourism, already severely challenged by the vastness of the region, are further constrained by the area of applicability and the ease in which transgressors may evade detection (Blay, 1992). For example, Kaye and Rothwell (1993) noted the difficulties inherent in a more rigorous application of Australian law in their claimant sector in Antarctica. Sabella (1992) maintains that a formal inspectorate and regulatory authority for compliance and monitoring are needed. Blay (1992) pointed out that before the Protocol was agreed tourism was not covered by any legally enforceable rules.

Liability

Liability issues for Antarctic activities are complex (Watts, 1986b) and present a major challenge to tourism policy makers. The sinking of the *Bahia Paraiso* less than 1 mile from Anvers Island, Antarctic Peninsula in January 1989 sparked considerable debate since the vessel was carrying 81 tourists; further, as an Argentine navy vessel it was not insured. The resulting spill of 600 000 litres of diesel fuel (Kennicut and Sweet, 1992), quick response team efforts (Kennicut *et al.*, 1990) and subsequent clean-up operations entailed financial and technical resources that far exceeded the capacity of Argentina's Antarctic programme. At the XVIIth ATCM it was agreed to convene a meeting of legal experts before the next ATCM to consider liability issues (Hay, 1993a) and a meeting was held in Heidelberg from 18 to 20 November 1993. At the XVIIIth ATCM a further meeting was planned for the autumn of 1994 at The Hague (ATCM, 1994a, p. 11).

Implementation

Long delays in implementing national legislation for instruments agreed in the ATS are not unusual and may be due to the low priority national policy accords Antarctic matters (Auburn, 1982), domestic policies and/or the political system involved. Therefore, new tourism regulations agreed in the ATS face the prospect of delayed implementation. Furthermore, ATS-related legislation, especially that implementing the Protocol, may vary in stringency among the respective Treaty states.

OTHER MATTERS

Given environmental, science and safety concerns and the actual manner in which tourism is conducted in the Treaty area, current regulatory measures provide a start, but are limited in scope and overall effectiveness; these subjects warrant further consideration. Other barriers to the effective regulation of Antarctic tourism include: the real and perceived political, cultural and economic differences between Treaty parties; the terminology employed in Treaty instruments and national legislation; non-compliance with reporting procedures; the lack of an administrative centre for Treaty matters; and the need for monitoring and further research on the environmental effects of tourism.

Political, cultural, environmental and economic differences between Treaty parties

Treaty parties represent nations with many different political, cultural, environmental and economic orientations. These factors influence negotiating positions in the Treaty forum and need to be considered to appreciate fully the achievements of the ATS's consensus system. Joyner and Ewing (1991) noted that ATCPs, especially the Latin countries, are not likely to accept any changes that degrade their prominence in the ATS, but shifts in traditional roles may be forthcoming given proper conditions and continued negotiation.

Terminology

Treaty documents do not employ consistent terminology that defines and clearly differentiates categories of Antarctic visitors (Boczek, 1988). For example, Recommendation VIII-9 (Heap, 1990, p. 2604) suggests that tour organisers oversee tours and expeditions when this may not be the case. Some terms used in the Protocol are ambiguous, such as the repeated use of the phrase 'to the maximum extent practicable' that leaves parties to interpret measures as they see fit (Blay, 1992) or undefined, such as minor or transitory impacts (Article 8). Boczek observed that there is no coherent set of rules governing tourists given the 'softness' of Treaty language and a lack of 'conceptual rigor' in regulations applicable to Antarctic visitors, and suggested they be placed 'in one Recommendation like the Agreed Measures' (1988, p. 489).

Non-compliance with reporting procedures

Treaty parties are required to report on Antarctic tourist activity organised in their home country. If operators fail to report to home governments as required, Treaty parties cannot comply in turn. Many operators do report, especially those based in the United States, but some (and most yacht owners) do not (Enzenbacher, 1992a). Of the 12 tour operators that offered Antarctic cruises during the 1992/93 season, five of the six required to report to the NSF did. Nevertheless, reported information may be incomplete or irregularly distributed (Nicholson, 1986; Boczek, 1988; Enzenbacher, 1992), while little is done to ensure compliance (Auburn, 1982; Foreman, 1992). Treaty Article VII(5) provides for the exchange of tourism and other relevant information between parties, but the quality, nature and amount of material exchanged vary considerably.

The lack of an administrative centre

There is no centralised source for the assessment, compilation or storage of reported tourism information. The administrative needs of the ATS were deliberately overlooked when the Treaty was first negotiated (Auburn, 1982). The need for permanent administrative arrangements and archival facilities for the ATS has long been recognised as one of its principal weaknesses (Myhre, 1986; Scully, 1988b; Foreman, 1992). The question of a small, cost-effective secretariat has been considered at ATCMs for many years (Hay, 1993a), but has long been rejected. However, recent progress has been made in negotiations calling for a modest secretariat.

The need for monitoring and further research on the environmental effects of tourism

Little is currently known about the effect tourist activity has on the Antarctic environment (Enzenbacher, 1992a). If parties are to ensure that tourists do not engage in activity contrary to the principles or purposes of the Treaty, tourism will need to be more closely monitored (Nicholson, 1986). Environmental monitoring programmes are needed to understand the effects of tourism on terrestrial and marine ecosystems (Champ et al., 1992). Further research conducted on a long-term basis will provide a better understanding of the role natural variation plays in environmental change versus change induced by human visitation. Until such factors can be clearly differentiated it will be difficult to draw any conclusions about environmental impacts caused by tourist activity or properly inform future policy making (Enzenbacher, 1992).

POSSIBLE ACTIONS

Given the current regulatory framework for Antarctic tourism and the need to know more about the nature, scale and environmental effects of tourist activity to regulate adequately, the following possible actions are offered as a means by which to address some issues that need further attention. Although voluntary guidelines supplement ATS efforts to regulate tourism by establishing a code of behaviour for Antarctic tourists and operators, they are not legal instruments. A coordinated ATS response is needed to address adequately tourism issues.

To date, the United States is the only Treaty nation to provide consistent, detailed information on Antarctic tours conducted by its operators. Non-compliance with Treaty reporting provisions highlights a major gap in policy that needs to be addressed if an accurate picture of Antarctic tourism is to emerge. The information exchange requirements under Protocol Annex I place substantial demands on Treaty parties and tour operators. How effectively this will be handled remains to be seen. For example, Nicholson (1986) suggested Treaty parties implement a system of registration or licensing of tour operators to encourage better reporting and provide closer control of tourist activity. An expansion of the NSF/Antarctic tour operators meeting into a Treaty-wide meeting would also address current gaps in communication and information exchanged between parties and tour operators and may improve cooperation between both sets of interests in the Antarctic.

Regulations covering Antarctic tourism would benefit from a clearer demographic picture of visitors. Operators routinely collect passenger data. However, some operators have refused to divulge such information on the grounds that it warrants commercial protection, although it is difficult to justify this position since many operators target different geographic segments of the population and data collected could remain confidential; once compiled it would not be possible to discern the statistics of any one operator. Tourism reporting requirements would be greatly facilitated by centralised administration since data on tourist activity could more readily be collected, organised, compiled and exchanged. The longer it takes to establish a secretariat, the greater the task to place the ATS on a sound administrative footing.

Recognising the variety of political systems and legislative machinery and procedures represented in the ATS, having parties ratify the Protocol in conjunction with implementing domestic legislation would affect the strongest collective outcome. Although it is not appropriate to distinguish between types of activity when applying environmental regulations in Antarctica or 'to give one use of Antarctica absolute and universal priority over others' (Heap and Holdgate, 1986, p. 209), activities unique to tourism need to be looked at to determine how they affect the environment and its ecosystems. An annex that applies statutory law on tourist activity may not be appropriate for the current size of the industry, but it may be appropriate to regulate vessels or operators in the form of a permit system, especially since future levels and forms of Antarctic tourism are difficult to predict.

An ATS tourism observer programme that covered all operators based in Treaty nations may well prove to be the best means by which to enforce regulations and promote compliance with tour operator and visitor guidelines; the financial burden for administering the programme could be shared between Treaty parties, tour operators and tourists.

Many IAATO members expend considerable effort and expense to provide a comprehensive shipboard education programme for Antarctic tourists, others may not. Efforts should be made to standardise the quality of tourist information. Similarly, the cooperative efforts of IAATO members should be extended to devise methods for gathering accurate data on the environmental effects of tourism (Enzenbacher, 1992). Tour operators have a vested interest in keeping the Antarctic clean 'because their stock-in-trade is the pristine environment' (Swithinbank, 1993, p. 108), but a balance needs to be struck when regulating conscientious operators and those that know little about the Antarctic or abide by well-established guidelines.

One IAATO member conducted a voluntary IEE and a second member conducted an environmental audit before requirements for tour operators had been clearly established (ATCM, 1994b, p. 3), the results of which appeared in papers tabled at the XVIIIth ATCM in Kyoto (ATCM, 1994c, d); such initiatives should be encouraged since they increase current knowledge of tourism operations. Yet, if operators will be required to conduct annual environmental impact assessments (EIAs) individually it remains to be seen how cumulative impacts will be addressed; joint EIAs have been mentioned, but as yet no clear description of how they should be conducted is available.

How effective and widely circulated the recently agreed guidance for visitors and those organising and conducting tourism in the Treaty area will be remains to be seen. The proliferation of codes of conduct for tourists may cause confusion. To date, the COMNAP guidelines are the only set approved by an official Treaty entity although these guidelines are not comprehensive, do not specifically address tour operators and are not available in many of the languages represented by tour groups. SCAR and Treaty publications are not readily accessible to the public, nor are they phrased for busy expeditioners or tourists (Stonehouse, 1990). Furthermore, with increasing numbers of nationals from many different countries visiting the Antarctic as tourists, more can be done to develop educational materials in languages that suit their needs.

CONCLUSIONS

The ATS provides a forum within which comprehensive regulations for Antarctic tourist activity can be agreed. Given the unique nature of Antarctica's environment and the need for its protection, the challenge to Antarctic policy makers to formulate appropriate tourism policy is considerable. Whether or not the collective political will exists to develop and coordinate tourism regulations remains to be seen. At present, there are no means of accurately determining future levels and forms of Antarctic tourism. Given recent tourism trends and developments (Enzenbacher, 1993a, b, 1994a) it makes sense to implement appropriate regulations now before issues have the chance to become even more complex and difficult to address. Some of the limitations of the ATS in regulating tourism are rooted in Antarctica's unique international status and the fundamental weaknesses of the negotiated regime. Others can more readily be addressed. The challenge to Antarctic policy makers is to identify the tourism issues that can be negotiated to the greatest effect within a consensus system, ensure regulatory appropriateness and move forward. Although the ATS has a long-established record of success in addressing difficult issues, prospects for more effective regulation of Antarctic tourism will be limited until hurdles in current negotiations are overcome.

Some issues unique to tourist activity require special attention if Antarctica is to be adequately protected. The political, cultural, economic and other differences between Treaty parties can be enormous; they affect Treaty negotiations at many levels. Comprehensive regulations for

Antarctic tourism can be achieved in the Treaty forum provided policies acknowledge these differences, consider the current scale and scope of tourist activity and remain flexible to respond to future levels and forms of tourism.

Given the limitations of the current regulatory framework for Antarctic tourism, trusting voluntary compliance with current guidelines to protect Antarctica's environment from the real and potential adverse effects of tourist activity would not be adequate or responsible. That is why considerable efforts are made by some Treaty parties to meet with tour operators, establish an observer programme to monitor Antarctic tour operations, and devote considerable resources to comply with Treaty reporting provisions covering tourist activity, assess tourism regulatory issues and table ATCM papers accordingly. These efforts underscore the continuing commitment Treaty parties undertake as stewards of Antarctica.

Cooperative efforts on behalf of all parties concerned with Antarctica can help pave the way to improved and informed environmental and tourism policies. The increase in the number of tourism papers circulated at Treaty meetings and the depth in which tourism issues are considered by some delegations are positive developments. SCAR functions could be enlarged to include liaison with operators through attendance at an annual ATS/Antarctic tour operators meeting, providing advice on the direction Antarctic tourism research should take and the coordination of its findings. The Antarctic environment stands to benefit by a swift response to this call.

Given the growing number of operators, ships, yachts, aircraft, tourists, expedition staff and other personnel entering the Treaty area, a coordinated, long-term, systematic approach to monitoring tourist activity and environmental change is needed. Findings will inform future tourism and environmental policies. Current efforts are recognised, but need to be enlarged. Continued cooperation between Treaty parties, tour operators, SCAR, NGOs and other interested parties is essential to the development of appropriate tourism regulations and the protection of the Antarctic environment.

ACKNOWLEDGEMENTS

I thank the American Friends of Cambridge University, the Australian Federation of University Women, the Brian Roberts Fund, the British Federation of Women Graduates, the British Foreign and Commonwealth Office Polar Regions Section, the Cambridge Overseas Trust, the International Federation of University Women and St Edmund's College, University of Cambridge for their generous support of this research. Thanks are also extended to Drs John Heap and Charles Swithinbank for helpful comments on draft versions of the text, to colleagues and staff members of the Scott Polar Research Institute, University of Cambridge and to Melissa Folks at the International Association of Antarctica Tour Operators for providing IAATO guidelines, by-laws and contact information.

APPENDIX A: ANTARCTIC TREATY SIGNATORIES WITH DATES OF ACCESSION AND SCAR (SCIENTIFIC COMMITTEE ON ANTARCTIC RESEARCH) MEMBERSHIP BY CATEGORY

| | Adherents and members (in alphabetical order with Y-M-D dates): | | | |
| | Antarctic Treaty | | SCAR | |
			Full	Associate
Argentina	1961-06-23		1958-02-3	
Australia	1961-06-23		1958-02-3	
Austria	1987-08-25			
Belgium	1960-07-26		1958-02-3	
Brazil	1975-05-16	(1983-09-12)	1984-10-1	
Bulgaria	1978-09-11			
Canada	1988-05-4			
Chile	1961-06-23		1958-02-3	
China, Peoples'				
Republic	**1983-06-8**	**(1985-10-7)**	**1986-06-23**	
Colombia	1989-01-31			1990-07-23
Cuba	1984-08-16			
Czech Republic*	1962-06-14			
Denmark	1965-05-20			
Ecuador	**1987-09-15**	**(1990-11-19)**	**1992-06-15**	**(1988-09-12)**
Estonia				1992-06-15
Finland	**1984-05-15**	**(1989-10-9)**	**1990-07-23**	**(1988-07-1)**
France	1960-09-16		1958-03-3	
Germany BRD†	1979-02-5	(1981-03-3)	1978-05-22	
DDR†	1974-11-19	(1987-10-5)	1981-09-9	
Greece	1987-01-8			
Guatemala	1991-07-31			

continued

APPENDIX A: *continued*

Adherents and members (in alphabetical order with Y-M-D dates):

	Antarctic Treaty		SCAR Full	SCAR Associate
			Full	Associate
Hungary	1984-01-27			
India	**1983-08-19**	**(1983-09-12)**	**1984-10-1**	
Italy	**1981-03-18**	**(1987-10-5)**	**1988-09-12**	**(1987-05-19)**
Japan	1960-08-4		1958-02-3	
Korea (Pyongyang)	1987-01-21			
Korea (Seoul)	**1986-11-28**	**(1989-10-9)**	**1990-07-23**	**(1987-12-8)**
Netherlands	**1967-03-30**	**(1990-11-19)**	**1990-07-23**	**(1987-05-20)**
New Zealand	1960-11-1		1958-02-3	
Norway	1960-08-24		1958-02-3	
Pakistan				1992-06-15
Papua New Guinea‡	1981-03-16			
Peru	**1981-04-10**	**(1989-10-9)**		**1987-04-14**
Poland	**1961-06-8**	**(1977-07-29)**	**1978-05-22**	
Romania	1971-09-15			
Russia§	**1960-11-2**		**1958-02-3**	
South Africa	**1960-06-21**		**1958-02-3**	
Spain	**1982-03-31**	**(1988-09-21)**	**1990-07-23**	**(1987-01-15)**
Sweden	**1984-04-24**	**(1988-09-21)**	**1988-09-12**	**(1987-03-24)**
Switzerland	1990-11-15			1987-06-16
United Kingdom	**1960-05-31**		**1958-02-3**	
United States of America	**1960-08-18**		**1958-02-3**	
Ukraine	1992-10-28			
Uruguay	**1980-01-11**	**(1985-10-7)**	**1988-09-12**	**(1987-07-29)**

The Treaty, made on 1 December 1959, came into force on 23 June 1961. SCAR, formed on 3 February 1958, is part of the International Council of Scientific Unions. Original signatories and members: the 12 states which made the Treaty and formed the Committee, are *italicised*; the Treaty dates given are those of the deposition of instruments of ratification, approval or acceptance. Consultative parties of the Treaty: 26 states (**emboldened**), the 12 original parties and 14 (formerly 15†) others which achieved this status after becoming actively involved in Antarctic research (with dates in brackets). In total, 41 states are adherents to the Treaty. SCAR members are 25 full (formerly 26†) and 5 associate; the dates in brackets for some recent full members are those of admission as an associate member.
* Formerly Czechoslovakia, represented by the Czech Republic from 1 January 1993.
† The two German states unified on 3 October 1990.
‡ Papua New Guinea succeeded to the Treaty after becoming independent of Australia.
§ Formerly the Soviet Union, represented by Russia from December 1991.
Source: Compiled by R.K. Headland, Scott Polar Research Institute, University of Cambridge.

APPENDIX B: ATCM 1994 RECOMMENDATION XVIII-1 ON TOURISM AND NON-GOVERNMENTAL ACTIVITIES

The Representatives,

Reaffirming the exceptional character of the Antarctic environment given in particular the fragility of its fauna and flora and of the setting which the Antarctic offers for the conduct of scientific activities;

Acknowledging the increase in the development of tourist activities in the Antarctic;

Noting that those who visit the Antarctic and organise or conduct tourism and non-governmental activities in the Antarctic are currently subject to legally binding obligations pursuant to national legislation implementing the Antarctic Treaty and associated legal instruments;

Noting further that such visitors or organisers will be subject to additional legally binding obligations upon entry into force of the Protocol on Environment Protection to the Antarctic Treaty;

Recognising the need for visitors and organisers to have practical guidance on how best to plan and carry out any visits to the Antarctic;

Recalling the Final Act of the Eleventh Special Antarctic Treaty Consultative Meeting, at which the Protocol was adopted, in which the signatories of the Final Act decided that the Annexes of the Protocol should be applied in accordance with their legal systems and to the extent practicable;

Desiring to ensure that those who visit the Antarctic carry out their visits or tours strictly in accordance with existing obligations and in so far as is consistent with existing national law, in accordance with the Protocol, pending its entry into force;

Desiring further to facilitate the early entry into force of the Protocol and of the implementation of its provisions in relation to those who visit or organise tours to the Antarctic.

Recommend to their governments that:

1. They circulate widely and as quickly as possible the Guidance for Visitors to the Antarctic and the Guidance for Those Organising and Conducting Tourism and Non-Governmental Activities in the Antarctic annexed to this Recommendation.
2. They urge those intending to visit or organise and conduct tourism and non-governmental activities in the Antarctic to act in accordance with the attached guidance consistent with the relevant provisions of their applicable national law.

Guidance for visitors to the Antarctic

Activities in the Antarctic are governed by the Antarctic treaty of 1959, and associated agreements, referred to collectively as the Antarctic Treaty system. The Treaty established Antarctica as a zone of peace and science.

In 1991, the Antarctic Treaty Consultative Parties adopted the Protocol on Environmental Protection to the Antarctic Treaty, which designates the Antarctic as a natural reserve. The Protocol sets out environmental principles, procedures and obligations for the comprehensive protection of the Antarctic environment, and its dependent and associated ecosystems. The Consultative Parties have agreed that, pending its entry into force, as far as possible and in accordance with their legal system, the provisions of the Protocol should be applied as appropriate.

The Environmental Protocol applies to tourism and non-governmental activities as well as governmental activities in the Antarctic Treaty Area. It is intended to ensure that these activities do not have adverse impacts on the Antarctic environment, or on its scientific and aesthetic values.

This **Guidance for Visitors to the Antarctic** is intended to ensure that all the visitors are aware of, and are therefore able to comply with, the Treaty and the Protocol. Visitors are, of course, bound by the national laws and regulations applicable to activities in the Antarctic.

(A) Protect Antarctic wildlife

Taking or harmful interference with Antarctic wildlife is prohibited except in accordance with a permit issued by a national authority.

1. Do not use aircraft, vessels, small boats, or other means of transport in ways that disturb wildlife, either at sea or on land.
2. Do not feed, touch, or handle birds or seals, or approach to photograph them in ways that cause them to alter their behaviour. Special care is needed when animals are breeding or moulting.
3. Do not damage plants, for example by walking, driving, or landing on extensive moss beds or lichen-covered scree slopes.
4. Do not use guns or explosives. Keep noise to the minimum to avoid frightening wildlife.
5. Do not bring non-native plants or animals into the Antarctic (e.g. live poultry, pet dogs and cats, house plants).

(B) Respect protected areas

A variety of special areas in the Antarctic have been afforded special protection because of their particular ecological, scientific, historic or other values. Entry into certain areas may be prohibited except in accordance with a permit issued by an appropriate national authority. Activities in and near designated Historic Sites and Monuments and certain other areas may be subject to special restrictions.

1. Know the locations of areas that have been afforded special protection and any restrictions regarding entry and activities that can be carried out in and near them.
2. Observe applicable restrictions.
3. Do not damage, remove or destroy Historic Sites or Monuments, or any artefacts associated with them.

(C) Respect scientific research

Do not interfere with scientific research, facilities or equipment.

1. Obtain permission before visiting Antarctic science and logistic support facilities; reconfirm arrangements 24–72 hours before arriving; and comply strictly with the rules regarding such visits.
2. Do not interfere with, or remove, scientific equipment or marker posts, and do not disturb experimental study sites, field camps or supplies.

(D) Be safe

Be prepared for severe and changeable weather. Ensure that your equipment and clothing meet Antarctic standards. Remember that the Antarctic environment is inhospitable, unpredictable and potentially dangerous.

1. Know your capabilities, the dangers posed by the Antarctic environment, and act accordingly. Plan activities with safety in mind at all times.
2. Keep a safe distance from all wildlife, both on land and at sea.
3. Take note of, and act on, the advice and instructions from your leaders; do not stray from your group.
4. Do not walk onto glaciers or large snow fields without proper equipment and experience; there is a real danger of falling into hidden crevasses.
5. Do not expect a rescue service; self-sufficiency is increased and risks reduced by sound planning, quality equipment, and trained personnel.
6. Do not enter emergency refuges (except in emergencies). If you use equipment or food from a refuge, inform the nearest research station or national authority once the emergency is over.
7. Respect any smoking restrictions, particularly around buildings, and take great care to safeguard against the danger of fire. This is a real hazard in the dry environment in Antarctica.

(E) Keep Antarctica pristine

Antarctica remains relatively pristine, and has not yet been subject to large scale human perturbations. It is the largest wilderness area on earth. Please keep it that way.

1. Do not dispose of litter or garbage on land. Open burning is prohibited.
2. Do not disturb or pollute lakes or streams. Any materials discarded at sea must be disposed of properly.
3. Do not paint or engrave names or graffiti on rocks or buildings.
4. Do not collect or take away biological or geological specimens or man-made artefacts as a souvenir, including rocks, bones, eggs, fossils and parts or contents of buildings.
5. Do not deface or vandalise buildings, whether occupied, abandoned, or unoccupied, or emergency refuges.

Guidance for those organising and conducting tourism and non-governmental activities in the Antarctic

Antarctica is the largest wilderness area on earth, unaffected by large scale human activities. Accordingly, this unique and pristine environment has been afforded special protection. Furthermore, it is physically remote, inhospitable, unpredictable and potentially dangerous. All activities planned in the Antarctic Treaty Area, therefore, should be planned and conducted with both environmental protection and safety in mind.

Activities in the Antarctic are subject to the Antarctic Treaty of 1959 and associated legal instruments, referred to collectively as the Antarctic Treaty system. These include the Convention for the Conservation of Antarctic Seals (CCAS) (1972), the Convention on the Conservation of Antarctic Marine Living Resources (CCAMLR) (1980) and the Recommendations and other measures adopted by the Antarctic Treaty Consultative Parties under the Antarctic Treaty.

In 1991, the Consultative Parties to the Antarctic Treaty adopted the Protocol on Environmental Protection to the Antarctic Treaty. This Protocol sets out environmental principles, procedures and obligations for the comprehensive protection of the Antarctic environment, and its dependent and associated ecosystems. The Consultative Parties have agreed that, pending its entry into force, as far as possible and in accordance with their legal systems, that the provisions of the Protocol should be applied as appropriate.

The Environmental Protocol designates Antarctica as a natural reserve devoted to peace and science, and applies to both governmental and non-governmental activities in the Antarctic Treaty Area. The Protocol seeks to ensure that human activities, including tourism, do not have adverse impacts on the Antarctic environment, nor on its scientific and aesthetic values.

The Protocol states, as a matter of principle, that all activities are to be planned and conducted on the basis of information sufficient to evaluate their possible impact on the Antarctic environment and its associated ecosystems, and on the value of Antarctica for the conduct of scientific research. Organisers should be aware that the Environmental Protocol requires that 'activities shall be modified, suspended or cancelled if they result in or threaten to result in impacts upon the Antarctic environment or dependent or associated ecosystems'.

Those responsible for organising and conducting tourism and non-governmental activities must comply fully with national laws and regulations which implement the Antarctic Treaty system, as well as other national laws and regulations implementing international agreements on environmental protection, pollution and safety that relate to the Antarctic Treaty Area. They should also abide by the requirements imposed on organiser and operators under the Protocol on Environmental Protection and its Annexes, in so far as they have not yet been implemented in national law.

Key obligations on organisers and operators

1. Provide prior notification of, and reports on, their activities to the competent authorities of the appropriate Party or Parties.
2. Conduct an assessment of the potential environmental impacts of their planned activities.
3. Provide for effective response to environmental emergencies, especially with regard to marine pollution.
4. Ensure self-sufficiency and safe operations.
5. Respect scientific research and the Antarctic environment, including restrictions regarding protected areas, and the protection of flora and fauna.
6. Prevent the disposal and discharge of prohibited waste.

Procedures to be followed by organisers and operators

(A) When planning to go to Antarctica. Organisers and operators should:

1. Notify the competent national authorities of the appropriate Party or Parties of details of their planned activities with sufficient time to enable the Party(ies) to comply with their information exchange obligations under Article VII (5) of the Antarctic Treaty. The information to be provided is listed in Attachment A.
2. Conduct an environmental assessment in accordance with such procedures as may have been established in national law to give effect to Annex I of the Protocol, including, if appropriate, how potential impacts will be monitored.
3. Obtain timely permission from the national authorities responsible for any stations they propose to visit.
4. Provide information to assist in the preparation of: contingency response plans in accordance with Article 15 of the Protocol; waste management plans in accordance with Annex III of the Protocol; and marine pollution contingency plans in accordance with Annex IV of the Protocol.
5. Ensure that expedition leaders and passengers are aware of the location and special regimes which apply to Specially Protected Areas and Sites of Special Scientific Interest (and on entry into force of the Protocol, Antarctic Specially Protected Areas and Antarctic Specially Managed Areas) and of Historic Sites and Monuments and, in particular, relevant management plans.
6. Obtain a permit, where required by national law, from the competent national authority of the appropriate Party or Parties, should they have a reason to enter such areas, or a monitoring site (CEMP Site) designated under CCAMLR.
7. Ensure that activities are fully self-sufficient and do not require assistance from Parties unless arrangements for it have been agreed in advance.

8. Ensure that they employ experienced and trained personnel, including a sufficient number of guides.
9. Arrange to use equipment, vehicles, vessels, and aircraft appropriate to Antarctic operations.
10. Be fully conversant with applicable communications, navigation, air traffic control and emergency procedures.
11. Obtain the best available maps and hydrographic charts, recognising that many areas are not fully or accurately surveyed.
12. Consider the question of insurance (subject to requirements of national law).
13. Design and conduct information and education programmes to ensure that all personnel and visitors are aware of relevant provisions of the Antarctic Treaty system.
14. Provide visitors with a copy of the **Guidance for Visitors to the Antarctic**.

(B) When in the Antarctic Treaty Area. Organisers and operators should:

1. Comply with all requirements of the Antarctic Treaty system, and relevant national laws, and ensure that visitors are aware of requirements that are relevant to them.
2. Reconfirm arrangements to visit stations 24–72 hours before their arrival and ensure that visitors are aware of any conditions or restrictions established by the station.
3. Ensure that visitors are supervised by a sufficient number of guides who have adequate experience and training in Antarctic conditions and knowledge of the Antarctic Treaty system requirements.
4. Monitor environmental impacts of their activities, if appropriate, and advise the competent national authorities of the appropriate Party or Parties of any adverse or cumulative impacts resulting from an activity, but which were not foreseen by their environmental impact assessment.
5. Operate ships, yachts, small boats, aircraft, hovercraft, and all other means of transport safely and according to appropriate procedures, including those set out in the Antarctic Flight Information Manual (AFIM).
6. Dispose of waste materials in accordance with Annex V of the Protocol. These annexes prohibit, among other things, the discharge of plastics, oil and noxious substances into the Antarctic Treaty Area; regulate the discharge of sewage and food waste; and require the removal of most waste from the area.
7. Cooperate fully with observers designated by Consultative Parties to conduct inspections of stations, ships, aircraft and equipment under Article VII of the Antarctic Treaty, and those to be designated under Article 14 of the Environmental Protocol.
8. Cooperate in monitoring programmes undertaken in accordance with Article 3 (2) (d) of the Protocol.
9. Maintain a careful and complete record of their activities conducted.

(C) On completion of the activities   Within three months of the end of the activity, organisers and operators should report on the conduct of it to the appropriate national authority in accordance with national laws and procedures. Reports should include the name, details and state of registration of each vessel or aircraft

used and the name of their captain or commander; actual itinerary; the number of visitors engaged in the activity; places, dates and purposes of landings and the number of visitors landed on each occasion; any meteorological observations made, including those made as part of the World Meterological Organisation (WMO) Voluntary Observing Ships Scheme; any significant changes in activities and their impacts from those predicted before the visit was conducted; and action taken in case of emergency.

(D) Antarctic Treaty system documents and information Most Antarctic Treaty Parties can provide through their national contact points copies of relevant provisions of the Antarctic Treaty system and information about national laws and procedures, including:

- The Antarctic Treaty (1959)
- Convention for the Conservation of Antarctic Seals (1972)
- Convention on the Conservation of Antarctic Marine Living Resources (1980)
- Protocol on Environment Protection to the Antarctic Treaty (1991)
- Recommendations and other measures adopted under the Antarctic Treaty
- Final Reports of Consultative Meetings
- Handbook of the Antarctic Treaty System (1994)
- Handbook of the Antarctic Treaty System (in Spanish, 1991 edition)

Attachment A: Information to be provided in advance notice

Organisers should provide the following information to the appropriate national authorities in the format requested.

1. name, nationality, and contact details of the organiser;
2. where relevant, registered name and national registration and type of any vessel or aircraft to be used (including name of the captain or commander, call-sign, radio frequency, INMARSAT number);
3. intended itinerary including the date of departure and places to be visited in the Antarctic Treaty Area;
4. activities to be undertaken and purpose;
5. number and qualifications of crew and accompanying guides and expedition staff;
6. estimated number of visitors to be carried;
7. carrying capacity of vessel;
8. intended use of vessel;
9. intended use and type of aircraft;
10. number and type of other vessels, including small boats, to be used in the Antarctic Treaty Area;
11. information about insurance coverage;
12. details of equipment to be used, including for safety purposes, and arrangements for self-sufficiency;
13. and other matters required by national laws.

APPENDIX C: IAATO GUIDELINES FOR TOUR OPERATORS

1. Thoroughly read the Antarctic Conservation Act of 1978 (US Public Law 95-541), abide by the regulations set forth in the Act, and brief your staff accordingly. Comparable legislation for non-US countries should be adhered to accordingly. Be mindful of your own actions and present the best example possible to the passengers.
2. Be aware that under the Act, it is prohibited to enter Specially Protected Areas (SPAs) and Sites of Special Scientific Interest (SSSIs) unless permits have been obtained in advance. Only those with 'compelling scientific purpose' are allowed permits to enter SPAs, as any entry could 'jeopardise the natural ecological system existing in such an area'. SSSIs are 'sites where scientific investigations are being conducted or are planned and there is a demonstrable risk of interference which would jeopardise these investigations'. Permits to enter SSSIs are only granted if the 'proposed entry is consistent with the management plan' for that particular site.
3. Enforce the IAATO Guidelines of Conduct for Antarctic Visitors in a consistent manner. Please keep in mind, however, that guidelines must be adapted to individual circumstances. For example, fur seals with pups may be more aggressive than without pups, and therefore passengers need to stay further away; gentoo penguins are more sensitive to human presence than chinstraps; penguins on eggs or with small chicks are more easily disturbed than moulting chicks.
4. Hire a professional team, including qualified, well-trained and experienced leaders, cruise directors, officers, and crew. Place an emphasis on lecturers and naturalists who will not only talk about wildlife, history and geology, but also guide passengers when ashore. It is recommended that at least 75 per cent of the staff have previous Antarctic experience.
5. Hire Zodiac drivers who are familiar with driving Zodiacs in polar regions. Zodiac drivers should take care not to approach too close to icebergs or other floating ice, or glaciers where calving is a possibility, or to steep cliffs where snow or ice may suddenly slip down into the sea. They should also use caution not to disturb wildlife, which can be very sensitive to engine noise.
6. Educate and brief the crew on the IAATO Guidelines of Conduct for Antarctic Visitors, the Agreed Measures for the Conservation of Antarctic Fauna and Flora, the Marine Mammal Protection Act of 1972 and the Antarctic Conservation Act of 1978, and make sure they are consistently enforced. We encourage tour operators to give slide illustrated talks to the crew and offer guided tours ashore, in order to stimulate the crew's interest in Antarctica and to make sure that they also understand the need for the environmental protection of the region. Unsupervised crew should not be ashore.
7. Have a proper staff-to-passenger ratio. Ensure that for every 20 to 25 passengers there is 1 qualified naturalist/lecturer guide to contact and supervise small groups ashore.
8. Limit the number of passengers ashore to 100 at any one place at any one time.
9. Brief all passengers thoroughly on the IAATO Guidelines of Conduct for Antarctica Visitors, the Agreed Measures for the Conservation of Antarctic Fauna and Flora, the Marine Mammal Protection Act of 1972 and the Antarctic Conservation Act of 1978. It is imperative that passengers and crew be briefed

about the Acts and Agreed Measures, as well as the specifics about the landing sites, prior to going ashore. Make certain that passengers understand both the ethical and legal responsibilities outlined in these documents.

10. When approaching whales or seals by ship or by Zodiac, the ship's officer on the bridge, or the Zodiac driver, should use good judgement to avoid distressing them.
11. Communicate your voyage itinerary to the other passenger vessels in order to avoid over-visitation of any site.
12. Give proper notice to all research stations: 72 hours advance notice and a 24-hour advance reconfirmation of the ship's estimated time of arrival at all Antarctic research stations.
13. Respect the number of visits which have been allocated by different stations, for example Palmer and Faraday, as agreed with the NSF and BAS, respectively. Comply with the requests of the station commander—for example, the commander at Arctowski requests that visits only be made in the afternoon.
14. Respect the work the scientists are conducting—do not disturb those working while visiting the stations.
15. It is the responsibility of the tour operator to ensure that no evidence of our visits remains behind. This includes garbage (of any kind), marine pollution, vandalism etc. Litter must never be left ashore.
16. Follow Annex 5 of the Marpol Agreement. Retain all plastic for proper disposal on the mainland. Wood products, glass and metal must be compacted and disposed of well away from land or returned to the mainland. Ensure that incinerators, if used, are functioning properly.
17. Refrain from dumping bilges or treated sewage within 12 nautical miles of land or ice shelves, or in the vicinity of research stations where scientific research is taking place. This might inadvertently affect the results of scientific investigations, and could potentially harm the wildlife.
18. Respect historic huts, scientific markers and monitoring devices.

Source: IAATO (1993c) (also National Research Council, 1993, pp. 101–103). Reproduced with the kind permission of the International Association of Antarctic Tour Operators, Office of the Secretariat, 11417 SE 215th Street, Kent, WA 98031, USA

APPENDIX D: IAATO GUIDELINES FOR VISITORS

Antarctica, the world's last pristine wilderness, is particularly vulnerable to human presence. Life in Antarctica must contend with one of the harshest environments on earth, and we must take care that our presence does not add more stress to this fragile and unique ecosystem.

The following Guidelines of Conduct have been adopted by all members of the International Association of Antarctica Tour Operators (IAATO) and will be made available to all visitors travelling with them to Antarctica. With your cooperation we will be able to operate environmentally conscious expeditions that protect and preserve Antarctica, leaving the continent unimpaired for future generations.

Please thoroughly study and follow these guidelines. By doing so, you will make an important contribution towards the conservation of the Antarctic ecosystem and minimise visitor impact. It will also help to ensure that you will have a safe and fulfilling experience in visiting one of the most exciting and fascinating places on earth.

1. Do not disturb, harass, or interfere with the wildlife

- Never touch the animals
- Maintain a distance of at least 15 feet (4.5 metres) from penguins, all nesting birds and true seals (crawling seals), and 50 feet (15 metres) from fur seals
- Give animals the right of way
- Do not position yourself between a marine animal and its path to the water, nor between a parent and its young
- Always be aware of your surroundings; stay outside the periphery of bird rookeries and seal colonies
- Keep noise to a minimum
- Do not feed the animals, either ashore or from the ship

Most of the Antarctic species exhibit a lack of fear which allows you to approach relatively close; however, please remember that the austral summer is a time for courting, mating, nesting, rearing young and moulting. If any animal changes or stops its activities upon your approach, you are too close! Be especially careful while taking photographs, since it is easy not to notice adverse reactions of animals when concentrating through the lens of a camera. Disturbing nesting birds may cause them to expose their eggs/offspring to predators or cold. Maintain a low profile since animals can be intimidated by people standing over them. The disturbance of some animals, most notably fur seals and nesting skuas, may elicit an aggressive, and even dangerous, response.

2. Do not walk on or otherwise damage the fragile plants, i.e. lichens, mosses and grasses

Poor soil and harsh living conditions mean growth and regeneration of these plants is extremely slow. Most of the lichens, which grow only on rocks, hard-packed sand and gravel, and bones are extremely fragile. Damage from human activity among the moss beds can last for decades.

3. Leave nothing behind, and take only memories and photographs

- Leave no litter ashore (and remove any litter you may find while ashore); dispose of all litter properly
- Do not take souvenirs, including whale and seal bones, live or dead animals, rocks, fossils, plants, other organic material, or anything which may be of historical or scientific value

4. Do not interfere with protected areas or scientific research

- Do not enter buildings at the research stations unless advised to do so
- Avoid entering all officially protected areas, and do not disturb any ongoing scientific studies

5. Historic huts may only be entered when accompanied by a properly authorised escort

- Nothing may be removed from or disturbed within historic huts

Historic huts are essentially museums, and they are all officially maintained and monitored by various governments.

6. Do not smoke during shore excursions

Fire is a very serious hazard in the dry climate of Antarctica. Great care must be taken to safeguard against this danger, particularly around wildlife areas, historic huts, research buildings, and storage facilities.

7. Stay with your group or with one of the ship's leaders when ashore

- Follow the directions of the expedition staff
- Never wander off alone or out of sight of others
- Do not hike onto glaciers or large snow fields, as there is a real danger of falling into hidden crevasses

In addition to the Guidelines of Conduct for Antarctica Visitors adopted by IAATO, all visitors should be aware of the Agreed Measures for the Conservation of Antarctic Fauna and Flora. This annex to the Antarctic Treaty of 1959 addresses the protection of the environment and conservation of wildlife. Citizens of any government that has ratified the Antarctic Treaty are legally bound by the following guidelines of conduct in the region south of latitude $60°$ South:

Conservation of wildlife

Animals and plants native to Antarctica are protected under the following five instruments outlined in the Agreed Measures:

1. *Protection of native fauna.* Within the Treaty Area it is prohibited to kill, wound, capture or molest any native mammal or bird, or any attempt at such an act, except in accordance with a permit.

2. *Harmful interference.* Appropriate efforts will be taken to ensure that harmful interference is minimised in order that normal living conditions of any native mammal or bird are protected. Harmful interference includes any disturbance of bird and seal colonies during the breeding period by persistent attention from persons on foot.
3. *Specially protected species.* Special protection is accorded to fur and Ross seals.
4. *Specially protected areas (SPAs).* Areas of outstanding scientific interest are preserved in order to protect their unique natural ecological system. Entry to these areas is allowed by permit only.
5. *Introduction of non-indigenous species, parasites and diseases.* No species of animal or plant not indigenous to the Antarctic Treaty Area may be brought into the Area, except in accordance with a permit. All reasonable precautions have to be taken to prevent the accidental introduction of parasites and diseases into the Treaty Area.

Additionally, the Marine Mammal Protection Act of 1972 prohibits US citizens from taking or importing marine mammals, or parts of marine mammals, into the USA. Both accidental or deliberate disturbance of seals or whales may constitute harassment under the Act.

Further, the Antarctic Conservation Act of 1978 (US Public Law 95-541) was adopted by the United States Congress to protect and preserve the ecosystem, flora and fauna of the continent, and to implement the Agreed Measures for the Conservation of Antarctic Fauna and Flora. The Act sets forth regulations which are legally binding for US citizens and residents visiting Antarctica.

Briefly, the Act provides the following:

In Antarctica the Act makes it unlawful, unless authorised by regulation or permit issued under this Act, to take native animals or birds, to collect any special native plant, to introduce species, to enter certain special areas (SPAs), or to discharge or dispose of any pollutants. To 'take' means to remove, harass, molest, harm, pursue, hunt, shoot, wound, kill, trap, capture, restrain, or tag any native mammal or native bird, or to attempt to engage in such conduct.

Under the Act violations are subject to civil penalties, including a fine of up to $10 000 and one year imprisonment for each violation. The complete text of the Antarctic Conservation Act of 1978 can be found in the ship's library.

Our ship's staff will make certain that the Antarctic Conservation Act and the above guidelines are adhered to.

By encouraging your fellow expeditioners to follow your environmentally conscious efforts you will help us to ensure that Antarctica will remain pristine for the enjoyment of future generations. Thank you in advance for your cooperation.

Source: IAATO (1993d) (also National Research Council, 1993, pp. 96–100).
Reproduced with the kind permission of the International Association of Antarctic Tour Operators, Office of the Secretariat, 11417 SE 215th Street, Kent, WA 98031, USA.

REFERENCES

Angelini, J., Mansfield, A., 1993, *Implementation of the Protocol on Environmental Protection to the Antarctic Treaty into United States law and practice*, University of California School of Law, Berkeley

Antarctic Treaty, 1985, *Final report of the thirteenth Antarctic Treaty Consultative Meeting*, 7–18 October 1985, Brussels

Antarctic Treaty, 1991, *Final report of the sixteenth Antarctic Treaty Consultative Meeting*, 7–18 October 1991, Bonn

Antarctic Treaty, 1993, *Final report of the seventeenth Antarctic Treaty Consultative Meeting*, 11–20 November 1992, Venice

ATCM (Antarctic Treaty Consultative Meeting), 1992a, *Tourism in Antarctica, Information paper 18 submitted by IUCN*, XVIIth ATCM, 11 November 1992, Venice

ATCM, 1992b, *The regulation of tourism and non-governmental activities in the Antarctic Treaty Area, Working paper 2 submitted by the United Kingdom*, XVIIth ATCM, 9 November 1992, Venice

ATCM, 1992c, *Provisional list of documents distributed, Information paper 53/rev.2 submitted by the Secretariat*, XVIIth ATCM, 18 November 1992, Venice

ATCM, 1992d, *Preliminary draft annex VI to the Protocol on Environmental Protection to the Antarctic Treaty: regulation concerning tourism and non-governmental activities. Working paper 1 submitted by Chile, France, Germany, Italy and Spain*, XVIIth ATCM, 9 November 1992, Venice

ATCM, 1992e, *A revised 'Code of guidance for visitors to the Antarctic', Working paper 3 submitted by the United Kingdom*, XVIIth ATCM, 9 November 1992, Venice

ATCM, 1992f, *The regulation of tourism and non-governmental activities in the Antarctic Treaty Area (II). Information paper 6 submitted by the United Kingdom*, XVIIth ATCM, 11 November 1992, Venice

ATCM, 1994a, *Draft final report of the XVIIIth Antarctic Treaty Meeting. Working paper 37 submitted by the Secretariat*, XVIIIth ATCM, 22 April 1994, Kyoto

ATCM, 1994b, *IAATO report of activities for XVIII ATCM—Kyoto. Information paper 96 submitted by IAATO*, XVIIIth ATCM, 20 April 1994, Kyoto

ATCM, 1994c, *Example of an environmental audit. Information paper 13 submitted by IAATO*, XVIIIth ATCM, 10 April 1994, Kyoto

ATCM, 1994d, *Draft initial environmental evaluation. Information paper 23 submitted by IAATO*, XVIIIth ATCM, 10 April 1994, Kyoto

Auburn, F.M., 1982, *Antarctic law and politics*, C. Hurst & Company, London

Barnes, J.N., 1991, Protection of the environment in Antarctica: are present regimes enough? In Jorgensen-Dahl, A., Ostreng, W., eds., *The Antarctic Treaty System in world politics*, Macmillan, London, pp. 186–228

Beck, P.J., 1990, Regulating one of the last tourism frontiers: Antarctica, *Applied Geography*, **10**(4): 343–356

Blay, S.K.N., 1992, New trends in the protection of the Antarctic environment: the 1991 Madrid Protocol, *American Journal of International Law*, **86**: 377–399

Boczek, B.A., 1988, The legal status of visitors, including tourists, and non-governmental expeditions in Antarctica. In Wolfrum, R., ed., *Antarctic Challenge III*, Duncker & Humblot, Berlin, pp. 455–490

Burgess, J., 1990, Comprehensive environmental protection of the Antarctic: new approaches for new times. In Cook, G., ed., *The future of Antarctica: exploitation versus preservation*, Manchester University Press, Manchester, pp. 53–67

Champ, M.A., Flemer, D.A., Landers, D.H., Ribic, C., DeLaca, T., 1992, The roles of monitoring and research in polar environments: a perspective, *Marine Pollution Bulletin*, 25(9–12): 220–226

Claus, J.E., 1990, *Promotional letter to Antarctic tour members from the Chief Operating Officer, Society Expeditions*, Society Expeditions, Seattle

COMNAP (Council of Managers of National Antarctic Programs), 1990, *Visitors' guide to the Antarctic/visits to scientific stations in Antarctica*, NSF 90-147, COMNAP, Washington DC

Cook, G., 1990, Possible future developments. In Cook, G., ed., *The future of Antarctica: exploitation versus preservation*, Manchester University Press, Manchester, pp. 95–103

Couratier, J., 1983, The regime for the conservation of Antarctica's living resources. In Vicuña, F.O., ed., *Antarctic resources policy: scientific legal and political issues*, Cambridge University Press, Cambridge, pp. 139–148

Cousteau, J., Charrier, B., 1992, Introduction: the Antarctic a challenge to global environment policy. In Verhoeven, J., Sands, P., Bruce, M., eds., *The Antarctic environment and international law*, Graham & Trotman, London, pp. 5–10

ECO, 1994a, Two and a half years on, ratification limps along . . ., *ECO*, 88(1): 12 April

ECO, 1994b, Ratification roll call, *ECO*, 88(4): 22 April

Enzenbacher, D.J., 1991, A policy for Antarctic tourism: conflict or cooperation? Unpublished M.Phil. thesis, University of Cambridge Scott Polar Research Institute, Cambridge

Enzenbacher, D.J., 1992, Antarctic tourism and environmental concerns, *Marine Pollution Bulletin*, 25(9–12): 258–265

Enzenbacher, D.J., 1993a, Antarctic tourism: 1991/92 season activity, *Polar Record*, 29(170): 240–242

Enzenbacher, D.J., 1993b, Tourists in Antarctica: numbers and trends, *Tourism Management*, 14(2): 142–146

Enzenbacher, D.J., 1994a, Antarctic tourism: 1992/93 season activity and recent developments, *Polar Record*, 30(172)

Enzenbacher, D.J., 1994b, NSF and Antarctic tour operators meetings, *Annals of Tourism Research*, 21(2): 424–427

Enzenbacher, D.J., 1994c, Tourism at Faraday Station: an Antarctic case study, *Annals of Tourism Research*, 21(2): 303–317

Foreman, E.F., 1992, Protecting the Antarctic environment: will a protocol be enough?, *American University Journal of International Law and Policy*, 7: 843–879

Hall, C.M., 1992, Tourism in Antarctica: activities, impacts, and management, *Journal of Travel Research*, 30(4): 2–9

Harris, C.M., Meadows, J., 1992, Environmental management in Antarctica: instruments and institutions, *Marine Pollution Bulletin*, 25(9–12): 239–249

Hay, L., 1993a, Environmental protection high on Venice meeting agenda, *ANARE News*, 73: 33

Hay, L., 1993b, Tourism issues unresolved by Antarctic Treaty Meeting, *ANARE News*, 73: 4

Heap, J., ed., 1990, *Handbook of the Antarctic Treaty System*, 7th edn, Polar Publications, Cambridge

Heap, J.A., Holdgate, M.W., 1986, The Antarctic Treaty System as an environmental mechanism—an approach to environmental issues. In *Antarctic Treaty System: an assessment*, National Academy Press, Washington DC, pp. 195–210

Holdgate, M.W., 1983, Environmental factors in the development of Antarctica. In Vicuña, F.O., ed., *Antarctic resources policy*, Cambridge University Press, Cambridge, pp. 77–101

IAATO (International Association of Antarctica Tour Operators), 1993a, *Guidelines of conduct for Antarctica tour operators as of November 1993*, IAATO, Kent

IAATO, 1993b, *Guidelines of conduct for Antarctica visitors as of November 1993*, IAATO, Kent

IUCN (International Union for Conservation of Nature and Natural Resources), 1991, *A strategy for Antarctic conservation*, IUCN, Gland

Joyner, C.C., Ewing, B.G., Jr., 1991, Antarctica and the Latin American states: the interplay of law, geopolitics and environmental priorities, *Georgetown International Environmental Law Review*, 4(1): 1–46

Kaye, S., Rothwell, D.R., 1993, Australian law in Antarctica, *Polar Record*, 29(170): 215–218

Keage, P.L., Dingwall, P.R., 1993, A conservation strategy for the Australian Antarctic Territory, *Polar Record*, 29(170): 242–244

Kennicut, M.C. II, Sweet, S.T., 1992, Hydrocarbon contamination on the Antarctic Peninsula: the *Bahia Paraiso*—two years after the spill, *Marine Pollution Bulletin*, 25(9–12): 303–306

Kennicut, M.C. II et al., 1990, Oil spillage in Antarctica: initial report of the National Science Foundation-sponsored quick response team on the grounding of the *Bahia Paraiso*, *Environmental Science and Technology*, 24(5): 620–624

Kiernan, V., 1993, Antarctica welcomes careful visitors, *New Scientist*, 139(1882): 7

Manheim, B.S., Jr., 1990, *Paradise lost? The need for environmental regulation of tourism in Antarctica*, Environmental Defence Fund, Washington DC

Manheim, B.S., Jr., 1992a, The failure of the National Science Foundation to protect Antarctica, *Marine Pollution Bulletin*, 25(9–12): 253–254

Manheim, B.S., Jr., 1992b, Gaps in management of Antarctic seaborne tourism under the Protocol, Paper distributed at the Antarctic Treaty Meeting on tourism, 9–10 November, Venice

Myhre, J.D., 1986, *The Antarctic Treaty System: politics, law and diplomacy*, Westview Press, Boulder

National Research Council, 1993, *Science and stewardship in the Antarctic*, National Academy Press, Washington DC

NSF (National Science Foundation), 1988, *US response to Antarctic tourism*, NSF, Washington DC

NSF, 1989, *Antarctic Conservation Act of 1978 (Public Law 95-451) with regulations, maps of special areas and application forms*, NSF, Washington DC

NSF, 1993, *USAP observer program summary 1992–93*, US NSF, Washington DC

Negroponte, J.D., 1987, The success of the Antarctic Treaty, *Department of State Bulletin*, 87(2123): 29–30

Nicholson, I.E., 1986, Antarctic tourism—the need for a legal regime? In Wolfrum, R., ed., *Antarctic Challenge II*, Duncker & Humblot, Berlin, pp. 191–203

NZARP (New Zealand Antarctic Research Programme), 1990, *New Zealand government policy on tourist and private Antarctic expeditions*, DSIR Antarctic, Christchurch

Oceanites, 1990/91, *Antarctic traveler's code for visitors and tour companies*, Oceanites Inc., Cooksville

Orrego Vicuña, F., 1986, Antarctic conflict and international cooperation. In *Antarctic Treaty System: an assessment*, National Academy Press, Washington DC, pp. 55–64

Orrego Vicuña, F., 1988, *Antarctic mineral exploitation: the emerging legal framework*, Cambridge University Press, Cambridge

Quigg, P.W., 1983, *A pole apart: the emerging issue of Antarctica*, McGraw-Hill, New York

Redgwell, C., 1990, Antarctica: the legal regime. In Cook, G., ed., *The future of Antarctica: exploitation versus preservation*, Manchester University Press, Manchester, pp. 81–94

Sabella, S.J. 1992, Upon closer inspection, *Marine Pollution Bulletin*, **25**(9–12): 255–257

SCAR (Scientific Committee on Antarctic Research), 1980, *A visitor's introduction to the Antarctic and its environment*, SCAR, Cambridge

Scully, R.T., 1986a, The evolution of the Antarctic Treaty System—the institutional perspective. In *Antarctic Treaty System: an assessment*, National Academy Press, Washington DC, pp. 391–411

Scully, R.T., 1986b, Institutionalisation of the Antarctic Treaty regime. In Wolfrum, R., ed., *Antarctic Challenge II*, Duncker & Humblot, Berlin, pp. 283–296

Scully, R.T., 1988, The institutional development of the Antarctic Treaty System: the question of a secretariat. In Wolfrum, R., ed., *Antarctic Challenge III*, Duncker & Humblot, Berlin, pp. 41–52

Stephenson, L., 1993, Managing visitors to Macquarie Island—a model for Antarctica?, *ANARE News*, **73**: 8–9

Stonehouse, B., 1990, A traveller's code for Antarctic visitors, *Polar Record*, **26**(156): 56–58

Suter, K., 1991, *Antarctica: private property or public heritage?*, Zed Books, London

Swithinbank, C., 1993, Airborne tourism in the Antarctic, *Polar Record*, **29**(169): 103–110

Triggs, G.D., 1987, The Antarctic Treaty System: some jurisdictional problems. In Triggs, G.D., ed., *The Antarctic Treaty regime: law, environment and resources*, Cambridge University Press, Cambridge, pp. 88–109

Trolle-Anderson, R., 1987, The Antarctic scene: legal and political facts. In Triggs, G.D., ed., *The Antarctic Treaty regime: law, environment and resources*, Cambridge University Press, Cambridge, pp. 57–64

US Congress, 1993a, H.R.964. *A bill to implement the Protocol on Environmental Protection to the Antarctic Treaty, to enact a prohibition against Antarctic mineral resource activities, and for other purposes. 103rd Congress, 1st session, 18 February*, US House of Representatives, Washington DC

US Congress, 1993b, H.R.1066. *A bill to implement the Protocol on Environmental Protection to the Antarctic Treaty, and for other purposes. 103rd Congress, 1st session, 23 February*, US House of Representatives, Washington DC

Vidas, D., 1992, *Antarctic tourism: a challenge to the legitimacy of the Antarctic Treaty System?* International Antarctic Regime Project (IARP) publication series, No. 6., Fridtjof Nansen Institute, Oslo

Watts, A.D., 1986a, *The Antarctic Treaty as a conflict resolution mechanism. In Antarctic Treaty System: an assessment*, National Academy Press, Washington DC, pp. 65–75

Watts, A.D., 1986b, Liability for activities in Antarctica—who pays the bill to whom? In Wolfrum, R., ed., *Antarctic Challenge II*, Duncker & Humblot, Berlin, pp. 147–161
Watts, A., 1992, *International law and the Antarctic Treaty System*, Grotius Publications, Cambridge

13 Tourist Impacts and Management in the Antarctic Peninsula Area

BERNARD STONEHOUSE AND KIM CROSBIE

INTRODUCTION: ANTARCTIC TOURISM

Antarctica and its neighbouring islands are growing tourist attractions. The Antarctic continent, Antarctic Peninsula, the nearby South Orkney and South Shetland Islands and South Georgia, for long the preserve of explorers and scientists, are now visited annually by tourists in search of adventure, unusual wildlife, scenic beauty, remoteness, history—or merely the vacation with a difference.

Antarctic tourism began in the mid-to-late 1950s. The first tourist aircraft to visit Antarctica left Punta Arenas on 23 December 1956 and overflew the South Shetland Islands and northern half of the Peninsula. The first Antarctic tourist ship explored a similar area in January 1958 (Reich, 1980; Codling, 1982). Since those early days numbers of tourists visiting annually have increased erratically, but in recent years surely. In 1992–93 over 7000 tourists are estimated to have visited Antarctica (Enzenbacher, 1993), and in 1993–94 the figure may reach 9000. These are small numbers compared with those visiting tourist venues elsewhere, but they represent over a threefold increase since 1990.

Currently about 19 out of every 20 Antarctic tourists are ship-borne adventure-travellers, with special interests in scenery and natural history (Hall and McArthur, 1993; Stonehouse, 1994). The remainder are airborne travellers interested in climbing, skiing, and visiting some of the remoter parts of Antarctica that are relatively or completely inaccessible by ship, for example, the South Pole, Vinson Massif (Antarctica's highest peak) and emperor penguin colonies bordering the ice-bound Weddell Sea (Swithinbank, 1993).

Airborne tourism was in the past more popular. From February 1976 Boeing 747s of Quantas and DC-10s of Air New Zealand carried several

Polar Tourism: Tourism in the Arctic and Antarctic Regions
Edited by C. Michael Hall and Margaret E. Johnston. © John Wiley & Sons Ltd, 1995

thousands of passengers in long flights to the Antarctic mainland, over-flying the continent without landing. Similar flights were made over Antarctic Peninsula from Chile (Boswall, 1986). Tourist overflights ended on 28 November 1979, when a low-flying Air New Zealand aircraft crashed on the slopes of Mount Erebus, Victoria Land, with the loss of 257 passengers and crew (Mahon, 1981).

Ship-borne tourists in the 1993–94 season will have had at least a dozen ships and more kinds of cruise to choose from. They may visit Antarctica in small Russian ice-breakers carrying fewer than 40 passengers, larger ice-breakers or liners of 90–200 passengers, still larger cruise liners carrying up to 450 passengers, or yachts with fewer than a dozen. A cheaper alternative is to travel as paying passengers on expedition ships; the ill-fated Argentine naval transport *Bahia Paraiso*, that sank off Anvers Island in 1989, carried over 80 tourists. Among dedicated tourist ships, the liners, which in other seasons cruise the Caribbean, Amazon or Mediterranean, provide luxury accommodation at the level of well-appointed international hotels. The larger ones have casinos, entertainers and other diversions; the smaller ones concentrate their passengers' attention more exclusively on the Antarctic experience. Ice-breakers offer simpler standards, though still very comfortable. Yachts are for the hardy, and for those who do not care to travel *en masse*.

In comparison with tours of similar duration elsewhere in the world, Antarctic vacations tend to be expensive. They seem likely to remain so, for most tourists live in the northern hemisphere, and have to fly to points of departure in the south, often with overnight hotel expenses included. Tourism is nevertheless expanding annually and showing an ever-widening range of standards, facilities and prices. In 1992–93 costs for a typical 15-day high-season (January) luxury cruise, including air passages to and from Miami, ranged from US$8000 to US$12 500 per head. A 22-day cruise by ice-breaker, including helicopter flights, cost from US$9000 to US$16 500 per head. The larger passenger liners on short runs offer some of the cheapest packages, currently ranging from about US$5000 upward for 10-day cruises.

These prices for seaborne tours are small compared with airborne adventure holidays. Camping and climbing for one to two weeks in the Ellsworth Mountains, for example, may cost up to six times as much as a seaborne tour of similar length. The main factor limiting expansion in this field is the high cost of safe and ecologically sound operations. Uptake is currently restricted to a few tours and a few dozen passengers per year. However, the recent realisation that many bare-ice runways are available in Antarctica (Swithinbank, 1993) has led to renewed interest in the possibilities of more widespread and cheaper forms of airborne tourism.

Despite high costs, ship-borne tourism is by no means restricted to the very wealthy. Visitors recently encountered by our team aboard Antarctic cruise ships have included many of modest means—including young professionals and public servants, and older retired schoolteachers and nurses—seeking the 'vacation of their lifetime', or forfeiting two or three more orthodox vacations in favour of a single, once-in-a-lifetime and never-to-be-forgotten Antarctic cruise. There are as yet no cut-price Antarctic cruises, but operators compete keenly, and many are seeking cheaper alternative ways of giving their clients a taste of Antarctica.

The areas most frequently visited remain those that are most readily accessible from neighbouring continents. The South Shetland and South Orkney Islands and the Antarctic Peninsula, which lie within two days' sailing from the ports of Ushuaia (Argentina) and Punta Arenas (Chile), and the sub-Antarctic island of South Georgia some three to four days away, currently attract over 90 per cent of all Antarctic tourists. To reach other areas of mainland Antarctica from South Africa, Australia or New Zealand involves voyages two to three times as long, and correspondingly more expensive. Though tours from New Zealand may include visits to historic sites linked with the names of D'Urville, Ross, Scott, Shackleton, Amundsen, Mawson and Byrd, they cross much wider stretches of the world's roughest and least hospitable oceans. Travellers afflicted with sea-sickness have longer to reflect on whether their holiday money was well spent.

A STUDY OF SHIP-BORNE TOURISM: PAC

Antarctica's wilderness is claimed by seven nations, though currently unprotected by sovereignty. Its conservation is managed by a consortium of nations, currently numbering the 24 consultative parties to the Antarctic Treaty, whose responsibilities arise from expression of scientific interest in the continent. Their environmental protection policies, recently revised, are embodied in the Environmental Protocol to the Antarctic Treaty, which seeks to protect Antarctica from adverse impacts of all human activities, including tourism.

Tourism in Antarctica is currently being studied by Project Antarctic Conservation (PAC), a six-year research and management programme based at the Scott Polar Research Institute, University of Cambridge, UK. The project, led by Dr Bernard Stonehouse and now in its third year, is funded largely by charitable trusts (see Acknowledgements). Philosophically neither for nor against Antarctic tourism, PAC accepts both the existence of the industry and its legitimacy, and aims (a) to study its development, evolution and environmental impacts, and (b) to make recommendations towards the management of the industry under the Antarctic Treaty

System, in ways that will allow its rational development towards sustainable levels.

Most of PAC's resources and efforts are currently directed towards ship-borne tourism, particularly in the Antarctic Peninsula region, though we are interested also in both ship-borne and airborne tourism developments elsewhere in Antarctica, and in parallel developments of tourism in the Arctic and other wilderness areas. Ten research objectives are identified:

1. To document the growth and development of Antarctic tourism;
2. To maintain a database covering both ship-borne and airborne forms of the industry;
3. To enquire into the motivations and expectations of Antarctic tourists;
4. To study methods used by tour operators in the field;
5. To establish a geographical and ecological database covering all known tourist landing sites, as a basis for management plans;
6. To study tourist impacts on wildlife, especially the long-term welfare of bird and mammal concentrations;
7. To study tourist impacts on vegetation, especially methods of rehabilitating impacted sites;
8. To test the validity of current methods of regulating tourism, and to model and test new methods of regulation;
9. To examine the effectiveness of current and developing Antarctic Treaty legislation covering tourism; and
10. To establish predictive models for the industry's future development and assess possible needs for future legislation.

Monitoring began in 1991–92 with a combined British and Argentine team based at Argentine station Teniente Camára, Half Moon Island, South Shetland Islands (Stonehouse, 1992). Field research continued in 1992–93, again with Argentine participation, at a small temporary station established for the purpose on Cuverville Island, Danco Coast, Antarctic Peninsula. In 1993–94 the UK team worked again at Cuverville Island, and for six weeks operated an additional station at Hannah Point, South Shetland Islands. All three sites were chosen because they were known to be popular with tour operators, and were considered likely to be vulnerable to tourist impacts (Stonehouse, 1993a, 1994). Simultaneously in each season opportunities were taken, through questionnaires and observation, to study the views and attitudes of tourists and tour operators, and to examine the industry's practices ashore and afloat. PAC began in isolation, but several other organisations are now involved in research on different aspects of tourism, notably the United States Office of Polar Programs, the National Science Foundation in Washington DC, and the International Centre for Antarctic Information and Research, Christchurch, New Zealand.

Ship-borne tourism: the Lindblad way

Preliminary enquiries among Antarctic tourists, based on PAC question-naires currently being analysed, reveal a variety of reasons for visiting Antarctica. A few tourists rate highly the fact that they have visited all other continents, and Antarctica is their seventh and last. For others, visiting Antarctica has been a long-standing ambition, now made possible by retirement, financial windfall, or the advent of cheaper tours in recent years. Many have been impressed by recent publicity (for example, articles in the *National Geographic Magazine*), and travel to enjoy the scenery, ice, wildlife (especially penguins, seals and whales), the remoteness and isola-tion, and the occasional historical evidence of mankind past and present. Many show evidence of deep interest in conservation, and concern for the future of the continent.

Tour operators meet their clients' aspirations by short cruises, usually lasting 10–20 days, involving 5–14 days in Antarctic waters. Most operators land passengers ashore at least once every day, using fleets of inflatable boats with outboard engines. Some, particularly those on the smaller ships, land twice or thrice daily. Except in areas set aside under the Treaty for scientific research (currently Specially Protected Areas, SPAs and Sites of Special Scientific Interest, SSSIs), and in the immediate environs of research stations, operators are free to land tourists virtually anywhere in Antarctica. However, most tend to converge on a number of sites of proven worth, while the more enterprising operators constantly seek new sites. In 1993–94 helicopters were used to land passengers on pack-ice and at emperor penguin colonies not easily reached by boat.

In the Antarctic Peninsula and Scotia Arc alone some 70 sites are known to be used. The less popular ones are visited only sporadically, but such popular landings as Half Moon Island, Cuverville Island and Hannah Point may receive visits every second or third day throughout the summer season of four to five months, bringing over 2500 passengers ashore. Some popular sites have now been visited regularly for over 30 years (Stone-house, 1992, 1993a, b, 1994).

While cruising south of latitude 60° S, ships and passengers come under Antarctic Treaty regulations, which provide guidelines for tourist opera-tions that require the environmentally benign behaviour of passengers and crew. However, from its earliest days, indeed long before such guidelines were drawn up, Antarctic tourism has been dominated by a strong ethic of environmental concern, based on the practices of its first entrepreneur, Lars-Eric Lindblad, and currently maintained by most operators (Codling, 1982; Zehnder, 1990; Stonehouse, 1994).

In the absence of more formal control measures, the 'Lindblad pattern' has for long provided the environment's most effective shield against tourist-induced damage. This pattern operates best with ships of up to about 140 passengers, guided ashore and afloat by experienced staff (Stonehouse, 1994). Each voyage becomes an 'expedition' with lectures, briefings and shore landings. Lecturers are often scientists or administrators, retired or vacationing, with long experience of Antarctic affairs. Passengers are briefed on the Antarctic Treaty and issued with a set of guidelines consistent with Treaty recommendations, covering behaviour ashore, possible hazards, the need to avoid interference with wildlife, and other points of conduct.

Tourists are usually issued with bright red jackets that ensure their visibility. Landed in parties of 10–15 (usually up to a total of 100 ashore at a time), under experienced supervision, they are mostly free to wander, but required to stay within easy reach of the embarkation point. Those who infringe the guidelines by approaching animals too closely or dropping litter are likely to be admonished by guides or fellow-passengers. Parties usually remain ashore for one to three hours. Such landings are interspersed with scenic boat tours among icebergs and islands. Evenings are often taken up with a 'recap' session to discuss the day's events and plans for the following day, and to reinforce the expedition spirit and conservation ethic.

This pattern of shipboard education, linked with guidelines that require visitors to avoid walking on vegetation, disturbing nesting birds and leaving litter, has recommended itself strongly to the kinds of tourists who have so far made up the majority in Antarctica. Many claim that they would avoid tours which did not feature similar levels of concern.

As a consequence of the Lindblad pattern, in an environment that has proved vulnerable to impacts from scientists, and that many regard as hypersensitive to visitor impact of any kind, there is so far remarkably little evidence of damage from tourism. That damage is not immediately apparent does not mean that it is absent. We still have to measure possible long-term effects, for example of multiple visits to breeding colonies of penguins, and indeed to establish the base-line data against which such long-term effects may be measured. However, the Lindblad pattern of tourist management has ensured high standards of behaviour among tour operators and tourists alike, and far less environmental damage than might have been expected had Antarctic tourism developed without it.

Changing patterns

Though the Lindblad way continues to appeal to tourists, and in principle to be favoured by most operators, changes within the industry, notably the advent of larger ships and more ships, bring serious challenges. In the largest ships, carrying up to 450 passengers, operators catering for a wider cross-section of passengers and interests find it more difficult to establish the single-minded conservation ethic on which the Lindblad way is based. Entertainments and alternative pastimes divert attention from the 'expedition' spirit: the presence of several language groups, even the need for two sittings for dinner, make briefings less intimate, and the important recap sessions less spontaneous and more difficult to organise.

As the industry grows, the expedition spirit itself becomes more tenuous and difficult to maintain. Despite increasing numbers of tours ships, following each other along well-worn routes from Tierra del Fuego to the South Shetlands and Antarctic Peninsula, cruises continue to be represented as 'expeditions' or 'voyages of exploration'. For example, a recent advertisement for a tour promoted by a prominent United States scientific institution announced an 'expedition' voyage in which travellers would experience a 'rare opportunity' to follow in the footsteps of research scientists and explorers, and perhaps even 'make significant discoveries' of their own in Antarctica. It is difficult to reconcile this image with the reality of a succession of ships, landing tourists in batches of up to 100, under the constant scrutiny of guides. During the high season of January and February ships have difficulty in keeping out of each others' sight, a problem that in our experience worries operators more than the tourists themselves, but reflects again the difficulties of maintaining an image of isolation in a relatively crowded seaway.

One large-ship operator has constrained landed passengers within a ring of traffic cones. This device might with advantage have been used by a novice operator who reputedly, in 1992–93, contravened both guidelines and common sense by landing several hundred passengers simultaneously on Deception Island (Sitwell, 1993).

A related problem is the difficulty of continuing to sell Antarctica as 'virgin' or 'near-virgin' territory. The more thoughtful tourists, many of whom list conservation among their concerns for Antarctica, find this confusing, and question the right of tour operators to be entering virgin territory by the shipload. Fortunately for their peace of mind, the image cannot long be sustained in the Antarctic Peninsula's agglomeration of research stations, abandoned huts, wind-scattered rubbish heaps and derelict navigation beacons. Tourists were in fact among the first to react vigorously against the rubbish that mars Antarctica's beauty, and press their national operators for clean-up campaigns.

As larger cruise ships enter the scene, voyages become cheaper, passengers more numerous, and the mean age of passengers falls. Guides and lecturers too tend to be younger, and 'old Antarctic hands', lecturing comfortably to near-contemporaries on history, natural history and exploration, are being replaced by more lively mentors more disposed to action and adventure. This shift of mode exposes a further limitation inherent in the traditional pattern. The Lindblad way is a means of enjoying Antarctica passively, but there are many other possible ways, including those already practised in airborne adventure tourism elsewhere in Antarctica.

After almost four decades of tourism, Antarctica has developed no capacity of its own for dealing with tourists. Ship-borne tourism within the limited Lindblad pattern has been accepted, but no provision has been made for alternative forms of tourism, or even for containing ship-borne tourism in areas where it can be handled effectively. For example, there are no provisions for passengers to camp ashore or stay overnight in huts, to take long back-packing walks, to climb, ramble, study, settle to several hours' bird-watching, to read in a resource centre. In short, to take part in any of the wide range of activities, both educative and life-enhancing, that are commonplace for adventure tourists elsewhere in the world.

In the north, the various government agencies and private operators who sponsor Arctic tourism provide infrastructure for these and many more activities. Antarctica has no tourist board, no indigenous community that stands to gain from developing tourism, and a reactive rather than proactive system of governance that, for environmental protection purposes, fails to distinguish between an advancing industry and a scientific sector that, at least during the current world depression, seems to be declining.

Individual states that claim Antarctic territory show more initiative in this respect. The Australian government some years ago took the unique step of sponsoring a thought-provoking report on tourism in the sector for which it claims responsibility (Commonwealth of Australia, 1989). The Chilean government, to which the Antarctic Peninsula is simply a southern extension of Chile itself, has led the way in sponsoring and encouraging airborne tourism, providing on King George Island both an airstrip and a hostel that, provided ostensibly for scientific researchers, are available for visiting tourists too.

Suggestions for developing tourist facilities in Antarctica are unlikely to be received kindly by those in authority. The Antarctic Treaty area has since 1960 been regarded by participating governments as a 'Special Conservation Area', and the recently negotiated Protocol on Environmental Protection further designates Antarctica as a 'natural reserve, devoted to peace and science', assuring the continuing protection of its 'wilderness and aesthetic values' (HMSO, 1992). Those seeking to develop Antarctic resources for any purpose are warned that all activities must be planned and conducted 'so as to accord priority to scientific research and to preserve the value of Antarctica as an area for the conduct of such research'. One could imagine tourist facilities that would not conflict with these aims, and indeed might enhance them: enterprising Australians have already suggested combined hotels and scientific centres, that could be run more economically than current operations in the Australian sector.

Antarctica has already been subject to massive development, carried out first by whalers, and more recently over the past 50 years by scientists and their supporters, and resulting, for example, in several settlements of small-town size (Stonehouse *et al.*, 1994).

Lack of official enthusiasm for Antarctic tourism did not prevent the development of either airborne or seaborne enterprises, and lack of facilities is not preventing adventure-minded operators from providing new diversions for their clients ashore. In the past two seasons, we believe for the first time, ship-borne parties of tourists have camped ashore in Antarctica, and helicopters have taken tourists to otherwise inaccessible places—experiments that, with or without official sanction, will no doubt be tried again.

If the Lindblad pattern of 'expedition' tourism loses ground in Antarctica, operators who sell only this form of tourism will clearly fail in competition with those who offer more adventurous or educational alternatives. Administrators will no longer be able to rely, as they have unknowingly relied for decades, on the protective values of the Lindblad pattern. They may need to ensure that, as other and possibly more environmentally threatening kinds of tourism develop, adequate means of environmental protection are available for coping with them.

Passenger landings

So far the consultative parties have not found it desirable to limit the sites where visitors may land, and tour operators make full use of their unusual freedom to land passengers virtually anywhere they please in the Treaty area. In 1989–90 the United States National Science Foundation (NSF) listed 33 sites in maritime Antarctic (Antarctic Peninsula and the South Orkney and South Shetland Islands) where passengers were landed. In that season 164 visits were made, involving 10 322 passenger landings. In 1990–91 170 visits were made to 34 locations, with just over 12 000 passenger landings. In 1991–92 356 visits were made to over 46 sites, 15 of which were new, involving over 24 000 passenger landings.

The 70-plus sites that we currently list, like the numbers of ships visiting and passengers landing, will no doubt continue to grow. The most popular sites, for example Whalers Bay, Deception Island and Port Lockroy, further south down the Peninsula, now have long (though mostly unrecorded) histories of visits. Others like Cuverville Island, Half Moon Island and Hannah Point, 'discovered' by operators less than a decade ago, have shorter histories of visiting, though with dramatic increases in recent years. NSF records show Cuverville to have received 8 visits with 883 passengers in 1989–90, 8 visits with 936 passengers in 1990–91 and 21 visits with 2565 passengers in 1991–92. In the same three years Half Moon Island received 10 visits with 1191 passengers, 9 visits with 1101 passengers and 25 visits with 2984 passengers. Similarly Hannah Point was only lightly visited during the first two of those years, but attracted 17 visits with over 1600 passengers in 1991–92. Popular sites are likely to be visited every second or third day throughout the Austral summer.

What makes a site attractive? Stonehouse (1992) identifies 11 factors ranging from offshore searoom for ships (a quality appreciated by ships' captains) to the presence of penguin colonies and relics of earlier human occupation. For tourists, sites without wildlife or human artefacts have little appeal, while those in spectacular settings of glaciers and mountains are particularly favoured. However, it is cruise directors who ultimately choose where landings are made. Each has a list of particular sites acceptable on grounds of safety, known to have proved popular before, and often favoured especially for such factors as reliability of weather or ease of landing. The most popular sites are those that feature on most of the cruise directors' lists.

As pressures grow on the well-known sites, the more adventurous cruise directors seek new places to land. At each discovery they may claim—and some who peddle the 'virgin territory' image make a point of doing so—to be landing clients where few or none have landed before. Though this delights some of the passengers, the more thoughtful ones again perceive the danger inherent in images of 'exploration' and 'virgin territory'. In an area where few sites have been surveyed ecologically, where only the first two or three are at this moment being subject to impact assessment studies, and where the true nature of human impacts is still open to question, the constant search for novelty exposes more and more sites to unmeasured levels of impact and potential damage.

The once-in-a-lifetime marketing image, an appeal to the adventure traveller, hides a similar environmental hazard that perceptive tourists readily detect. The one-time visit to an undiscovered or rarely visited area carries an implication of minimal commitment or responsibilities. We have met many Antarctic tourists whose travels were marred by a feeling that their visit, believed to be almost unique, must in some way be ruining the environment. Most are reassured to know that, despite the advertisements, their journey is far from unique, that the beauty they see around them persists despite the hundreds more tourists simultaneously in the area, not to mention the tens of thousands who preceded them.

It will perhaps signify a welcome maturity (and must surely be better for business) when Antarctic tour operators urge their clients to visit Antarctica not once, but again and again, and to discover and cherish within it values more wholesome than doubtful virginity and questionable adventure.

Monitoring human impacts

The 1991 Protocol decrees a need for the comprehensive analysis of environmental impacts of all human activities, whether of scientists, tourists, ships' crews, or any other category of visitor. These activities differ in kind and in the degree to which monitoring is possible. Activities at research stations are localised, and there is often a complement of scientists in residence capable of establishing projects and controls. In contrast, tour operators are free to unload their clients at any point, other than scheduled areas and operating scientific stations. Though they are required to report all landings to their governments, some admit to a falsification of records, in the interest of keeping particular landings secret from rivals.

Scientists of PAC take every opportunity to monitor activities at all landings aboard the cruise ships on which they travel, but their major monitoring effort is concentrated at popular sites where visits are frequent. Studies of impacts ashore focus on wildlife and vegetation, prime attractions to visitors. The actual parameters deemed to represent impact must be chosen with care. While a decline in overall breeding population of a penguin colony is often considered a critical indicator of significant detrimental human impact (e.g. Benninghoff and Bonner, 1985), relying solely on population size or breeding success is fraught with problems. Persistent visits to a colony may barely affect breeding populations, but have considerable impact on young birds prospecting for nests. Penguin breeding populations anyway vary considerably (up to 20 per cent) from year to year, probably in response to fluctuations in food supply and other factors operating far from land (Trivelpiece et al., 1990; Whitehead et al., 1990).

Experimental variables of human behaviour and environmental response must be sufficiently defined to provide the information required. Scientific literature often refers to very broad variables such as 'human activity' or 'disturbance' in relation to 'population decline' (Croxall et al., 1981; Jouventin et al., 1984; Scientific Committee on Antarctic Research, 1984). If a monitoring study seeks changes in the environment due to 'human activity', then any detrimental impacts detected can be avoided only by preventing all visits. Alternatively, if the study is capable of indicating exactly which human activities under which conditions produce what effects, then innocuous tourist activities can be identified and encouraged.

A monitoring study must aim to provide a broad yet detailed understanding of the interaction between people and the environmental component in question. The information produced must allow prediction of how that interaction might change if other relevant variables, such as frequency of visits or location of breeding site, were to change. Pragmatic behavioural guidelines of the kind produced by IAATO (Stonehouse, 1991) are useful at present while little environmental monitoring has been done. However, they have not been produced from a wide body of research-generated knowledge, and better guidelines may be expected when monitoring studies have achieved better understanding of human and wildlife interactions.

Field techniques used to measure human impacts may themselves generate impacts, and great care must be taken that the generated impacts are negligible compared with the effects to be measured. This is particularly true in work on penguins and seals. Techniques that involve handling or marking animals must be avoided, as likely to impose greater impacts than any number of visits from tourists that approach and comport themselves according to the guidelines. PAC is developing non-invasive techniques (Nimon and Stonehouse, 1994) designed to derive as much information as possible with minimal interference.

PROTECTED AREA MANAGEMENT

On a worldwide canvas, concepts of protecting natural areas have evolved through stages, representing different points of balance between the conflicting aims of human recreation and environmental protection. The Commission on National Parks and Protected Areas, a commission of the International Union for the Conservation of Nature and Natural Resources (IUCN) (1990), recently summarised the objectives of national parks and protected areas in the following terms:

> To fulfil private, local, national and international responsibilities in marine and terrestrial protection; and to recognize, protect and present, both directly and indirectly, places which are significant examples of the world's heritage in ways that encourage public understanding, appreciation, enjoyment and use of this heritage in a sustainable manner.

From its inception in 1959 the Antarctic Treaty, in developing its own system of area protection, concentrated on two issues—the protection of scientific research and, somewhat secondarily, protection of the environment (Stonehouse, 1993). To these ends it provided for the nomination of two categories of protected areas—Sites of Special Scientific Interest (SSSIs) and Specially Protected Areas (SPAs)—and also for 'historic monuments'. Many such sites and monuments have been designated and marked on maps. Sadly, few protected sites are marked in the field, and several have been damaged by accident or carelessness as scientific programmes have proliferated.

By contrast, provision made for Sites of Special Tourist Interest (SSTI) was allowed to lapse without use. Though conceived less for the gratification of tourists than for their control and monitoring, no SSTIs were ever designated—an omission representing many missed opportunities for gathering information on the growth, development and impacts of tourism during its early years (Stonehouse, 1993b, 1994).

The Protocol on Environmental Protection to the Antarctic Treaty 1991 (often referred to as the Madrid Protocol), takes protected area management a stage further, for the first time introducing concepts of active management. Annex V to the Protocol, dealing specifically with issues of area protection and management, requires all who propose activities—whether scientific programmes, tourist operations or other—to file preliminary statements from which judgement can be made on the possible environmental impacts of their proposal. If the intended activities are judged to have more than transitory impacts, then a full environmental impact assessment is required. As with other activities under the Treaty, no central authority provides agreed uniformity of standards or norms. Each state regulates the activities of its own nationals to its own environmental standards.

The Protocol dispenses with SSSIs, SPAs and the non-functional SSTIs, providing instead for the creation of more rigorously defined Antarctic Specially Protected Areas (ASPAs) and Antarctic Specially Managed Areas (ASMAs), for which management plans are required. This requirement is at present minimal: the prescription for management plans expresses little more than a sparse framework for the bureaucratic regulation of human activities that may damage the environment. The Protocol does not require area management plans involving the kinds of detail that—elsewhere in the world, for example throughout most of the Arctic—are now considered mandatory wherever wilderness is managed in response to human intrusion.

The park concept in Antarctica

Antarctica has many areas set aside for scientific research, but no 'parks'—in the American sense, areas preserved in a natural state for recreational use. Though agencies outside the Treaty system have from time to time suggested the need for Antarctica to share the system of parks, sanctuaries and reserves that serves the rest of the world, including the Arctic, difficulties both conceptual and semantic appear to have intervened. The case for Antarctic parks appears not to have been established to the satisfaction of the Antarctic Treaty System.

Proposals that the whole of Antarctica be given park status proliferated during the 1980s, at the time when mining on the continent remained a possibility (see Hall and Wouters, Chapter 10). Should Antarctica become an 'international park' as suggested by some environmental groups, a 'world park' as suggested by the government of Australia and IUCN, a 'wilderness reserve' as mooted by France, or an 'international wildlife reserve' as suggested by Russia? These notions have on the whole been disregarded as impracticable. How would such a park or reserve be maintained: who would fund it, and who would be the park-keepers? These are not trivial questions: there are currently no international parks elsewhere in the world, least of all on this scale, and an area so vast and unusual as Antarctica seems hardly the right place for experimentation.

Would a park concept be right for smaller areas of Antarctica? Here we are on more familiar ground, for Iceland, Greenland, Siberia, North America and Scandinavia all have designated Arctic parks on scales ranging from a few thousand hectares to practically the whole northern third of Greenland. These are national parks, developed by single nations for special purposes, in Canada, for example, to represent the gamut of Arctic landscape diversity, and in Greenland to focus the attention of tourists and other visitors on a small number of relatively manageable sites. For national parks there is no southern equivalent. Before the Treaty came into being, no national authority saw the need for such parks, for 'park' implies visitors, and Antarctica was not a feasible venue for normal travellers. Tourism had started when the Treaty gathered strength in the 1960s, and by the negotiation of the Protocol in 1991 tourists were beginning to match and even outnumber scientists in Antarctica. Was there no case for parks to be reconsidered then?

Parks established *de novo* in Antarctica cannot be 'national', for a single nation setting up a national park today would almost certainly be deemed to be violating the spirit of the Antarctic Treaty. But sadly, even non-national parks, set up by consensus and managed by multinational management groups, lie beyond the scope of the Treaty system as it stands. Parks require day-to-day management, and neither the Treaty itself nor the Protocol provides for organisational systems that depend on intensive management.

Setting aside the limitations of the Treaty system, successful management requires agreement on objectives, and the term 'park' is open to many interpretations. Would parks with recreational facilities, for example information centres and safe areas where visitors can camp, wander freely, and learn from their own experiences, be justified in Antarctica? Or should area management continue to be limited to the protection of science and ecosystems—to the provision, in effect, only of refuges, reserves and sanctuaries?

These dilemmas of definition highlight the more general question of just what activities are deemed appropriate in Antarctica, and where a reasonable balance may lie between managing human activities and conserving ecosystems. Many different models of visitor impact management are to be found in parks, sanctuaries and reserves throughout the world: against this wide spectrum of possibilities, provisions under the Protocol—limited as they are by lack of management possibilities—seem curiously restricted.

DISCUSSION AND CONCLUSIONS

Antarctic tourism is a growing industry: tourists already outnumber scientists and their support staff in Antarctica, and prudent management must take into account the strong possibility that growth will continue. Most Antarctic tourism is currently ship-borne, and conforms to an environmentally benign pattern of behaviour established at the outset by its founder, Lars-Eric Lindblad. This pattern still has strong appeal among many tourist operators. However, two factors militate against it. The first is the difficulty of promoting its 'expedition spirit', (a) on the larger ships that, for economic reasons, are becoming more popular, and (b) now that so many ships are involved. The second is its inherent passiveness: it does not allow for activities other than rigorously controlled visits ashore, and there are already growing demands for such other kinds of adventure tourism as hiking, climbing, bird-watching and photography—currently catered for in airborne parties—that seem likely to intensify.

Project Antarctic Tourism is monitoring current trends in Antarctic tourism, and drawing parallels with other forms of world tourism to which it might ultimately conform. Tourism elsewhere is generally welcomed and catered for by an infrastructure of parks, reserves, information centres, and promoting tourist boards and authorities that see the industry as a legitimate use of natural resources. Not so in Antarctica, for the governing Antarctic Treaty is dedicated to conservation and science. Nevertheless tourism is already there, growing and diversifying, and already shows signs of developing in ways parallel to those already seen in the Arctic, where facilities ashore are commonplace. Lack of management control has already resulted in diffusion, with tour operators free to land passengers almost anywhere, and no management strategies available for any landing site. It remains to be seen whether the Antarctic Treaty System can cope, reactively or proactively, with future developments in this lively industry.

ACKNOWLEDGEMENTS

We thank Amanda Nimon and Pamela Davis for their contributions both to this research and to this chapter. PAC's first field season was made possible by a grant from the World Wide Fund for Nature. Development of the research during the second and third seasons was generously funded by the Jephcott Charitable Trust, whose support provided the continuity that made long-term studies feasible. In the first two seasons the project received generous logistic support from Instituto Argentino Antártico and the Argentine Navy. Tour operators Society Expeditions, Ocean Cruise Lines, Quark, Clipper Cruises, Mountain Travel Sobek and TransOcean Tours have assisted generously by providing passages for researchers and equipment, and other acts of logistic help and courtesy. Ms Nimon's research is funded by an Australian Commonwealth Scholarship, Ms Crosbie's by the Triangle 1949 Trust: other researchers have received support from the Cambridge Commonwealth Trust, the Cambridge Overseas Trust, the Brian Roberts Fund, the TransAntarctic Expedition Fund, the United Kingdom Foreign and Commonwealth Office, and the government of British Antarctic Territory.

REFERENCES

Benninghoff, W.S., Bonner, W.N., 1985, *Man's impact on the Antarctic environment*, SCAR/ICSU Press, Cambridge

Boswall, J., 1986, Airborne tourism 1982–84: a recent Antarctic development, *Polar Record*, **43**(123): 187–191

Codling, R.J., 1982, Sea-borne tourism in the Antarctic: an evaluation, *Polar Record*, **21**(130): 3–9

Commonwealth of Australia, 1989, *Tourism in the Antarctic. Report of the House of Representatives Standing Committee on Environment, Recreation and the Arts*, Australian Government Publishing Service, Canberra

Croxall, J.P., Rootes, D.M., Price, R.A., 1981, Increases in bird populations at Signy Island, South Orkney Islands, *British Antarctic Survey Bulletin*, **54**: 47–56

Enzenbacher, D., 1993, Tourists in Antarctica: numbers and trends, *Tourism Management*, **14**(2): 142–146

Hall, C.M., McArthur, S., 1993, Ecotourism in Antarctica and adjacent sub-Antarctic islands: development, impacts, management and prospects for the future, *Tourism Management*, **14**(2): 117–122

HMSO, 1992, *Protocol on Environmental Protection to the Antarctic Treaty, with Final Act of the Eleventh Antarctic Treaty Special Consultative Meeting*, Cm 1960, Miscellaneous Report No. 6, HMSO, London

IUCN, 1990, *Framework for the classification of terrestrial and marine protected areas*, IUCN/Commission on National Parks and Protected Areas, Geneva

Jouventin, P., Stahl, J.C., Weimerskirch, H., Mougin, J.L., 1984, Seabirds of the French subantarctic islands and Adelie Land: their status and conservation. In Croxall, J.P., Evans, P.G.H., Schreiber, R.W., eds., *Status and conservation of the world's seabirds*, Cambridge, ICPB Technical Publications, **2**: 609–625

Mahon, P.T., 1981, *Report of the royal commission to inquire into the crash on Mount Erebus, Antarctica, of a DC-10 aircraft operated by Air New Zealand Ltd*, Government Printer, Wellington

Nimon, A., Stonehouse, B., 1994, Penguin responses to humans in Antarctica: some issues and problems in determining disturbance caused by tourist parties. In Dann, P., Norman, I., Reilly, P., eds., *Recent penguin research*, Surrey, Beatty and Son, Melbourne

Reich, R.J., 1980, The development of Antarctic tourism, *Polar Record*, **20**(126): 203–214

Scientific Committee on Antarctic Research, 1984, *A visitor's introduction to the Antarctic and its environment*, British Antarctic Survey, Cambridge

Sitwell, N., 1993, A safe course through southern waters, *New Scientist*, **140**(1895): 45–46

Stonehouse, B., 1991, IAATO: an association of Antarctic tour operators, *Polar Record*, **28**(167): 322–324

Stonehouse, B., 1992, Monitoring shipborne visitors in Antarctica: a preliminary field study, *Polar Record*, **28**(166): 213–218

Stonehouse, B., 1993a, Shipborne tourism in Antarctica: Scott Polar Research Institute studies 1992–93, *Polar Record*, **28**(167): 330–332

Stonehouse, B., 1993b, Tourism and protected areas. In Lewis Smith, R.I., Walton, D.W.H., Dingwall, P.R., eds., *Improving the Antarctic protected areas*, IUCN, Cambridge, pp. 76–83

Stonehouse, B., 1994, Ecotourism in Antarctica. In Cater, E.A., Lowman, G.A., eds., *Ecotourism: a sustainable option?*, John Wiley and Royal Geographical Society, London, pp. 195–212.

Stonehouse, B., Crosbie, K., Girard, L., 1994, Sustainable ecotourism in the Arctic and Antarctic, *Geographical Journal*

Swithinbank, C.W., 1993, Airborne tourism in the Antarctic, *Polar Record*, **28**(169): 103–110

Trivelpiece, W.Z., Trivelpiece, S.G., Geupel, G.R., Kjelmyr, J., Volkman, N.J., 1990, Adelie and chinstrap penguins: their potential as monitors of the Southern Ocean marine ecosystem. In Kerry, K.R., Hempel, G., eds., *Antarctic ecosystems: ecological change and conservation*, Springer-Verlag, Heidelberg, pp. 191–202

Whitehead, M.D., Johnstone, G.W., Burton, H.R., 1990, Annual fluctuations in productivity and breeding success of Adelie penguins and fulmarine petrels in Prydz Bay, Antarctica. In Kerry, K.R., Hempel, G., eds., *Antarctic ecosystems: ecological change and conservation*, Springer-Verlag, Heidelberg, pp. 214–223

Zehnder, W., 1990, Tourism in Antarctica, *Anare Club Journal*, **10**(1): 22–25

14 The Management of Tourism at Historic Sites and Monuments

JANET HUGHES AND BRUCE DAVIS

INTRODUCTION: TOURISM AT HISTORIC SITES

Annex V to the Protocol on Environmental Protection of the Antarctic Treaty (AT) provides for the identification, registration and protection of historic sites and monuments, also that Specially Protected Areas may include sites or monuments of registered historic values. These basic provisions, however, merely state that historic sites and monuments shall not be 'damaged, removed or destroyed'. There are no established criteria for determining historic sites and monuments, no clear philosophy about 'conservation', 'restoration', removal or 'interpretation' and no Antarctic Treaty-recognised visitor guidelines.

Tourism at historic sites in Antarctica and the sub-Antarctic islands can be classified into two main types. First, organised cruises with paying passengers visiting well-known sites and monuments. The sites most commonly visited include the Scott and Shackleton huts in the Ross Sea, whaling stations at Deception Island and South Georgia and less frequently Cape Denison (Mawson's huts) and Cape Adare (Borchgrevink and ruined Campbell huts). These all date from the so-called 'heroic age' of Antarctic exploration and all except those at Deception Island are protected historic sites under Recommendation I-IX of the Antarctic Treaty (Swithinbank, 1992). The second form of tourism is visits by national expedition personnel on recreational trips or by private expeditions to sites which include sites above, but which also include a wider variety of other locations, frequently more recent historic sites, most of which are not protected. Valued more for curiosity or souvenirs they are often regarded as 'blots on the landscape' rather than historic resources.

The major concentrations of historic sites and monuments in Antarctica and the sub-Antarctic islands, including unregistered sites (Table 14.1), are the Ross Dependency and the Antarctic Peninsula and their adjacent sub-Antarctic islands. There are problems in managing both classes of visit.

Polar Tourism: Tourism in the Arctic and Antarctic Regions
Edited by C. Michael Hall and Margaret E. Johnston. © John Wiley & Sons Ltd, 1995

Table 14.1. Cultural resources attracting significant tourist numbers in Antarctica and sub-Antarctic islands

Site	Location	Type	Date	Significance	Listing
Wilkes	65°51'S 53°41'E	IGY	1956–61	?	Unlisted on A
Casey					Unlisted, removed
Proclamation Islands	67°25'S 60°47'E	Exploration	1930	P	AT (Australia)
Cape Bruce	68°22'S 78°33'E	Exploration	1931	Cairn	AT (Australia)
Walkabout Rocks	66°32'S 93°01'E	Exploration	1939	Cairn	AT (Australia)
Dobrovolski	66°32'S 93°01'E	Pillar for gravity studies	1956(IGY)	Scientific	AT (Poland)
Dobrovolski	67°00'S 142°42'E	Magnetic observatory	1956(IGY)	Scientific	AT (Poland)
Cape Denison	77°38'S 166°07'E	Heroic	1913	Memorial	AT (Australia)
Cape Denison	77°38'S 166°24'E	Heroic	1912	Huts	AT (Australia)
Cape Royds	77°38'S 166°24'E	Heroic	1908–9	Hut	AT (NZ)
Cape Evans	77°51'S 166°37'E	Heroic	1911–13	Hut, scientific	AT (NZ)
Cape Evans	77°51'S 166°37'E	Heroic	1914–16	Memorial cross	AT (NZ)
Hut Point		Heroic	1901–4	Hut	AT (NZ)
Hut Point		Heroic	1904	Memorial	AT (NZ)

Location	Latitude	Longitude	Period	Date	Description	
Observation Hill	77°51'	166°40'E	Heroic	1913	Memorial	AT (NZ)
Cape Crozier	77°32'	169°18'E	Heroic	1911	Hut	AT (NZ)
Cape Adare	71°17'S	170°15'E	Heroic	1899	Huts	AT (NZ)
Cape Adare	71°17'S	170°15'E	Heroic	1899	Memorial	AT (NZ)
Framnesodden, Peter Island Øy	68°47'S	90°42'W	Exploration	1929	Hut, plaque	AT (Norway)
Barry Islands, Marguerite Bay	68°10'S	67°08'W	Exploration	1951	Huts, memorial	AT (Argentina)
Megalestris Hill, Petermann Island	65°10'S	64°10'W	Heroic	1909	Cairn with plaque	AT (UK?)
Port Chacot	65°03'S	64°01'W	Heroic	1904	Cairn with pillar and plaque	AT (France?)
Whaler's Bay, Deception Island	62°59'S	60°34'W	Whaling	1906–30	Cairn and plaque	AT (?)
Whaler's Bay, Deception Island	62°59'S	60°34'W	Whaling	1906–30	Memorial plaque	AT(?)
Potter Cove, K. George Island	62°13'S	58°42'W	?	1874	Plaque	AT (?)
Snow Hill Island	64°24'S	57°00'W	Heroic	1902	Hut	AT (Argentina?)
Hope Bay	63°24'S	56°59'W	Heroic	1903	Hut	AT (Sweden?)
Paulet Island	63°35'S	55°47'W	Heroic	1903	Hut, grave	AT (Sweden?)
Scotia Bay, Laurie Island	60°46'S	44°40'W	Heroic	1903	Hut, meteorological hut, magnetic observatory, graveyard	AT (Argentina?)

Table 14.1. (*continued*)

Site	Location	Type	Date	Significance	Listing
Port Martin, Terre Adelie	66°49'S 141°24'E	Exploration	1950	Huts and installations (burnt by fire)	AT (France)
Ile des Pétrels, Terre Adelie	66°40'S 140°01'E	Exploration	1952	Hut	AT (France)
Ile des Pétrels, Terre Adelie McMurdo	66°40'S 140°01'E	Exploration	1957	Memorial cross	AT (France)
Stonington Island East Base	68°11'S 67°00'W	Exploration	1940–41 and 1947–48	Buildings and artefacts	AT (US)
Waterboat Pt	64°49'S 62°52'W	Exploration	1921–22	Remains of hut	AT (Chile?)
List of UK sites Other unlisted sites					
Sub-Antarctic islands historic sites					
Marion and Prince Edward Islands		Sealing, penguining	18?–1947	Sites listed by Cooper and Avery 1986	S. Africa
Marion Island		Exploration	1947	Proclamation post and plaque	? France
Crozet Islands		Sealing, shipwrecks	18?	Trypots, hut remains?	? France
Kerguelen Islands		Whaling, sealing?, exploration	18?	Whaling station	? France

Heard Island	Sealing,	1853–1929,	Sealing,	ANARE/HIMI, Australia
Macquarie Island	ANARE Sealing, penguining, AAE, ANARE	1947–54 1821?–1922?, 1947–	base Sealing, penguining, ANARE	Tasmanian legislation
Campbell Island	Sealing, shipwrecks, science station	?	Sealing, whaling, exploration	?NZ
Auckland Islands	Sealing, whaling, shipwrecks, science stations	18?–1945	Sealing, castaway depots	NZ legislation
South Georgia	Sealing, whaling, heroic	?–19	Whaling, graves, church, ?German station	UK legislation
Bouvet Øya	Whaling exploration	?	Small hut	?

Key to table:
Heroic: Heroic era in Antarctica, 1898–1922.
Sealing: Sealing for all species including fur seals and elephant seals.
Penguining: On Macquarie, King and Royal penguins were exploited for oil and to a much lesser extent on other sub-Antarctic islands, some species were exploited for skins used for muffs (Auckland Islands) and decorative clothing (Marion Island).
Exploration: 1922–57 in Antarctica.
IGY: International Geophysical Year.
Memorial: Usually a cross, with or without burial.

While the historic and scientific merits of later bases are debated, there seems general acceptance, reinforced by the Antarctic Treaty (and by national legislation on the relevant Sub-Antarctic islands), that *registered* historic sites should be respected and preserved.

Given increased tourism on the Antarctic continent and associated sub-Antarctic islands, it is a matter of urgency that management strategies for historic huts and other cultural sites be developed. This chapter provides suggestions as to the documentation, conservation and interpretation of historic sites and monuments, stressing the value of multidisciplinary approaches to evaluation, and proposes forms of international collaboration. This chapter also discusses pragmatic measures for dealing with tourism, such as guided tours, the role of operators, on-site interpretation and visitor surveys.

WHAT IS HISTORIC?

While it may appear a digression to discuss the philosophy and methodology of cultural conservation, it is essential to indicate the practical problems as well as dispel some of the myths pertaining to Antarctic historic sites and monuments. A fundamental point is to determine what is 'historic'. There has been little development of criteria relating specifically to polar regions and it is useful to identify current limitation of knowledge.

Perhaps the most comprehensive listing of all Antarctic historic sites and monuments and criteria for their classification is given by Warren (1989). Individual assessments have been completed for many sites, some in great detail (see references), most including an analysis of their significance. Most examination has focused on early sealing and whaling sites and the 'Heroic Age' rather than later sites, such as International Geophysical Year 1957–58 (IGY) era huts, with notable exceptions being the studies of Wilkes and Casey stations (Clark and Wishart, 1989) and East Base (Broadbent, 1992). Archaeological examinations of sites on sub-Antarctic islands have also been detailed, with perhaps a greater focus on scientific and exploitation issues (Townrow and Shaughnessy, 1988, 1991; Cooper and Avery, 1986; Graham, 1989; Basberg and Naevestad, 1990) rather than social history which seems favoured at later sites on continental Antarctica.

Warren (1989, p. 89) argued that an Antarctic historic resource includes 'Any place which was the location of, or is fundamentally associated with, an original and significant event in Antarctic discovery, exploration or science *prior* to the IGY' and which 'represents a unique international achievement [or] symbolises an important artistic, national, religious or cultural interest'. Warren (1989) found that no sealing site in Antarctica was listed and that there are sufficient historic and/or scientific criteria for the listing of Petermann Island, inhabited by Charcot in 1909, as well as post-'Heroic era' sites including Dobrovolski, East Base and Wordie House. The authors believe there are some post-IGY sites which would also meet these criteria.

The Antarctic Treaty Recommendation I-IX and the Madrid Protocol (Annex 5) state that declared historic sites and monuments must be preserved. This is given greater status under the Area Protection and Management Annex of the Environment Protocol. Abandoned buildings which are not declared historic must be removed (Madrid Protocol Article 1(5) of the Waste Management Annex) by the generator of the 'waste' and the user of the site except where removal would cause more damage than allowing it to remain. However, there is a danger that some Treaty signatories might declare abandoned buildings as historic sites rather than face the expensive problem of removal. This should be prevented by strict adherence to the Protocol to ensure preservation is actually carried out. Nevertheless, there has been no insistence on action by the Antarctic Treaty System even for sites of acknowledged importance such as Cape Denison, despite extensive publicity following tourist visits. Greater environmental damage can be done in some cases by removal from the site or by insensitive repair than if the sites were left to the gradual attrition by the Antarctic weather (see later comment).

Stonehouse (in Monteath, 1992) reacted to the perceived lack of action in cleaning up abandoned sites by Antarctic Treaty nations by encouraging tourists to remove whaling material during a visit to the South Sandwich Islands. However, this must be resisted since tourists are not qualified to assess the dangers of some materials (e.g. batteries, asbestos, explosives) nor the historic value of some artefacts (e.g. sealing relics).

Warren (1989, pp. 10–11) identified lack of interim protection as a major problem and concluded that 'Interim protection should apply to all sites where physical remains which date prior to the International Geophysical Year exist'. Interim protection should be followed as soon as possible by a professional assessment of the site. There is no apparent rationale for the lack of interim protection which is common in heritage legislation in most nations and a political urgency to 'clean up the environment' should not risk damage to cultural resources.

Unesco specifies the types of expertise needed for assessment of cultural and natural heritage, but some Antarctic and sub-Antarctic sites have not been assessed by professionals in the relevant fields (Barr, 1990; Shears and Hall, 1992). As Warren (1989, p. 14) concluded, 'treatment of historic resources in the Antarctic is significantly affected by the lack of involvement by professional archaeologists and conservators'. Many nations seem reluctant to pay for this expertise and expect it to be done through inadequate granting systems which often fail to even meet the expenses of the person carrying out the work. SCAR (the Scientific Committee on Antarctic Research) has little involvement in the conservation of historic sites and monuments, arguing that this is not a 'scientific' issue. However, SCAR's assessment is incorrect. Materials conservation in Antarctica does involve a considerable scientific challenge and scientists themselves should insist on the conservation of artefacts that reflect significant developments in scientific technology and methods of investigation (Shroeter et al., 1993).

Archaeologists and conservators need to recognise broader dimensions than documentation, including the value of materials conservation experimentation and the retention of historic materials for scientific study (Greenfield, 1980, 1981; Dougherty, 1985; Mabin, 1985). For example, items such as seal carcasses from earlier expeditions at East Base and other sites should be retained both as artefacts and as a scientific resource.

It may not always be essential to retain buildings and monuments: some may only require documentation and removal (Lazer and McGowan, 1989). Site assessments by Clark and Wishart (1991) and by Broadbent (1992) have generally been urgent preliminary studies as part of an environmental impact assessment, prior to removal of buildings or to the clean up of sites. At Old Casey Station outdated buildings, which are expensive to maintain and to heat, were removed for re-erection in a museum display in Australia. In general, items considered for museums must be of significance to justify the effort and expense of display; but if they are sufficiently significant for repatriation for a museum display then there must be clear reasons for not preserving them in situ in Antarctica.

Most tourists go to the southern polar regions to see wildlife and enjoy the adventure of one of the world's rare wilderness areas with polar history being an important, but secondary, interest (Hughes, 1994). Nevertheless, it is understandable that visitors view some abandoned sites as 'untidy', without realising the significance of why remains are there or why action has not been taken (usually a matter of cost).There is generally insufficient interpretation for visitors to understand the significance of a site. Therefore poorly informed judgements, mostly based on personal aesthetics, are often reached. However, aesthetic value alone should not determine the fate of historic resources and the historical and scientific reasons for retention of an unattractive site needs to be explained to visitors and the Antarctic community generally.

Some stations were vacated when it was determined that human occupation was affecting the wildlife that the base was established to study (e.g. Cape Hallett, Taylor Glacier Field Hut). Animals damage historic sites in some locations. For example, elephant seals on Macquarie Island wallow and roll against buildings. There has been considerable adverse comment from tourists and ANARE personnel about fencing off sites which many would prefer to see 'given back to the wildlife' (Disney, personal communication, February 1993).

It is not tourists alone who suffer myopia about historic sites and monuments. Many expeditioners and polar planners fail to recognise the significance of sites. Warren (1989) provides examples of designated monuments which have not been included in rationales for SSSI designation (e.g. Cape Royds) nor in management plans, nor does any mechanism exist to deal with issues of conflict or incompatibility between such designations. Warren (1989) recommends the inclusion of archaeologists and conservators in SCAR's group of specialists in environmental conservation (GOSEAC) but so far no attempt has been made to implement such a suggestion. Indeed, there appears to be some reluctance within the Antarctic Treaty System to face the issue of historic sites and monuments. Neither within SCAR nor COMNAP is the matter afforded any priority; it is only through individual dedication that heritage conservation receives any recognition.

PRINCIPLES AND PRACTICE OF HERITAGE CONSERVATION

Increased visitation by tourists now provides philosophical support for preservation *in situ* whereas, in the past, the extreme remoteness and difficulty of carrying out work led to some calls for repatriation, often without detailed consideration of the inherent technical problems. While the Madrid Protocol has now enshrined preservation *in situ*, it gives no guidance as to how this difficult task can be achieved in such extreme conditions.

Movable cultural heritage such as artefacts inside buildings have frequently been removed, sometimes for display in a museum (e.g. from Old Casey Station to Queen Victoria Museum in Australia, and from Snow Hill Island to the National Museum of Argentina) and sometimes for conservation and return to Antarctica (e.g. artefacts from Scott and Shackleton huts). This issue is not addressed by the Antarctic Treaty though removal not sanctioned by government has resulted in diplomatic action (Warren, 1989), but souveniring by national expeditioners still continues in some places (Graham, 1989). The increasing number of former national expeditioners returning to their bases as tourists may lead to an increased appreciation of the disappearing way of life of these scientific outposts, especially with the end of the husky era. Many of these buildings have their own special character and interest, such as the old paint store at Davis Station which is the only remaining polygonal building in good condition from the first ANARE base on Heard Island.

Documentation and monitoring

Documentation of historic sites and monuments varies greatly in level of detail, and in focus (e.g. industrial archaeology vs social history)

(Harrowfield, 1988; Ritchie, 1990; Bonner, 1993). Two of the primary needs are an accurate survey and cataloguing of sites and a statement of significance (Pearson, 1992). Given new technological capacities in site recording it appears desirable to move towards GIS (geographical information systems) rather than rely upon sketches and excavation drawings as in the past. Global positioning systems (GPS) permit accurate identification of locations and boundaries while coded markers can be unobtrusive but invaluable aids to monitoring. Aerial photography, satellite imagery and photogrammetry also facilitate documentation and monitoring. These and other tools will be invaluable in the essential and urgent task of documenting sites before tourist impacts arise and also provide information of interest to visitors, which is frequently overlooked.

There is an especial need to provide this information on features of sites outside the huts since there is generally only one expert guide available for tourist visits. Visitors who are ashore but not inside the huts are often unaware of the interesting material surrounding the huts and also unaware that they may be unintentionally damaging it by handling or trampling. Many visitors seem to treat the 'outdoor' artefacts as being less valuable when, in fact, they are essential and evocative elements of the site. For example, the uniform, grey, oxidised surface of hay bales at Cape Royds has been damaged by visitors picking at it, exposing the 'fresh' straw colour inside, which results in accelerating attrition.

Materials conservation issues

The Antarctic environment poses special problems for materials preservation. Some of the issues requiring examination include humidity levels within buildings, the impact of snow drift and meltwater, wind loading assessments, corrosivity, corrasion (aeolian erosion) and salt deposition, fungal treatments, protective barrier coating, the use of vapour barriers and data logging of climatic variation (Hughes, 1992a, b). Remedial work on some Antarctic buildings, plus the removal of interior ice, appears to have caused new forms of deterioration rather than solving problems.

Generally, it appears likely that damage caused by visitation is less serious than that caused by severe environmental conditions. However, deterioration due to changes in environmental conditions caused by removal of ice in the Ross Dependency is primarily due to a desire to make the buildings accessible to visitors (Harrowfield, 1990). Many visitors to Cape Denison publicise calls to remove the ice from Mawson's huts (which is not favoured by heritage professionals) to allow presentation similar to that of huts in the Ross Dependency. Few visitors have detailed understanding of the preservation problems of the site, though preservation work itself is of interest to visitors if well explained which will then hopefully promote financial support for this work.

Guidelines for visitors

The New Zealand government insists official representatives accompany tourist visits to the Ross Dependency and has recently established a detailed policy on numbers ashore at each site (Antarctic Heritage Trust, 1993). Because most visitors to the Ross Sea area go aboard large tourist vessels this stipulation can be readily met by restricting access to the huts' keys for entry, though visitors can still walk around the sites unsupervised. Greater difficulty arises when small private expeditions and NGOs visit these sites since it is difficult to insist on them having government representation. These visitors tend to be present for a longer duration and so have a potentially greater individual effect. Visits to Macquarie Island and the New Zealand sub-Antarctic islands are controlled by government permits; 600 tourists are allowed per annum at two designated sites on Macquarie Island which both include historic features (Stephenson, 1993) (see Wouters and Hall, Chapters 15 and 16).

A code of behaviour for visitors to Cape Denison was drafted by the author for the Project Blizzard visit of 1985/86, which was updated by the Australian Heritage Commission and the Antarctic Division. These revised guidelines are included on the map of the historic site of Cape Denison (AUSLIG, 1990). A limit of 20 ashore at any one time at Cape Denison has been imposed because of severe katabatic winds in this region. This appears somewhat restrictive but does permit closer supervision of activities around the huts. This is essential because this important site is still not adequately documented archaeologically and because it is the least altered and disturbed of the 'Heroic era' sites and many scientific and historical features have not yet been recorded fully (Pearson, 1992). The control of visitors at historic sites on the Antarctic Peninsula, such as Snow Hill Island, Deception Island and East Base on Stonington Island does not appear to include national staff supervision although visits to whaling stations on South Georgia are controlled by local staff who can supervise access to the museum at Grytviken (Bonner, 1993).

In order to assess the growth of tourism numbers and likely impacts, accurate records of site visitation are essential. Visitor books at sites in the Ross Dependency have given useful qualitative data, however, there is insufficient detail for understanding visitors' expectations of historic sites. Most tourism questionnaires only survey cruise passengers, not national expeditioners and private expeditions and most focus on nature conservation rather than historic sites. There is clearly a need to understand visitor expectations better, the quality and accuracy of interpretation and the meaning of follow-up response surveys.

The numbers and characteristics of visitors to historic sites and monuments in Antarctica have been reported by several commentators (Townrow, 1988; Graham, 1989; Harrowfield, 1989; Enzenbacher, 1992;

Shears and Hall, 1992; Hughes, 1992b, 1994). However, while such research is valuable there is clearly a need for greater comparability of results from visitor surveys, perhaps through the use of a common, comprehensive visitor survey for each major destination.

Interpretation should also be an essential element of visitor management at Antarctic sites. Interpretation includes all on-site information available to tourists, including signs, guidebooks and tours. It is an essential element in conveying the significance of the site and thereby aids its protection. Interpretation at historic sites and monuments is not specified by the Antarctic Treaty apart from having a sign in the four Antarctic Treaty languages at designated sites.

Leaflets and booklets have been prepared for Macquarie Island, the New Zealand sub-Antarctic islands and sites in the Ross Dependency as well as a map for Cape Denison, but there appears to be little interpretive material for the most visited historic sites in the Antarctic Peninsula. The map of Cape Denison performs a multiple role as souvenir, information sheet and visitor guideline. The modern aluminium signs on New Zealand sub-Antarctic islands were sometimes of unsympathetic appearance and some were inappropriately attached to grave markers, though obviously durable in harsh conditions. Some signs on huts in the Ross Dependency have stained the timber and it is preferable not to attach signs directly on to the buildings.

STRATEGIC NEEDS

The two principal strategic needs for the conservation of historic sites and monuments throughout Antarctica are for an integrated management strategy and an agreed code of conduct for tourist and national expeditioner visits to these sites. Elements required for an integrated management strategy include:

- accurate professional documentation of sites;
- preparation of a statement of significance;
- preparation of a management plan and code of conservation practice;
- monitoring of site dynamics and the effectiveness of management practice;
- investigation of preservation needs, and development of techniques;
- heritage education and site interpretation guidelines for national expeditioners as well as other visitors.

Much more progress is required to achieve these ideals though significant advances have been made in the Ross Dependency. Considerable damage arises from enthusiastic amateurs and indifferent bureaucrats seeking simplistic solutions to what are complex and often difficult conservation problems (Hughes, 1992).

In terms of tourist visitation there are three principal needs which need to be recognised:

- accurate documentation of sites so that significance can be explained and visits regulated to minimise human impacts, visits should not be encouraged to sites which have not been documented;
- monitoring of visits so that practices can be improved, carrying capacities determined and the success of conservation measures assessed;
- a more systematic approach to the entire spectrum of issues relating to the identification and conservation of historic sites and monuments for the whole continent with special emphasis on preservation and interpretation needs.

However, in devising and implementing a tourism strategy for visitation to these sites a number of questions must be addressed; these are dealt with below.

Sustainability and carrying capacity

The number of visitors to historic sites and monuments is increasing rapidly without any knowledge of the threshold limits before damage occurs and with few means of ensuring restrictions at some sites, especially those near bases. There is an urgent need to develop strategies for ensuring historic resources are sustained for future visitors. This involves identifying causes of deterioration, determining appropriate materials conservation techniques and priorities for treatment before developing regulations but these will be pointless unless visitors are educated to respect sites and treat them with care. Clear concise guidelines should be written to cover all visitors, especially expeditioners and small private groups who are perhaps less regulated than cruise passengers.

Damage relative to numbers

There is little current evidence linking deterioration or damage to specific tourist numbers, but a monitoring programme including periodic photographic assessment may yield some useful information. Souveniring is still a problem at some sites, such as Marion Island (Graham, 1989) and at Wilkes, although these examples are not due to paying tourists but from national expeditioners. Trampling and contamination of scientific specimens are a significant concern since most visitors are unaware of which areas are of importance and these zones are not always specifically marked.

The 'user pays' principle

Although tourist visits are levied at some sites by a charge per passenger on cruise ships (Antarctic Heritage Trust, 1993), this is more to reimburse administrative costs, licence fees or the distribution of visitor codes, than to meet major logistic and conservation costs. Indeed, some Treaty nations claim that although they would like to ensure the preservation of these sites, many other needs and priorities apply. A number of private foundations have attempted to obtain donations for conservation work in Antarctica, but this is not easily achieved and there have sometimes been conflicts with government bodies over the nature of the preservation work carried out.

A 'user pays' approach may increasingly be employed for tourist visits but it will constitute only a small element of fiscal needs in heritage conservation which requires more capital equipment and labour than for most other visitor sites in Antarctica. The building of walkways and provision of guides on Australia's Macquarie Island and New Zealand's Campbell and Auckland Islands was financed by tourist levies, though some tour operators complain about the cost (Stephenson, 1993; Hall and Wouters, 1994).

The government role in funding conservation

The Antarctic Treaty Consultative Meeting (Canberra, 1961) Recommendation I-IX states that historic sites and monuments must be preserved by their nominator. Therefore, New Zealand has taken responsibility for preserving British sites in the Ross Dependency and Argentina has conducted work at Nordenskjold's hut on Snow Hill Island (Comerci) because of an Argentine participant, Sobral, in that expedition. Mawson's huts are on the Australian Register of the National Estate, although there has been little funding of preservation work (about A$50 000 through Project Blizzard) and a Cabinet submission requesting funding of an estimated A$400 000 for the project was rejected. The New Zealand government funds travel to the Ross Dependency sites for personnel, but this is more logistically feasible than for more remote places such as Cape Denison. Britain has some potential nominations for historic sites and some 'restoration' has commenced (Shears and Hall, 1992) though none of these sites is yet listed. In the current era of financial constraint, funding for conservation of historic sites and monuments will remain scarce, with a consequent deterioration in the condition of significant relics of the 'Heroic Age' of Antarctic exploration.

Justifications for conserving these sites

Preservation of historic sites in Antarctica is inextricably involved in three major current issues in Antarctica: management of special areas, tourism and clean-ups of abandoned bases. Historic sites have an important educative role in informing all visitors about polar history and science and an appreciation of the past is invaluable for providing insights to the future. Visits to historic sites provide a great contrast to present station visits where modern buildings and scientific instruments, motorised transport and electronic communications contrast with artefacts of the era of dogs, pemmican and Morse code. Historical assessment is also an important element of scientific investigation, especially in documenting areas where alien species might have been introduced (van Klinken and Green, 1992), what native species were exploited (Townrow and Shaughnessy, 1991) and in what numbers (Cooper and Avery, 1986; Graham, 1989) since it is often difficult to determine from written historic records.

Levying national expeditioners

National expeditioners on recreational trips at present are not currently levied for visiting historic sites and monuments. While it appears appropriate for *all* visitors to make a modest contribution towards the upkeep of historic sites, it is unlikely that Treaty parties would levy such charges on their own expeditioners, moreover there is no Treaty mechanism for dealing with such matters. While there are no specific costs for providing a guide as with cruise visits, differences in visitor impact between paying tourists and national expeditioners are probably negligible and there is a case for requesting contributions from *all* visitors.

Tourism code of practice

In recent years Antarctic tourism operators have made laudable attempts to develop minimum impact codes and guidelines for site visitation (Herr and Davis, 1993). Indeed, their thought processes have often appeared well ahead of Treaty nations in this regard. None the less there is genuine concern that less respectable operators may enter the market and that private expeditions will ignore any form of voluntary regulation (Naveen, 1993). Other commentators are also worried about liability in situations where safety standards are not always high, the climate is severe and the terrain difficult. A written code of practice needs to be backed up by meticulous attention to procedures and a willingness to improve where deficiencies are identified (see Enzenbacher, Chapter 12).

Table 14.2. Elements of an action plan for Antarctic tourism at historic sites and monuments

---

Managing the resource

- There is a need for detailed and accurate documentation of historic sites and monuments prior to tourism activities and tourism should be discouraged at undocumented sites in the same way that there is agreement that there should be no visits to areas where there had been no opportunity for scientific documentation (ref). Documentation must include a statement of significance
- Management plans are required, including accurate interpretive information, installation of site markers and notices in official Antarctic languages. The management plan should include provisions for site monitoring, including all human impacts
- Education programmes should be adjusted to the levels of responsibility of those involved in management of groups of visitors (tour operators, national expeditions) and for each individual. There should be a basic level of information for each individual covering the points of interest and significance of the site and explaining the need for individual care to protect cultural values. Information is required in greater detail for those responsible for groups of visitors to ensure they fully understand and accept the need for certain restrictions and precautions in managing all visitors
- Provision of training courses for tour guides and government representatives regarding the preservation problems of sites should be discussed with tour operator organisations. This would improve the accuracy of information given to tourists and hence promote support for preservation work
- Antarctic Treaty consultative parties (ATCPs) should establish prioritised conservation measures for all historic sites and monuments within their jurisdictions based upon best international practice for cultural conservation and careful scientific development of reversible conservation techniques
- A register of expertise and research papers should be compiled and circulated to all ATCPs
- Interim and long term conservation strategies should be devised and enforced via appropriate statutory provisions and policy determinations
- Buffer zones may be required to protect some sensitive sites and visual encroachments should not be permitted in future

Managing the tour operators

- ATCPs should establish and promulgate clear guidelines for tourism operations in Antarctica. Such guidelines should include approval procedures for historic site visits, permitted numbers ashore, codes of conduct and safeguards on site and post-visit reportage
- The primary responsibility of tourism operators is to ensure passenger safety and compliance with legislation and guidelines. Permit systems should specify the degree of discretion available if deteriorating weather or other conditions render amendment of visits essential
- Structured discourse between tour operators and relevant government agencies should be encouraged and welcomed. Procedures for handling complaints between ATCPs and tour operators should be established

Table 14.2. (*continued*)

- Disaster plans for historic sites (such as fire plans) should be discussed and developed for circulation
- Government representatives should accompany and monitor site visits for all passenger cruises and methods should be investigated for ensuring and improving the compliance of small expeditions and NGOs

Managing the visit

- All tourist visits to historic sites should be ship-based with no overnight stays except in an emergency. Aircraft-based tourism involves special conditions and a code of operations must be devised by ATCPs to cover such operations
- Cooperation between tour operators and relevant government agencies is required to develop site manuals for the more frequently visited areas
- Pre-visit interpretation prepared by an appropriately qualified person should be provided to ensure the significance and fragility of the sites and artefacts are fully explained
- Surveys are needed to identify visitor expectations and assess the quality of visits to historic sites
- Groups of visitors coming ashore should be limited to numbers specified when management plans are developed. Carrying capacity of historic sites must be determined considering both hut interiors and surrounds
- Visitor guidelines should include concise instructions to follow specified routes, to clean footwear before entering buildings and 'etiquette' regarding photography
- Areas which are especially vulnerable may be designated 'off limits' to visitors and these should be marked on maps or explained at pre-visit briefings
- Reinforcement of the prohibition against souveniring or removal of artefacts, geological specimens and 'debris' is important in pre-visit briefings. Proposals to remove artefacts for scientific study must have official approval and the advice of archaeologists (who frequently maintain the only artefacts records) and conservators (who can provide specialist advice and preservation and handling of specimens) should be sought by ATCP governments
- Tour operators should enforce sanctions against passengers who consistently ignore the approved code of conduct
- Tourists should not undertake 'clean-ups' of abandoned sites but could help to inform and encourage action by government and environmental organisations by taking photos and accurate notes of affected areas
- Signs should not be attached directly to buildings since this often results in stains and adversely affects appearance. Some huts and abandoned bases contain hazardous materials such as unlabelled chemicals, old explosives and the like. All visitors should be warned of the existence of these materials until they can be disposed of following documentation of the site

continued

Table 14.2. (*continued*)

International obligations

- ATCPs must urgently address the issue of identification, conservation and interpretation of historic sites and monuments, including tourism aspects. A long-term strategy is required to meet the objective of Annex V of the Madrid Protocol
- The most urgent need is to exchange information (as was agreed by the Antarctic Treaty signatories in 1961) to prevent repetition of mistakes and duplication of research efforts
- A working party of representatives of tour operators, archaeological and scientific expertise and Treaty parties should be established to draw up visitor guidelines for consideration at an Antarctic Treaty consultative meeting
- The lack of an interim protection provision in the Antarctic Treaty for abandoned bases pre-dating the IGY should be urgently addressed
- There should be no clean-ups of abandoned bases pre-dating the IGY without assessment by relevant heritage professionals including archaeologists, architects and conservators, preferably working together as a team
- Specific questions relating to visits to historic sites should be attached or included in surveys and interviews to obtain data on tourist expectations and experiences to aid site management
- It is difficult to envisage means for controlling yacht visits to historic sites without regulatory powers other than by improving education and stressing to these most independent of tourists that they have potentially the greatest impact on these sites because of their longer stays ashore. These visitors should be discouraged from staying ashore close to sites for lengthy periods especially now overwintering by private expeditions is becoming more common, adding to the difficulty of identifying and limiting inappropriate conduct

From the broad discussion above it can be seen that there are both specific needs to be addressed and positive opportunities which can be realised to improve the visitors' experiences at Antarctic and sub-Antarctic historic sites and monuments. Hall and McArthur (1993) have noted that as far as tourism is concerned, it is the quality of the site visit which is paramount and to achieve this management of both the resource and the visitor must be simultaneously achieved. Some elements of an action plan to achieve these complementary objectives are listed in Table 14.2.

CONCLUSION

The future of tourism in Antarctica is likely to bring a general increase in passenger numbers and more yacht visits. Cruise ships, especially Russian ice-breakers, are capable of getting to more unspoilt wilderness areas and to remote locations previously protected by their isolation. Their passengers seem less demanding of luxury and are of a wider age range and agility. The possibility of mass tourism is now much greater with ships, such as the *Marco Polo*, carrying more passengers than can possibly be handled at most Antarctic historic sites.

Fortunately to date the principal tour operators have provided a self-regulatory code of conduct which appears to conform to the major safety and environmental protection requirements. While much effort has been expended in considering the impacts on and management of the natural environment, the needs of cultural resources have not received a high priority by ATCPs, yet they should be considered to be an integral part of environmental management, especially where tourism is concerned.

This prospect of increased tourism, with a high proportion of visitors landing at registered and unregistered historic sites throughout the Antarctic continent and adjacent islands, should prompt urgent consideration of the issues raised in this chapter. However, these problems are by no means insoluble with some of the remedies being able to be readily implemented with minimal cost given the will by all parties to act.

REFERENCES

Antarctic Heritage Trust, 1993, *Minutes of the Conservation Advisory Group Meeting of the Antarctic Heritage Trust*, Antarctic Heritage Trust, Christchurch

AUSLIG (Australian Surveying and Land Information Group), 1990, *Cape Denison Historic Site Map*, Catalog Number CU90/077, Department of Administrative Services, Canberra

Barr, S., 1990, Antarctica's cultural heritage: can ICOMOS help?, *ICOMOS Information*, April–June: 30–35

Basberg, B.L., Naevestad, D., 1990, Industrial archaeology at South Georgia, *Norsk Polarinstitutt Meddelelser*, **113**: 21–26

Bonner, N., 1993, Museums and the Antarctic. In *SCAR/IUCN Workshop on Environmental Education and Training in the Antarctic*, SCAR/IUCN, Gorizia

Broadbent, N., 1992, Reclaiming US Antarctic history: the restoration of East Base, Stonington Island, *Antarctic Journal of the United States*, **27**(2): 14–17

Clark, L., Wishart, E., 1989, Historical recording of Wilkes, *Aurora*, **9**(1): 4–6

Clark, L., Wishart, E., 1991, History or rubbish? A study of Wilkes Station, *Historic Environment*, **8**(1 and 2): 25–27

Cooper, J., Avery, G., 1986, *Historical sites at the Prince Edward Islands*, Council for Scientific and Industrial Research, Pretoria

Dougherty, G.J., 1985, Analysis of motor spirit from Captain Scott's Antarctic Expedition 1910, *NZ Antarctic Record*, **6**(2): 43–44

Enzenbacher, D.J., 1992, Tourists in Antarctica: numbers and trends, *Polar Record*, **28**(163): 17–22

Graham, T., 1989, Cultural resource management of the Prince Edward Islands, Unpublished thesis, BA Hons in Archaeology, University of Cape Town, Cape Town

Greenfield, L.G., 1980, A note on magnetotactic bacteria in Antarctica, *NZ Antarctic Record*, **3**(1): 16

Greenfield, L.G., 1981, Pathogenic microbes in Antarctica, *NZ Antarctic Record*, **3**(3): 38

Hall, C.M., McArthur, S., eds., 1993, *Heritage management in New Zealand and Australia: interpretation, marketing and visitor management*, Oxford University Press, Auckland

Hall, C.M., Wouters, M., 1994, Managing nature tourism in the Sub-Antarctic, *Annals of Tourism Research*, **21**(2): 355–374

Harrowfield, D.L., 1988, Historic sites in the Ross Dependency, Antarctica, *Polar Record*, **24**(151): 277–284

Harrowfield, D.L., 1989, The historic huts on Ross Island—an important recreation/tourism resource, *NZ Antarctic Record*, **9**(2): 65–73.

Harrowfield, D.L., 1990, Conservation and management of historic sites in the Ross Dependency, paper presented at Antarctica 150: Scientific Perspectives—Policy Futures Conference, University of Auckland, Auckland

Herr, R.A., Davis, B.W., 1993, The regulation of Antarctic tourism: a study in regime effectiveness. In *International Antarctic Regime Project Meeting*, Nansen Institute, Oslo

Hughes, J.D., 1992a, Deterioration problems requiring investigation to develop methods for in situ preservation of cultural heritage at Mawson and Davis Stations. In *Symposium on Antarctic Heritage Values*, Australian Antarctic Division, Kingston

Hughes, J.D., 1992b, Mawson's Antarctic huts and tourism: a case for on-site preservation, *Polar Record*, **28**(164): 37–42

Hughes, J.D., 1994, Antarctic historic sites: the tourist implications, *Annals of Tourism Research*, **21**(2): 281–294

Lazer, E., McGowan, A., 1989, *Heard Island archaeological survey (1986–1987)*, Department of Architectural Science, University of Sydney, Sydney

Mabin, M.C.G., 1985, C^{14} ages for heroic era penguin and seal bones from Inexpressible Island, Terra Nova Bay, North Victoria Land, *NZ Antarctic Record*, **6**(2): 24–25

Monteath, C., 1992, Voyage to the South Sandwich Islands, *Antarctic*, **12**(10): 359–363

Naveen, R., 1993, General principles regarding the management, education and training of all Antarctic tourists and visitors. In *SCAR/IUCN workshop on environmental education and training in the Antarctic region*, SCAR/IUCN, Gorizia, pp. 1–22

Pearson, M., 1992, Expedition huts in Antarctica: 1899–1917, *Polar Record*, **28**(167)

Ritchie, N.A., 1990, Archeological techniques and technology on Ross Island, Antarctica, *Polar Record*, **26**(159): 257–264

Shears, J.R., Hall, J., 1992, Abandoned stations and field huts: The British approach to management. In *Proceedings of the Fifth Symposium on Antarctic Logistics and Operations*, Instituto Antarctic Argentino, Buenos Aires

Shroeter, B., Green, T.G.A., Seppelt, R.D., 1993, The history of Granite House and the western geological party of Scott's Terra Nova expedition, *Polar Record*, **29**(170): 219–224

Stephenson, L., 1993, Managing visitors to Macquarie Island—a model for Antarctica? *ANARE News*, **73**: 8–9

Swithinbank, C., 1992, *Conservation areas of Antarctica—a list of SPAs, SSSIs, historic sites and monuments, SRAs, MUPAs, sealing zones and seal reserves*, Scott Polar Research Institute, Cambridge

Townrow, K., 1988, Sealing sites on Macquarie Island: an archaeological survey, *Papers and Proceedings of the Royal Society of Tasmania*, **122**(1): 15–25

Townrow, K., Shaughnessy, P.D., 1991, Fur seal skull from sealers' quarters at Sandy Bay, Macquarie Island, Southern Ocean, *Polar Record*, **27**(162): 245–248

Van Klinken, R.D., Green, A.J.A., 1992, The first record of Oniscidea (terrestrial Isopoda) from Macquarie Island, *Polar Record*, **28**(166): 240–242

Warren, P.A., 1989, Proposal for the designation and protection of Antarctic historic resources, Unpublished MA thesis, University of Washington, Seattle

15 Managing Tourism in the Sub-Antarctic Islands

MARISKA WOUTERS AND C. MICHAEL HALL

Experience reveals that the natural environments of these southern oceanic islands are readily disturbed and destroyed but virtually impossible to rehabilitate or replace . . . managers have an awesome responsibility to secure island protected areas against the deleterious influences of man. In recent years the expansion of commercial interests in fishing, mineral exploration and tourism, and increased scientific activity, are inexorably eroding the isolation of the southern islands and pose problems for their effective management as protected areas (Clark and Dingwall, 1985, p. 4).

INTRODUCTION

Consisting of 22 major islands and island groups, the sub-Antarctic islands number 800 individual islands and have an area double that of the Hawaiian island group (Clark and Dingwall, 1985). All are oceanic, far from continental land masses and each other, with climates strongly influenced by the Southern Ocean which surrounds them (Walton, 1985; Selkirk *et al.*, 1990). The sub-Antarctic islands are rich in plant life, marine mammals and avifauna and are among the last 'bastions of nature in a world beset by massive and rapid change through human activity' (Higham, 1991, p. 58). The islands are characterised by limitations of space, restricted habitats, impoverished floras and faunas compared to continental areas of similar ecological diversity, and a high degree of species endemism due to their geographical and ecological isolation (Clark and Dingwall, 1985; Hall, 1992a; Hall and McArthur, 1993; Hall and Wouters, 1994).

Their isolation means that they are ideally suited as refuges for threatened plants and animals; however, as the island biota is often specialised, it is consequently highly vulnerable to external disturbance, especially human-induced impacts. 'The evolution of the island biota is of great international

Polar Tourism: Tourism in the Arctic and Antarctic Regions
Edited by C. Michael Hall and Margaret E. Johnston. © John Wiley & Sons Ltd, 1995

taxonomic and ecological interest, and the islands are of immense value for scientific study' (Higham, 1991, p. 10).

Maintenance of these island ecosystems in their natural state is of great importance to global conservation and science. Because the islands are unique, there are considerable difficulties in managing them to preserve their uniqueness (Selkirk et al., 1990). Their isolation was their best protection for many millennia, however, that remoteness and wildlife is making them increasingly attractive for nature-based tours.

Although not as well recognised as tourism on the Antarctic continent, sub-Antarctic visitation has been increasing rapidly in recent years. Visitors to the sub-Antarctic islands are generally propelled by the same motivations as visitors to the Antarctic: the wilderness and isolation of the sub-Antarctic islands, their wildlife, and the brief, but highly exploitative, human history. However, sub-Antarctic tourism has additional components which do not occur in Antarctic tourism management. The major difference between Antarctica and the sub-Antarctic islands is the pattern of jurisdiction. Whereas Antarctica is administered under the Antarctic Treaty System, the sub-Antarctic islands are administered by individual nations. Some of the islands in the sub-Antarctic also have a human population aside from research staff, for example, on Tristan da Cunha and South Georgia. These inhabitants may also partake in tourist activities.

Although the sub-Antarctic islands are sovereign territories, the management strategies brought to bear in visitor management are still relevant to the Antarctic situation and to the broader issues of tourism management in polar regions. This chapter examines the nature of sub-Antarctic tourism, its impacts and management. The chapter is divided into four main sections. First, a discussion of the problems in defining what constitutes the sub-Antarctic. Second, an examination of the impacts of tourism on the sub-Antarctic islands. Third, an overview of the tourism policies and management strategies which have been put into place to control visitation in the various sub-Antarctic territories. Finally, the chapter concludes with a discussion of the sub-Antarctic tourism management regime and its future prospects in the light of increased tourist visitation.

THE SUB-ANTARCTIC ISLANDS: DEFINITION AND LOCATION

The sub-Antarctic islands lie close to the Antarctic Convergence in the Southern Ocean, an important oceanographic boundary where cold water from the ocean to the south meets warmer water from the north (Selkirk et al., 1990). The northern boundary of the sub-Antarctic region is known as the Sub-tropical Convergence, where the surface waters of the Southern Ocean meet the warmer sub-tropical waters of the Pacific, Indian and South

Atlantic Oceans. The southern boundary is known as the Antarctic Convergence (Fraser, 1986). Various systems of classifying these southern islands have been used, based on latitudinal, climatic or vegetational criteria. The island areas discussed in this chapter are derived from the discussion of Clark and Dingwall (1985), who used the term insulantarctica, comprising the sub-Antarctic, maritime Antarctic and cool temperate islands (Table 15.1). This chapter employs the term 'sub-Antarctic' to embrace all these island groups. However, this classification is very general, and in fact encompasses islands which have different bio-geographical identifications. The concept of grouping the world's southern islands is useful for defining ecologically based conservation regions, but is too broad in terms of the wide-ranging climate, oceanographic and biological factors which characterise these islands. However, this characterisation facilitates the analysis and discussion of management, in particular for tourism, of the islands in the Southern Ocean (Hall and Wouters, 1994).

The sub-Antarctic islands generally include Iles Crozet, Macquarie Island, Marion Island and Prince Edward Island to the north of the

Table 15.1. Classification of the sub-Antarctic islands

Classification	Location	Island groups
Cool temperate	Northern limit approximately the Sub-tropical Convergence, southern limit north of the Antarctic Convergence	● Tristan da Cunha Islands, Ile Amsterdam, Ile Saint-Paul ● New Zealand shelf islands: Antipodes Islands, Auckland Islands, Bounty Island, Campbell Islands, Snares Islands ● Falkland Islands
Sub-Antarctic	Islands in the vicinity of the Antarctic Convergence	● Iles Kerguelen, Iles Crozet, Heard Island, MacDonald Islands, Macquarie Island, Marion Island, Prince Edward Island, South Georgia
Maritime Antarctic	Islands appreciably south of the Antarctic Convergence, but outside the Antarctic Treaty area	● South Sandwich Islands, Bouvetøya

Source: After Clark and Dingwall (1985, pp. 186–187).

Antarctic Convergence; Heard Island, MacDonald Islands and South Georgia to the south; and Iles Kerguelen which straddle it. These islands experience cool, wet, windy conditions, with considerable variation in daylight hours between summer and winter. North of the above sub-Antarctic islands lie the cool temperate islands: Antipodes, Auckland, Bounty, Campbell and Snares Islands in the New Zealand region; Gough, Inaccessible, Nightingale, and Tristan da Cunha Islands in the southern Atlantic Ocean; and Iles Amsterdam and Iles St Paul in the southern Indian Ocean. The South Sandwich Islands and Bouvetøya are regarded as maritime Antarctic islands (Walton, 1985; Fraser, 1986; Selkirk et al., 1990).

The islands range widely in their latitudinal extent, from the Tristan da Cunha group at latitude $37°$ S and north of the Sub-tropical Convergence, to the South Shetland Islands, at latitude $62°$ S and enclosed by pack-ice for much of the year (Clark and Dingwall, 1985). The Southern Ocean has a strong influence on their ecosystems. The remoteness of the islands, the often limited areas available for establishment, and the cold summers have all tended to limit biodiversity in both the flora and fauna (Walton, 1985). Consequently, the islands have extremely important conservation values, particularly as refuges for rare and threatened species. However, the islands are also very vulnerable to loss through disturbance and are difficult to restore (Molloy and Dingwall, 1990). Table 15.2 provides an analysis of the islands' characteristics.

Table 15.2. Sub-Antarctic island characteristics

Island Group	Sovereignty	Total area (km^2)	Snow-free area (km^2)	Maximum elevation (m)	Latitude (° S)
South Georgia	UK	3 755	1 500	2 934	54
South Sandwich	UK	618	85	1 370	56–59
Tristan da Cunha	UK	111	—	2 060	37
Falkland	UK	13 000	—	705	51–52
Bouvetøya	Norway	50	4	780	54
Prince Edward and Marion	South Africa	335	335	1 230	46
Iles Amsterdam	France	55	—	911	37
Iles Saint-Paul	France	7	—	272	38
Iles Crozet	France	233	233	934	46
Iles Kerguelen	France	3 626	2 900	1 960	49
Heard and MacDonald	Australia	380+	70	2 745	53
Macquarie	Australia	118	118	433	54

Sources: Clark and Dingwall (1985, p. 170); Walton (1985, p. 294).

TRENDS IN SUB-ANTARCTIC TOURISM

Tourist visitation to the sub-Antarctic has been less frequent than that to the Antarctic and is mainly limited to private expeditions and commercial educational cruises (Booth, 1990; Hall and Wouters, 1994). Tourist vessels such as *World Discoverer* and *Lindblad Explorer* have visited many of the islands, including Falkland, South Georgia, South Sandwich and Macquarie Islands as well as the southern islands of New Zealand (Clark and Dingwall, 1985). Nevertheless, tourism at Prince Edward and Marion Islands has not been encouraged by the South African government, nor at the Iles Kerguelen by the French, possibly because of the islands' military facilities (Hall, 1987; Hall and McArthur, 1993).

The rate of visitation to the Australian, British and New Zealand sub-Antarctic islands has increased considerably in recent years (Hall, 1992b). Despite the growing interest by operators in visiting the islands, specific data on tourist numbers to the sub-Antarctic islands are generally not available. Macquarie Island was visited by 564 people in the 1990–91 summer. There were no tours in 1991–92 (Hall, 1992b). However, several tours for the 1992–93 season included Macquarie Island in their itinerary (Quark Expeditions, 1992–93; Seaquest Cruises, 1992, p. 22). More specific data on sub-Antarctic island visits may possibly become available with more rigorous reporting by commercial Antarctic tour operators who include sub-Antarctic island visits in their itineraries (Wouters, 1993).

The growth in sub-Antarctic tourism may be due to several factors (Hall and Wouters, 1994). First, there has been an increase in public awareness of remote tourism destinations through increased public exposure to wildlife documentaries, membership of conservation organisations, and advertising. Second, the relative tourist overcrowding of the Antarctic Peninsula is leading some operators to search for other remote destinations which can convey an Antarctic experience for visitors without other tourists being seen. Third, improved transport technology makes ship travel through the Southern Ocean smoother and safer for tourists. Finally, the overall expansion of the Antarctic and sub-Antarctic tourist market may generate growth.

A contributing factor to visitor growth may be the increase in private boat ownership. The exact numbers and destinations of these tourists are difficult to determine, because, similar to yacht visits in Antarctica, sub-Antarctic tourists are able to visit a wide range of localities. Nevertheless, yacht-based cruises have grown substantially. In the 1970s only one or two yachts were operating in the Southern Ocean; this figure had grown to 6 in the early 1980s, and to over 20 in the 1990/91 season (Poncet and Poncet, 1991, p. 6). However, 'the proliferation of private yachts in the Southern Ocean has added a new and largely unwelcome element to the tourist problem. The activities of these yachts seem at the moment, to be beyond any general control' (Bonner and Walton, in Poncet and Poncet, 1991, p. 6).

Airborne tourism does not appear to exist in the sub-Antarctic islands: landing is extremely difficult at most of the islands, although overflights would be possible. The use of planes may not be commercially viable as the islands are at great distances from each other; however, some Antarctic cruise ships carry helicopters which could be used for aerial sightseeing and landing passengers at more remote locations.

TOURISM IMPACTS

Sub-Antarctic tourism is a relatively recent phenomenon, and there is little information on the actual impacts tourism has had on the sub-Antarctic islands. The most serious concern surrounding tourism in these islands is the potential adverse impacts tourism may have on the physical environment. A number of the sub-Antarctic islands have already suffered marked human impact through the exploitation of whale, seal and fisheries resources for most of the past 300 years (Clark and Dingwall, 1985; White, 1994). Generally, however, the islands of the Southern Ocean have not been permanently inhabited and exploitation periods have been short. Several southern island groups have not been modified by humans at all. Clark and Dingwall (1985, p. 4) believe that 'they are among the few remaining terrestrial areas of the world unaffected by man [sic]—and hence are of great importance'. The sub-Antarctic islands contain some of the world's least human-impacted biotas, and their relative isolation has been their greatest conservation asset, but it is these same harsh conditions which are now attracting visitors in increasing numbers. Their fragility means that even minute changes brought about by human impacts, such as tourist activity, may have long-term impacts on ecosystem stability (Hall, 1992b).

The types of impact by visitors on and around islands include inadequate waste disposal, litter, vegetation trampling, disturbance to wildlife, and the potential threats of fire and the introduction of pests, particularly rodents (Booth, 1990). But, as in the case of Antarctic tourism, environmental impacts on the islands depend on the nature of the activity. Overflights generally provide minimal disturbance of the environment, although low overflights of wildlife colonies may panic the birds or marine animals. For example, in June 1990, around 7000 King penguins stampeded, piled up on top of each other and died from suffocation when an Australian Air Force Hercules circumnavigated Macquarie Island at an altitude of 250 metres (Swithinbank, 1993). The impacts of ship-based tourism are more controversial. Cruise travel occurs in the Austral summer, coinciding with the peak breeding periods of many species, and may disturb breeding sites. Ships can also pollute over a large area through oil spill, and indiscriminate disposal of waste and sewage (Hall, 1992b).

Given the specialisation of the island biota, the islands are highly vulnerable to external disturbance and environmental change, especially human-induced impacts (Hall and Wouters, 1994). The extinction of species is particularly common on islands when new competitors or physical conditions are introduced. One of the greatest threats to island biota is therefore the introduction, accidental or deliberate, of alien plants and animals, in particular through seed dispersal or the transfer of mammals such as rats and mice. Careless behaviour by tourists would certainly increase this threat, and excessive disturbance of plants and animals by tourist visits, as has occurred in areas of the Falkland Islands, must be avoided (Clark and Dingwall, 1985).

Impacts of tourism in the sub-Antarctic are mainly associated with the physical environment, but there is also concern over the conservation of cultural heritage. A number of early European sites associated with farming, sealing and whaling, exist on the islands, and some early exploration bases are of substantial historical significance (Hall, 1992b; Hughes, 1994). The cultural history is part of the attraction of the islands to tourists, and is used by tour operators as a major visitor drawcard. However, the isolation of the islands means that it is extremely difficult for authorities to regulate access to cultural and natural heritage sites and even though the majority of operators are very careful about their activities, there is little control, if any, over the activities of visitors on private yachts.

TOURISM POLICIES

All of the sub-Antarctic islands fall outside the Antarctic Treaty area, and are therefore not subject to any of its provisions. Each island or archipelago is subject to national sovereignty. South Georgia and the South Sandwich Islands are British, Prince Edward and Marion Islands are South African, Macquarie, Heard and MacDonald Islands are Australian, Bouvetøya is Norwegian, and Iles Kerguelen, Crozet, Amsterdam and Saint-Paul are French. The New Zealand sub-Antarctic islands, which consist of the Antipodes, Auckland, Bounty, Campbell and Snares Island groups, are discussed in Chapter 16 by Wouters and Hall (also see Cessford and Dingwall, 1994; Hall and Wouters, 1994; Sanson, 1994).

Historically, South Georgia has had a resident population for longer than any of the other islands and industrial relics in the form of abandoned whaling stations still litter the island (Walton, 1985). However, the scientific importance of the island has been recognised and the new conservation legislation enacted by the Falkland Islands government is now as stringent as that applying within the Antarctic Treaty area. Heard, MacDonald, Prince Edward and Marion Islands are also covered by specific conservation legislation. However, the French have continually and deliberately introduced a wide range of herbivores into Kerguelen, resulting in major degradation of large areas of vegetation, so that there is little on the main island sufficiently undamaged to be worth protecting (Walton, 1985). Therefore, national jurisdiction can be advantageous to the management of the islands, but at the same time may also be detrimental. For example, if islands are inhabited, then provision for the island's people by using its resources may be more important than the preservation of the island for its unique features. If the islands are uninhabited, then national agencies may easily forget their existence, and not include specific manage- ment plans for the protection and conservation of the islands, such as control over access to them. This can pose problems for the effective management of tourism. The following section will discuss the varying tourism management problems of the sub-Antarctic islands. New Zealand's sub-Antarctic tourism policy will be reviewed in Chapter 16 by Wouters and Hall.

Tristan da Cunha Islands

The Tristan island group includes Tristan da Cunha, Inaccessible, Nightingale and Gough Islands. Tristan da Cunha is British territory and is a Dependency of St Helena. Apart from a seven-person South African meteorological team on Gough Island, these last three islands are uninhabitable by humans (Wouters, 1993). Essentially, they are nature reserves for sea- birds, seals and penguins. The entire population of 300 people lives on Tristan da Cunha in a village called Edinburgh.

The Tristan da Cunha Conservation Ordinance 1976 is the basis of con- servation on the islands, which are the responsibility of the Administrator of Tristan da Cunha. The entire group is protected but the degree of protec- tion varies from island to island. A formal management plan does not exist (Clark and Dingwall, 1985). The Administrator advises that Tristan da Cunha has no tourist industry and none of the facilities such an industry would demand (Wouters, 1993). The RMS *St Helena* is the only regular passenger ship, calling at the island *en route* from England to Cape Town just once a year. The occasional cargo or naval ship may call, but these are infrequent, and depend upon special cargoes. Fishing boats are the normal method of getting to the island, but they carry only 8–10 passengers and priority is given to islanders and those travelling on government business. There does not appear to be a tourism management policy.

Falkland Islands

The Falkland Islands is an archipelago of over 300 islands, inhabited by 2200 residents of predominantly British origin. Sovereignty is claimed by both the United Kingdom and Argentina and was the subject of a short, though bloody, conflict between the two nations in 1981, although Poncet and Poncet (1991) argue that the islands remain British in their administration, population and way of life.

Tourism is well-established with visits having frequently been made to the Falklands by cruise ships such as the *Lindblad Explorer*. Landings, although controlled, appear to have caused some localised disturbance to sea-bird colonies (Clark and Dingwall, 1985). There is currently no legislation which controls the movement of tourists within the islands, other than with regard to access to government-owned nature reserves (Wouters, 1993). The Falkland Islands Tourism Board encourages 'responsible development of tourism' and produces a number of publications which recommend appropriate behaviour when in areas of environmental importance and sensitivity. The Falkland Islands Tourism Office in Stanley retails several tourist booklets, including a *Country Code* of recommended environmental 'dos and don'ts' (Poncet and Poncet, 1991).

The number of cruise ship visits is increasing quite substantially, and as many of the islands visited are privately owned, the owners use their own judgement on the controls which need to be applied (Wouters, 1993). In June 1992, the owners of Bleaker and Sea Lion Islands decided to restrict cruise ship access to ships carrying no more than 130 passengers, and that only one ship per day be allowed to visit the locations. In addition, there must be a ratio of one trained guide to every 35 clients, and clients must not stray further than 100 metres from the guide. Walking routes have to be agreed in advance (Wouters, 1993).

Iles Amsterdam, Iles Saint-Paul, Iles Crozet and Iles Kerguelen

The islands form part of a *parc national antarctique français*. Management details are not fully known (Wouters, 1993). The islands are state-owned territories, part of the Territoire des Terres Australes et Antarctiques Françaises (TAAF) (Walton, 1985). The majority of the islands have been declared a *parc national de refuge dans les possessions australes françaises*, and a National Park Act protects marine mammals, some bird species, and plants (Poncet and Poncet, 1991). The Antarctic and sub-Antarctic Lands Act (decree 1966) covers human activities on the islands. According to Clark and Dingwall (1985, p. 34) commercial tourist interest in these islands is low, although it appears as if the islands will become part of

commercial circumpolar voyages which have been proposed for introduction for the 1993–94 Austral summer (Hall and Wouters, 1994). In
addition, private yachts are increasingly starting to visit the islands.
Vessels are requested to ensure that their first port of call is at the TAAF
station of each island group, where the *chef de district* can be contacted.
There are several Specially Protected Areas (SPAs) and Sites of Special
Scientific Interest (SSSIs). Access to these is restricted and by permit only,
issued by the *chef de district* (Poncet and Poncet, 1991).

Heard and MacDonald Islands

Heard Island is close to its natural state and the MacDonald Islands are in
pristine state (Bonner and Lewis Smith, 1985), and were proposed for
World Heritage listing in 1990 (Poncet and Poncet, 1991; Hall, 1992c).
There are no introduced mammals or plants on the islands and their
natural state contrasts markedly with most other sub-Antarctic islands,
making them extremely important areas for conservation and science
(Poncet and Poncet, 1991). Although a staffed station was run for a short
time by Australia on Heard Island, this was abandoned in 1955 and both
Heard and the uninhabited MacDonald Islands are now very rarely visited
(Clark and Dingwall, 1985; Walton, 1985).
  Heard and MacDonald Islands are Australian federal government
responsibilities and as external territories are subject to the same legislation
as the Australian Capital Territory (ACT). The various Heard Island and
MacDonald Island Acts (1957–73) give power to the Governor-General to
make ordinances for the peace, order and the good government of the
Territory. A number of ordinances of the ACT apply some limited nature
conservation measures. These include the National Parks and Wildlife
Conservation Act 1975, Wildlife Protection (Regulation of Exports and
Imports) Act 1982, Environment Protection (Impact of Proposals) Act 1974
(Hall 1992b), but there is no specific management plan although guidelines
for visits have been produced (Clark and Dingwall, 1985).
  Under the Australian Heritage Commission Act 1975, federal ministers
and authorities are required to refer to the Commission for comment any
action which will affect a place in the Register of the National Estate to a
significant extent. Both the Heard and MacDonald Islands, and Macquarie
Island are listed on the register. Although not subject to cruise ship visits,
there have been a number of private expeditions to the Heard and
MacDonald Islands. Furthermore, the proposed nomination of the islands
to the World Heritage List may well encourage visitor interest. Therefore,
Hall (1992b) believes that it would seem imperative that the Commonwealth develop a management plan for the islands.

Macquarie Island

Macquarie Island is one of eight islands or groups of islands which is truly sub-Antarctic. It is the only one of these eight islands or groups which is wholly protected, comprising 28 per cent of the protected area found on these islands (Department of Parks, Wildlife and Heritage (DPWH), 1990). Macquarie Island is administered by the Tasmanian Department of Parks, Wildlife and Heritage, and is subject to Tasmanian state legislation on park use and protection. Overall administration of the island is carried out by the Tasmanian Department of Parks, Wildlife and Heritage through the National Parks and Wildlife Act 1970 and subsequent regulations.

Initially protected as a sanctuary under the Tasmanian Animals and Birds Protection Act 1928, it was proclaimed a wildlife sanctuary in 1933. Macquarie Island became a conservation area in 1971, and in 1972 it became a state reserve. The Tasmanian National Parks and Wildlife Service declared Macquarie Island a nature reserve in 1978, equivalent in status to a national park, and renamed it Macquarie Island Nature Reserve. The island is permanently occupied by scientists at the meteorological and research station (Bonner and Lewis Smith, 1985; Clark and Dingwall, 1985; Rounsevell and Copson, 1985; DPWH, 1990; Selkirk et al., 1990).

In 1977, Unesco accepted this sub-Antarctic island as a biosphere reserve in the 'Man and the Biosphere' programme (Davis and Drake, 1983; Selkirk et al., 1990). A biosphere reserve is an area set aside so that human impact on the environment as compared with unaltered ecosystems can be monitored. It differs from a national park in that it is a representative example of a particular terrain and species, whereas a national park is intended to conserve unique or spectacular sites and species (Davis, 1983; Bonner and Lewis Smith, 1985; Rounsevell and Copson, 1985). It is the only island in the Southern Ocean to have been declared a biosphere reserve.

The Tasmanian Department of Parks, Wildlife and Heritage has prepared a management plan for Macquarie Island. Hall and McArthur (1993) have provided a detailed discussion of this plan. One of the plan's objects is 'to permit tourist visits under strictly controlled operations which allow visitors to experience the natural values of the island without compromising them'. However, while the plan recognises that 'in the long term it is only with public understanding and support that the world's wildlife, habitats and natural ecosystems can be protected', tourism should only be encouraged in so far as it does not conflict with the objects of management, first of which is 'to protect and manage the reserve as a natural habitat for its indigenous flora and fauna and in order to achieve ecosystem conservation'. In order to achieve these goals the prescription for management states: 'Tourist visits will be ship-based but limited facilities such as walkways, viewing platforms and interpretation material may be provided in selected areas to protect the wildlife, environment, historical and/or scientific values of the reserve'. In addition to setting guidelines for the protection of scientific programmes and the safety of visitors and personnel, the Guidelines for Tourism Operations at Macquarie Island Nature Reserve set nine directives for the protection of the environment (Hall and McArthur, 1993) as shown in Table 15.3.

There is no airstrip, the only access to the island being by sea. Entry to the reserve is by permit (DPWH, 1990). Visitors are landed on the Isthmus and at Sandy Bay between 7am and 7pm and are met by staff of the Department of Parks, Wildlife and Heritage. There are wooden walkways and viewing platforms to make both places easily accessible for visitors (DPWH, 1990, p. 20). Information for the visitor to Macquarie Island provided by the Department of Parks, Wildlife and Heritage is presented in an attractive folder detailing visitor regulations, history, flora and fauna, with excellent photos to aid the identification of wildlife. Indeed, the abundant and spectacular wildlife is one of the most appealing features to Macquarie Island visitors, as it is one of the richest wildlife sanctuaries in the world (DPWH, 1990, p. 25).

Table 15.3. Directives for the protection of the environment, Macquarie Island Nature Reserve, Tasmania

---

- All tourist operations will be ship-based with no overnight stay on the island except in an emergency. Shore visits will only be permitted between the hours of 0700 and 1900 local station time
- The landing and pick-up of personnel will only be at beaches designated by the Department
- The areas which may be accessed on foot will be designated by the Department and all shore parties are to be in two-way radio communication with the ship and must not be more than one hour walking time from the beach where they are to be picked up
- Shore parties to be organised in groups of no more than 10 people including one leader/guide with each party
- Strict quarantine procedures will be enforced to prevent exotic species being taken ashore in equipment or clothing
- Any food and drink items to be consumed during visits ashore are to be unopened, prepacked, processed food or drinks, previously approved by the Department
- No food items are to be given to wildlife
- All rubbish and unused food items are to be returned to the ship. No ship-borne rubbish, including food items are to be disposed of in Tasmanian territorial waters
- No collecting of flora, fauna, historical sites or artefacts, geological specimens or objects is permitted

---

Source: Hall and McArthur (1993, p. 121).

The New Zealand sub-Antarctic island management plans (see Chapter 16) have greatly influenced the management of Macquarie Island by the Tasmanian Department of Parks, Wildlife and Heritage, which has adopted similar costing and management strategies, and guidelines for tourism operations (Hall, 1992b; Hall and Wouters, 1994). However, Hall and McArthur (1993, p. 121) believe that the success of the guidelines in meeting both the conservation objectives and providing a satisfying tourist experience is still to be examined. The A$100 charge per visitor under the management plan may place substantial economic burdens on smaller tourist operations and thereby further restrict tourist access. The current limit on ships is four ships and approximately 600 people per Austral summer (Hall, 1992b). However, this may lead to some difficulties in implementation, as four ships with 150 passengers each will of course produce more revenue than four commercial operators on yachts with only 25 people each.

From a biophysical perspective, the guidelines may well be extremely appropriate for the management of visitation to sub-Antarctic islands and may also meet the requirements of the proposed World Heritage Listing for Macquarie Island (Hall 1992b). However, the assessment of tourist activities would require a far more thorough consideration of sub-Antarctic ecology and the relation to human impacts than has hitherto been the case.

Marion and Prince Edward Islands

These two islands are administered by the Department of Environment Affairs of South Africa (Wouters, 1993), although legislated for separately in the national parliament (Walton, 1985). They are managed as a nature reserve (Clark and Dingwall, 1985; Poncet and Poncet, 1991) and are covered by specific conservation legislation (Walton, 1985, p. 315). The Department is currently in the process of drawing up a management plan concerning South Africa's sub-Antarctic islands (Wouters, 1993).

Conditions imposed by the South African authorities on tourists visiting the islands are quite stringent (Poncet and Poncet, 1991, p. 33). The current policy on tourism and private expeditions to Marion and Prince Edward Islands states that tourism and private expeditions are not encouraged and will not be supported by the South African government (Department of Environment Affairs, n.d.). Tourism to the islands will only be authorised under permit of the Department, and visitors are only allowed on Marion Island. Several reasons are given for this: all available resources (including domestic facilities and search and rescue services) are used mainly for the conduct of official meteorological and research activities; the domestic facilities available at the base station are sufficient only for those engaged in official activities, and the fragility of the island ecosystems necessitates a limitation on the number of persons present on the island (Department of Environment Affairs, n.d.).

South Georgia and the South Sandwich Islands

Britain is the responsible authority for the islands of South Georgia and South Sandwich. The volcanic South Sandwich Islands are very rarely visited by tourists, as they are remote, barren and inaccessible. Landing is extremely difficult without helicopters (Wouters, 1993). On the other hand, South Georgia has been frequently visited by tourists since 1970, and interest is increasing (Walton, 1985, p. 316). The tourists come principally in organised cruise ships, although there has been a considerable number of private and commercial yacht visits. South Georgia is a Crown Colony, administered by a Commissioner and organised by the Foreign and Commonwealth Office in London (Wouters, 1993). It is the sub-Antarctic island with the longest period of continuous habitation and economic history, but it presently has no permanent inhabitants, although there is a station at Husvik and a small year-round British Antarctic Survey (BAS) biological base at Bird Island (Bonner and Lewis Smith, 1985; Wouters, 1993).

South Georgia has no management plan, but it does have wildlife protection ordinances. There are three forms of designated area for conservation: Specially Protected Areas (SPAs) are designated to preserve their natural ecological systems from any interference; Sites of Special Scientific Interest (SSSIs) are designated to prevent scientific investigations being jeopardised by disturbance. Permits to enter these areas are issued only for compelling scientific reasons which cannot be served elsewhere (Bonner and Lewis Smith, 1985). There is no published tourist management scheme (Wouters, 1993), although a third category of protected area, Areas of Special Tourist Interest (ASTIs), have been designated, which are selected areas that are representative of wildlife and scenic beauty where the effects of tourist activity may be systematically assessed (Bonner and Lewis Smith, 1985; Wouters, 1993). Tourism is limited to ASTIs and is well regulated (Clark and Dingwall, 1985). In addition to the normal entry formalities required at Grytviken, it is prohibited to land on South Georgia for mountaineering or other 'recreational' purposes except in ASTIs, unless granted a special permit to visit other places (Bonner and Lewis Smith, 1985). ASTIs which have been designated are:

- Grytviken: the area bounded by Moraine Fjord, Hamburg Glacier, Mt Sugartop and Lyell Glacier. This area covers the port of entry and principal settlement, the remains of the oldest whaling station, Sir Ernest Shackleton's grave and examples of almost all the plant communities found in South Georgia.

- Bay of Isles: the area between Cape Buller and Cape Wilson inland to the height of land, together with all the islands and rocks in the bay. This area covers king penguin and gentoo penguin rookeries, wandering albatross colonies and many other bird species, as well as substantial glaciers and fine scenery (Bonner and Lewis Smith, 1985, p. 282).

Tour ships normally clear through the magistrate at Grytviken, visit the whaling station where there is now a small museum, and the cemetery where Sir Ernest Shackleton is buried, before proceeding on to other stops to view wildlife. Some consideration has been given to a small tourist tax of $10 per person (Levich and Fal'kovich, 1987, p. 97). Clark and Dingwall (1985) believe that designation of areas of 'Special Tourist Interest' appears to be an effective method to control small numbers of tourists as long as adequate supervision exists.

Bouvet (Bouvetøya) Island

Bouvetøya has never been inhabited (Walton, 1985). The island and its surrounding waters are a nature reserve administered by the Norwegian Ministry of Environment (Wouters, 1993). The regulations setting the management guidelines for the island state that the island is designated a nature reserve with its adjacent territorial waters. The primary aim of the regulations appear to be concerned with the protection of the flora and fauna, although there is allowance for scientific research (Walton, 1985; Poncet and Poncet, 1991; Wouters, 1993). Activities on the island are governed by permit, and the use of vehicles or the landing of aircraft is forbidden except by permit (Poncet and Poncet, 1991, p. 32). It would appear that due to its remoteness and inaccessibility, Bouvetøya has not been visited by tourists (Wouters, 1993).

THE SUB-ANTARCTIC ISLAND TOURISM MANAGEMENT REGIME

It is apparent from the above discussion that there is a wide variation in the administration of tourism in the sub-Antarctic islands. In general terms, legislation attempts to restrict the introduction of alien species, prohibit the harvesting of any living resources except under special licence, and protect the native flora and fauna from interference and disturbance (Walton, 1985). However, the Australian sub-Antarctic islands are subject to a more stringent management regime, which has been developed in close relation to the policies developed by New Zealand for its sub-Antarctic islands (Cessford and Dingwall, 1994; Hall and Wouters, 1994; Sanson, 1994). A summary of the policies is provided in Table 15.4.

Table 15.4. Summary of sub-Antarctic island tourism policies

Island (Group)	Tourism policy	Details
Tristan da Cunha	No	No tourist industry
Falkland Islands	Yes	Government-owned nature reserves: legislation controlling tourist movements. Several privately owned islands: owners have placed restrictions on cruise ship access to ships carrying no more than 130 passengers. Only 1 ship per day allowed to visit. Ratio of 1 guide per 35 clients required. Clients must not stray more than 100 m from guide. Walking routes have to be agreed in advance.
Iles Amsterdam, Iles Crozet Iles Kerguelen, Iles St Paul	Unknown	Low tourist interest
Heard and MacDonald	No	Guidelines for visits only
Macquarie Island	Yes	To permit tourist visits under strictly controlled conditions which allow visitors to experience the natural values of the island without compromising them
Marion and Prince Edward	Yes	Tourism and private expeditions are not encouraged and will not be supported. By permit to Marion Island only
South Georgia and South Sandwich	No	Designation of ASTIs: selected areas which are representative of wildlife and scenic beauty where effects of tourist activity may be systematically assessed
Bouvetøya	No	No tourist visits

Therefore, although there are national provisions for conservation on the islands not all are comprehensive and their enforcement is fragmentary. Increasing tourist interest in these islands, particularly South Georgia, will require more vigorous prosecution of the laws if they are to be of any use. The proliferation of private yachts in the Southern Ocean has added a new element to the management equation. The activities of these yachts seem, at the moment, to be beyond any general control, regulation and enforcement.

The sub-Antarctic islands have already suffered from human exploitation. Regimes to reduce this impact are necessary, but whereas in the Antarctic implementation of such a regime is difficult due to its unique transnational structure, it is paradoxically complex in the sub-Antarctic *because* of the number of sovereign nations and lack of a single enforcement agency. The joint SCAR/IUCN workshop on the biological basis for conservation of sub-Antarctic islands encouraged national authorities to develop and implement conservation policies and plans, devised specifically for each island or island group, and incorporating a full consideration of the control of the human impact on the natural ecosystem (Walton, 1985). The workshop concluded that 'although achievement of the objectives of conservation plans will be subject mainly to self-assessment, the use of independent observers appointed by each national authority is likely to contribute greater success' (Walton, 1985, p. 107). The workshop also recommended that national authorities be encouraged to consider which areas might be proposed for international designation as World Heritage sites or biosphere reserves.

Booth (1990) believes that the challenge to island managers is to maximise the benefits from recreation and minimise the detrimental impacts. As in the case of many current Antarctic tourist operators, sub-Antarctic commercial operators and private recreation entrepreneurs may also become conservation advocates. Impacts of considerable numbers of people in one place must be minimised. Clark and Dingwall (1985, p. 179) believe that 'managing authorities need to ensure appropriate supervision of visits, to provide detailed information on the islands and their conservation needs'. In addition, they stated that designation of ASTIs such as on South Georgia should be considered. International cooperation to allow a wide range of islands to be visited would enhance the viability of tourist operations. Moreover, if sufficient numbers of sites were available, areas could be rested periodically from tourist schedules, especially if adverse effects became evident.

The exchange of information is as much a problem in the administration of sub-Antarctic tourism as in Antarctica. Management must be based on adequate knowledge if it is to be truly effective. Ecological studies and long-term monitoring are required, in particular interaction of human activities with the sub-Antarctic ecosystems. Activities must be regulated to avoid unnecessary disturbance to wildlife and the environment. This requires active and extensive research. Information flow can be improved when national authorities, operating agencies and scientists promote free and full exchange of all information and data, especially on those aspects which concern conservation and environmental protection of these unique islands (Walton, 1986; Enzenbacher, 1992). To encourage responsible and controlled tourism, both scientists and administrators should provide public education on the significance and value of the sub-Antarctic islands. Each nation should encourage both scientists and administrators to provide public education on the significance and value of the sub-Antarctic islands; and to encourage responsible forms of tourism.

The management of tourism in the islands of the Southern Ocean poses special challenges. 'With adequate precautions and international cooperation in regulating tourist operations, tourism should be compatible with scientific and conservation objectives in protected areas on islands of the Southern Ocean' (Clark and Dingwall, 1985, p. 179). However, there will be no more second chances, mistakes will be paid for in accelerated loss of species.

The sub-Antarctic islands have high conservation significance, and Holdgate (1970, cited in Clark and Dingwall 1985, p. 168) identified three principal objectives to aid their management:

1. The general protection of scenic beauty and the biota of the Antarctic region south of 60° S latitude.
2. The protection of remaining undisturbed ecosystems of oceanic islands north of 60° S, and as far as possible the restoration or stabilisation of those ecosystems that have been disrupted by actions of man.
3. The wise management of the biological resources of the Southern Ocean, to enable a sustainable harvest to be taken.

The first two objectives are particularly important for the management of tourism in Antarctica and the sub-Antarctic islands (Hall, 1992b). The isolation of the islands can no longer be regarded as adequate protection for the islands. Tourism has become a reality in the management of the island ecosystems. Somewhat optimistically, O'Connor and Simmons (1990, p. 192) argue that 'In itself, the image of the last islands of nature in a spoiled world promotes a nature tourism use'. However, evidence from other polar regions suggests that wise and careful use is not always the outcome of nature-based tourism visitation.

The sub-Antarctic islands are not isolated independent units. Marine mammals and sea-birds migrate over large distances between the islands and numerous animal and plant species are endemic to island groups or to the whole Southern Ocean region (Clark and Dingwall, 1985). Many cruise ships visit a number of sub-Antarctic islands during one voyage, as well as visiting Antarctica. Management of tourism to Antarctica and the sub-Antarctic islands should thus be considered an entity. Despite the variations of sovereignty, Antarctic and sub-Antarctic tourism are invariably linked. Present management programmes vary among different nations, and international cooperation and coordination will be required to produce a regulatory system for tourism operations encompassing both the sub-Antarctic and the Antarctic.

ACKNOWLEDGEMENTS

The authors would like to gratefully acknowledge the assistance of the following in providing information for this chapter: G.L. Bound, Falkland Islands Tourism,

Falkland Islands; Tore Ising, Head of Section, Ministry of Environment, Oslo, Norway; P.H. Johnson, Administrator, Tristan da Cunha, South Atlantic; Fe Van Rensburg, Director-General, Department of Environment Affairs, Pretoria, South Africa; Dr D.W.H. Walton, Head, Terrestrial and Freshwater Life Sciences Division, British Antarctic Survey, Cambridge, United Kingdom.

REFERENCES

Bonner, W.N., Lewis Smith, R.I., eds., 1985, *Conservation areas in the Antarctic*, International Council of Scientific Unions, SCAR, Scott Polar Research Institute, Cambridge

Booth, K., 1990, Restoration, a positive force for island restoration. In Towns, D., Daugherty, C., Atkinson, I., eds., *Ecological restoration of New Zealand islands*, Conservation Sciences Publication No. 2, Department of Conservation, Wellington, pp. 278–283

Cessford, G.R., Dingwall, P.R., 1994, Tourism on New Zealand's Sub-Antarctic islands, *Annals of Tourism Research*, **21**(2): 318–332

Clark, M.R., Dingwall, P.R., 1985, *Conservation of islands in the Southern Ocean*, International Union for Conservation of Nature and Natural Resources, Cambridge University Press

Davis, B.W., 1983, Australia's Biosphere Reserves: the role of Macquarie Island, *Australian Ranger Bulletin*, **2**(3): 93

Davis, B.W., Drake, G.A., 1983, *Australia's biosphere reserves: conserving ecological diversity*, Australian National Commission for UNESCO, Australian Government Publishing Service, Canberra.

Department of Environment Affairs, n.d., *Marion and Prince Edward Island—policy on tourism and private expeditions*, Department of Environment Affairs, Pretoria

DPWH (Department of Parks, Wildlife and Heritage), 1990, *One of the wonder spots of the world: Macquarie Island Nature Reserve*, Department of Parks, Wildlife and Heritage, Tasmania

Enzenbacher, D.J., 1992, Tourism in polar areas: a symposium, *Polar Record*, **28**(166): 246

Fraser, C., 1986, *Beyond the roaring forties: New Zealand's Sub-Antarctic islands*, Government Printing Office Publishing, Wellington

Hall, C.M., 1987, Tantamount to an act of war? Australians fear French move to new nuclear test site, *Alternatives: Perspectives on Science, Technology and the Environment*, **14**: 70–71

Hall, C.M., 1992a, Tourism in Antarctica: activities, impacts, and management, *Journal of Tourism Research*, **30**(4): 2–9

Hall, C.M., 1992b, Ecotourism in the Australian and New Zealand Sub-Antarctic islands, International Geographical Union Commission on Leisure and Recreation Symposium, Telluride, August

Hall, C.M., 1992c, *Wasteland to world heritage: preserving Australia's wilderness*, Melbourne University Press, Carlton

Hall, C.M., McArthur, S., 1993, Case-study: ecotourism in Antarctica and adjacent Sub-Antarctic islands: development, impacts, management and prospects for the future, *Tourism Management*, **14**: 117–122

Hall, C.M., Wouters, M., 1994, Managing nature tourism in the Sub-Antarctic islands, *Annals of Tourism Research*, **21**(2): 355–374

Higham, T., ed., 1991, *New Zealand's Sub-Antarctic islands—a guidebook*, Department of Conservation, Invercargill

Hughes, J., 1994, Antarctic historic sites: the tourism implications, *Annals of Tourism Research*, **21**(2): 281–294

Levich, S.V., Fal'kovich, N.S., 1987, Recreation and tourism in the Southern Ocean and Antarctica, *Izvestiya Vsesoyuznogo Geograficheskogo Obshchnestva*, **119**(2): 168–174

Molloy, L.F., Dingwall, P.R., 1990, World Heritage values of New Zealand islands. In Towns, D., Daugherty, C., Atkinson, I., eds., *Ecological restoration of New Zealand islands*, Conservation Sciences Publication No. 2, Department of Conservation, Wellington, pp. 194–206

O'Connor, K.F., Simmons, D.G., 1990, The use of islands for recreation and tourism: changing significance for nature conservation. In Towns, D., Daugherty, C., Atkinson, I., eds., *Ecological restoration of New Zealand islands*, Conservation Sciences Publication No. 2, Department of Conservation, Wellington, pp. 186–193

Poncet, S., Poncet, J., 1991, *Southern Ocean cruising handbook*, Government Printing Office, Stanley, Falkland Islands

Quark Expeditions, 1992–93, *Journeys to the far side of Antarctica*, Travel brochures, Quark Expeditions

Rounsevell, D., Copson, G., 1985, Southern Ocean sanctuary, *UNESCO Review*, **10**: 9–11

Sanson, L., 1994, An ecotourism case study in Sub-Antarctic islands, *Annals of Tourism Research*, **21**(2): 344–355

Seaquest Cruises, 1992, Antarctica, *New Explorer: Journal of Explorations Aboard Seaquest Cruises*, Fall: 22–24

Selkirk, P.M., Seppelt, R.D., Selkirk, D.R., 1990, *Sub-Antarctic Macquarie Island—environment and biology*, Cambridge University Press

Swithinbank, C., 1993, Airborne tourism in the Antarctic, *Polar Record*, **29**(169): 103–110

Walton, D.W.H., 1985, The Sub-Antarctic islands. In Bonner, W., Walton, D., eds., *Key environments: Antarctica*, Pergamon Press, Oxford, pp. 351–369

White, K.J., 1994, Tourism and the Antarctic economy, *Annals of Tourism Research*, **21**(2): 245–268

Wouters, M.M., 1993, Promotion or protection: managing the paradox—the management of tourist visitation to Antarctica and the Sub-Antarctic islands, the New Zealand situation as a case study, Unpublished master's thesis, Massey University, Palmerston North

16 Tourism and New Zealand's Sub-Antarctic Islands

MARISKA WOUTERS AND C. MICHAEL HALL

The world today has lost all interest in the Auckland Islands ... as far as can be seen, the islands will have no future history. The bleak climate, the unproductive soils, and the isolation of the Auckland Islands under the changed conditions of a modern world, suggest that, in the loneliness of the Sub-Antarctic Ocean, they will be 'world forgetting, by the world forgot' (McLaren, 1948, pp. 102–103).

Last century, New Zealand's sub-Antarctic islands were touted as a farming resource. Today they are the subject of a new kind of economic activity, nature tourism, which is demanding a completely different style of management (Peat, 1991, p. 38).

New Zealand administers 5 of the 22 islands or island groups in the Southern Ocean (Fraser, 1986), and was the first country to establish reserves for the protection and preservation of sub-Antarctic flora and fauna when it introduced protective legislation for Adams Island in 1910 (Brewster, 1982). This status was subsequently applied to all New Zealand's sub-Antarctic islands. New Zealand's five sub-Antarctic island reserves include the Antipodes, Bounty, Auckland, Campbell and Snares Island groups. These island reserves contain some of the world's last remaining areas of vegetation mostly unmodified by people or introduced animals. Each of the reserves has a distinctive flora and fauna of international scientific importance. They provide habitat and breeding areas for birds and marine mammals peculiar to the sub-Antarctic regions (Department of Conservation, 1992, p. 1). Nevertheless, despite the emphasis on their protection, Sanson and Dingwall (1992, p. 15) believed that 'tourism has undoubtedly become one of the key issues in the management of the sub-Antarctic islands'.

It is often claimed that New Zealand's competitive advantage in the international tourism market is its clean, green image (Shultis, 1989; Hall et al., 1993). Nevertheless, 'there is an inherent potential for conflict between increasing recreational and tourism use of conservation areas and

Polar Tourism: Tourism in the Arctic and Antarctic Regions
Edited by C. Michael Hall and Margaret E. Johnston. © John Wiley & Sons Ltd, 1995

the preservation of those conservation values on which such activity depends' (Fyson, 1991, p. 22). This is particularly relevant to the management of sub-Antarctic tourism, where increasingly there is greater pressure to allow visitation, without creating undue disturbance to the natural values of the islands (Peat, 1991). Tourism to New Zealand's sub-Antarctic islands is not new; fare-paying passengers were often carried on government steamers in the nineteenth century (Fraser, 1986). However, visitation of New Zealand's sub-Antarctic islands is becoming increasingly popular and underlines the need for careful management (Cessford and Dingwall, 1994; Hall and Wouters, 1994; Sanson, 1994).

This chapter will discuss the unique values of the New Zealand sub-Antarctic islands and their attractiveness to visitors. Past human impact and present New Zealand efforts to protect the islands from further human modification are discussed. The management guidelines for tourism are reviewed with a discussion of their potential as a model for management of the sub-Antarctic islands. The chapter concludes by discussing the implications of sustainable forms of tourism for management in the New Zealand sub-Antarctic islands.

LOCATION AND DESCRIPTION

Biogeographically, the New Zealand sub-Antarctic islands fall within the province of InsulAntarctica, one of the 227 provinces identified in a classification scheme to encompass the world's biogeographical diversity. Although referred to in this chapter as 'sub-Antarctic', the southern New Zealand islands are more appropriately considered as representative of a cool-temperate zone, characterised by a mean annual air temperature generally above 5°C, supporting vegetation, including trees and woody plants, and lying generally between the Sub-tropical and Antarctic convergences (Molloy and Dingwall, 1990; Higham, 1991). However, Fraser (1986) asserts that the five New Zealand groups as well as Gough Island and Macquarie Island are the world's only true sub-Antarctic islands, as they are influenced only by the ocean and are properly situated between the Antarctic and Sub-tropical convergences. Higham (1991, p. 9) believes that 'both physically and biologically, the New Zealand islands are widely representative of their biogeographical realm, and are therefore of international significance'.

The islands provide restricted habitats, and although there is a high degree of species endemism, ecological diversity is limited (Clark and Dingwall, 1985; Fraser, 1986). The islands host a number of endangered species, and have significant breeding colonies of marine birds and mammals (Hall, 1992b). However, the islands are also very vulnerable to disturbance and are difficult to restore (Molloy and Dingwall, 1990).

The Antipodes are the most remote of the New Zealand sub-Antarctic islands. Campbell Island is the most southerly of the islands at 52°53′ S, and with its weather station is New Zealand's only inhabited sub-Antarctic island. It is also the world's major breeding ground of the majestic southern royal albatross. The Auckland Islands are by far the largest group and lie between latitudes 50°30′ and 50°60′ S. They have the most varied bird and insect life of all the groups. They are large enough to have elements of most of New Zealand's other sub-Antarctic islands, and a wider range of native flora and fauna than anywhere else in the sub-Antarctic, making them a very popular visitation site. The Snares Islands are the closest to New Zealand. North East Island, the largest of the Snares, is just over 3.5 kilometres long, but is home to an estimated 6 million sooty shearwaters. The barren Bounty Islands are situated at 47°45′ S and 179°02′ E. All the islands are heavily weathered and eroded. There is little soil for vegetation, and the islands provide very few landing places. When the sea-birds leave at the end of the breeding season, the Bounties become the desert islands of the Southern Ocean (Fraser, 1986; Higham, 1991; Peat, 1991). The biota of the sub-Antarctic islands is a culmination of a long history of geographic isolation, species dispersal, climatic factors, community interaction, and minimal human interference until very recently (Higham, 1991).

HUMAN HISTORY AND IMPACT

The New Zealand sub-Antarctic islands have not been permanently inhabited, but nevertheless have a rich human history which extends over 200 years. Past human activities include sealing, whaling, exploration, colonisation and settlement, shipwrecks of the sailing era, farming, research, tourism and reserve management (Higham, 1991; Peat, 1991; Sanson and Dingwall, 1992). All these activities have left their imprint and are of considerable historical interest and cultural value. Maori visited the Snare Islands and possibly other New Zealand sub-Antarctic islands for food-gathering purposes (Hall, 1992b). Auckland Island was inhabited by a small group of Maori from about 1842 until 1856. In addition to the castaway depots established for the survivors of the not infrequent shipwrecks, there were attempts at settlement in Port Ross and on Enderby Island by English settlers from 1849 to 1852. Associated with these activities were the introduction of cattle, goats, pigs and sheep (Fraser, 1986).

The first major impact of people in the sub-Antarctic was that of exploitation, in particular the slaughtering of marine mammals. Moreover, with the activities of sealers, colonists and farmers came rats, cats and mice (Clark and Dingwall, 1985; Fraser, 1986; Higham, 1991; Hall and Wouters,

1994). On the main Auckland Island, pigs that were put ashore and abandoned cats created havoc with the vegetation and ground-nesting birds, and rats similarly wiped out most of the ground-burrowing sea-birds on Campbell Island (Fraser, 1986). Only the Bounty and Snares Islands have been spared from the introduction of exotic animals and thus are largely unmodified (Clark and Dingwall, 1985). Adams Island (Auckland Islands group) is considered to be the largest island in the world today spared the introduction of mammalian predators (Peat, 1991). The islands also lacked the selection pressures of moa browsing and grazing which occurred on mainland New Zealand (Foggo, 1990). The New Zealand sub-Antarctic islands therefore comprise an almost unlimited opportunity for understanding the dynamics of vegetation processes in the absence of herbivorous vertebrates and with a mere 200 years of human interference.

Fraser (1986, p. 131) believed that 'the handful of truly unspoilt sub-Antarctic islands are those which have been too small, remote, or dangerous to exploit in the past'. Among these are the sheer-sided offshore stacks such as Jacquemart Island in the Campbell Group and Leeward Island in the Antipodes, or some of the steeper Bounty Islands. Apart from these few islands there are effectively no places people have reached which they have not changed or affected to some extent. Nevertheless, compared to many continental regions, the New Zealand sub-Antarctic islands are essentially pristine (Hall, 1992b). The Bounties and Antipodes are virtually unscathed; Disappointment Island, Adams Island and the Snares have no introduced animals or rodents and have evolved more or less undisturbed since their creation. Such places are extremely rare and are of enormous ecological importance (Fraser, 1986). Significantly, their wilderness character has become a major factor in the development of the tourism potential of the New Zealand sub-Antarctic islands, both on their own and in conjunction with visits to the New Zealand Ross Dependency.

SUB-ANTARCTIC ISLAND MANAGEMENT POLICY

Responsibility for management of New Zealand's sub-Antarctic island nature reserves lies with the Department of Conservation (DoC). Under the Conservation Act 1987, the Department's mission is to conserve the country's natural and historic heritage (Edmonds, 1990). Policy development originates from Head Office in Wellington, and the management of the conservation estate is administered by 14 regional conservancies. The Southland Conservancy (based in Invercargill) is responsible for the management of the sub-Antarctic island reserves (Sanson and Dingwall, 1992). Public participation in the management of the sub-Antarctic islands is enhanced through the role of the Southland Conservation Board. Members of the board are appointed by the Minister of Conservation to approve and review conservation management strategies and plans and to monitor the effectiveness of these documents. The New Zealand Conservation Authority, which is a separate statutory body appointed by the Conservation Minister, provides a national overview in the approval process of conservation management strategies and plans (Sanson and Dingwall, 1992).

As stated above, New Zealand was the first country to establish reserves to protect and preserve the sub-Antarctic flora and fauna. Adams Island (Auckland Islands) was the first flora and fauna reserve in the New Zealand sub-Antarctic in 1910, although at that time land was still being farmed on Campbell Island and the main Auckland Island. The rest of the Aucklands were set aside for conservation purposes in 1934, and gradually the other islands followed (Brewster, 1982; Fraser, 1986). By 1961, all five of New Zealand's sub-Antarctic groups were flora and fauna reserves. In 1978, they were gazetted as nature reserves, restricting landings and visitation on the islands, and in 1986 they became national reserves. As declared national nature reserves, New Zealand's sub-Antarctic islands receive the highest form of statutory protection available, a status which is only accorded to areas whose natural ecosystems are of outstanding scientific value. The status of national reserves requires an Act of Parliament to alter any conditions pertaining to the reserve (Fraser, 1986; Molloy and Dingwall, 1990).

The management of the islands is governed by the Reserves Act 1977. This Act provides for the protection in perpetuity of the indigenous flora and fauna, ecological associations and natural environment, and for extermination as far as possible of exotic flora and fauna of these islands. The overriding aim of management of national nature reserves is to safeguard numbers, natural distributions and interactions of indigenous plants and animals (Peat, 1991; DoC, 1992). These aims are contained in a set of management plans. Other uses, such as tourism, can only be allowed provided that the primary management objective of protecting the natural ecological values of the islands is not imperilled (Sanson and Dingwall, 1992).

All the island groups have individual management plans. Management plans have been prepared, approved and published for the Auckland, Campbell and Snares Island groups. The plans for the Antipodes and Bounties have not been published, but they are recognised as statutory documents (Fraser, 1986; Sanson and Dingwall, 1992). These plans detail management measures regarding granting of permits, activities permissible on the islands, construction of buildings, frequency of visits, precautions against introductions of animals and plants, economic exploitation, transport on and near the islands, waste disposal, pollution and management of adjacent waters (Clark and Dingwall, 1985). A conservation management strategy is currently being written for all New Zealand's sub-Antarctic islands (Wouters, 1993). This aims to set longer-term objectives of the Department's integrated management of natural and historic resources, tourism and other conservation purposes consistent with existing New Zealand government legislation.

DoC is not only responsible for the protection of the islands' natural features, but has also written a draft historic resource management strategy for the historic sites on the sub-Antarctic islands (Wouters, 1993). The strategy identifies three key components; survey, evaluation and protection of the resource. It concentrates on a theme approach with active conservation measures designed to protect the best remaining example of each. A conservation plan is to precede any on-site or active conservation management, and should be consistent with the overriding principle of preservation with minimum alteration to the historic places as found. Priority will be given to keeping historic artefacts *in situ* on the islands except where off-site conservation measures are necessary to ensure the protection of the resource (Peat, 1991; Sanson and Dingwall, 1992; DoC, 1993).

TOURISM IN NEW ZEALAND'S SUB-ANTARCTIC ISLANDS

With the recent boom in 'nature tourism', the Auckland Islands, along with Campbell, Bounty, the Antipodes and the Snares, are becoming popular destinations for the more adventurous (Pope, 1990, p. 105).

The New Zealand sub-Antarctic islands have been the subject of tourist visitation since the end of the nineteenth century, although commercialised tourist visitation to the islands did not commence until the late 1960s. Fare-paying passengers were often carried on government steamers which supplied castaway depots during the nineteenth and early twentieth centuries. In the summer of 1969–70, the Danish ship *Magga Dan*, chartered by Lars Lindblad, took tourists to both Auckland and Campbell Islands *en route* to Antarctica (Williams, 1990). Between 1968 and 1993, an estimated 2850 people have visited the islands on ship-based tours (Sanson, 1992) (Table 16.1). However, this figure is almost certainly an underestimate as numerous yacht and fishing vessel visits have occurred in the past two decades which have either not received approval by the relevant management authority or been observed by scientific and meteorological staff based on the islands.

Visitation to sub-Antarctic islands is a major component of Antarctic cruise tourism. Many cruise ships which pass through New Zealand *en route* to Antarctica, also visit its southern islands (Peat, 1989). However, the New Zealand sub-Antarctic islands received only infrequent visitation from commercial tourism vessels such as the *Lindblad Explorer* (Lindblad Travel)

Table 16.1. Known tourist visits to New Zealand's sub-Antarctic islands, 1969–93

Cruise season	No. of ship visits	No. of passengers
1967–68	2	45
1969–70	—	—
1970–71	2	160
1971–72	—	—
1972–73	—	—
1973–74	1	90
1974–75	—	—
1975–76	—	—
1976–77	—	—
1977–78	—	0
1978–79	—	—
1979–80	1	90
1980–81	1	90
1981–82	2	180
1982–83	2	179
1983–84	2	190
1984–85	—	—
1985–86	1	100
1986–87	1	125
1987–88	3	45
1988–89	3	47
1989–90	5	72
1990–91	12	812
1991–92	2	15
1992–93	9	600[*]
1993–94	11	240
Total	60	3090

[*] Proposed figure for the 1992/93 season.
Sources: Sanson (1992, 1994); Sanson and Dingwall (1992); Wouters (1993).

and *World Discoverer* (Society Expeditions) before the mid 1980s. Since then, New Zealand-based companies, such as Discovery Charters South Seas and Southern Heritage Tours, are marketing yacht-based tours to the islands alone for up to a maximum of 20 passengers. Two types of tourist operators may be identified in the New Zealand sub-Antarctic:

- International cruise ships visiting the islands *en route* to and from Antarctica carrying 90–160 passengers that visit two or three sites only.

- New Zealand boats carrying up to 25 passengers on 10–20 day tours of principally Auckland and Campbell Islands, with numerous site visits (Sanson and Dingwall, 1992, p. 15).

Both types of tourist vessel are increasingly visiting the sub-Antarctic islands (Peat, 1989). Over the years a steady trickle of private motor boats and yachts have also visited the sub-Antarctic islands.

The total applications for the 1992–93 season were 13 cruises with 750 passengers (Sanson and Dingwall, 1992). The figures for the 1992–93 season are illustrated in Table 16.2. Campbell Island received a record eight visits from tourist ships. The *Pacific Ruby* chartered by the New Zealand company Southern Heritage Tours, visited the new sub-Antarctic islands five times. During the 1992–93 season, the *Frontier Spirit* and the *Kapitan Khlebnikov* also visited the sub-Antarctic islands. Visits by these last two vessels were usually of half a day's duration and their passengers were confined to the boardwalk areas of both Campbell and the Auckland Islands. Visits by the smaller vessels (about 20 passengers) were usually extended a little beyond the boardwalk areas. Each vessel carried a New Zealand government representative and lecturers (New Zealand Antarctic Society, 1993, p. 395).

Tourism attractions

Islands attract visitors for their isolation, high biological and scenic values, and the sense of adventure that an island visit holds. . . . Islands, particularly those under some form of restoration or protection, offer the nature-seeking recreationist an inspiring environment (Booth, 1990, p. 278).

Booth (1990, p. 278) asserts that it is likely that the designation of an island under protection or restoration status will increase the number of visitors wishing to go there. This assertion is highly applicable to tourism to the New Zealand sub-Antarctic islands, and may be one of the strongest factors for those who visit the island reserves.

Table 16.2. New Zealand sub-Antarctic island tourist numbers, 1992–93

Ship	No. of voyages	No. of passengers
(Quark) *Kapitan Khlebnikov*	1	85
(Seaquest) *Frontier Spirit*	3	(Voyage 1) 95
		(Voyage 2) 107
		(Voyage 3) 118
(NZ Nature) *Pacific Ruby*	5	76
Total	9	481

Source: Wouters (1993).

Historic sites are of attraction to visitors. Among them are a cemetery at Port Ross, Auckland Island, which represents the short-lived whaling-based Hardwicke settlement of the 1850s; a Second World War coast watch lookout on Auckland Island, a castaway depot on Enderby and another on Antipodes; whaling relics on Snares and Campbell Islands; and the remains of the old sheep farm on Campbell Island (Peat, 1991). Campbell Island is also the only site in the New Zealand sub-Antarctic where people are permanently based at the meteorological station (McKenzie, 1989).

The sub-Antarctic islands are notable for the abundance of wildlife they support. In particular the populations of birds on the islands are immense. The Snares are estimated to harbour over 6 million breeding sea-birds, which is comparable to the total number of sea-birds around Great Britain and Ireland. The Auckland Islands support the world's largest breeding populations of wandering albatross and shy mollymawk, and Campbell Island accommodates the world's largest breeding population of royal albatross. The Auckland Islands are also the principal breeding ground of one of the world's rarest seals, the Hooker's sea lion (Higham, 1991). Molloy and Dingwall (1990) believed that the scenic quality of the islands and their aesthetic appeal have an emotional impact on all who visit them.

As in the Antarctic and the other sub-Antarctic islands, the summer cruises to New Zealand's sub-Antarctic islands coincide with breeding times. This creates both an attraction for tourists as well as a problem. Some sites are more sensitive than others, such as Enderby Island, where sea lions are easily disturbed (Peat, 1991). The recognition that any visit can put the natural ecosystems of the islands at threat, principally through the risk of accidental introduction of rodents or new flora and disturbance to breeding animals, has resulted in the development of a set of guidelines setting out strict management procedures for both types of operation (Sanson and Dingwall, 1992).

Tourism guidelines

DoC does not see its role as a promoter of tourism in the sub-Antarctic, but rather its vocation is to manage tourism so that it has the least impact (Peat, 1991). The Department has prepared specific guidelines on tourism to the New Zealand sub-Antarctic islands to elaborate the policies on tourism contained in the management plans. The management plans have general recommendations for visitation management. The tourism policy for the Auckland Islands is

> To permit visits to selected areas of the reserve by tourists but under such controls as deemed necessary to ensure protection of its natural features, ecosystems and cultural values. . . . Cruising expeditions must have a genuine

educational or inspirational purpose relating to better appreciation of nature.
... Often the most spectacular sight-seeing is obtained from the sea, and this
activity is not restricted (Department of Lands and Survey, 1987).

A similar policy exists for the Campbell Islands. It is the intention of the
DoC that both island groups will be managed according to 'wilderness-type
visiting codes, visits are limited in number, the landings are supervised by
a representative of the department, are under strict supervision and are of
short duration' (Department of Lands and Survey, 1983). Visits to the
Bounty Islands are limited to specialised interest groups which have
received permission from DoC (Peat, 1989) but the Snares Islands are not
open for tourism.

A quota of 500 tourists per season was permitted for the Campbell and
Auckland Islands in 1990/91 and a maximum of 600 people were permitted
to land at any one designated tourist site in 1992/93 (Peat, 1991; DoC, 1992).
A maximum of 20 visitors to one guide is maintained for all landings, except
on the Bounty Islands where the ratio is one guide per 10 visitors. No overnight stays on the islands are allowed unless specially authorised. Most of
the visitation occurs on the main Auckland and Campbell Islands and on
Enderby Island. However, to reduce visitor impact on the most popular sites
(such as Enderby Island), several new sites have been made available, for
example Lake Hinemoa track and Hadfield Inlet on Auckland Island
(Sanson and Dingwall, 1992).

Tourist visits are by entry permit only (Reserves Act 1977) to designated
sites on modified islands, and have to be accompanied by a DoC representative. These representatives are there to ensure the strict regulations are
complied with (Williams, 1990). The representatives aim to encourage
cooperation and greater understanding of what the visitor is seeing, and the
need for reserve management. People ashore have to be carefully controlled
as the ground is easily damaged because of the wet climate and peat soil,
and is slow to recover (Fraser, 1986). Visitors to Campbell Island and
Auckland Island generally support the concept of boardwalks to protect the
fragile environment, although some found the spacing between the slats too
wide (Cooper, 1993; Cessford and Dingwall, 1993; Mahoney, 1993). Upon
completion of the voyage, a report on the cruise and recommendations
where necessary are made. However, Wouters (1993) believes that it is
important to formalise the standard of reporting, as there appears to be
some variation among the cruise reports examined.

No landings are permitted on pristine or near pristine islands (e.g. Snares,
Antipodes, Adams and Disappointment Islands) (Peat, 1991; DoC, 1992). A
maximum cruise ship size of 160 passengers has been established for cruise
ships visiting the islands and a visitor monitoring programme has also been
in place since 1990 (Sanson and Dingwall, 1992).

DoC charges a permit fee and a visitor impact fee. The visitor fee varies according to the size of the vessel. For the 1992/93 season the fees were: cruise ships (30–180 persons maximum), NZ$135 per passenger; tour boats (30 persons maximum), NZ$190 per passenger (minimum fee of NZ$2800); and private yachts (1–10 persons), NZ$190 per crew member. These fees are directed towards management programmes such as the construction of over a kilometre of boardwalk on Campbell Island to allow tourists to visit an albatross colony with minimal impacts on the environment, visitor impact monitoring, guidebooks, the provision of a New Zealand government representative, a rodent contingency plan to prevent the accidental introduction of rodents on to the islands, and the payment of a DoC resource rental (Peat, 1991; Sanson, 1992; Sanson and Dingwall, 1992). For the 1992–93 financial year, approximately 0.34 per cent of the total DoC budget is being spent on sub-Antarctic management, of which about 16 per cent should be returned as revenue, that is as tourism impact fees (Wouters, 1993). There is increasing interest in visits by private yachts to the islands, but all visitors are treated similarly for entry permit procedures (Sanson and Dingwall, 1992). Overseas tourist ships are required to have a current deratting exemption certificate as part of the permit to land on the islands.

There are general guidelines with which visitors have to comply, as well as specific conditions and restrictions for visits within a particular island group (Peat, 1991). For example, the Department does not allow helicopter landings and overflying without separate prior approval. The guidelines are intended to assist the DoC as manager of the reserves, tourism operators, and others wishing to visit the reserves. Key elements of the Department's strategy for tourism are given in Table 16.3.

In addition to the more traditional forms of visitation, people also participate in other activities around New Zealand's sub-Antarctic islands, such as diving and kayaking (Williams, 1990). The abundant wildlife makes diving attractive, although it can be hazardous. Sea kayaking is rated as a 'hard' adventure due to the dangerous coastlines, the huge waves, and the usually constant heavy swells. Campbell Island has been circumnavigated by kayak. These forms of activity add another element to the management of sub-Antarctic tourism.

DoC places great emphasis on education and has produced a code of visitor conduct. Individual copies of the sub-Antarctic Island Guidebook are given to each tourist visiting the islands as part of their entry permit and to assist in interpretation (Sanson and Dingwall, 1992) as well as a copy of the SubAntarctic Islands Minimum Impact Code which is presented as a small, easy-to-carry leaflet. A very important role of the departmental representatives is to ensure that visitors are well aware of plant quarantine measures adopted by the department to ensure the ultimate protection of the islands from new introductions (Sanson and Dingwall, 1992). DoC believes that the policy of

Table 16.3. Department of Conservation management strategy for tourism

Strategy	Details
Guidelines on tourism/entry permits	A set of guidelines on tourism is given to each tourism operator containing conditions reinforced in the signed entry permits
Limitation on islands and sites	No visits are permitted to any of the less modified or unmodified islands which have high conservation values (e.g. Snares, Adams and Antipodes Islands) although zodiac cruising is allowed at these locations. Elsewhere a series of visitor sites has been established and a maximum limit of 600 visitors per site introduced. The majority of visits occur on the main Auckland, and Campbell Islands and on Enderby Island. Several new sites have been made available (e.g. Lake Hinemoa track and Hadfield Inlet) to reduce visitor impact of the most popular sites (e.g. Enderby Island)
Departmental representatives	The presence of a departmental representative on each tour boat is regarded as the key to compliance with the Department's visitor guidelines and the emphasis on rodent and plant quarantine measures and confining visits to environmentally acceptable sites. The representatives also act in an interpretation and guiding capacity, while operators must comply with guiding ratios of 1 guide to 20 visitors
Managing impacts	A maximum cruise ship size of 160 passengers has been established for cruise ships visiting the islands and a visitor monitoring programme has also been in place since 1990. On potentially high impact sites (e.g. Campbell Island) extensive boardwalks (2.3 km long) have been constructed at considerable expense to provide access for visitors while minimising disturbance to wildlife, vegetation and soils. A minimum viewing distance of 5 metres is enforced when viewing wildlife with all animals given the right of way. Rodent quarantine precautions are rigidly enforced and a full set of rodent bait stations is maintained in Invercargill for deployment in case of accidental introduction of rodents
Tourism revenue	The Department recovers costs of managing visitor impacts, quarantine, the provision of a departmental representative and resource rental through its tourism impact and facilities fee
Permit application fee	NZ$56.25 per cruise
Tourism impact facilities fee	Small ships (<30 passengers) NZ$190 per passenger ($2800 min. fee). Cruise ships (<160 passengers) NZ$135 per passenger. This money is spent directly on the management of the reserves and human impacts

Source: Sanson and Dingwall (1992, pp. 15–17).

insisting on a guide for every 20 visitors is central to successful management (Peat, 1991), although Hall and Wouters (1994) have argued that there is no scientific basis for the selection of the figure of 20 visitors.

DoC's tourism strategy has adopted ideas from the Galapagos Islands National Park (Peat, 1991), which is a World Heritage site in Ecuador. In turn, the New Zealand sub-Antarctic island management plans have greatly influenced the management of Macquarie Island. DoC has established a close association with the Tasmanian Department of Parks, Wildlife and Heritage which administers Macquarie Island, which has adopted similar costing and management strategies, and guidelines for tourism operations. The two departments have worked closely on devising tourism guidelines for sub-Antarctic tourism because after visiting the New Zealand islands some cruises also visit Macquarie Island (Peat, 1991; Hall *et al.*, 1992; Sanson and Dingwall, 1992).

The sub-Antarctic programme advocated by DoC receives substantial support from operators. However, the pricing policy employed by DoC is seen by several small-scale operators as discriminating against them in favour of the larger cruise ships (Hall and Wouters, 1994). The smaller operations feel that their own operations are more environmentally friendly than that of the large cruise ships, yet it is felt that the DoC pricing policy acts against their own ventures and fails to appreciate the commercial context for small-scale special interest tourism operations. Furthermore, several operators have argued that their knowledge of the islands either matches or is better than those of the New Zealand government represent-ative that they have to take on board. Thus the requirements of electing a government representative may have to be changed. However, should the small-scale tour operator be allowed to act as a DoC representative, a conflict of interest may occur.

Environmental monitoring and compliance

Monitoring and regulation of tourist, and other, ships are extremely difficult. The isolation of the islands and potential for unauthorised landings pose a real dilemma for protection. DoC relies very heavily on the surveil-lance carried out by the Royal New Zealand Air Force and Navy. Recent defence cutbacks have reduced New Zealand's operational surveillance capability in the Southern Ocean and on the sub-Antarctic islands, at the same time that human activity such as commercial tourism and fishing have increased. For example, DoC's monitoring boat *Renown* only has operational capacity to the Snares Islands (Sanson and Dingwall, 1992).

The management emphasis in the New Zealand's sub-Antarctic islands is on ecosystems or habitat protection and enhancement and removal of introduced flora and fauna (Sanson and Dingwall, 1992), although the ecological basis for the plans is vague (Wouters, 1993). DoC uses observational experience, in particular to ensure that the environment is not harmfully affected. For monitoring, a lot of reliance is placed on voluntary compliance by tourist operators (Wouters, 1993). For example, the cruise ship *Kapitan Khlebnikov* which visits the sub-Antarctic islands *en route* to Antarctica, carries helicopters for ice reconnaissance as well as sightseeing purposes (Quark Expeditions, 1992–93). DoC forbids the use of helicopter landings for tourism purposes on its sub-Antarctic islands. However, it has jurisdiction only over the island reserve. Should a helicopter fly at 1000 feet above the island, it can only interfere if there is apparent disturbance to the wildlife (Wouters, 1993).

SUSTAINABLE TOURISM ON NEW ZEALAND'S SUB-ANTARCTIC ISLANDS

Rapid increases in tourist numbers and failure of management practices have often led to the deterioration of natural areas in New Zealand (Ministry of Tourism (MoT), 1992). The New Zealand sub-Antarctic is not immune from this possibility. Present guidelines may well be appropriate for the management of current levels of visitation to the sub-Antarctic islands. However, as Codling (1982, p. 7) observed, 'all forms of control, whether zoning or other management techniques, raise questions as to the timing of their introduction, effective enforcement and monitoring of their effect'. The assessment of tourist activities requires a far more thorough study of Antarctic ecology and the relation to human impacts than has hitherto been the case. Consideration of the impact of tourism on the interaction of the ecology of the sub-Antarctic has often been limited to a concern about its effect on a particular species or vegetation (Hall and Wouters, 1994). This has limitations for the sustainable management of tourism to these areas, in particular as the dominant form of tourism is that of eco-tourism, which has as its primary motivation the interaction in a responsible manner with nature.

From an ecological perspective, sustainable tourism means conserving the productive basis of the physical environment by preserving the integrity of the biota and ecological processes and producing tourism commodities without degrading other values (Hall and Wouters, 1994). A New Zealand Ministry of Tourism paper on tourism sustainability (1992, p. 5) has put forward several points which can be adapted to indicate the importance of tourism sustainability in Antarctica and the sub-Antarctic islands. These include:

- supporting the maintenance and improvement of the Antarctic and sub-Antarctic environment and heritage and ensuring its preservation for future generations;

- bringing satisfaction and enrichment to visitors and strengthening a respect for these natural areas and their historic places;
- generating jobs and wealth, diversifying regional economies, widening economic opportunities and stimulating appropriate investment; and,
- improving the quality of community life by widening choice, supporting local services and infrastructure, and bringing social contact.

New Zealand already has domestic legislation, the Resource Management Act, which encourages sustainable management of resources. Under this legislation, the Resource Management Act (RMA) 1991 (Part 2, Section 5), 'sustainable management' means 'managing the use, development, and protection of natural and physical resources in a way, or at a rate, which enables people and communities to provide for their social, economic, and cultural wellbeing and for their health and safety'.

Sustainable management as embodied in the RMA involves three inter-related factors; sustained resource use, protecting ecological systems and maintaining environmental quality. This means that natural assets have to be maintained for future generations, development has to ensure that ecosystems continue to function and the intrinsic value of resources has to be protected (MoT, 1992). The MoT (1992) believes that the RMA is directly relevant to sustainable tourism development.

Having no form of tourism in the Antarctic or sub-Antarctic may well be the most advisable management strategy from the perspective of ecological conservation (Hall, 1992b). However, this is also unrealistic. Paradoxically, to ensure the preservation of wilderness, people must be allowed to visit these areas. This is necessary in order to persuade policy makers that the conservation status of these areas should be preserved. Documentaries, books and museums are important for education and publicity, but are not sufficient to create a groundswell of public opinion for preservation. Tourism is currently the only form of economic exploitation of the sub-Antarctic islands and Antarctica. Since ecological appreciation alone is not enough to give wilderness value, eco-tourism to the Antarctic and sub-Antarctic islands can provide the economic argument to ensure their preservation (Hall and Wouters, 1994).

In conjunction with providing an enriching experience to visitors, Antarctic and sub-Antarctic tourism is also economically significant to New Zealand cities which benefit from tourism to these areas. Bluff in particular is associated with Antarctic tourism as a stage post for cruise ships departing or arriving *en route* to the continent. The development of the sub-Antarctic interpretation centre in the nearby city of Invercargill is an additional attraction for Antarctic travellers. Christchurch has in the past also been used by cruise ships, but currently appears to be used by smaller organisations travelling primarily to New Zealand's sub-Antarctic islands

(Wouters, 1993). Its Antarctic visitor centre creates tourist revenue by providing an Antarctic experience for the public who will not visit Antarctica itself (Hall and Wouters, 1994).

Eco-tourism can therefore fill the hiatus that exists between preservation and economic development. As the management regimes established by DoC aim to ensure the sustainable use of the sub-Antarctic islands as a tourist resource, they may serve as a model to other nations. With the sub-Antarctic precedent, and the application of the RMA, New Zealand may offer extensive guidance to the creation of an appropriate tourism management regime for all the sub-Antarctic islands and, possibly, the Antarctic itself.

CONCLUSION

> If people do not use these island areas and learn to feel strongly about them, the preservation system may ultimately lack the support which is essential for its functioning (O'Connor and Simmons, 1990, p. 192).

Establishment of a tourist management regime for New Zealand's sub-Antarctic islands is relatively easy because national sovereignty is undisputed. Sovereignty also allows for regulation and control over the activities of both tourists and tour operators. Hall (1992a), however, argues that 'the appropriateness of the New Zealand management models is still to be tested, particularly as some tourism operators have had little opportunity to contribute to the development of management strategies'. However, DoC is currently producing a *conservation management strategy* for the islands, in which public participation is a major component.

In New Zealand, the management of tourism in the sub-Antarctic Islands has been based on concern over the potential impacts of visitation. The management regimes are strongly weighted in favour of ecological considerations. However, managers face a paradox. In order to maintain support for their management strategies, they need to be able to give people access to the resource. Even controlled, that access will affect the ecological resource, however minimally. Management agencies therefore have to find a level at which ecological change is acceptable and which is in keeping with the commercial nature of both small and large tourism operations. In order to achieve this, managers need to understand the impact of visitation on ecological processes. Managers also need to be able to regulate the activities of tourism operations in such a way that commercial viability is not threatened (Hall and Wouters, 1994). At present, DoC is only at the very early stages of these processes. Until the effects are fully understood, the policy process will not be completely effective.

DoC has also been criticised for a lack of consistency in their sub-Antarctic management, making long-term planning and tour promotion difficult (Hall and Wouters, 1994). To enable both conservation of the resource and commercial viability, it is essential that tour operators are involved in the planning process. However, it is argued that some tourist operators have had little opportunity to contribute to the development of management strategies. Further conflict between private operators and DoC concerns the appropriate level of visitation to the islands. DoC has allocated only three sites to ships carrying more than 30 passengers. Visits to these sites are specific to the site quota. The Department will consider applications to other sites on Auckland Island and Campbell Island by vessels carrying less than 30 passengers (Wouters, 1993). Southern Heritage Expeditions have argued that the DoC should not be the only body responsible for eco-tourism development and instead have called for a management body to be established which consists of private sector operators, tourism industry representatives and conservation organisations as well as DoC representation (Russ, 1992).

The development of larger Antarctic cruise ships and the expansion of the Antarctic/sub-Antarctic cruise ship market will also place greater pressure on management authorities whose primary goals are conservation, while also facing demands from tourist authorities who are promoting eco-tourism to provide access to visitors and from smaller operators who wish to reduce the costs imposed by the Department. However, the efforts of the DoC are much more substantial than that by other authorities in sub-Antarctic islands who allow visitation. Indeed, with regards to tourism DoC 'is really between a rock and several hard places—required to foster it, control it, protect the environment from its depredation and also, if possible, in compliance with user pays, to make revenue' (Chamberlain, 1992, in Wouters, 1993, p. 164). Nevertheless, with increased stakeholder consultation and experience, the management plans for the New Zealand sub-Antarctic islands should provide adequate protection while allowing visitation.

REFERENCES

Booth, K., 1990, Restoration, a positive force for island restoration. In Towns, D., Daugherty, C., Atkinson, I., eds., *Ecological restoration of New Zealand islands*, Conservation Sciences Publication No. 2, Department of Conservation, Wellington, pp. 278–283

Brewster, B., 1982, *Antarctica—wilderness at risk*, Friends of the Earth/A.H. & A.W. Reed, Wellington

Cessford, G.R., Dingwall, P.R., 1993, *Assessing shipborne tourists visiting New Zealand's Sub-Antarctic islands*, Department of Conservation, Wellington

Cessford, G.R., Dingwall, P.R., 1994, Tourism on New Zealand's Sub-Antarctic islands, *Annals of Tourism Research*, **21**(2): 318–332

Clark, M.R., Dingwall, P.R., 1985, *Conservation of islands in the Southern Ocean*, International Union for Conservation of Nature and Natural Resources/ Cambridge University Press, Cambridge

Codling, R.J., 1982, Sea-borne tourism in the Antarctic: an evaluation, *Polar Record*, **21**: 3–9

Cooper, W., 1993, *Report on MS frontier spirit cruise #58 Jan–Feb 1993*, New Zealand representative, Department of Conservation Field Centre Manager

Department of Lands and Survey, 1983, *Management plan for the Campbell Islands Nature Reserve*, Management Plan Series No. NR13, Department of Lands and Survey, Wellington

Department of Lands and Survey, 1987, *Management plan for the Auckland Islands Nature Reserve*, Management Plan Series No. NR19, Department of Lands and Survey, Wellington

DoC (Department of Conservation), 1992a, *New Zealand's Sub-Antarctic islands— guidelines on tourism*, Southland Conservancy, Invercargill

DoC, 1993, *Historic resource management strategy*, Southland Conservancy, Invercargill

Edmonds, A., 1990, Partnerships in island restoration. In Towns, D., Daugherty, C., Atkinson, I., eds., *Ecological restoration of New Zealand islands*, Conservation Sciences Publication No. 2, Department of Conservation, Wellington, pp. 284–285

Foggo, M.N., 1990, The botanical values of the New Zealand subantarctic islands. In Towns, D., Daugherty, C., Atkinson, I., eds., *Ecological restoration of New Zealand islands*, Conservation Sciences Publication No. 2, Department of Conservation, Wellington, pp. 215–216

Fraser, C., 1986, Beyond the roaring forties: New Zealand's sub-antarctic islands, Government Printing Office Publishing, Wellington

Fyson, H., 1991, Wooing the tourists? *Terra Nova*, December: 22–24

Hall, C.M., 1992a, Tourism in Antarctica: activities, impacts, and management, *Journal of Travel Research*, **30**(4): 2–9

Hall, C.M., 1992b, Ecotourism in the Australian and New Zealand Sub-Antarctic islands, International Geography Union Commission on Leisure and Recreation Symposium, Telluride, August

Hall, C.M., 1993, Case-study: ecotourism in Antarctica and adjacent Sub-antarctic islands: development, impacts, management and prospects for the future, *Tourism Management*, April: 117–122

Hall, C.M., Keelan, N., Mitchell, I., 1993, The implications of Maori perspectives on the interpretation, management and promotion of tourism in New Zealand, *Geojournal*, **29**(3): 315–322

Hall, C.M., McArthur, S., Spoelder, P., 1992, Ecotourism in Antarctica and adjacent Sub-Antarctic islands: development, impacts, management and prospects for the future. In Weiler, B., ed., *Ecotourism*, Bureau of Tourism Research, Canberra, pp. 156–164

Hall, C.M., Wouters, M.M., 1994, Managing nature tourism in the Sub-Antarctic islands, *Annals of Tourism Research*, **21**(2): 355–374

Higham, T., ed., 1991, *New Zealand's Sub-Antarctic islands—a guidebook*, Department of Conservation, Invercargill

McKenzie, R., 1989, Life on Campbell island, *New Zealand Geographic*, **1**: 20–38

McLaren, F.B., 1948, *The Auckland Islands: their eventful history*, A.H. & A.W. Reed, Wellington

Mahoney, P., 1993, *Report on Sub-Antarctic and Antarctic cruise*, Senior Conservation Officer, Department of Conservation, Wellington

Molloy, L.F., Dingwall, P.R., 1990, World heritage values of New Zealand islands. In Towns, D., Daugherty, C., Atkinson, I., eds., *Ecological restoration of New Zealand islands*, Conservation Sciences Publication No. 2., Department of Conservation, Auckland

MoT (Ministry of Tourism), 1992, *Tourism sustainability—a discussion paper*, Issues Paper No. 2, MoT, Wellington

New Zealand Antarctic Society, 1993, Antarctic, *New Zealand Antarctic Society Bulletin*, **12**(11/12)

O'Connor, K.F., Simmons, D.G., 1990, The use of islands for recreation and tourism: changing significance for nature conservation, In Towns, D., Daugherty, C., Atkinson, I., eds., *Ecological restoration of New Zealand islands*, Conservation Sciences Publication No. 2, Department of Conservation, Wellington, pp. 186–193

Peat, N., 1989, Sweeps made over rock clusters in the cause of life, *The Press*, 27 March

Peat, N., 1991, Treading softly in the Sub-antarctic, *Terra Nova*, **5**: 38–43

Pope, L., 1990, Wild splendour, *New Zealand Geographic*, **8**: 83–106

Quark Expeditions, 1992–93, *Journeys to the far side of Antarctica*, Quark Expeditions travel brochure

Russ, R., 1992, New Zealand ecotourism: the role of the private sector—player and referee. In Hay, J.E., ed., *Ecotourism business in the Pacific: promoting a sustainable experience, conference proceedings*, Environmental Science Occasional Publication No. 8, University of Auckland, Auckland, pp. 190–194

Sanson, L., 1992, New Zealand's sub-antarctic islands: a case study in the development of ecotourism policy. In Hay, J.E., ed., *Ecotourism business in the Pacific: promoting a sustainable experience, conference proceedings*, Environmental Science Occasional Publication No. 8, University of Auckland, Auckland, pp. 141–150

Sanson, L., 1994, An ecotourism case study in Sub-Antarctic islands, *Annals of Tourism Research*, **21**(2): 344–354

Sanson, L.V., Dingwall, P.R., 1992, Progress in the conservation of New Zealand's subantarctic island nature reserves (1987–1992), Department of Conservation, Paper prepared for presentation at the SCAR/IUCN workshop on Protection, Research and Management of Subantarctic Islands, 27–29 April 1992, Paimpont, France

Shultis, J.D., 1989, Images and use of New Zealand's protected areas by domestic and international visitors, *Geojournal*, **19**(3): 329–335

Williams, K., 1990, The subantarctic islands, *Adventure*, **46**(June–July): 25–35

Wouters, M., 1993, Promotion or protection: managing the paradox—the management of tourist visitation to Antarctica and the Sub-Antarctic islands, the New Zealand situation as a case study, Unpublished master's thesis, Massey University, Palmerston North

17 Visitor Management and the Future of Tourism in Polar Regions

MARGARET E. JOHNSTON AND C. MICHAEL HALL

> Science, politics, human puzzles and vexations and beyond them the polar regions themselves—the cold Arctic basin ringed by tundra, the vast dome of Antarctica with its fringe of islands. Their beauty touches everyone who sees them. Their presence is commanding, their scale magnificent. They are of immense value to the world. We have gained much and learned much from polar regions, and damaged both in the process. Perhaps now, in maturity, we are learning to care for them. If not, the gains will stop, and we shall learn no more (Stonehouse, 1990, p. 207).

Tourism in polar regions has grown substantially in recent years, and will continue to grow. In the Antarctic and sub-Antarctic we can expect increasing numbers and visitor pressure at existing sites, and perhaps the development of new locations for shore visits. The Antarctic Peninsula and surrounding islands will continue to be the focal point for tourism in the Antarctic. However, the Ross Sea area will receive a gradual increase in tourist traffic to and from Australia and New Zealand. The development of circumpolar tourism in the Antarctic Ocean will also place pressure on sub-Antarctic islands and parts of the Antarctic continent which have received little previous tourist visitation. In addition, increased demand for Antarctic tourism experiences may well see the recommencement of airborne flights from Australia and New Zealand.

Tourism in the Arctic and sub-Arctic has the potential to grow disproportionately more than its current large share of polar travel would suggest. Tourism increases will be experienced in greater numbers at existing sites and routes, and in the development of new opportunities. For example, cruising potential throughout the Arctic will be realised increasingly in the next decade, as companies take advantage of the vast, untapped cruising market in the northern hemisphere, and Antarctic cruising companies, in

Polar Tourism: Tourism in the Arctic and Antarctic Regions
Edited by C. Michael Hall and Margaret E. Johnston. © John Wiley & Sons Ltd, 1995

the 'off' season, deploy their vessels in the the Arctic (Marsh and Staple, Chapter 4; Smith, 1993). Cruises in the Arctic may well take on more importance as health-conscious tourists flee the traditional sun-oriented cruises. But the greatest impetus for the increase in cruise tourism is the opening up of the Russian Arctic to tourists. Marketing for cruises, as well as for airplane tours, undoubtedly will use to advantage the theme of the unity of the Arctic Ocean and the circumpolar world. This will encourage an expansion of multi-country destination cruises as well as specialised cruises stopping only in Russian ports. Cruise tourism in the Arctic may benefit as well from the present levels of publicity around Antarctic cruises.

The development of cultural tourism related to indigenous peoples and historic tourism based on Arctic exploration and industrial development will also increase. The recent past of exploration, coal-mines, military installations and community modernisation is rising in interest. For example, a proposed territorial park in the Northwest Territories was deemed meritorious for numerous tourism-related reasons; its historical appeal includes: 'the establishment of the Hudson Bay Co. post in 1911, the establishment and growth of the community associated with the Anglican church, [and] the RCMP [Royal Canadian Mounted Police], [and artefacts related to] . . . Dewey Soper's [Dominion surveyor, naturalist and explorer] investigations' (Downie, 1993, p. 53). The boom in cultural tourism will take advantage of tourists' thirst for knowledge about aboriginal peoples' traditions, pasts, and present lifestyles, and the quest for cultural souvenirs (see Smith, 1993). However, great care will have to be to taken to ensure that the tourism product is appropriate to indigenous values, that it reflects local community wishes in terms of number of visitors (if any) and type of tourism, and that aboriginal people themselves obtain the economic benefits that they desire. This may well be the major challenge in Arctic tourism in the next decades.

Established tourism destinations will grow as greater numbers of people seek wilderness landscapes. This will be particularly noticeable in the road-accessible parts of the Arctic and sub-Arctic where saturation (as a frontier or wilderness) could occur. In Europe, economic unity should increase the appeal of northern Scandinavia, though Jacobsen (1994) suggests that as tourist numbers increase, the character of this region will change:

> several parts of the European Arctic will continue for some time to be a desti-nation for adventurous tourists who search for rare experiences. The rapid developments in tourism to Northern Scandinavia indicate that large parts of this region will not be a tourist frontier much longer, at least not in the peak of the summer season. In the summer, the new tourist frontiers of the European Arctic appear to be Svalbard, Greenland and parts of Iceland and Northern Russia (Jacobsen, 1994, p. 14).

If the same process occurs in North America, it may well cause displacement of tourists from the more heavily used areas of the southern Yukon, southwestern Northwest Territories and southern Alaska, to the currently lesser used routes like the Dempster Highway and the Canol Road, which, in turn, might then come under considerable tourist pressure. Corresponding to the Scandinavian situation, there may be some displacement to the less easily accessible Arctic mainland in Canada, the Canadian Arctic Archipelago, northern Alaska, and perhaps Greenland. However, these destinations require water or air travel, which is expensive, particularly beyond the regional hubs (Anderson, 1991). The relative cheapness of road-based tourism has been an important part of its appeal and popularity; this may encourage the vast majority of tourists to stay within the road network even as numbers rise. Displacement might also serve to expand the tourist season beyond the months of June to September, to April, May and October and perhaps even the winter months, though this growth will likely be minimal (Hinch and Swinnerton, 1992). Greater success in de-seasonalisation should continue in northern Scandinavia, especially in late winter adventure and cultural tourism (Jacobsen, 1994).

VISITOR MANAGEMENT AND VISITOR CODES

Although tourist visitation to the polar regions is extremely low in comparison to total world tourist arrivals, its impact on the environment and local residents can be substantial. As we have seen in various chapters in this book, there is great concern about the impacts of tourism; this concern will grow along with the increased numbers and new destinations (Mason, 1994). There are a variety of visitor management strategies in place in the polar regions, but they vary in terms of formality and comprehensiveness. Furthermore, these strategies are affected by such factors as sovereignty and other forms of political control, operator interest, tourist awareness, understanding and compliance, opportunities for enforcement, and the particular focus of the strategy. Despite these differences and the distinct physical conditions of the northern and southern polar areas, the development of operator and visitor codes of conducts, and an appropriate management regime may benefit from the comparative study of polar tourism (Government of Norway, 1992). Both regions are characterised by fragile ecosystems and a reliance on nature-based tourism; both are experiencing increased visitor growth which is expected to continue in the foreseeable future. The development of continent-wide visitor guidelines and an operator code of ethics in the Antarctic by a group of tourism operators shows tremendous promise for control of tourism. Consideration has been given to the creation of a general Arctic visitor code which is very similar to the Antarctic code (Mason, 1994). Codes for operators from other contexts (e.g. an eco-tourism association) may be in use by individual companies in the Arctic and sub-Arctic.

Specific concerns have been raised about the impacts of tourism on polar environments, particularly as tourism tends to be concentrated at certain attractions and in the summer season. For the most part, tourists follow established routes and choose, to a greater or lesser degree, from a number of available experiences and sites, resulting in concentration rather than dispersion of numbers. This spatial concentration is particularly a problem in areas where access is by air or sea. For example, Reich (1980, p. 203) noted that, despite the enormous size of the Antarctic continent, 'tourism is not evenly spread and the question of the scale of the activity may well arise if it continues to be concentrated in a few relatively small areas'. The scale of activities is, of course, relative, and its nature highlights the need for detailed environmental impact assessment of tourism activities (Nicholson, 1986). Similarly, '"tourism impact" is a relative concept, for what may be too much in one area may be quite manageable in another' (Anderson, 1991, p. 209). It could be argued that spatial concentration allows certain areas to be consigned to the 'sacrifice' pile while enabling the better protection of others. Similarly, concentration might help contain tourist impacts temporally, allowing local populations, be they scientists or native hunters, to resume their regular daily lives following the visiting season. Bonner and Lewis Smith (1985) suggested that in the Antarctic situation, it would make sense to focus visitation on the relatively few locations that afford safe landing sites in one particular area, in order to make it easier to control tourist impact.

For some human impacts, such as disturbance of animals, the impact of tourism may not be different from that of community residents or of state-sponsored activities such as scientific research. However, the impact may differ in its intensity or pattern of incidence. For example, although staff from national Antarctic programmes are just as likely as tourists to disturb skua breeding colonies, disturbance by tourists may be compressed into a much shorter period and involve more people (Wouters, 1993). Hemmings et al., (1991, p. 5) assert that it is the 'placement of large numbers of people (perhaps 100) in environmentally sensitive locations (e.g. alongside a penguin colony) for short periods (a matter of hours)' which is character-istic of commercial Antarctic tourist visits. Although most tourists are genuinely concerned about protecting Antarctica, their visits are often loca-lised due to limited access to areas, these are repetitive and frequently occur at breeding grounds for seals, penguins and other sea-birds, placing additional stress on these species (Manheim, 1990).

Tourism in polar regions requires a high quality environment since it is the landscape itself that serves as a major drawcard for tourist activities whether they be educationally, culturally or adventure oriented. Even heavily used destination areas will need to meet tourist expectations of polar wilderness, however that may be defined for the particular destination. If the image and the reality do not match for the tourist because of obvious environmental damage, the experience itself can be negatively affected, as can the industry. Degradation is already evident in the polar regions to varying degrees. In some places, disturbances are minimal and rare; in others, they occur regularly and are having a cumulative effect. There is also evidence that impact thresholds for resident communities have been reached in some cases (see Marsh and Staple, Chapter 4). It is apparent that tourism requires close monitoring and regulation if it is to be sustainable in polar regions. If tourism continues without appropriate regulation, restriction and guidance on conduct of visitors and operators, the polar environment may become degraded to the extent that it no longer has appeal for visitation.

Visitors to polar regions generally advocate their preservation (Marsh, 1991; Wouters, 1993; Marsh and Staple, Chapter 4). This is not only due to the effect of the pristine splendour of the polar landscape, but also to the rigorous education programmes undertaken by many tour operators, and the visitor guidelines most polar operators use. Nevertheless, environmental education may become less important in Antarctic tourism, for example, as the number of operators rises and larger vessels are increasingly used. With increasing numbers, and particularly the potential for an increase in land-based tourism, there will be challenges to industry self-policing: 'will IAATO have the strength and sufficient government support to retain its now important role?' (Smith, 1993). To prevent environmental degradation and to maintain a high standard of tourist operation in Antarctica there must be a comprehensive set of enforceable regulations for tour operations and visitor activities which runs parallel to the existing operator and visitor codes of conduct. In the Arctic, there are various legislative and other regimes in place to regulate tourist behaviour and tour operators, though there is no widely used code for visitors and operators. In both polar regions, visitor management takes place within political frameworks: the Antarctic Treaty System in the case of Antarctic tourism, and national and regional legislation and policies in the case of Arctic, sub-Arctic and sub-Antarctic tourism.

THE ANTARCTIC TREATY SYSTEM

As a functional system the ATS has many impracticalities which often result in the delayed implementation of measures (see Enzenbacher, Chapter 12). The destruction of several protected areas has demonstrated that 'on the ground activities' in Antarctica move more quickly than Treaty negotiations (Wouters, 1993). The decision process is fragmented and several years may be required to implement measures or to make amendments to those already in place. Existing measures have evolved in a piecemeal fashion over the last 20 years, and are now often regarded as inadequate (IUCN, 1991, 1992; Beck, 1994). Difficulties in accessing Antarctic Treaty information also complicates the regulation of tourism. As Beck (1990, p. 348) noted, 'the effective management of any activity is primarily a function of information, and recent ATCMs [Antarctic Treaty Consultative Meetings] have noted the manner in which advance details about tourism and private expeditions have been supplied either inconsistently or not at all'. The Protocol on Environmental Protection appears to establish a necessary baseline for appropriate human conduct in Antarctica. However, there are several insufficiencies. First, although the Protocol already refers to 'tourism', it is not included in Article 1 (Definitions). Hemmings et al. (1991, p. 8) note that 'if references are to be made to "non-governmental activities" (which we see no reason for), then rigorous definition is also required, reflecting the diverse nature of such activities'. Liability is one of the major contentious issues in Antarctic management, and also affects the regulation of Antarctic tourism. Liability for any operator in Antarctica has not been considered in the Protocol, and should be addressed with priority. Due to the differing legal status of state and non-state operators, separate treatment may be necessary. The IUCN (1992, p. 4) believes that 'it is vitally important to complete these outstanding matters, and to find ways of placing legally binding obligations on all who conduct and participate in tourist ventures in the Antarctic'. In summary, the development of Antarctic tourist regulations has been *ad hoc*, and has resulted in a rather disjointed and inconsistent accumulation of agreements. Although the various measures relating to tourism and non-governmental activities have been assembled in the *Handbook of the Antarctic Treaty System* (Heap, 1990), there is still no systematic and comprehensive legal regime in place to manage Antarctic tourism (IUCN, 1992; Wouters, 1993; Beck, 1994). The developments of Antarctic visitor codes can be seen as filling a perceived gap in the Antarctic Treaty System, and inadequacies in the existing regime of regulating visitors which make no specific reference to tourism (Beck, 1990). However, there is a clear need for greater efforts to disseminate visitor information (Enzenbacher, 1991) and establish a coherent tourism management system.

Antarctic codes of conduct

Unlike the sub-Antarctic islands where national sovereignty allows for the implementation of regulatory strategies for tourist visitation (see Wouters and Hall, Chapters 15 and 16), the Antarctic Treaty System does not detail adequate regulation for Antarctic tourism; most of the tourist cruise companies working in Antarctica have been self-policing. To formalise existing shipboard practices, three North American Antarctic ship tour operators issued joint environmental guidelines for their cruising expeditions in 1989 (IAATO, 1991, 1992) (see Enzenbacher, Chapter 12). These companies (Mountain Travel, Society Expeditions, Travel Dynamics) introduced environmental guidelines for both passengers and tour operators, now widely used in the industry, which address traveller conduct around wildlife, respect of historic relics and sites, and the unauthorised removal of keepsakes. IAATO's members strongly believe that environmental and educationally oriented tourism to Antarctica will benefit the continent's future preservation. Its members have carried the large majority of all visitors who have travelled to Antarctica over the last 25 years. The director of planning and operations at Society Expeditions, Peter Cox, believes that their passengers, 'after having been indoctrinated, prior to their trip through the literature they receive and during their trip through lectures on board and experience in the field, become staunch ambassadors for Antarctica' (cited in Wouters, 1993, p. 73). In accordance, IAATO (1991) states that:

> Environmentally-sound and educational travel to Antarctica will continue to be an essential element in creating public support for protective legislation and in guarding against future attempts to exploit the mineral wealth and the rich wildlife of this continent and the surrounding seas.

Thus, it is nature-based tourism which should ensure the continued protection of Antarctica and the sub-Antarctic islands from other forms of economic exploitation such as mining and whaling. This role can be illustrated by a personal account of a passenger on one cruise, emphasising the operator's perseverance with educating its guests:

> Tourists, coached unremittingly by their tour leaders and wildlife lecturers, are obsessively careful to leave nothing but footprints. Most of them have made the long and expensive journey to enjoy and appreciate the pristine environment. At least 3,000 people cruised the Antarctic Peninsula the summer before our visit, yet we saw not one piece of rubbish which could be attributed to them (Raymond, 1990, p. 33).

Despite their efforts to date, IAATO is concerned that profit-driven opportunist tour operators might come in with inadequate ships, inexperienced staff and unprepared passengers which may put the environment as well as visitors at risk (Wouters, 1993). In order to achieve the highest quality of environmental practices among tour operators, IAATO invites new operators to become members and thus adopt the guidelines so that all are conducting tourism in an equivalent and environmentally responsible manner (Wouters, 1993). Commercial operators undoubtedly have a responsibility to protect the polar environment, and therefore tourist operators need to have an input into the policy-making process. In the case of the Antarctic, the resolution of the issue of official assistance to tourist and non-governmental expeditions will require far greater involvement from operators than has hitherto been the case (Nicholson, 1986; Hall, 1992a). Tourist operators must be encouraged to feel a degree of 'owner-ship' over polar resources in order to assist their resolve to manage and protect them (Davis, 1984; Hall and Wouters, 1994). As Codling (1982, p. 9) observed,

> It is in the interest of tour operators, who intend to return to the continent, to cooperate with the treaty nations, and they should be closely involved in any action taken to resolve pressures or conflict. Their own commercial interests are best served if their clients are satisfied, and there is value in seeking to understand and respond to visitors' requirements.

Although the self-policing by Antarctic operators has only been to the benefit of the Antarctic environment, it is not enough, as this system may not be so effective in the regulation of private yachts and expeditions; further, tourism requires continual monitoring of its environmental impacts (Wace, 1990; Enzenbacher, 1991; Sanson and Dingwall, 1992). Antarctic tour operators are required to be self-sufficient under the Antarctic Treaty. However, the current self-regulatory nature of Antarctic tourism does not require tour operators to meet defined minimum standards (Enzenbacher, 1991, Chapter 12). Companies that insure their operations and provide for emergency back-up do so of their own volition. Generally, companies establish safety standards to comply with insurance requirements rather than because regulatory provisions require them. Tour operators maintain that current guidelines are adequate, yet it is not clear that self-regulation is sufficient to address all issues arising from tourist activity (Enzenbacher, 1992). As Wouters (1993, p. 77) concluded, 'The present spirit of cooperation amongst the major tour operators should be encouraged, but may need to be supplemented by more formal measures which also provide an enforcement mechanism'.

VISITOR MANAGEMENT IN THE ARCTIC AND SUB-ARCTIC

Cooperation among tour operators is less common in the northern polar regions, probably because it has not seemed necessary or possible. However, there has been both self-regulation and governmental regulation of tourism in the Arctic and sub-Arctic, and many jurisdictions are involved in controlling particular aspects of tourism. In addition to the

eight countries with circumpolar territory, there are other political units, such as the territories in Canada, and aboriginal groups in Russia and Greenland, for example, with control over designated lands. Two examples will be considered here. The management of tourist behaviour in Svalbard, Norway is comprehensive. A strict system has been established in order to ensure visitor compliance with regulations and to help ensure visitor safety, a concern which certainly is much greater in the Arctic given the many independent, and self-guided tourists than it is in the Antarctic which has a stronger operator component of control. The other example is the Northwest Territories, where a variety of regulations for tourists exists in a framework which is still being established.

Visitor management in the Northwest Territories

Individual pieces of legislation in the Northwest Territories which regulate tourism are either specific to tourists or potentially affect all persons in the territory. For example, under the Wildlife Act hunting licences are required to hunt game, and in the case of big game, non-residents must hire a guide licensed under the Travel and Tourism Act. (Yukon Territory has similar legislation.) However, in emergency situations, threatening animals, including polar bears, may be shot by anyone, although even in self-defence, such an action is seen as extremely serious and there are special reporting requirements. Specific legislation for the protection of designated sites or areas in the north also controls visitor movements. For example, visitors are required to obtain permission to visit the nationally and territorially established ecological sites 'because of the stress that their presence can place on life in the very short breeding season' (Department of Indian Affairs and Northern Development, 1992, pp. 35–36). Commercial tourism and the industry is regulated, in part, under the Travel and Tourism Act of the Northwest Territories which defines tourist establishments, outfitters and guides, and indicates the licences and permits required for the provision of tourist services and facilities. Additionally, the final agreement for dividing the Northwest Territories into two separate jurisdictions (to occur in 1999) provides for private Inuit-owned land; all persons intending to undertake activities, including tourism, on these private lands would require a land use permit.

These pieces of legislation comprise the essential regulatory framework for tourism. A legislative regime also exists in national parks, a potentially easier environment in which to control visitors because of the defined physical space, the limited number of access points, and the existence of enforceable regulations with prescribed penalties. There are currently four national parks (or national park reserves) in the Northwest Territories which were visited by about 11 000 people in 1991 (Department of

Economic Development and Tourism, 1993). Two of these are in the Arctic, and combined, they receive about 1000 visitors per year (Department of Economic Development and Tourism, 1993). Outside the parks, the Royal Canadian Mounted Police operate a voluntary wilderness travel registration system (Department of Indian Affairs and Northern Development, 1992), while in these park reserves there is a mandatory registration system and a required visitor orientation programme. Educational brochures give information about the rules and regulations of the park with explanations. For example, one brochure notes the requirement to pack out all litter and garbage, and states: 'In the Arctic environment, litter may endure for decades' (Environment Canada Parks Service, 1992, p. 6). Readers are told: 'Please remember that plants and animals in national parks are protected. Picking plants lessens the opportunities of others to see them. Plants grow so slowly there that you will destroy many years of plant life by picking a single plant' (Environment Canada Parks Service, 1992, p. 3).

There is also considerable emphasis on the need for visitor self-sufficiency and the lack of emergency services for visitors. This relates to an important distinction between tourism in the Arctic and in the Antarctic: in the Arctic, there is a considerably higher number of independent, self-guided visitors who travel far beyond the general access points. These individuals are outside the informal control and the well-specified safety measures of tourist operators. They do not have the benefit of that particular form of guidance and education for safe and appropriate behaviour. In an information brochure, one national park reserve informs visitors that:

> Due to the remote nature of the park, and for your own safety, you must register at the park office in Pangnirtung or Broughton Island before going to the park AND when you have completed your trip. ... Park staff can provide only limited ground assistance in case of emergencies. They are not able to perform 'mountain' rescues. In bad weather, help may be slow arriving. ... Mountain climbers and persons hiking off the main trail must have self-rescue capability. All costs of air evacuation, if necessary, are the responsibility of the visitor and not of the Canadian Parks Service (Environment Canada Parks Service, 1992, p. 6).

Beyond the structure of park visitor management strategies, there is a larger concern for the safety of self-guided wilderness travellers that has been voiced among agencies in the Northwest Territories and in the federal government (Johnston, 1993). It resulted in the updating and publication of a *Guide for expeditions to northern and Arctic Canada* (Department of Indian Affairs and Northern Development, 1992). This small booklet gives a description of all the guidelines, rules and regulations that affect visitors in the north, and it is intended to aid people planning adventure

expeditions or other self-guided trips into remote areas. This booklet represents a kind of visitor code, although one which clearly is aimed at a specialised group of tourists. Certainly, it goes beyond the basic ideas of minimal impact tourism which are covered in Mason's (1994) draft visitor code and the Antarctic visitor code. It provides detailed information that could be of practical use in planning an expedition and information that could help wilderness travellers during their trip or in emergencies. For example, information is given on ways to prepare for cold temperatures and polar bears, and it explains how to deal with frostbite, snow blindness and hypothermia. It also brings together all the applicable legislation, including those related to firearms, pollution, fishing, hunting, and archaeological and historical resources.

The overriding focus of this booklet is the safety of travellers. Less prominent is the concern regarding tourism impacts, however, it is still evident: 'Visitors to the Arctic are strongly encouraged to take every precaution to ensure that neither the fragile ecosystems nor northern residents are disturbed in any way' (Department of Indian Affairs and Northern Development, 1992, p. vii). The particular focus and approach reflect the target market for the brochure—adventure travellers/expeditionists —and the activities they are likely to be involved in. Concerns over search and rescue, environmental impacts and disruption of archaeological sites have been at the forefront of the search for a management strategy for Arctic adventurers which might be resolved through formal regulation, licensing and insurance requirements (Johnston, 1993). Though search and rescue of visitors are potentially equally important in Antarctica, this management issue has not yet been approached in a comprehensive way (Smith, 1993).

Visitor management in Svalbard

Svalbard is unique in the Arctic world. It has a series of strict and far-reaching regulations which govern travel and environmental protection in the archipelago which are quite distinct from those in the rest of Norway. The regulations (first outlined in 1983) were established in order to 'protect the archipelago's natural environment and historical remains; ensure compliance with other laws and regulations; [and] provide for the safety of tourists and other travellers' (Ministry of Justice, 1993, p. 3). Not only do the regulations require that travellers and tour operators undertake certain actions, but also they give considerable discretionary power to the Governor of Svalbard.

The regulations make tour operators responsible for the safety of their participants and for ensuring that the participants comply with applicable laws regarding their behaviour. Operators are required to have insurance or to have guarantees to cover any expenses associated with search and rescue regardless of negligence. The Governor determines the amount of insurance needed, and may require insurance or a guarantee of individual travellers. The most interesting aspect of the regulations relates to the notification of travel plans. Each tour operator must provide details of their tour plans, and vessels sailing into national parks or nature reserves (covering a substantial portion of the archipelago) must provide a sailing schedule indicating any planned landings. Individual travellers must notify the Governor of their travel plans if they are intending to travel in a national park or nature reserve. Finally, under certain conditions, the Governor is entitled to order a change in travel plans. The circumstances under which this is allowed relate to the potential for damage to the environment or cultural artefacts, pressure on protected areas, physical danger to individuals, and harm to lawful activities. Indeed, the Governor has the right to prohibit completely travel which is considered inappropriate under these regulations (Ministry of Justice, 1993).

There are other regulations which assist in visitor management, including those regarding hunting and fishing, and the temporally defined or complete prohibition of access to particularly significant parts of the archipelago (Ministry of Environment, 1992a). Protection for elements of cultural heritage was established in law in 1992 (Ministry of Environment, 1992b). In addition to brochures which outline these regulations affecting tourists, Svalbard has produced numerous informational brochures which provide practical advice for intending travellers. Environmental and tourist regulations are summarised in these brochures. Like the Canadian guide to the Arctic, the information prepared for Svalbard emphasises the importance of being prepared for polar bears. All people who travel beyond the settlements are advised to take a rifle for protection against bears. However, in both countries, shooting a bear is serious and travellers are advised on the many ways they can stay away from dangerous situations. Other particular areas of emphasis on Svalbard are the need to bring all refuse back to the settlements, the prohibition of driving motorised vehicles on thawed ground, and the need to avoid disturbing birds and mammals (Ministry of Environment, 1992a). This strict management regime is appropriate to this particular context given the increasing tourist pressures: 'We wish to preserve the natural environment of Svalbard, and tourism must therefore be regulated and restricted' (Ministry of Environment, 1992a, p. 5).

CONCLUSION: THE END OF THE FINAL TOURIST FRONTIER

The Ice dissolves into a black veil. Beyond it there is nothing more (Pyne, 1986, p. 389).

Since the early eighteenth century tourists have travelled outwards from the tourist-generating regions of Europe and North America, and later Asia, in ever-increasing numbers. From the 1960s, increased wealth and leisure time in both the traditional tourist-generating areas and in the recently developed nations of the Pacific Rim have, in combination with advances in transport technology, led to an even greater boom in international travel. Wave after wave of tourists has advanced over the globe, consuming landscapes and the many perfect images of the tourism marketer. In the search for authentic and unique experiences, the vanguard of the tourist horde has moved from one destination to the next.

No part of the globe is now untouched by tourism, but by their very isolation the polar regions have been relatively immune from the effects of tourism. However, the isolation which has long served the polar regions is now the very feature that attracts tourists to visit these places. The polar regions, particularly the non-road accessible areas, are still among the world's last tourism frontiers. However, advances in transport technology and greater disposable income are enabling greater numbers of people to visit these remote polar destinations. Regularly scheduled and charter aircraft and cruise ships of varying sizes facilitate relatively easy access for those who can afford them. Perhaps even more detrimental to the frontier quality of the polar regions is the network of roads that make the sub-Arctic and Arctic accessible to huge amounts of vehicular traffic in North America and Europe. The incremental access that has come in conjunction with resource development and settlement has opened vast areas of wilderness to what, in the polar context, essentially amounts to mass tourism.

The growth in visitor numbers to the polar regions, especially in the north, is testimony to the disappearance of the tourist frontier and the changing nature of these environments for tourism. The regular appearance of the North and South Pole on the world's television sets makes the polar environment seem all the more accessible and, perhaps, even more desirable to visit. However, though more accessible vicariously and in reality, the polar regions are still fragile and sensitive, and there is great potential for tourists to disrupt the natural environment and the human inhabitants. It is almost impossible to halt the growth in tourist visitation to these regions. Therefore, there is an urgency in formulating sustainable approaches to tourism at the poles. Sustainable tourism means conserving the productive basis of the physical environment by preserving the integrity of the biota, ecological processes and cultural values, and at the same time, producing tourism commodities without destroying other aspects of land use such as indigenous peoples' activities (Hall and Johnston, 1992). Although it might make ecological sense to reduce tourism substantially or to prohibit it completely in all polar regions or in some selected areas, this is unrealistic given the ever-increasing public demand and the impossibility of halting access in most cases. It is also unrealistic given national interests in both regions and the economic expectations of indigenous peoples and residents in northern latitudes. Additionally, and paradoxically, by allowing people to visit polar wilderness, we can encourage an interest in polar conservation by the public who then might attempt to persuade policy makers and governments to maintain or designate protected area status. Vicarious appreciation through books and documentaries is important, but it is not necessarily sufficient to create a groundswell of public support for preservation (Hall, 1992b; Hall and Wouters, 1994). The development of a tourism industry also provides a useful economic argument in helping ensure that the polar areas are maintained in their relatively pristine state for future generations rather than being exploited completely for other natural resource uses. Nevertheless, now that isolation is less a factor in limiting visitor arrivals, it is essential that appropriate management regimes are put in place to regulate tourist activity. As this chapter and various others throughout this book have indicated, visitor and operator codes of conduct are and will continue to be an integral component of any polar tourism management regime. However, they are not enough. Regulatory frameworks also need to be implemented to ensure that there is a complementary system of compliance.

In the northern polar and sub-polar regions, and in the sub-Antarctic islands, legislative powers exist for the development of management regimes. The examples of regulation in Svalbard and in the Canadian north illustrate the various approaches that can be taken. Nevertheless, there is a need for an international agreement on tourism which enables countries to work together to manage tourism in the Arctic and sub-Arctic as part of overall resource management. This is particularly important now as the essential physical unity of the circumpolar world is being enhanced by a growing political cooperation. In the transnational space of the Antarctic, the Antarctic Treaty System is slowly reaching a point at which regulation of tourist activities is becoming possible through formal enforcement mechanisms. However, in both polar regions, the development of appropriate tourist management regimes will fundamentally depend on the political will of stakeholders, and of governmental authorities in particular.

Government, industry, conservation groups and communities which depend on polar tourism have all revealed a desire to conserve the Antarctic and Arctic environments. In particular, tour operator voluntary codes of conduct in the Antarctic indicate a recognition of the need to protect the resource which sustains their businesses and attracts tourists in the first place. Nevertheless, the number of both operators and tourists is rapidly increasing, making it extremely difficult for voluntary codes of conduct to be as effective as they have been to this point. Operators in the Arctic and sub-Arctic can learn from the experience of their counterparts to the south (see Smith, 1993). In some cases, these are the same people, and so there is plenty of opportunity for similar progress to be made in the north. However, the world abounds with examples of unrestrained tourism growth which damages cultural and environmental resources, and has negative social impacts on local communities. Some of these examples are in the polar regions, but certainly there is considerable potential, as tourist numbers increase and activities become more invasive, for great damage here as well. Undoubtedly, government and supragovernmental authorities will be faced with decisions about controls on tourism in the polar environment. It is hoped that the present volume will provide a basis on which some of those critical policy and management decisions will be based.

REFERENCES

Anderson, M.J., 1991, Problems with tourism in Canada's eastern Arctic, *Tourism Management*, **12**(3): 209–220

Beck, P.J., 1990, Regulating one of the last tourism frontiers: Antarctica, *Applied Geography*, **10**(4): 343–356

Beck, P.J., 1994, Managing Antarctic tourism: a front-burner issue, *Annals of Tourism Research*, **21**(2): 375–386.

Bonner, W.N., Lewis Smith, R.I., eds., 1985, *Conservation areas in the Antarctic*, International Council of Scientific Unions, SCAR, Scott Polar Research Institute, Cambridge

Codling, R.J., 1982, Sea-borne tourism in the Antarctic: an evaluation, *Polar Record*, **21**: 3–9

Davis, B., 1984, Australia and Antarctica: aspects of policy process. In Harris, S., ed., *Australia's Antarctic policy options*, Centre for Resource and Environmental Studies, Australian National University, Canberra, pp. 339–354

Department of Economic Development and Tourism, 1993, *Quick facts about the Northwest Territories tourism industry*, Government of the Northwest Territories, Yellowknife, Canada

Department of Indian Affairs and Northern Development, 1992, *Guide for expeditions to northern and Arctic Canada*, Minister of Supply and Services Canada, Ottawa, Canada

Downie, B., 1993, Katannilik Territorial Park: an Arctic tourism destination. In Johnston, M.E., Haider, W., eds., *Communities, resources and tourism in the north*, Lakehead University Centre for Northern Studies, Thunder Bay, pp. 51–60

Environment Canada Parks Service, 1992, *Auyuittuq National Park Reserve*, Minister of Supply and Services Canada, Ottawa, Canada

Enzenbacher, D.J., 1991, A policy for Antarctic tourism: conflict or cooperation? Unpublished Master of Philosophy in Polar Studies, Scott Polar Research Institute, University of Cambridge, Cambridge

Enzenbacher, D.J., 1992, Antarctic tourism and environmental concerns, *Marine Pollution Bulletin*, **25**(9–12): 258–265

Government of Norway, 1992, *Tourism in the high north, management challenges and recreation opportunity spectrum planning in Svalbard, Norway (Submission)*, XVII ATCM/INFO 16, 17 November, Government of Norway, Oslo

Hall, C.M., 1992a, Tourism in Antarctica: activities, impacts, and management, *Journal of Travel Research*, **30**(4): 2–9

Hall, C.M., 1992b, *Wasteland to world heritage: preserving Australia's wilderness*, Melbourne University Press, Carlton

Hall, C.M., Johnston, M., 1992, Pole to pole: polar tourism policy and development in Australia, Canada and New Zealand, paper presented at the Association for Canadian Studies in Australia and New Zealand Conference, Wellington, New Zealand, 14–16 December

Hall, C.M., Wouters, M.M., 1994, Managing nature tourism in the Sub-Antarctic islands, *Annals of Tourism Research*, **21**(2): 355–374

Heap, J., ed., 1990, *Handbook of the Antarctic Treaty System*, 7th edn, Polar Publications, Cambridge

Hemmings, A.D., Cuthbert, A., Dalziell, J., 1991, *Non-governmental activities and the protection of the Antarctic environment, a paper for the government of New Zealand*, Antarctic and the Southern Ocean Coalition (NZ), Wellington

Hinch, T., Swinnerton, G., 1992, Tourism and Canada's Northwest Territories: issues and prospects, paper presented to the IGU Symposium on Recreational Resources and Leisure in Geographical Perspective, Telluride, Colorado, 14–22 August

IAATO (International Association of Antarctica Tour Operators), 1991, *Antarctica visitor guidelines; Antarctica tour operator guidelines; Antarctica tour operators form association, Press release*, IAATO, Kent

IAATO, 1992, *Tourism in Antarctica—guidelines for a low-impact presence (Submission)*, XVII ATCM/INFO 65, 16 November, IAATO, Kent

IUCN (International Union for Conservation of Nature and Natural Resources), 1991, *A strategy for Antarctic conservation*, IUCN, Gland

IUCN, 1992, *Tourism in Antarctica*, XVII ATCM/INFO 18, 11 November, IUCN, Gland

Jacobsen, J.K.S., 1994, *Arctic tourism and global tourism trends*, Research Report No. 37, Lakehead University Centre for Northern Studies, Thunder Bay, Ontario

Johnston, M., 1993, Tourism and the regulation of adventure travel in the Canadian Arctic, paper presented at the Arctic Tourism and Ecotourism Symposium, 5th World Wilderness Conference/1st Northern Forum, Tromso, Norway, 24 September–1 October

Manheim, B.S., Jr., 1990, *Paradise lost? The need for environmental regulation of tourism in Antarctica*, Environmental Defense Fund, Washington DC

Marsh, J.S., 1991, The characteristics of a sample of tourists visiting Antarctic, paper prepared for the Annual Meeting of the Ontario Division of the Canadian Association of Geographers, Ottawa, 26 October

Mason, P., 1994, A visitor code for the Arctic, *Tourism Management*, **15**(2): 93–97

Ministry of Environment, 1992a, *Experience Svalbard on nature's own terms*, Ministry of Environment, Norway

Ministry of Environment, 1992b, *Regulations concerning the cultural heritage in Svalbard*, Ministry of Environment, Norway

Ministry of Justice, 1993, *Regulations to tourism and other travel in Svalbard*, Ministry of Justice, Norway

Nicholson, I.E., 1986, Antarctic tourism: the need for a legal regime? *Maritime Studies*, **29**: 1–7

Pyne, S., 1986, *The ice: a journey to Antarctica*, Ballantine Books, New York

Raymond, R., 1990, Frozen assets, *Panorama*, April: 30–34

Reich, R.J., 1980, The development of Antarctic tourism, *Polar Record*, **20**(126): 303–314

Sanson, L.V., Dingwall, P.R., 1992, Progress in the conservation of New Zealand's subantarctic island nature reserves (1987–1992), Department of Conservation. Paper prepared for presentation at the SCAR/IUCN workshop on Protection, Research and Management of subantarctic Islands, 27–29 April, Paimpont, France

Smith, V.L, 1993, What have we learned from Antarctica: a tourism case study, paper presented to the Arctic Tourism and Ecotourism Symposium, 5th World Wilderness Conference/1st Northern Forum, Tromso, Norway, 24 September–1 October

Stonehouse, B., 1990, *North Pole South Pole: a guide to the ecology and resources of the Arctic and Antarctic*, Prion, London

Wace, N., 1990, Antarctica: a new tourist destination, *Applied Geography*, **10**(4): 327–341

Wouters, M., 1993, Promotion or protection: managing the paradox—the management of tourist visitation to Antarctica and the Sub-Antarctic islands, the New Zealand situation as a case study, Unpublished master's thesis, Massey University, Palmerston North

Name Index

Place Index

Subject Index